Here's an engaging story of a controversial plant and the people who rely on it. If you've ever finished a mystery novel and realized you've effortlessly learned history, pharmacology, sociology, psychology, and a warm appreciation for real characters, get ready to have a comparable experience. The authors depict the humanity of all their participants while weaving details of the data into a riveting narrative. Readers from diverse backgrounds can learn a lot from this text. Seasoned cannabis researchers are bound to appreciate the nuanced look at the lives of patients. Citizens new to the field will relish many surprises that will likely defy their stereotypes, and fellow patients will find the tales of their brothers and sisters extremely validating. In addition, the book is a superb series of lessons on the utility, challenges, and delights of qualitative research. Anyone interested in finding out more about any underground population and communicating the information in a compelling way now has a stellar example for how to do so.

**Mitch Earleywine**, Ph.D., Author of *Understanding Marijuana* (Oxford University Press) and Professor, University at Albany, SUNY

Authors Newhart and Dolphin have provided an in-depth sociological study of the patient experience with cannabis in the USA that examines the real-life obstacles, stigma, and legal tightrope that people must negotiate to treat their illnesses in the face of continued federal recalcitrance. Readers will learn details of the history and legal underpinnings related to the cannabis controversy, and hear the stories of 40 patients in their own words, thus putting a human face on this complex topic. It is a highly accurate and welcome addition to the available literature.

**Ethan Russo**, M.D., Author of *Cannabis: From Pariah to Prescription* (Routledge) and Director of Research and Development at the International Cannabis and Cannabinoids Institute

With the definitions and uses of marijuana changing rapidly, this is an important and timely book. It brings together policy, experience and especially medicalization in a rich analytical fashion. It should become a benchmark work on impacts of medical marijuana i

**Peter Conrad**, P of
*Society* (The d
Pro ster

# The Medicalization of Marijuana

Medical marijuana laws have spread across the U.S. to all but a handful of states. Yet, eighty years of social stigma and federal prohibition creates dilemmas for patients who participate in state programs.

*The Medicalization of Marijuana* takes the first comprehensive look at how patients negotiate incomplete medicalization and what their experiences reveal about our relationship with this controversial plant as it is incorporated into biomedicine. Is cannabis used similarly to other medicines? Drawing on interviews with midlife patients in Colorado, a state at the forefront of medical cannabis implementation, this book explores the practical decisions individuals confront about medical use, including whether cannabis will work for them; the risks of registering in a state program; and how to handle questions of supply, dosage, and routines of use.

Individual stories capture how patients redefine and reclaim cannabis use as legitimate—individually and collectively—and grapple with an inherently political identity. These experiences help illustrate how stigma, prejudice, and social change operate.

By positioning cannabis use within sociological models of medical behavior, Newhart and Dolphin provide a wide-reaching, theoretically informed analysis of the issue that expands established concepts and provides new insight on medical cannabis and how state programs work.

The authors are a husband-and-wife team with more than thirty-five years collective experience writing on cannabis and drug policy topics, including contributions to more than two dozen books.

**Michelle Newhart**, Ph.D., teaches Sociology and works as an instructional designer at Mt. San Antonio College. Previously, she has taught at the University of Colorado, Boulder. She is the co-author of *Understanding Research Methods* (10th ed.) from Routledge.

**William Dolphin** has taught English and Composition at San Francisco State University, Rhodes College, Azusa Pacific University, and the University of California, Berkeley. He currently teaches in the College of Arts and Sciences and the Graduate School of Education at the University of Redlands.

# The Medicalization of Marijuana

## Legitimacy, Stigma, and the Patient Experience

Michelle Newhart and
William Dolphin

Routledge
Taylor & Francis Group

NEW YORK AND LONDON

First published 2019
by Routledge
711 Third Avenue, New York, NY 10017

and by Routledge
2 Park Square, Milton Park, Abingdon, Oxon, OX14 4RN

*Routledge is an imprint of the Taylor & Francis Group, an informa business*

*Library of Congress Cataloging-in-Publication Data*
A catalog record has been requested for this book

ISBN: 978-1-138-32087-1 (hbk)
ISBN: 978-1-138-32088-8 (pbk)
ISBN: 978-0-429-45046-4 (ebk)

Typeset in Bembo
by Apex CoVantage, LLC

Visit the eResources: www.routledge.com/9781138320888

MIX
Paper from
responsible sources
FSC® C013056

Printed and bound in Great Britain by
TJ International Ltd, Padstow, Cornwall

# Contents

# Illustrations

## Figure

## Tables

# Acknowledgments

There are many people to thank for their assistance with this book. First, all the medical cannabis patients who volunteered for interviews. Your stories encouraged us to rethink many ideas, and we are grateful for your many generosities. We owe special thanks to the larger medical cannabis community in Colorado, especially in Denver and Colorado Springs, who welcomed us to events, helped with networking, and provided many useful suggestions, and generally supported this research with their interest and encouragement. Thanks to John Carnahan for patiently reviewing many versions of this work. We are both especially grateful to Ed Rosenthal and Jane Klein, who introduced us to the world of cannabis advocacy and to each other.

A special thanks to my lifelong mentor in sociology, Mary Jo Neitz, who shaped my path as a sociologist and intellectual, and who continues to serve as mentor, supporter, and inspiration. Thanks also to my parents, Rick and Cathy Newhart, who believed in me. I appreciate the chairs and members of my dissertation committee, Jane Menken, Stefanie Mollborn, Amy Wilkins, and Stefan Timmermans, for their guidance and assistance in this work.

—Michelle Newhart

My contributions to this book reflect the inspiration and influence of too many people to name, but it all began with Fausto Alegado, a dear departed friend whose generosity extended to confiding the benefits of his medical cannabis use and his fear of being caught. My investigation of his predicament led me to a crash course on marijuana jurisprudence via Ed Rosenthal's federal trial, which segued into work with advocates such as Steph Sherer, who introduced me to a host of physicians, scientists, and—most importantly—medical cannabis patients of all types who have made me privy to their struggles and triumphs. Like Michelle, I owe much to their courage and can only hope to have done it justice here.

—William Dolphin

# Preface

I didn't choose marijuana; marijuana chose me. In 2010, I was completing my Ph.D. in sociology in Boulder, Colorado. Every day, new green crosses indicated that another medical marijuana dispensary had opened. They popped up at such a prolific rate that no one could seem to resist the comparison with Starbucks. I had thought that coming to graduate school in Colorado would be a chance to get away from all things cannabis. Instead, it felt like marijuana was following me around.

For most of my life, it was assumed that if you had any connection to marijuana, you were probably an enthusiastic user, a stoner, a part of the culture—or one of the subcultures—who affiliated with it. Why else would you be talking about it? Its associations carry considerable cultural baggage, and the stereotypes surrounding it are deeply ingrained and encompassing. The implication used to bother and embarrass me. Now I see that it also turns out to be *exactly* what makes marijuana interesting. As the first chapters in this book describe, the conventional understanding of cannabis and cannabis users is an elaborate, deliberate social construction a century in the making.

Behind the one-dimensional social construction of cannabis lies a remarkably multilayered topic with a surprising number of associations and interconnections to other social issues and cultural phenomenon: identity politics, culture wars, aging and generational trends, social movements, embodiment, modern policing, global economies, ecological concerns, addiction studies, the translation of science into policy, and of course, health, medicine, the expansion of pharmaceutical drugs and of complementary and alternative medicine. The last two decades have been marked by the start of a radical transformation of the social construction of cannabis, one that promises to change both medicine and society.

\*\*\*

In 1999, I was working in book publishing. I answered an advertisement for a job in a San Francisco Bay Area newspaper for a part-time publisher's assistant and ended up working for Ed Rosenthal. Perhaps you've never heard of Ed

Rosenthal. I hadn't, but it turns out that Ed is one of the most prominent marijuana authors and activists of the past half-century. Pretty much every cannabis enthusiast in the country—and many around the world—knows Ed from his books and long-running column in *High Times* on cannabis cultivation. His first book (with Mel Frank), *Marijuana Grower's Handbook*, got a positive review in the *New York Times Book Review* in 1978 and helped start his publishing company. When I worked for him, Ed lived and worked with his wife Jane out of the rambling hilltop Victorian he and Mel had bought in Oakland, California. On a clear day, the Bay Bridge and the Golden Gate could be seen from the back patio.

Before working for Ed, I knew about cannabis the kind of things that you learned from small talk between college students. It was the 1990s. I didn't really learn about it in my college classes, except to absorb that it was not regarded as a serious academic topic among the sociologists I knew. Even if it had been, it likely wouldn't have reached me. Lots of other topics were ahead of drug policy in my academic interests.

Still, I chose to accept the job with Ed because it scratched a sociological "itch" for me. Like many curious social science types, I was pulled in by the adventure, and intrigued to get access to what was then an underground culture. Also, I liked Ed. Working for him was like the best parts of doing fieldwork. Proposition 215 had just passed a few years before, ushering in the first state medical marijuana program. Bill Clinton was just being replaced with George W. Bush. California was arguably the battlefront on the issue, and I had somewhat accidentally wandered in to a front row seat.

In my eight years as Ed's editor, I learned a great deal about cannabis. I traveled to interesting places around the world and met advocates, physicians, patients, owners of some of the first Bay Area cannabis clubs, Dutch cannabis breeders, and longtime underground growers. These were not people you could look up in the phone book. They were a mixture of hippies, farmers, clean-cut types, odd ducks, and renegades. Some were exiles from other states or lived as exiles outside of America. Many used pseudonyms and were careful about who knew their exact location. It was a small world, and because nearly everyone in it knew Ed, I had a calling card. I got the opportunity to interview many of them for book projects, and over the course of years, some became friends.

In 2002, during my third year at the publishing company, Ed Rosenthal was arrested for his role in the city of Oakland's medical marijuana program. Ed was in the *New York Times* once again, but this time it was the front page, and it was his case they were covering. The trial became an influential pivot point in the national conversation on medical access[1]. As a federal case, the defense was not allowed to discuss medical matters, state law, or even how the City of Oakland had attempted to work within federal law, greatly distorting the facts that were presented. In 2003, the jury reached a guilty verdict. Ed was convicted on three felony counts, but in a dramatic departure from the more than five years of mandatory prison time prosecutors demanded, Ed was sentenced to just one day, with credit for time served awaiting bail after his arrest.

The person hired to work media relations during Ed's case was William Dolphin, my co-author on this book, who, through a twist of fate, would become my friend, confidant, and, fourteen years after that first meeting, my husband. William worked on Ed's landmark trial, after which he edited and contributed to various projects with Ed and I over several years before he moved on to work at the University of California at Berkeley. After Ed's trial, William began more than a decade of work for Americans for Safe Access (ASA), the leading nonprofit advocacy organization for medical marijuana patients, writing and producing publications on medical research and public policy, as well as a newsletter for advocates that reaches nearly 40,000 readers each month. William's name is familiar to many patients and activists from this newsletter and the various pamphlets on treating medical conditions he produced for patients and physicians.

In 2006, I left the job with Ed to attend graduate school in sociology at CU-Boulder. After finishing my coursework, I started working on my dissertation. I was interested in activism, decision-making behaviors, and health. I started a proposal to study how individuals use over-the-counter nutritional supplements as self-treatment for health problems, a trend that had grown significantly since changes to the laws in the late 1990s. Then the medical cannabis "green rush" began. The articles I was reading at the time were replete with statistics and theories about who takes herbal supplements, and when, and for what reason, and to what effect. I started thinking that medical cannabis was a lot like these herbal supplements, but with some important differences—namely, its legacy as a recreational substance. I could make that my dissertation. But the idea of turning my culminating graduate school work back to cannabis gave me pause. I had only become interested in cannabis because of sociology. In grad school, I could do sociology about any topic I chose. I spent time debating.

Given my background, medical cannabis might seem an obvious dissertation choice. After all, I had extensive knowledge on the topic, and an existing network of friends and colleagues associated with medical cannabis to help me get started. These are huge advantages to draw upon. It wasn't that I was bored by the idea, something that I'd expected to happen after the eight years I'd already spent immersed in the topic. In truth, its complexities held my interest, and I was as curious as ever to find out what was going on in Colorado and where it would end up.

The reasons *not* to write my dissertation on cannabis may be less obvious. From my years of editing Ed's books, I had learned that cannabis stigma has a long reach. It had not exempted me then, and it likely would not do so now. It did not matter that my role was editor, or researcher. I worried that what *would* matter was the succession of work on the issue, establishing a pattern and making me forevermore unemployable. I might point out here that the stigma applies regardless of whether I *actually use* marijuana or not. Any involvement implies it and is awkward to deny. Stigma punctures the neutrality of research or editorial work with its implication of bias, self-interest, and a lack of seriousness around the topic. If I doubled down and wrote my dissertation about cannabis, what was I bringing upon myself? Would I ruin the very chances I was chasing?

In trying to decide whether to write my dissertation about medical cannabis, I started talking to friends and family. One of my first calls was to William. I called my parents, and other colleagues too. They all encouraged me to do it, sharing insights and helping me find my way forward. Much like the patients interviewed for this book, my decision to pursue this project was reached through deliberation among my close network, those who have long known me and understood what I was up to. Their suggestions and support helped me to go for it, and I'm glad I did. It was strangely liberating. After years of trying to manage, explain, or excuse how cannabis fit into my identity, I stopped trying to justify it and started working with a new sense of purpose on understanding it. I hope my work helps you to make better sense of it too.

\*\*\*

Once I decided to write my dissertation about medical cannabis, I contacted some of the industry professionals I knew in California. I was not sure how interconnected networks were across states, or whether California connections would help me reach key people in Colorado. In September 2010, I kicked off my data collection by attending a medical marijuana conference in Denver. I had attended many similar events over the years, and it was immediately clear when I walked into this event that change was underway. It was the first time I had been at a cannabis event at which people wore name tags with their real first and last names on them. Now not only were attendees wearing their full legal names, freely visible, but many also had the names of cannabis businesses on them, and people were handing around business cards. The mundaneness of name tags and business cards in a conference setting may seem unremarkable, but, to me, it signaled a real shift in attitudes and norms, a move away from paranoia and secrecy toward legitimacy.

Nearly everyone I talked with welcomed research, some eagerly. Rather than being met with suspicion, or needing an OG like Ed to introduce me around, I was welcomed by people who thanked me, even before I had completed a single thing. I was invited to events and included in informal networks quite readily. I had entered the field anticipating that my "cannabis credentials" from California would be critical for entry, but it turned out that my university affiliation was at least as important as, if not much more important than, the "friend of a friend" networks I had expected to rely on. Academic credentials signaled serious, professional work, and in an industry seeking professionalization and legitimacy, the prospect of being treated seriously was welcome.

I expected to find a patient-driven social movement underway. After all, in California, the pioneering laws to allow medical cannabis were structured to keep profit out of the equation, and it was mostly patients who led the way. I soon realized that this was not the way things were unfolding in Colorado. Most events consisted of the networking activities of an emergent industry in the midst of negotiating its transition out of the underground or gray market. Public activity around medical cannabis in Colorado was not coordinated or attended primarily by patients in their role as patients or as citizens volunteering in a social movement. To be sure, many who attended events were registered medical marijuana patients, but they were not solely patients or activists—they were small business entrepreneurs invested financially in the newly forming medical marijuana industry: dispensary owners, infused product developers, or providers of one of the many secondary services that cannabis businesses require to function. Some were seriously ill, chronically ill, or disabled and, radicalized by the relief cannabis had brought them, were now looking for where they fit. Some were old-school "outlaw" growers looking to turn legit in a market where their expertise had extraordinary value. A handful were old hippies who had adopted this issue long ago and stayed the course. Some were younger countercultural types, many of whom served as front-line employees in the service and manufacturing sectors of this new industry.

One contingent not composed of patients was the refugees from the financial and real estate industries who had left these sectors as a result of the economic downturn—entrepreneurial types who had sniffed out the need for their skills in the emerging medical cannabis sector. They were enticed by the potential to work for something meaningful, and—every entrepreneur's dream—to get in "on the ground floor." Many mentioned their passionate feelings about the issue, but it was also clear that they found it thrilling to be part of the creation of a legitimate industry where literally nothing had existed before. Many felt a sense of accomplishment in helping to shape that industry in its early days, to be a part of history. Of course, many also hoped to hit the right niche, build successful companies, and make handsome amounts of money. The prospect of making money while doing something meaningful held a strong allure and gave many events the feeling of civil rights meets alternative health care meets dot-com boom.

In conversation, people told stories about their own therapeutic experiences or about the recovery of people close to them. But on stage, events typically revolved around industry talk: interpreting the latest rules that had come down the pike, learning about security or tracking systems available for dispensaries, or figuring out how to conduct banking when regular, federally insured banks refused them service out of fear of federal reprisals. Despite looking for more patient-centered events, it turned out that most of the visible, public activities related to medical cannabis revolved around businesses development, and the population they were meant to serve—the patients—remained largely invisible. I found myself wondering—where *are* the patients this new industry is serving? The result of my search to find the patients, learn their stories, and share their experiences is here. To the patients and advocates who participated in this research, and all the others who shared their experiences, thank you for telling me your stories. They have helped me find the courage to write this book.

# Marijuana, Cannabis, and Hemp: A Note on Terms

This book uses the botanical term *cannabis* to refer to both the plant and the many consumable products made from it. The word *marijuana* also appears in many places throughout these pages because it was used by many of the individuals interviewed, and it is the word used in many proper names and laws. As simple as that may sound, the terms themselves tell a story that bears on the patient experiences recounted here.

As with all things involving contested social construction, dispute over what to properly call the plant comes with the territory. And as a forbidden intoxicant, it attracts more slang and code names than most—from "muggles" and "weed" in the 20s, "reefer" and "pot" in the 30s, and "grass" in the 40s to today's "dank" and "chronic." Putting aside colloquialisms, the three terms commonly used in the U.S. are marijuana, cannabis, and hemp. For at least the last half-century, *marijuana* has been the most prevalent term, but *cannabis* is gaining currency and marks the speaker as among the cognoscenti. The participants in this study used both *marijuana* and *cannabis* to refer to the plant, with most calling it marijuana, the name used in Colorado state law and regulations, as well as federal law. That is consistent with the prevalence of the terms in general usage, even in relation to medical use, as reflected in the Google search results produced for the terms in January 2018: "medical marijuana" appears roughly 1,750,000 times to a "mere" 567,000 hits for "medical cannabis."

Regardless of a term's prevalence, those affected by it can be sensitive about its use and implications, as has been the case with names historically associated with stigmatized groups. Among patient advocates, there has been a concerted effort to decouple medical use of the plant from the stigma and stereotypes that attach to *marijuana*. Many patients in this study described making strategic choices about which term to use, often choosing *cannabis*, as chapter 5 discusses. *Cannabis* is a term gaining increasing acceptance as the appropriate term, but it's also an ancient Latin word that has been used in English since the sixteenth century and the botanical name used by Carl Linnaeus in his 1753 taxonomy, *Species Plantarum*.

Some activists have argued for making distinctions between the terms based on uses of the plant, such that *cannabis* refers to medical use, while *marijuana* refers to recreational use. More have adopted the stance that any use of the word *marijuana* is pejorative and perpetuates racist tropes about Mexican immigrants to the U.S. This is an emerging view. However well-founded in the historical record (as discussed in chapter 3), this interpretation of the term is not shared by all, or even most, activists, as seen in the names of leading organizations. The oldest advocacy group concerned with the issue is the National Organization for the Reform of Marijuana Laws (NORML), founded in 1970, and the organization that has driven many of the successful state initiative campaigns over the past twenty years is the Marijuana Policy Project.

Legislation has driven contemporary terminology in many respects. In the early twentieth century, the plant is named *marijuana* or *marihuana* in federal and state laws. When Congress and the various states first enacted laws targeting consumption of this "new" drug marijuana, they effectively obscured its identity as the plant widely known at the time as *hemp* or sometimes *cannabis*. *Marijuana* became the word used to refer to the plant in its illicit, smoked form in the press and public discourse.

In recent years, *cannabis* is being used increasingly in not just conversation but legislation. California's recent history provides an illustration: The first mention of *medical cannabis* comes during the 2011–2012 legislative session, appearing once in a bill that uses the term *medical marijuana* a dozen times.[2] In the next session, there were four bills that used *medical cannabis* to fifteen that called it *medical marijuana*. The 2015–2016 legislative session was the tipping point, with the introduction of ten bills related to *medical marijuana* and ten others related to *medical cannabis*. The 2017–2018 session, underway as this book went to press, has seen thirty-four *medical cannabis* bills introduced and eighteen that refer to *medical marijuana*. This shift in terms is captured in the changing name of California's comprehensive regulatory system enacted in 2016, which started as the Medical Marijuana Regulation and Safety Act but was renamed, as of January 1, 2017, the Medical Cannabis Regulation and Safety Act. The regulatory agency the legislation created likewise went from being called the Bureau of Medical Marijuana Regulation to the Bureau of Medical Cannabis Regulation, which then, with the passage of the voter initiative legalizing all adult use, became the Bureau of Cannabis Control.

Similarly, and perhaps more pointedly, in 2017, the Hawaii Senate and Assembly unanimously passed SB278, which finds "the term marijuana originated as a slang term to describe the genus of plants that is scientifically known as cannabis" and "[m]arijuana has no scientific basis but carries prejudicial implications rooted in racial stereotypes from the early twentieth century."[3] By the end of 2019, all references to medical marijuana are to be replaced with medical cannabis.

The change in terms may mark an apt end to an era. The term *marijuana* or *marihuana* doesn't appear in the American lexicon until around 1918, the time of moral panic that also produced the Harrison Narcotics Act and alcohol prohibition. In the 1930s, *marihuana* was the term of choice for the yellow journalists employed by William Randolph Hearst, who produced lurid stories of axe-murdering Mexican migrants made insane by consuming the new and dangerous drug. The varying spellings (also *marig hwane* and *mariguan*) suggest attempts at phonetic spelling of Spanish, but even in that language it was at best regional slang.

*Hemp* was the word Americans knew and used. *Hemp* had been the term in English for the plant at least as long as the language has been written, dating back through Old English to before 1000 AD. Chaucer wrote of hemp as plants long cultivated for fiber, and seventeenth-century landowners in Virginia and other American colonies were directed by law to grow it. By the early nineteenth century, the plant called hemp was being described by Yeats and others as something consumed for its effects. British physicians working in India were reporting on the traditional Ayurvedic medical practices they observed there,[4] including the plant's uses as an analgesic and antispasmodic. Extracts of the plant suspended in alcohol were manufactured by pharmaceutical companies and sold in pharmacies as *hemp tinctures* from the 1850s until it was dropped from the *U.S. Pharmacopoeia* in 1942. Even so, San Francisco's fateful 1991 municipal voter initiative, Proposition P, which would set the stage for California's statewide Proposition 215 in 1996, was the "Hemp Medicine" measure. Nonetheless, *hemp* is a term now reserved for distinguishing phenotypes cultivated for fiber properties from those rich with cannabinoids that are grown for the medical and recreational markets, despite the fact that it was the original name for the medicine.

We use the term *marijuana* in the book's title because it best captures what is currently being medicalized: the twentieth-century construction of the plant and its uses as deviant and destructive.

## Notes

1. Dean E. Murphy covered the issue in the *New York Times*, which included the articles, "Clash On Medical Marijuana Puts a Grower in U.S. Court" (January 21, 2003; https://www.nytimes.com/2003/01/21/us/clash-on-medical-marijuana-puts-a-grower-in-us-court.html), "A California Cultivator of Medical Marijuana Is Convicted on Federal Charges" (Feb 1, 2003; https://www.nytimes.com/2003/02/01/us/a-california-cultivator-of-medical-marijuana-is-convicted-on-federal-charges.html), and "Jurors Who Convicted Marijuana Grower Seek New Trial," (Feb 5, 2003; https://www.nytimes.com/2003/02/05/us/jurors-who-convicted-marijuana-grower-seek-new-trial.html).

2. California Senate Bill SB-129. Medical marijuana: qualified patients and primary care-givers: employment discrimination. Introduced by Senator Leno, January 27, 2011. http://leginfo.legislature.ca.gov/faces/billNavClient.xhtml?bill_id=201120120SB129

3. Hawaii Senate Bill 786. Passed 7–12.2017 (Act 170). https://legiscan.com/HI/text / SB786/id/1604401

4. O'Shaughnessy, W.B. 1843. "On the Preparations of the Indian Hemp, or Gunjah (Cannabis Indica)." www.ncbi.nlm.nih.gov/pmc/articles/PMC2490264/pdf/provmedsurgj 00865-0001.pdf

# Introduction

## A Tale of Two Patients

As my husband and I raised our kids, we felt like we were going to raise them in a drug-free environment, you know? We didn't smoke, we didn't drink, we went to church, and we were just very law-abiding citizens. We just wanted to live in a small community like we do. We wanted to know where our children were all the time, and I was fortunate enough that I was able to say home and raise our kids and not work outside of home except . . . until later on.

(Karen)

### Karen's Story

Now in her early fifties, Karen is a Hispanic wife and mother who lives with her husband Mateo and their two children in a small bedroom community on the outskirts of the Boulder–Denver metro area in Colorado. Back in the 1970s, when Karen and her husband were in their teens and early twenties, they were social cannabis users. When asked about the first time she tried cannabis, Karen says:

I was probably sixteen. And it was just really recreational—weekends, or after work, whatever. My husband and I were married for seven years before we had kids so it was just the two of us and we had a good time. We had money, we both had good jobs, and I'm not much of a drinker anyway. I've never wanted to experiment with other drugs. Once we started having a family and planning our own family, you know, it was time to settle down, grow up, be responsible.

For Karen and her husband, that meant leaving behind cannabis to be suitable parents and build a wholesome family life.

It has now been thirty years since they got married. Their children are now the age Karen and Mateo were when they last used cannabis socially, and, until the last few years, cannabis was more a distant memory for the couple than a part of their day-to-day world or social circle. Karen knew little about its medical applications and had no reason to believe it might be a viable alternative to pharmaceutical drugs. Trying cannabis medically to treat her migraines never would have crossed Karen's mind if it weren't for the car accident that befell Mateo and its aftermath, which would change their lives.

Back in 2000, Mateo was driving home from work when a driver ran a stop sign and t-boned the front end of his car, spinning his vehicle around until it landed on its side in a ditch. As dramatic as the impact was, the damage appeared to be mostly to the vehicles. Mateo, a healthy and athletic man, walked away from the accident seemingly unscathed. When the ambulance arrived on the scene, he declined medical treatment, but within days it was evident that there was more wrong than it had at first seemed. As Karen remembers:

> The accident happened on a Thursday. He called his boss and told him what had happened, and he said, "Take the day off, come in Monday, we'll call it good." So, my husband spent the weekend at home, felt pretty good, went back to work on Monday. By Monday, he called me at noon and said, "get me into a doctor. I have the worst headache." I can't even imagine his pain. It was just excruciating. We got him in to the doctor that afternoon. Right away they ran x-rays, EKG, and MRI—all kinds of stuff—and they said, "Well, from what we can tell, there isn't much going on here, but we'll send you to [a specialist]." And it turned out that . . . discs in his neck were ruptured. He was diagnosed with a closed head injury.

The injury generated a great deal of suffering for Mateo: blinding headaches and unyielding back and neck pain that upended his life. He was forced to quit working. At first, the accident seemed like a temporary crisis, but as time passed and Mateo did not recover, it slowly sank in: There was no "going back to normal." From the beginning, Mateo's ordeal was his family's ordeal. For most of their marriage, Karen had been a stay-at-home mom who was involved in her church and the PTA and volunteered with underprivileged children, but after the accident, she had to forego many of these activities and find ways to pull in income. She took over many family responsibilities while also managing her husband's health care—getting him to doctor's appointments, filling prescriptions, keeping records, filing insurance paperwork. Karen describes it as five years of hell, during which little changed for the better. Mateo's medical treatment after the accident was involved, and required a great deal of coordination, record-keeping, and financial stress.

> For five years, we did everything. . . . [Before the accident, my husband was] extremely healthy, very active. And so, when all of that happened, you know it was like: trigger-point injections, Botox injections, muscle stimulator machine, physical therapy, prescription medications, you

know, OxyContin, pharmaceuticals. I mean, the list of pharmaceuticals is just a mile-long. . . . Then he started suffering from depression. And then, of course, the pills have their side effects, and so, for all of the side effects they give you another pill, and then the pill has a side effect, so it's just a vicious circle of lots of medications, to the point of where, I mean, I would literally carry around a backpack full of bottles for him. They tried different antidepressants; they tried different pain pills; they tried different acid reflux pills, nausea pills. You know, the list is just literally endless. Endless! Our insurance company spent over $100,000 on his medical care in a five-year time frame. He had surgery, and it was actually the last resort. Surgery was the last resort.

I watched Mateo go from being so active and being a huge part of our family—then lost his job. You know, because of the pain and whatnot, I mean, we really, really almost lost everything. We've lived in this home for over twenty years, actually over twenty-five years, and when you have a guy come in with the tow truck and try to take your vehicles, you feel like you've hit bottom at that point. They started fore-closure proceedings. I mean, we had to do everything to keep our heads above water—cash out our 401(k)s, cash out our life insurance policies—just . . . everything. Everything. And then, we filed for disability for Mateo because eventually he just couldn't go back to work. It was just horrible. . . . I think what made it worse, though, was all of the pills he had to take.

Some drugs rendered Mateo zombie-like. Others transformed him into a Jekyll and Hyde of unpredictably angry moods. It became impossible to interact with him in a normal way. He moved into a basement room of the house. A few years in, he began to struggle with dependency on the medications that had been prescribed to manage chronic pain. Karen recounts that he twice had to go to a weeklong inpatient treatment to manage addiction problems related to the OxyContin and oxycodone prescribed to him.

Those were opiates. You know, it would relieve the pain, but it made him. . . . You couldn't even have a conversation with him, couldn't even talk to him. . . . He would sleep, have diarrhea, nausea, constipation . . . be the worst man—I mean, you didn't even want to be around him. He was so loopy, you couldn't even talk to him, honestly! He would make no sense. . . . It was awful.

Initially, when Karen's nephew, who was using medical cannabis for a diges-tive disorder, suggested that Mateo should try it, Karen dismissed the idea as idiotic. Despite her initial skepticism, the nephew persisted. Eventually, more out of an exhaustion of options than any genuine belief that it would work, Karen and Mateo decided that he should try medical cannabis. Much to his and Karen's shock, it worked. Medical cannabis gave Mateo a new level of control over his neuropathic pain. He was able to reduce his prescribed pain medications, which also lessened their significant, problematic side effects. He returned, if not to his former athletic self, at least to a far more functional state, the most "normal" life he had experienced since the accident.

> I honestly have been thinking about, for the longest time, writing a book and calling it "Medical Marijuana Saved My Husband's Life." Literally, because it did. It literally saved his life, you know? It saved our marriage. It really did, which is kind of crazy to think of, but if you had known us when we were going through all that, you just went like, "Wow, these people have—an awful life." It was an awful life, because honestly all he did was. . . . We used to have these huge barbecues in our backyard for the Fourth of July, and all of these people would come over and do things together. . . . That first [Fourth of July after the accident], he just spent the entire day in the basement sleeping. He was totally . . . he couldn't socialize with anyone anymore. You can't do anything. And so, when my nephew approached me and said how about trying this, I thought. . . . Actually, it was almost out of a moment of desperation, where I thought, "You know what? I've done it all. I've tried everything else. Maybe we need to consider this." Because . . . what? It can't get any worse!

Once Karen saw what cannabis did for her husband, she began to do research on it. Because of their financial situation, Karen and her husband decided that the most economical choice would be to grow his supply themselves, in a room in their basement. Karen and Mateo had been foster parents before his accident, but this was no longer possible. Still, between foster parenting and Mateo's accident records and disability claim, Karen was accustomed to navigating bureaucracies and keeping meticulous records. With some trial and error, they got their legal garden set up with Karen as Mateo's caregiver.

Karen became more willing to accept that cannabis might work for other conditions, but when she learned that it could be used to treat the migraines she experienced, she was very reluctant to try it herself. It made sense for Mateo because his situation had been dire, and other treatments were producing terrible side effects. Karen's situation was different. Karen's migraines could be quite severe, but the idea of "getting high" to treat them just seemed wrong to her. Karen was the one who managed everything, and her memories of using cannabis socially from her teens and twenties were of giggling, munchies, and carefree times with few responsibilities. That didn't seem appropriate now. Nonetheless, cannabis was always in the house for her husband's care.

> I have actually suffered from migraines since high school. My doctor . . . I had gone for a physical one day, and she said, "You know, Karen, you've

got the medicine. Why don't you use it?" And I said, "Because! It's pot!" You know, I was like, "I can't!" Because I had been . . . you know, I mean the government's done a really good job of teaching us that "Just Say No." And I raised my kids that way. And I just kept, I mean, literally, I grew [marijuana as a caregiver for my husband] for two years before I [was willing to try it]. I kept saying, "I can't!" You know, I was so brainwashed: "You just cannot do this." You know, I'd be a horrible mother; I'd be a horrible wife; I'd be a horrible parent. I mean, I'd be a bad daughter, you know? I mean, just . . . "You can't do this."

One day, as a migraine was setting in, Karen could not find her prescription migraine medication. She could tell that the migraine was going to be a nasty one.

The pain is so excruciating. You throw up. Light hurts your eyes. You really just want to go into a dark, dark room where you can't even see your hand in front of your face and just lay there and hopefully sleep through it. . . . And when the migraine is over, you're just totally drained. You have no energy. It literally takes almost thirty-six hours to recover from a migraine for me, in my experience.

When she failed to find her prescribed medication that day, the knowledge that cannabis could be used to treat migraines, knowledge she'd carried around for months, led her to the impulsive decision to try cannabis this time.

The first time I tried it, it made a believer out of me because . . . within seconds, I was pain-free. It totally knocked me off my chair. And you know, it was really hard for me, because I'm just in my basement, locking my bedroom door, trying to be sneaky and quiet, you know? I didn't want anybody to know what I'm doing. It's hard when you're not used to that kind of a lifestyle. . . . When it worked, I just went, "Wow, this is weird!" I was just in such disbelief. . . . I just couldn't believe it. And talking with people and doing the research on the internet, doing the books, reading about it, you know, it just was like maybe there really is something to this.

Not only did cannabis immediately halt the progression of Karen's migraine, it caused fewer side effects and had none of the "hangover" that her prescription migraine medications often left in their wake. While she remained secretive when using cannabis in her home for migraine relief, she was quick to spread the news among her close network of family and friends that "this works." The combination of witnessing Mateo's improvement and her own experience of relief radicalized Karen, turning her from a skeptic to an advocate. She is now open about her family's success with medicinal cannabis and welcomes the opportunity to share their story. Because Karen sees herself and her family as deviant in no other way, she believes her willingness to be open about medical cannabis use helps to dispel some of the misperceptions that surround its use and users, misperceptions she acknowledges she also held before this experience.

Karen offers assistance to others exploring cannabis as a medical option, and when new patients experience success with cannabis, it only adds to her conviction about the importance of this issue. In an attempt to save money and be more self-sufficient, she decided to provide cannabis for a few other patients in addition to her husband, an option that was within the rules for legally designated caregivers. That led to some interactions with the law. Federal agents from the Drug Enforcement Administration (DEA) came to her house after an anonymous tip, which Karen believes was probably from an electrician who had worked at the house.

> I was too shocked to be scared. . . . Everybody always told us if you're going to grow, you don't have to let them in, you just put your card in the window and say, "Bring me a warrant and I'll let you in, but without a warrant—bye." Well, we open the door and let them in. I thought, "I'm doing it legally. . . . If I don't have anything to hide [I] might as well let them in and cooperate. . . ." They kind of did that good cop, bad cop thing. I've seen enough *Law and Order* to see what's going on here. We let them into our grow room and show them everything. They took pictures and saw the plants and saw our licenses, and they basically gave me a thumbs-up and said, "Well, you're doing it the way you're supposed to be, so it's all good." It was a very huge relief and a huge shock because I had thought, "I'm going to jail! My God! That's it. It's done." Because again, it's still a federal offense.

The agents found her small garden in compliance with state law and left it undisturbed but said they would report her to local authorities. So, Karen went to the local police station herself and offered to help educate them about medical use.

> The next morning, I woke up and I thought, maybe you should go and talk to them first. Because I thought, well, if they're going to talk [to the local authorities] . . . I really didn't want them to know. I just . . . I didn't want them to know what I was doing because there's a stigma. Even though I have my card. Even though I had a recommendation. I kind of wrestle with, do I let my local law enforcement know? After the DEA came, I thought, I have no choice.

Karen admits that she and her husband now sometimes choose to use cannabis as a part of their social lives. She was never much of a drinker, even when she was younger, and now she and her husband find they prefer cannabis when they have a party at their home, or every so often to unwind at the end of a particularly hectic day. While Karen's views have changed, one of her two children, a freshman in college, still disapproves of his parents' use of cannabis.

> I remember asking [my son] one day, what would you think if I started smoking, and he flat-out said, "Mom," he says, "I think you'd be a horrible mother if you did." And that was his attitude. He won't touch it. He will not touch it. He'll drink. But he's a [college] student. He gets federal money for student financial aid. He would lose his financial aid. You know because it's federal money, and it's a federal offense. And there's been times where he's been in pain, and I'll say *mijo*, let me put some of this [cannabis lotion] on, and [in a whisper-yell]: "NO!!!" He won't. He'll just lay there and suffer rather than use it. Because that's how he was raised, and that's his belief system. And I told him, I said, I totally respect you for that. It is totally your choice. Maybe someday you will come around, you know? I'd rather see you smoking than drinking. . . . But that's society for you!

## Dale's Story

> I worked in the oil fields, where I was a safety supervisor. I remember standing up and saying, "There's nothing medical about marijuana." And boy was I wrong!
>
> (Dale)

Born and raised in Missouri, Dale has the slow scruffy drawl of so many hardworking roughneck blue collar guys in their fifties. He spent years working in the oil fields in locations around the country. As a frequent user of alcohol and all sorts of recreational drugs during his younger years, which had even entailed a brief stint in jail for methamphetamines, Dale was quite sure that he had enough expertise in the area of drugs to call bullshit when he heard it. He was confident that medical cannabis was nothing more than a clever ploy.

Dale came up in the working class with two siblings: one sister and one brother. His brother died young as a soldier fighting in Vietnam. Their dad traveled a lot in his work as a salesman, leaving mom at home to take care of the kids. Dale refers to his family life as pretty stereotypical of the 1950s and 1960s. Alcohol was ever-present social lubrication, but cannabis was morally opposed as the "devil's weed." Maybe it was his rebellious personality or just growing up in the heyday of the sex, drugs, and rock-and-roll epoch, but Dale began his career as a juvenile delinquent early. He started smoking and drinking at age eleven, trying cannabis along with anything else he could get his hands on.

> When I was a little bluegill, eleven years old, that's when I started kind of checking out pills, and I found that my mom, she was the best connection I ever had. I used to go in there and steal her Valiums and stuff like that.

He was already running afoul of the law within the year. At age twelve, he was arrested for stealing pills from a doctor's office. In 1973—the same year that Nixon launched the DEA—Dale was thirteen and on house arrest. At sixteen, still on probation, Dale's parents found an ounce of pot and handed it over to his probation officer, who pressured him to move out from his family's home or be reported for violating his probation. After Dale left home, his choice of friends and lifestyle made recreational drugs a normal feature of social life. In high school, Dale got arrested for possession of a pound of marijuana. Later, in his twenties, he got busted in Texas with 25 pounds of weed, which resulted in jail time and a felony record. "You know, that has followed me around the rest of my life," Dale said. It leaves him ambivalent about whether or not recreational use should now come with no penalties, since he feels he paid so many. On the one hand, it seems capricious that others would face no consequences, but, after thinking about it, he also says that he would not want others to have to go through the same thing.

In his late twenties, Dale had to go and find work because he got married and had two children: a boy and a girl. Dale's felony record made finding work a challenge. He got a commercial driver's license and ended up working the oil pipelines, jumping around to different locations based on where jobs were available. "Eventually I had to go out and make a living and stuff, and every time I turned around I had to take a drug test." In Dale's line of work, drug testing was standard, and if you didn't pass, you were out of work. Many drugs pass quickly out of the system within a day or two, or even within hours, but the metabolites from cannabis can linger in the system for up to a month, making it the most common reason for a failed drug test. Dale couldn't afford that, which meant cannabis was out.

Through his thirties, Dale still indulged in drugs and drank a lot of beer. He tried meth, which he now regards as a regrettable choice.

> You know, I got strung out on it [in the early 90s], and I'll never take it again now that I've been away from it for so long. It's some of the worst stuff there is. I stayed strung out for about eight months, and—well see, I was all strung out, and then my aunt died, and I found out I was inheriting some money. So, I thought, screw this doing [meth] all the time; I'll make it. It's a lot cheaper. So, I started doing that . . . and you know, I got caught. Then I went to prison [for four years], and I thought, well, I'll just have to leave that stuff in [my old town], and that's why I [live in a

different town now], because I just left that speed crap in [my old town]. I haven't done it since 2000.

While these are the highlights—or, perhaps more accurately, the low points—in Dale's drug history, he does not seem to connect the dots on how much the substances and their penalties have influenced his life. Whether using street drugs, pilfered pharmaceuticals, or just drinking beer, he presents it all in an unapologetic, matter-of-fact manner.

After the jail stint, Dale slowed down in his forties. He decided to stop drinking but needed help. His doctor administered a minor tranquilizer called Librium to aid Dale's detox from alcohol. Dale says that he became dependent on Librium, but it was effective. Dale stayed away from alcohol after that and tapered off the Librium under guidance from his physician. Next, he had a series of work-related injuries, in which he damaged the anterior cruciate ligament (ACL) in his right knee, followed by problems with the cartilage in his left knee. For each knee, it took many months to go through the insurance claim processes in the workplace to get treatment. After several surgeries in 2005 and 2006, multiple rounds of physical therapy, slews of pharmaceutical painkillers, and a stack of medical bills that were paid out by his employer, Dale was let go from work and given a $5,000 settlement. He spent six months unable to walk. Now, instead of taking drugs for fun, he was taking them to control pain.

The opioids he was prescribed screwed up his stomach and left him feeling zoned out. In relation to the pharmaceutical painkillers he was prescribed, Dale says, "I've always liked them. Drugs are good, but they're like fire, you know? If you take too much, they're bad for you. And I took too much, and it was bad for me, I guess." Because of stomach issues from the opioids, Dale barely ate. He started losing a lot of weight.

> I would just sit in front of the TV, you know. I'd get up in the morning and put on a DVD, something I'd watched ten times before, but it was a new adventure every day because I never remembered it because of the narcotic drugs.

Friends and family became concerned about him. His weight loss was alarming, and he seemed withdrawn. At some point, Dale's ex-wife's adult son, whom he considered a good friend, dropped by with groceries and a joint, insisting that he should smoke it and eat something. Dale smoked the joint and, for the first time in months, ate with real gusto. Impressed that the cannabis eased his stomach and helped his appetite, he was still not completely convinced that the "munchies" could be considered a "medical" effect of cannabis. However, he started using cannabis to improve his appetite and ultimately returned to a normal weight.

Since he planned to keep using it for appetite support, Dale looked into a doctor's recommendation. He lived on the western slope of Colorado, which is a conservative area where dispensaries were under a moratorium at that time. He thought that having his paperwork in order might help him stay out of trouble with local cops. To get a license, he had to go to Denver. After getting the recommendation, Dale teamed up with a buddy who was running a dispensary in a nearby town. He started working at the dispensary and getting discounts on his own supply as a result. When his daughter, now a devout Christian in the health care profession living in the mid-Atlantic region, learned that he was using cannabis, the two quit speaking to one another. Dale shrugs and says that she can believe what she wants, but her lack of acceptance is her own personal problem, which he clearly does not feel reflects on his choices.

Cannabis helped not only with appetite but also with pain management. While Dale liked the pain relief from the opioids, he hated the side effects. It had been a constant balancing act, but now he could substitute cannabis and reduce the number of painkillers he took. His stomach improved as a result.

> At first, I was taking it with the opiates and stuff, because it enhanced [the medication's effects]. And then I just did it by itself because—I don't know, I just did it by itself. I just lost interest in taking the pain pills.

Then Dale learned that cannabis could be used to treat Hepatitis C, a virus that is spread through blood-to-blood contact. Dale reports being diagnosed with Type 1A Hepatitis C in 1996. He believes he could have gotten it through intravenous drug use or from getting tattoos. The Hepatitis C virus comes in different variants, and may show no symptoms, but the disease scars the liver, causing damage and impairing its ability to function. It can eventually result in cirrhosis, but about 25 percent of cases resolve themselves. Baby Boomers are at the highest risk of this condition, with one in thirty contracting the disease (Gilead 2017a, 2017b). When Dale was diagnosed, he was told that Hepatitis C was typically treated with Interferon, but his type could not effectively be treated with this medication. He believed it to be a permanent condition that would eventually cause his liver to fail.

After learning that cannabis could treat Hepatitis C, Dale decided to "flood his system" with cannabis. He also began taking a supplement made from algae that a patient at the dispensary recommended to him for his liver. Later he added ginger, gingko biloba, and cayenne pepper to his dietary supplements, based on advice from friends and other patients.

Dale did not feel he was going overboard with his cannabis use, but he admits that he used a lot over the first few months. According to Dale, "I was taking so much because it settled my stomach, [which was upset] from the Hepatitis C. It just settled my stomach from the surgeries, and you know, it made me feel a lot better." His friends expressed worries that he was being excessive and urged him to be more moderate. After a few months, he scaled back to a modest level. He cut down smoking tobacco. He had already quit using other recreational drugs.

After using cannabis therapeutically for six months, Dale's functional health measurements had improved significantly, especially his liver function. Dale reports that when he went to the doctor after six months of using medical cannabis, the physician insisted that his liver enzymes were normal. He no longer had Hepatitis C. He says that the physician was scratching his head over it, but Dale attributes it directly to his medical cannabis use.

Dale's long trajectory of drug use includes a history of arrests and legal problems that are entirely a result of drug use, drug sales, or other decisions made in connection to drugs. Given his lifelong problematic relationship with substances across the spectrum, Dale is a dubious poster child for medical cannabis. In fact, Dale's story seems more a cautionary tale for the deleterious effects that drugs can have on a life. Some might even argue that Dale is the type of person who raises concerns among the general public about medical users in the first place. Yet despite his checkered past, he devotes a considerable amount of energy to advocating for medical cannabis. He claims that local police have harassed him over his activism. After participating in one such event, he was pulled over for a suspected DUI. Even though he no longer drinks and was sober at the time, he refused to submit to a urine test for drugs, unaware that this would cause him to lose his commercial driver's license for life. Dale is a die-hard libertarian who says he loves his country but hates his government. He advocates for medical cannabis because, as he sees it, the issue is just one more example of government overreach.

## Karen, Dale, and Medical Cannabis Patients at Midlife in Colorado

Karen and Dale are two of the forty middle-aged medical cannabis patients in Colorado who were interviewed for this book. Their stories provide a glimpse into the wide range of attitudes and experiences to be found among patients who use medical cannabis at midlife.[1] We have focused this book on patients for several reasons. First, the obvious: Patients are at the center of the medical cannabis issue. While several good books have addressed the overall policy landscape, industry development, or research on cannabis as a medicine, few have focused on the patients, their experiences of the system, their struggles, and their needs. The patient role is a self-selected identity, but it is also defined by formal rules for who can claim this identity and who cannot. Understanding who participates in the medical cannabis system becomes useful for assessing its successes and failures.

In the chapters that follow, we explore the ways in which the experiences reported by Karen, Dale, and the other patients in this study are shaped by the fact that cannabis is not fully accepted as a modern medical treatment, a situation that can be described as incomplete medicalization. *Medicalization* is a term introduced by sociologists in the 1970s to describe the process by which a previously nonmedical issue comes to be defined and treated as medical (Conrad 2007, 5). On the one hand, medicalization is a process of incorporation within the system of biomedicine. On the other, it is about the cultural acceptance of medical categorization. Because cannabis is not fully medicalized, it straddles legal, cultural, and institutional boundaries. This partial medicalization creates opportunities and pressures for those who participate in the emergent medical cannabis programs—patients, doctors, providers, and other stakeholders—to construct legitimacy where institutions and social norms do not yet confer it.

Medical cannabis use remains contested largely because the historical construction of rhetoric around marijuana use has reflected bias and prejudice more than science and fact, distorting the politics and policies surrounding it. The "official story" of marijuana use over the last eighty years has been a totalizing one in which all use is treated as deriving from deviant motives with the sole intent of intoxication. Medicalization troubles the single story of cannabis in which users are characterized as deviants seeking intoxication, making evident that use is more diverse than this oversimplified story suggests.

The first two chapters provide an overview of the forces, both cultural and structural, that shape the attitudes, stereotypes, and legal dilemmas faced by the contemporary medical cannabis patient. Chapter 1 recounts the evolution of cultural attitudes about marijuana leading up to the modern medical cannabis movement, from Killer Weed to Dropout Drug to the science and pseudoscience of recent years. Chapter 1 ends with a description of research on medical cannabis programs and patient populations.

The complex, interconnected layers of local ordinance, state and federal laws, and even international treaties that patients discover and navigate is the focus of chapter 2, The Landscape of Cannabis Policy. A look at the major shifts in federal policies over the twentieth century and the numerous attempts to amend federal law are coupled with a summary of the introduction of current state medical cannabis programs and the federal government's various attempts to squelch them. The chapter ends with a look at public opinion on medical cannabis and an introduction to important aspects of Colorado's law, regulations, and program that directly affected the participants in this study.

Readers who would like a background of the cultural and legal history of cannabis will benefit from these chapters, but it is also possible to skip ahead to chapter 3, where the book resumes analysis of patient experiences, starting with the decision to try cannabis medically. As the stories of Karen, Dale, and others show, medical cannabis patients vary considerably across social class, lifestyles, and prior use of illicit drugs, but an experience they share is a shift in attitude toward cannabis, both as a medicine and as a cultural object. Some medical cannabis patients start out like Karen. They may have used cannabis briefly in their youth, or they may have had no previous experience with recreational use. In either case, cannabis use was not considered an acceptable social activity for adults with professional jobs and kids to raise. Others, like Dale, had no moral objections to cannabis or other drugs and, in fact, had used drugs liberally, for better or worse, well into adulthood. In these cases, cannabis was only avoided when there was practical necessity, in order to evade risks connected to its use, such as drug testing for employment.

In looking at how patients initially explore medical cannabis, how they interact with physicians around the recommendation process, and how they organize their use to fit medical criteria, we borrow several important theories used in sociology and medical sociology to frame patient experiences and behaviors. These include Habermas' concepts of *system* and *lifeworld*, which explain the different logics used by actors working within institutions and those making decisions related to everyday life. In *Medicines and Society*, Nicky Britten applied Habermas' schema to medicine, which provides a useful point of comparison between medicinal use of cannabis and the use of pharmaceuticals more generally.

At the start, most patients shared a deep initial skepticism that cannabis possesses true medicinal value beyond placebo, distraction, and the appetite stimulation well known as the "munchies." This was true regardless of prior experience with recreational use. Certainly, many had no expectation that it could be effective on par with prescription medications. Some resemble Dale. They are less concerned with the legal and cultural status of cannabis but start out doubting that it has medical value. Others, like Karen, struggle with both the idea of cannabis as a medicine and with maintaining propriety and legality. They worry about the stereotypes of users and how cannabis use might reflect on their reputations, or struggle with how it might affect self-image. Karen not only rejected the idea of medical value when her nephew suggested it; she judged him for using it. When her husband tried cannabis with good results, she amended her ideas about its medical value, but the stereotypes were still ingrained strongly enough that Karen resisted using it herself. It felt too much at odds with her mature, parental identity and seemed hypocritical in light of how she'd raised her children. Chapter 3, Becoming a Patient, describes how patients first learned that they qualified for medical cannabis; how they mitigated risks associated with participating in a medical cannabis program and balance that against potential rewards of beneficial medical treatment; and how the decision to register with the state as a patient is a decision that is separable from cannabis use.

Chapter 4 describes the roles of physicians, identity work, and legitimation in the patient experience, beginning with approaching a physician to obtain the formal recommendation all states require to participate in a medical cannabis program. Similar to contested diagnoses, patients found variability in the willingness or ability of their primary physicians to recommend cannabis for their conditions. Some doctors rejected cannabis; others expressed a neutral or supportive attitude, citing bureaucratic or administrative restrictions that limited their ability to recommend cannabis for medical use. The vast majority of patients in this study obtained a recommendation with cannabis specialists, who are often derided as "doctor mills." The role of these specialized professionals is examined in the context of medicalization, where their actions bridge a gap between biomedicine and more informal patient-driven models of care. Many patients cared about doctor professionalism, and the management of impressions plays a part in the integrity and legitimacy of the medical cannabis designation. Yet the role of physicians is necessarily limited. Patients are often left to figure out how to use medical cannabis on their own.

Patients differ in their knowledge of cannabis starting out. Some have never used cannabis, others have only done so decades before and in a social context. Learning happens through fellow patients, online resources, and informal consultation with dispensary staff. In learning to use cannabis medically, patients acquire a new system of interpretation for effective use. These routines for using cannabis medically are laid out in chapter 5. The key theory that anchors our analysis is usually referred to as "drug, set, and setting." In this tripartite framework—elaborated across chapters 5, 6, and 7, respectively—a drug's effects are due to not just the drug's chemical composition but also its interaction with each individual's physiological and psychological "set," as well as the setting in which the drug is being consumed. A central premise of this book is that the redefinition of cannabis from a social inebriant to a medicine results in substantial changes to all three of these dimensions.

Chapter 5, Medical Cannabis Use in Everyday Life, examines how placing cannabis within a medical context changes the drug itself, its modes of ingestions, the interpretation of effects, and the settings in which it is used. It may come as a surprise to learn just how much innovation has transformed and diversified the cannabis plant for medical use instead of recreational use. By examining how patients arrived at their use routines, we show that patient concerns revolve around common, everyday concerns for holistic health and the ability to function in the individual's various roles.

Chapter 6, Changing the Set: Creating Medical Routines of Cannabis Use, proposes that, in the context of self-care, many of the differences between social use and medical use are in the behaviors and routines that accompany consumption rather than any other factor. However, differences between therapeutic and pleasant effects often blur, stressing that such designations are less appropriate at the individual level. Medical and recreational designations are a system-level distinction. Karen and Dale both reported social use in their late teen and early adult years prior to having children. Their use later in midlife is different in context and purpose. In chapter 7, The Power of Place: Changes to Setting, we argue that phases of the life course can serve as a type of setting, and midlife is a different setting than adolescence. Especially when combined with medical intentions, taking account of age dramatically alters how cannabis is used, understood, and represented.

The last chapters of the book turn from medical use to management of the medical cannabis identity, followed by two appendices. The first details the research methods used to collect and analyze the data in this book, and the second offers an annotated list of the patients interviewed to help readers track individual stories throughout the book.

Chapter 8 details the significant practical risks faced by medical cannabis patients, then turns to the topics of stereotype and stigma, exploring how cannabis use and medical conditions are each stigmatizing and intersect with other aspects of identity to affect perceptions of an individual's medical cannabis use. How patients cope with stereotypes and risks is explored in chapter 9, Strategies for Managing and Changing Cannabis Stigma. Patients have adopted both individual and collective strategies similar to those used by other groups for managing concealable stigmas. Many cannabis users resist stigma, and, like those advocating for gay marriage, work to reclaim a spoiled identity with some success. Out of this, a "thought community" has arisen that shares a common group style when interpreting medical cannabis use.

When Mateo, and then Karen, adopted medical use, their family's upstanding reputation allowed Karen to counteract the stigma associated with cannabis. Indeed, Karen's decision to be vocal about it was in part based on her self-awareness of the power her otherwise normative position lent to her story. She and her husband could advocate for the legitimacy of medical cannabis, even to the police themselves, because of their confidence in the strength of their social standing in the community. Dale also chose to be vocal about medical cannabis, but given his lengthy history of drug use, addiction, and arrest, his support was less likely to persuade others, least of all the police with whom he continued to have negative interactions. Members of the medical cannabis community face a conundrum in working with representatives like Dale, when establishing legitimacy for this issue is difficult. All patients face decisions about how publicly to adopt the medical cannabis user label based on the reputational risks that involve intersections of identity by race, gender, social class, and relationship to mainstream or subcultural groups that may alter the setting for medical cannabis use and affect how it is interpreted.

Karen and Dale illustrate how the setting for medical cannabis use extends to what sociology calls "strong networks," those information-carrying social ties largely composed of family and friends. Patient interviews show that responses to adverse health events and assessments about medical cannabis use are not isolated, individual choices but instead are intimately connected to one's family and social networks. Decisions about managing illness and treatment are almost never made alone. In both Karen and Dale's case, someone in their close networks persistently recommended cannabis for medical purposes. Many patients had a person like Karen's nephew or Dale's ex-wife's son—a personal connection who made the initial suggestion and sometimes kept making it with great persistence. Some patients witnessed firsthand the therapeutic effect of cannabis, as Karen did with Mateo. The success of others enabled the eventual decision to become a registered patient. Some, like Dale, were prodded into impromptu self-experimentation to determine by direct experience if cannabis was medically useful. Patients with more recent social use may not have required these prompts but nonetheless often describe a shift or transition during which they tested its medical efficacy and began a discussion with family or friends about the legitimacy of medical use. Once the barriers to trying medical cannabis were overcome and some success was experienced, patients often felt compelled to share this with others, essentially taking on the role of the person who had initially prompted them. This distribution of information along social networks plays a key role in introducing patients to cannabis. Some patients went beyond their close networks by participating in more public forums for education or advocacy, though many chose to keep their medical cannabis patient status private or restricted to their network of family and friends because public identification remained undesirable or represented unacceptable practical risks, whether legal, professional, or reputational.

Since cannabis is often a medicine of last resort, many patients present their medical cannabis use in the context of long experience with other treatments and the shortcomings of the U.S. health care system. Often, they report problems with overmedication or mistakes with prescribing or diagnosis. Karen, Dale, and other patients formed strong opinions about these experiences, and their stories illuminate how patients see the relationship between cannabis, pharmaceuticals, and overall goals of health and wellness. In the final chapter, Beyond Medicalization: Healthism and Pharmaceuticalization, we examine how patient interpretations of medical cannabis use contribute to and reflect larger societal trends toward healthism and pharmaceuticalization. Healthism helps explain how patients view their cannabis use in relation to health benefits and risks of harm, how mood and pain are intertwined, and the ways in which cannabis becomes a tool for enlightened health, supporting healthier choices. This contrasts sharply with patient concerns about the safety of pharmaceutical drugs and the influence big pharma exerts on physicians' prescribing practices. In every estimation that patients made about the relative safety of cannabis, they were adamant that it was far safer and often more efficacious than the pharmaceutical drugs they had been prescribed.

Our focus on patient experience contrasts with how cannabis use has been commonly considered: as a manifestation of criminality or addiction. By situating therapeutic cannabis use within a process of medicalization and the diverging trends of pharmaceuticalization and healthism, we examine the deeper issue: What defines a substance as a medicine? Is it chemical structure or formal designation or is it the behaviors that surround use?

## Note

1. For the purposes of this study, middle age, or midlife is defined as between the ages of thirty and sixty-five.

## References

Conrad, Peter. 2007. *The Medicalization of Society*. Baltimore, MD: The Johns Hopkins University Press.

Gilead Sciences, Inc. 2017a. "Understanding Your Hep C." *HepCHope.com*. Retrieved August 2017 (www.hepchope.com/about-hep-c).

Gilead Sciences, Inc. 2017b. "Reasons to Get Tested: Baby Boomers at Risk." *HepCHope.com*. Retrieved August 2017 (www.hepchope.com/).

# Chapter 1

# The Social Construction of Cannabis Use

The cannabis plant's legal and cultural status has been highly contested terrain over the last hundred years, shifting from its largely uncontroversial use as a folk medicine and natural resource at the advent of the twentieth century to its designation as a heavily criminalized drug by its end. This transition was at least in part accomplished by narrowing the definition of cannabis to equate with one use and one use only—illicit use for the "high," a use attributed no benefits, only harms. Other traditional uses—as medicine, food, fuel, and fiber—were subsumed by the focus on its potential dangers as an addictive, mind-altering substance. Policies across all levels of government enforced this single story[1] in ways that affected science, culture, and criminality. Mainstream culture, and in large part the social, medical, and natural sciences, adopted this singular definition. Despite intermittent protest and dissenting professional opinions, debates over cannabis were successfully and repeatedly reduced to the frame of use for nonmedical, sensation-seeking purposes, and anyone who fought to retain its historical uses or otherwise revise, expand, or reframe it to suggest benefit from this plant's use, or even less severe harm, was characterized as illegitimate and a potential "drug user" (Ferraiolo 2007).

Not only were the uses of cannabis as a traditional medicine stripped away, but the narrowed definition of cannabis use as deviant treated all use as equivalent. In reality, cannabis is used with different frequencies and purposes, and in different contexts. Naïve use is different than experienced use, and use by the young may differ substantially from use among the middle-aged or older adults. As a society, we know how to make these distinctions and regulate accordingly. We do so already in the case of alcohol, deeming some uses acceptable and others problematic based on age, context, amount, and frequency. With "marijuana," no such distinctions are made; all use is treated as equally problematic (Benoit 2003; Zinberg 1984). In this sense, it is not the plant but its users or potential users around which the issue centers. Over the past century, cannabis users have been routinely characterized in negative and stigmatizing ways (Ferraiolo 2007; Almanzar 2003). Framing users through a lens focused only on harm has mattered greatly for how the public perceives cannabis and its place in society (Almanzar 2003).

## From Hemp Medicines to Marijuana and Moral Panic

The approach to cannabis use in the first half of the twentieth century can be characterized as a transition from indifference to moral panic. The "patent medicines" of the past centuries gave way to a professionalizing and standardizing field of medicine. It is easy to forget, now that Americans spend $200 billion a year on pharmaceuticals, that only in the twentieth century has medicine been organized around standardized drugs. The proprietary medicines of the last century were typically based on some mixture of opiates, alcohol, and cannabis, in addition to other herbs and various substances. As U.S. society migrated from agrarian life toward cities, the introduction of revolutionary technologies and theories were fundamentally changing how medicine was practiced and by whom. Medical training and medicines were heading on a path of regulation and standardization that would create modern biomedicine.

Leading up to this time, the landscape of medicine was far different. Medical education and credentials were diverse, where they existed at all, and untested proprietary medicines were widely available. Medical concoctions were unregulated and very popular. With national campaigns, "snake oil" medicines were marvels of marketing and packaging, an entrepreneurial fast track that produced what Oliver Wendell Holmes referred to as "toadstool millionaires" (Tomes 2016). These proprietary medicines—commonly known as patent medicines—relied not on patents but on copyright and trademark law, which allowed them to protect their brand name, logo, and packaging without divulging their ingredients for others to copy (or for patients and doctors to evaluate).

As the relatively new germ theory for the transmission of illnesses gained acceptance through the middle of the nineteenth century, diagnoses based on the individual's unique attributes, personality type, and environmental conditions gave way to a view of diseases as discrete, mechanical, and treatable with only limited consideration of the individual characteristics of the patient. This new understanding of medical conditions was accompanied by the development of new techniques for drug manufacture. Aspirin was successfully standardized in the 1890s by a chemist at Bayer in Germany. First distributed through physicians in powder form, it only became a hit as an over-the-counter tablet in 1915 (Jeffreys 2004). Aspirin was followed by standardized drugs for syphilis, insulin treatments for diabetes, and then penicillin for infections in 1928. These "magic bullet" drugs offered targeted and highly effective treatment for some diseases when compared with what had come before. As new forms of mass-produced, standardized medications proved effective and medical professionalization began to create a new expert class of physicians, concerns increased with regard to the widespread and unchecked use of patent medicines, which could result in abuse, addiction, and toxicity causing injury or death (Bonnie and Whitebread 1999). Following Britain's lead, U.S. lawmakers enacted food and drug laws that became the precursors to modern drug regulation (Tomes 2016).

The first anti-drug campaign was concerned with opiates. Much like alcohol and cannabis, opium and drugs derived from it have been in use for much of known human history. The addictive quality of opiates was known, and in the mid-nineteenth century, the introduction of the concentrated opiate, morphine, and the new method of using hypodermic needles led to extensive use in the treatment of soldiers suffering injuries in the Civil War. Opiate withdrawal was so associated with this application that it was nicknamed the "army disease" (Bonnie and Whitebread 1999; Conrad and Schneider 1998 [1980]). It was also possible for unsuspecting customers who used patent medicines with unknown quantities of opiates to become addicted without knowing the contents of what they were consuming. Finally, the presence of deviant, underground opium smoking and trafficking of opium racialized the drug. Opium prohibitions began in the western U.S. during the 1880s and 1890s, and were closely tied to the perception of its users as immigrant Chinese who smoked this drug for the purposes of intoxication (Bonnie and Whitebread 1999). Attitudes toward opiate addiction shifted radically in the first two decades of the twentieth century (Conrad and Schneider 1998 [1980], 121). With new laws and regulations, the chances of accidental addiction became less probable, and those who persisted in using nonmedical formulations of opiates were increasingly characterized as deviants: "dope fiends" or "street users." As Bonnie and Whitebread (1999) point out, "what had been formerly viewed as an unfortunate sickness with organic causes was now viewed as yet another immoral behavior of the criminal class" (Bonnie and Whitebread 1999, 21). This change created problems of its own, as it gave rise to a criminal subculture with its own networks for supply (Conrad and Schneider 1998 [1980]; Bonnie and Whitebread 1999).

Opiates were categorized as narcotics, a class of drug that was medically defined based on the ability to dull a person's senses and cause drowsiness or sleep (Bonnie and Whitebread 1999, 28). In this era, many psychoactive substances were quickly grouped into the narcotics family, including plants from the belladonna group, cannabis, and peyote. Opiates were standardized and woven into formal medicine over the first half of the century, and synthetic opioid analogs were developed mid-century, but with ongoing concerns with their addictive and toxic potential. The recent epidemic of opioid-related deaths, especially among white middle-aged males in the working class, has created a new wave of concern for their place in medicine and society. Despite these concerns, opioids form an entire class of widely used and valued pharmaceutical medicines in their proper applications. The original moral panic over opiates may be seen as a template for what happened to cannabis. Much of the rhetoric about the dangers of "marihuana" was lifted directly from propaganda of the period from the 1870s to the

1900s that propelled the first great drugs scare over opiate use (Bonnie and Whitebread 1999; Chasin 2016; Himmelstein 1983; Harrison 1988).

Moral panics typically entail an outsized emotional reaction about an issue that does not correspond to actual harm, damage, or threat suggested by the evidence. In a moral panic, there is little evidence of significant practical consequences, but the sense of moral threat leads to public sensitization, exaggeration, distortion, and stereotyping (Goode 2008). The active period of concern is usually short, but actions taken in response to moral panics can be institutional and long-lasting (Goode and Ben-Yehuda 1994).

The first half of the twentieth century included a period of moral panic over cannabis, driven largely by the yellow journalism of Hearst newspapers, leading to the plant's criminalization in a transition that has been well documented by others (Ferraiolo 2007; London 2006; Gerber 2004; Booth 2003; Bonnie and Whitebread 1999; Goode 2008; Goode and Ben-Yehuda 1994; Himmelstein 1983; Cohen 1980). By the time the temperance movement was in full swing in the 1920s, cannabis remedies had fallen out of favor (Fox, Armentano, and Tvert 2009). Then, when Harry Anslinger was named the first chief of the newly created Federal Bureau of Narcotics (FBN) in 1930, the era of reefer madness commenced (Chasin 2016; Ferraiolo 2007). Anslinger would remain at the helm of the FBN for thirty-two years. During that time, he led the charge against marijuana, creating propagandistic literature on its dangers, falsely testifying to highly exaggerated negative effects, invoking racially charged stereotypes, and instigating policy changes at various levels of government that effectively criminalized marijuana— all of which contributed to cannabis losing its designation as a medicine in the U.S. Pharmacopoeia (Ferraiolo 2007; Galliher, Keys, and Elsner 1998). Anslinger and the FBN controlled drug-related research, repressed findings that did not match their agenda, exerted influence on the media, and ultimately shaped the discourse on cannabis for most of the twentieth century (Chasin 2016).

During the "reefer madness" era prior to mid-century, users were depicted as menacing, criminal, sexually deviant, and even potentially murderous or insane (Bostwick 2012; Gerber 2004; Almanzar 2003; Booth 2003; Bonnie and Whitebread 1999). The appellation "Killer Weed" derived its claims from opiate rhetoric, erroneously suggesting that cannabis use could result in death or induce users to commit murder (Himmelstein 1983).

The success of this morality campaign is largely attributed to the fact that most Americans had little firsthand experience with cannabis as a drug (Gerber 2004; Almanzar 2003). Only sixteen states had laws that made cannabis possession and sale a crime in the 1930s, and even in states with such laws, enforcement was lax (Goode and Ben-Yehuda 1994). In the early 1930s, breathless newspaper accounts employed the term "marihuana" instead of the more common and readily recognizable terminology of the time, "hemp" or "cannabis." Those stories included fanciful accounts of the ravages of this "new" and "dangerous" drug, a rhetorical choice that helped to transform public perceptions of the plant, as did associations with migrant workers from Mexico and immigrants from the West Indies, as well as jazz musicians (Bonnie and Whitebread 1999).

## From Killer Weed to Dropout Drug

After social uses of cannabis were popularized in the 1960s and 1970s, the sensational characterizations of earlier in the century became difficult to maintain. Many more people had tried cannabis or knew people who used it without suffering any dire consequences. Modern claims of harm shifted away from the most outrageous exaggerations but maintained a quality of disproportionality that is characteristic of moral panics (Goode 2008; Cohen 1980). The new claims of harm not only differed in their specifics but also transformed the "general image of the drug and its users" (Himmelstein 1983, 13). Instead of "killer weed," cannabis came to be known as the "dropout drug," which in turn reorganized the political actors involved in drug control (Himmelstein 1983, 13).

In this era, associations between cannabis and youth subcultures emerge (Hammersly, Jenkins, and Reid 2001). The new propaganda characterizing cannabis as a "dropout drug" expressly contradicted many of the prior claims made during reefer madness. As "killer weed," cannabis had been said to induce mania, leading to frenetic activity and extreme acts of depravity. The new dropout version claimed that its use led to apathy and a complete lack of motivation. Cannabis might no longer be characterized as instigating murderous insanity, but one thing remained the same: Cannabis use was still a subversion of mainstream culture and behaviors. While some people felt that cannabis use and users were harmless, stereotypes of cannabis users became interwoven with political divides, fueling jokes and derision in popular culture, even as it could serve as a sign of membership in counterculture. These stereotypes were intentionally reinforced and exploited by the Nixon administration in its launch of the war on drugs, as discussed in chapter 2.

Cannabis use has often been interwoven with stereotypes of its users, from jazz musicians and Mexicans to hippies and other groups whose association with cannabis indicates an oppositional edge. The hippie counterculture of the 1960s and 70s was the largest youth subculture to adopt cannabis, and its influence on college campuses accounts for how most Baby Boomers were introduced to it in the 1970s (Almanzar 2003; Harrison 1988). More recent groups to affiliate with cannabis use include hip-hop culture, skateboarders, and a more loosely defined frat-boy party subculture depicted in movies. The connection between cannabis and these groups evokes stereotypes that are mutually discrediting (Stolick 2009; Ferraiolo 2007; London 2006; Bonnie and Whitebread 1999). Within these subcultures, cannabis use often becomes a multilayered symbol signaling a deliberate subversion of mainstream values, a rebellion against social control and authority, and a marker of "cool" or devotion to a partying lifestyle. These meanings are intentional; creating distinction from mainstream norms is the point (Williams 2011).

Depictions of cannabis use often combine stereotypes of these groups with stereotypes of "stoned" intoxication, either in morality tales or for humorous effect (Goode and Ben-Yehuda 1994). Cannabis use becomes the cultural punch line to an inside joke that reinforces its relationship with undesirable personality and social group traits, such as lack of motivation, lower intelligence, poor judgment, or other characteristics that lead to marginalization and social or financial failings. This is not unique to cannabis. Joking often functions to define group or moral boundaries and serves as a form of informal social control (Fine and De Soucey 2005). This follows a well-worn rhetorical pattern of exaggerated, stereotyped representations of stigmatized groups serving as a basis for comedy (Schaefer 1999).

Undesirable qualities associated with cannabis or with specific groups that are considered cannabis friendly, such as hippies or gangs, discourages casual or occasional users from adopting cannabis use as a marker of identity. To do so might imply membership in a cannabis-friendly subcultural group, or suggest they share stigmatizing qualities with users or groups (Williams 2011; London 2006; Hammersly, Jenkins, and Reid 2001). Occasional users may only feel weakly connected to cannabis and downplay their use, or only disclose their use to specific people or in contexts where it would result in positive rather than negative social judgments (Hathaway, Comeau, and Erickson 2011). Those who use cannabis consistently or who identify with a subcultural group that glorifies its use are more inclined to identify themselves as cannabis consumers. In this sense, the framing of cannabis is tied to its legitimacy, and these factors influence who publicly identifies with it.

Starting in the dropout-drug era fifty years ago, age has been a significant criterion for cannabis use. Cultural and structural changes to society since then have gradually extended the adolescent and young adult phase of the life course into the college years, especially for "mainstream," white, middle-class Americans (Furstenberg et al. 2004; Arnett 2000). This longer period of young adulthood has been accompanied by new worries about experimentation with risky or deviant behaviors that are typically initiated during adolescence and young adulthood, such as sexual activity and drug use.

Settersten's (2004) work on the life course describes how age structuring includes timing of behaviors based on age, which matters for how those behaviors are interpreted. The 2016 report from the University of Michigan's ongoing Monitoring the Future study showed that cannabis use reports remain highest among the nineteen to twenty-two age group, with 25 percent reporting cannabis use in the last month (Schulenberg et al. 2017). After age twenty-two, use rates decline gradually with age, inching down a few percentage points for each successive age group, until it flattens out around age forty-five at 7 percent. Based on the 2012 report, which includes adults over age fifty-five, use rates drop off precipitously among the oldest categories, basically among those on the other side of the Baby Boom generation, who were already out of their teen years at the time when cannabis was popularized (Johnston et al. 2012).

Many "age out" of deviant behaviors, including the social use of cannabis when life-course hallmarks such as graduation, job, marriage, or children prompt different lifestyle choices. Others fall prey to the consequences of these youthful indiscretions, being arrested, getting pregnant outside of marriage, contracting STDs, becoming addicted to substances, or essentially derailing a successful progression to the next stage in the life course (Johnston et al. 2012; Sampson and Laub 1992). Some individuals will maintain a deviance career, but there is a drop in deviant behaviors with age, as individuals desist from these activities (Giordano, Cernkovich, and Holland 2003; Kazemian 2007; Warr 1998). This is not simply a reflection of aging but shows strong connections to life-course transitions, including marriage, work life, parenting, and changes in friendship networks and their activities (Adams and Markus 2001; Giordano, Cernkovich, and Holland 2003).

Activists in the 1970s believed that opposition to legalizing cannabis for medical or other uses was purely generational. As members of the flower-child generation aged and assumed positions of political power, and the older folks who had not seen or participated in cannabis use in their college years died off, support for legalization would steadily increase. They were right that the percentage of the U.S. population with direct experience of cannabis would grow steadily until roughly half of adults report using it at least once in their lifetime (Swift 2017; SAMHSA 2017). But the ratio of those opposed to or in favor of cannabis legalization did not change. The reason appears to be parenting, as shown in Nate Silver's (2010) statistical analysis of changes from 2000 to 2008 in the General Social Survey. As individuals moved into midlife and assumed the responsibilities of career and, more importantly, parenting, their attitudes on cannabis shifted. Opposition to legal access came to correlate most closely to having children in the home. Concern for the wellbeing of one's children is nothing surprising, and government messaging on marijuana has consistently exploited this fear.

## From Dropout Drug to Just Say No

Most sociological work on cannabis since the intensification of drug criminalization in the 1980s has focused on adolescent use and its negative short- and long-term effects. The adoption of cannabis by those in college during the 1960s and 1970s, and its trickle down to high schoolers shifted prevention efforts in the Reagan era to cannabis' influence on teens (Harrison 1988). This era saw massive funding increases to drug education and the introduction of DARE (Drug Abuse Resistance Education) and Nancy Reagan's infamous "Just Say No" campaign (Hudak 2016). In this time period, drug education programs worked from the premise that children are impressionable and incapable of making well-considered decisions (Earleywine 2010). In their view, if children become involved in use of cannabis, development and chances for success in life will be negatively affected. Showing concern for children reduces the need for immediate evidence and rationalizes efforts to maintain or increase criminality because reducing penalties has a hypothetical potential to increase supply to children (Earleywine 2010; Zimmer and Morgan 1997). Recent evidence refutes these predictions, but they still have moral and symbolic power to influence policymaking (Reed 2016; Anderson, Hansen, and Rees 2015; Lynne-Landsman, Livingston, and Wagenaar 2013).

Ironically, the *therapeutic* potential for children drove the passage of limited medical cannabis laws in more than a dozen states in a span of little more than a year. This potential came to public awareness in 2013 as a result of a CNN Special Report by medical correspondent Sanjay Gupta, M.D., the neurosurgeon who was under consideration by the Obama administration for the position of Surgeon General until he withdrew his name. The special described the case of Charlotte Figi, a then-six-year-old girl with Dravet syndrome, a severe form of epilepsy that produced up to 300 damaging grand mal seizures a week and left her confined to a wheelchair. Charlotte's desperate parents had signed a do-not-resuscitate order for their young daughter before they turned to cannabis as a medicine of last resort. In the first week of being treated with cannabis, Charlotte, who had been experiencing dozens of seizures a day, had none.

Charlotte's story, along with the advances in research that the show publicized, galvanized parents whose children were suffering from similar conditions. Within days, state legislators across the country were hearing from desperate parents pleading for legal access to this medicine. On April 1, 2014, less than eight months from the airing of the report, Alabama became the first state to enact what has come to be known as a CBD-only law, allowing legal use of a cannabis extract that is predominantly or exclusively CBD for treating seizure disorders. By the end of that month, Georgia, Kentucky, Mississippi, and Wisconsin had followed suit, and within little more than a year there would be seventeen states with such laws.[2] These "CBD-only" states are notable for their conservative politics and legislative resistance to drug policy reform. Added to the states that allow access to a broader range of whole-plant cannabis medicines, as of July 2018, forty-six states and the District of Columbia, as well as the U.S. territories of Puerto Rico and Guam, provide for the legal therapeutic use of cannabis in some form. That total includes Arkansas Oklahoma, and North Dakota, where ballot initiatives were not yet implemented as of the time of this writing. The four holdouts of Idaho, Kansas, Nebraska, and South Dakota have each actively considered medical cannabis legislation, with South Dakota having enacted a CBD-only law that is currently unworkable because it requires FDA approval.

The effect on teen use of this proliferation of state medical cannabis programs is coming into focus. The continuing collection of usage data from long-term studies such as Monitoring the Future, the National Survey on Drug Use and Health (NSDUH), and other surveys all show that providing medical access does not increase teen use. If anything, the effect is the opposite. Several studies have found teen use rates were unchanged or dropped after medical cannabis programs were enacted (Mauro et al. 2017; Grucza et al. 2016; Schmidt, Jacobs, and Spetz 2016; Lynne-Landsman, Livingston, and Wagenaar 2013). A 2012 study that compared use rates in states with and without medical cannabis laws found that while teen use increased in states without such laws, there was no change in teen use in states with medical cannabis laws. A 2015 study of twenty-one states with medical cannabis laws similarly found no significant difference in adolescent cannabis use rates from 1991–2014 (Hasin et al. 2015). In Colorado, the teen cannabis use rate is below the national average, and 2015 data from the Department of Public Health and Environment's biannual survey of 17,000 high school students reveals that cannabis usage dropped among teens when the state made all adult use legal (CDPHE 2015; 2017b). National data compiled by the federal government shows that in 2016 cannabis use among adolescents aged twelve to seventeen was lower than in most years from 2009 to 2014, and the number classified as having "marijuana use disorder" has dropped steadily.

Where state medical cannabis programs do show an effect on cannabis use rates is among those age twenty-six and over, whose use has increased (Anderson, Hansen, and Rees 2015). Uses for medical purposes at midlife radically change the "set and setting" of cannabis use, which in turn radically alters the experience of use. Timing matters. Age may affect the experience of cannabis in physiological as well as social ways. Cohorts create different referents related to cannabis use.

## From Stoner Culture to Skewed Science

Over the past four decades, the cultural subtext and stereotypes for cannabis use have become taken for granted. Public rhetoric still implies connections between cannabis and stereotypical groups and behaviors but has moved more into the language of authority: science and medicine.

Many of the modern arguments of harm caused by cannabis use share a common challenge. Each requires that clear distinctions be determined between correlation and causation. Teasing out such relationships takes time and research. Scientific research on cannabis has been skewed, because research whose aim is to prove harm has been well funded, but research meant to discount harm or show benefits has been successfully delayed or blocked and has not been eligible for financial support from most funding sources (Werner 2011; Aggarwal 2010; Cohen 2009; Gerber 2004). This imbalance has allowed questions of harm to frame the entire debate. Very little public discourse includes considerations of both health and harm, and those who wish to present both sides are often hamstrung by the lack of scientifically rigorous evidence. The large preponderance of negative studies allows for the easy but false inference that there is more evidence of harm than benefit. Scientific discourse has trickled down to set the terms of popular culture discourse in many respects. Topics about physical harm, mental harm, gateway theories, and amotivational effects dominated media and common understandings of cannabis among the public (Vickovic and Fradella 2011; Stolick 2009; Zimmer and Morgan 1997).

Specific claims to harm are based on purported negative effects to mental and physical health, as well as negative social judgments. These have included theories that combine social and physiological causes in their explanations, such as the *gateway effect* and *amotivational syndrome*. The gateway theory suggests that an effect of using cannabis is a progression to more seriously addictive and damaging drugs. Amotivational syndrome suggests that chronic cannabis use induces an indolent and unmotivated state, causing individuals to cease pursuit of their goals, or even stop maintaining their own appearance and health (Stolick 2009; Chapkis and Webb 2008; Iversen 2008; Joy, Watson, and Benson 1999; Zimmer and Morgan 1997; Lynne-Landsman, Livingston, and Wagenaar 2013). Neither has been shown to have a basis in evidence.

## Breakthroughs in Basic Science

Despite significant obstacles to clinical research on cannabis as a medicine in the United States, there have been important developments in basic scientific research, mostly from outside the United States, since the beginning of the 1990s (Werner 2011; Hazekamp and Grotenhermen 2010; Grant 2010; Aggarwal et al. 2009; Vettor et al. 2008). The most important development has been the identification in the early 1990s of the receptor system in the body with which cannabis interacts (Werner 2011; Vettor et al. 2008; Russo 2002).

Research on the endocannabinoid system (ECS) is opening the door to better understanding this plant's therapeutic and intoxicating effects. Some liken the activity of the ECS to the body's other receptor systems, such as the gland-based endocrine system, by which hormones are regulated (Iversen 2008). These basic scientific findings about cannabis show that this system plays an essential regulatory role for a large number of bodily functions. So far, the ECS has been related to regulating homeostasis in the body, including modulating immune function, influencing learning and memory, and affecting pain perception (Danovitch 2012; Werner 2011).

These functions are tied to two types of receptors distributed throughout the body and brain that interact with at least two naturally occurring ligands, or endocannabinoids, named anandamide and 2-AG (Danovitch 2012). The first type of cannabinoid receptor identified, CB1, is found primarily in the brain, while CB2 receptors are concentrated in the immune system. The CB1 receptors in the brain are further localized, with high concentrations in areas corresponding to the acute effects of cannabis use, such as memory, and very low concentrations in regions that control autonomic functions, such as respiratory centers of the medulla (Mackie 2008). The paucity of cannabinoid receptors in areas of the brain associated with breathing and heartbeat may help explain why cannabis is unusually safe. Many have proclaimed the research findings on the ECS as critical developments that will lead to the next generation of treatments (Vettor et al. 2008; Eddy 2009; Bostwick 2012; Aggarwal 2010; Mechoulam 2012). According to clinical researchers, cannabis has the potential to serve as the basis for an entire class of medications, just as the opium poppy plant has.

## The Evolution of Professional Medical Opinion

While researchers and professional medical associations are warming to the therapeutic potential of cannabis, members of the practicing medical community are much more divided over using the plant in its current form as a therapy (Kondrad and Reid 2013; Vettor et al. 2008). The most prestigious of America's professional medical associations have only recently adjusted their positions to more favorable but still tempered (Aggarwal 2010; Joy, Watson, and Benson 1999; Eddy 2010; Danovitch 2012). Opinions among individual medical professionals range from rejection of cannabis' medical uses and skepticism about even its palliative benefits, to full-fledged support for cannabis use across multiple scenarios that include palliative, ameliorative, and even preventive or maintenance use in conditions such as multiple sclerosis and epilepsy (Barthwell et al. 2010; Kondrad and Reid 2013; MacDonald 2009). Doctors in specialties such as oncology, anesthesiology, and neurology are more likely to be aware of research on the efficacy of cannabis and endorse its use by their patients. Even before any state had passed a medical cannabis law, Harvard researchers found that more than 44 percent of oncologists were encouraging their patients to try cannabis, despite its illegality (Doblin and Kleinman 1991). When *The New England Journal of Medicine* conducted an online debate in 2013 about medical cannabis using a cancer case study, they found 76 percent support among the 1,446 physicians representing seventy-two countries and fifty-six states and provinces in North America, despite the fact that such use would be illegal in many of the countries (Adler and Colbert 2013).

Physicians who criticize medical cannabis have expressed concerns that cannabis patients are gaining entry to the system based on largely self-reported subjective symptoms associated with pain (Caplan 2012; O'Brien 2013). However, pain is also one of the areas where biomedicine's solutions are limited and one of the reasons patients most often turn to forms of complementary and alternative medicine or CAM (Barnes et al. 2004). The prevalence of chronic pain has led to not just an exponential increase in CAM but also a fourfold increase in opioid use since the mid-1990s (Ayers and Kronenfeld 2010; Kessler et al. 2001). According to the Centers for Disease Control and Prevention (CDC), "enough prescription analgesics were prescribed in 2010 to medicate every American adult around the clock for a month" (CDC, 44). Some individuals make false claims of pain to obtain analgesic medications such as opioids or cannabis for improper uses; this is why doctors are assigned as gatekeepers to assess patient need. Safety is a central concern in making decisions about the use of analgesics, as approximately 17,000 Americans died from overdosing on prescribed opioids in 2016 alone, according to the Centers for Disease Control and Prevention (CDC 2017).

Ironically, the federal government's opposition to medical cannabis limits the influence of expert medical opinion (Bostwick 2012). The federal government has imposed unique barriers to medical research on cannabis, and maintains pressure up and down the legal chain from international law to state and local policies, which is discussed in the next chapter (Hudak and Wallack 2015). This undermines the ability of policymakers to base decisions on sound scientific expertise and medical evaluation and marginalizes the role of medical experts and professional associations. Instead, ideology is pitted against science and the will of the public. These choices have constrained the pathways for patients, doctors, advocates, and policymakers when it comes to setting medical cannabis policy and have played a critical role in ensuring its medicalization remains incomplete.

## The Process of Medicalization

When an issue that was previously defined as deviant or problematic is reframed as medical it is termed "medicalization." Sociologists have studied processes of medicalization since the late 1960s when it was first used to explain the incorporation of deviance into medicine, such as the classification of homosexuality and alcoholism as conditions (Conrad 2007). Early medicalization studies focused on the reframing of deviance, but this concept has since been applied to a wide range of human problems that came to be incorporated within medical jurisdiction (Conrad 2007, 4). Over the latter part of the twentieth century, medicalization has rapidly expanded, and many types of human problems have been redefined as medical issues.

Simply put, medicalization is the term used when something previously not treated as a medical problem comes to be treated as within the medical domain. This includes a definition of the problem using medical terms, using medical language, and adopting a medical framework or interpretation, and treating the problem with a medical intervention (Conrad 2007, 5).

Medicalization is seen as both a form of social construction and a form of collective action.

Just as cannabis use has a social construction that actively frames it with specific meanings, medicalization as a social construction is much more than labeling use as "medicating." It involves cultural, institutional, and interactional changes in response to these altered definitions. To accomplish this requires collective action and risks taken by patients, doctors, researchers, and stakeholders in government. Medicalization is not an immediate process, nor is it an either/or phenomenon. It is better understood in degrees, and it can coexist with other competing definitions that rely on other forms of social control, such as the law (Conrad and Stults 2008; Conrad and Schneider 1998 [1980]).

Historically, doctors and medical institutions have been central drivers in medicalization processes, but this is not simply to say that they have been selling new medical labels to unsuspecting patients—rather, patients and other lay people actively, often eagerly, collaborate in the interest of medicalization because, in many cases, it provides a more desirable interpretation of a problem and access to much-needed solutions that directly affect them or their families.

Just as medicine changes, medicalization processes also change (Conrad 2006). The concept has also been expanded to consider how medicalization processes are affected by the rise of biotechnological intervention, the increasing focus on health as an individual pursuit, the effect of the internet on health information, the effects of health insurance and managed care, and the exponential growth of pharmaceutical use, accompanied by power that pharmaceutical companies can exert by directly engaging consumers (Conrad and Stults 2008; Conrad 2005; 2006; Clarke et al. 2003; Schnittker 2009; Barker 2008).

Medicalization is most commonly applied to diagnoses and illnesses such as fibromyalgia, chronic fatigue syndrome, male menopause, or attention deficit/hyperactivity disorder (ADHD) (Conrad 2007, 2005; Conrad and Barker 2010; Conrad and Leiter 2004; Figert 2011; Turner 2004; Watkins 2007; Williams and Calnan 1996). Medicalization has also been applied occasionally to treatments, including opiate use (Conrad and Schneider 1998 [1980]), hormone replacement therapy, and complementary and alternative medicine (CAM) (Conrad 2007; Conrad and Leiter 2004). In these cases, the treatment is often the subject of scrutiny, although it also involves labeling those who use the treatment when it is not yet considered a legitimate medical intervention. A few studies have applied the theory specifically to medical cannabis (London 2006; Taylor 2008; Pedersen and Sandberg 2013; Hathaway, Comeau, and Erickson 2011; Chapkis and Webb 2008).

In *Deviance and Medicalization: From Badness to Sickness*, Conrad and Schneider (1998 [1980]) proposed a five-step model by which deviant behaviors come to be medicalized. The five steps, which are also summarized in Table 1.1 for easy reference, are (1) defining a behavior as morally deviant; (2) "prospection," or the emergence of a medical definition for a behavior, even if it may not be clearly defined as medical; (3) moral entrepreneurship, in which various lay or professional interest groups organize and attempt to fully claim medical territory for the issue by emphasizing its seriousness, scope, and its connection to "rights"; (4) legitimacy and consolidation, in which the state recognizes the medicalized status and begins to construct its management in these terms through legislation, court actions, and task forces; and (5) institutionalization, in which the medical definition becomes the dominant paradigm. This opens access to diagnosis and treatment, research through major institutions, and insurance reimbursement, as the public and media adopt and promulgate the view as normative (Conrad and Schneider 1998 [1980], 266–70).

In these instances, behaviors or complaints become connected, labeled, and defined as part of a problem that is constructed as medical in nature in phases 1 and 2. In the later phases, these new constructions seek acceptance and recognition from the institutions and their representatives, who can offer legitimacy. When medicalization is completed, it can be difficult to remember that the problem was constructed another way—it seems to simply be a "fact," and its incorporation into medical treatment is uncontroversial.

Many published case studies on medicalization describe problems that have reached the final phase of institutionalization. Cannabis has not reached that point. Currently, it may be best characterized as negotiating phases 3 and 4, as patients and their advocates push local, state, and federal officials to create systems for legal access. Moral entrepreneurs seek to establish the value

Table 1.1  Phases of the Medicalization Model[3]

| Phase 1: definition | Defining a behavior as morally deviant in a publicly recognized sense. This may include formal laws that restrict behaviors on this basis. |
|---|---|
| Phase 2: prospection | Emergence of medical categorization of the deviant behavior. New terminology may be introduced to distinguish the turn toward medical definition. |
| Phase 3: moral entrepreneurship | Medical territory is expanded through the work of moral entrepreneurs who emphasize the issue's importance, seriousness, and scope. These groups may benefit directly and/or professionally from expansion. |
| Phase 4: legitimacy consolidation | Proponents of medicalization seek recognition from the state through court rulings, legislation, or other actions. This stage helps to determine how the issue will be managed and defined. |
| Phase 5: institutionalization | The medical definition becomes the dominant paradigm, defining the issue among the public as "fact." It is incorporated into medical institutions, and alternative or opposing viewpoints are suppressed. |

of cannabis, but much of the public dialog has not shifted to one of "benefit" and remains anchored in debates about relative levels of harm, even for those using the drug under a doctor's supervision.

Similarly, phase 4, legitimacy consolidation, remains controversial in Colorado, even as the state has enshrined a medicalized status for cannabis in the state's constitution. Many other states have created patient legitimacy through enacting medical cannabis laws that provide legal and civil protections as well as systems for accessing cannabis, and yet others have taken approaches that are largely symbolic, distinguishing those with narrowly defined conditions from criminal users but offering no legal means of production or access. U.S. federal agencies and international bodies have actively rejected pressure from patients to acknowledge any cannabis use as therapeutic.[4]

Medicalization processes are not removed from everyday life; they involve contest and negotiation between medical professionals, patients, and the government (Conrad and Stults 2008). In the case of cannabis, medicalization is also tied to its relationship with other institutions—most importantly, its criminalization within the legal system, a relationship that will be further explored in the next chapter (Fair 2010; Conrad and Stults 2008).

## The Demedicalization of Cannabis

Conrad and Schneider's (1998 [1980]) case study on opiate use outlines the continuous, century-long debate over the appropriate management of opioids, drugs that have both medical utility and a high potential for abuse (Conrad and Schneider 1998 [1980]). Cannabis has also faced challenges in defining acceptable boundaries of practice, but it differs substantially from opioids in the qualities of intoxication, abuse potential, toxicity, and medicinal benefit. Some applications, such as analgesia, overlap, but cannabis has a far broader therapeutic potential than opioids or, for that matter, almost all other drugs. Opioid and cannabis use can each result in some degree of dependency, but the rate and severity is markedly different, with cannabis dependence ranked as roughly equivalent to being hooked on caffeine. The biggest difference is perhaps toxicity, with opioid use resulting in more than 53,000 deaths in the U.S. in 2017 alone, while cannabis is safer than many foods we commonly consume (Young 1988). Yet opiate medications such as morphine have never been banned, and the FDA has allowed the aggressive marketing of opioids such as OxyContin and oxycodone. Even so, the risks associated with opioid use is presented more accurately than those presented on cannabis. The differences between how opioids and cannabis are treated reflects the degree to which all these qualities have been actively misrepresented to accomplish moral, cultural, and political aims.

The re-incorporation of cannabis into medicine has been slow, in part because the standardization of dosage and purity modern medicine expects is more difficult to acheive with botanical products, but also because the path has been littered with obstacles that are unique to cannabis research. Since cannabis presents much lower risks across the physiological spectrum than other drugs, policies toward recreational and medical uses have been more determined by politics and culture than by threats to public health.

While medicalization implies a contest between a deviant identity and a legitimate medical one, this fails to fully capture the relationship between medical and recreational use. Distinctions between types of use may at times seem vague, but therapeutic use and recreational use are not synonymous. Nor do they always share the same goals. Let's look at what we know about those who use cannabis for medical reasons.

## Medical Cannabis Patients and Programs: What We Know

Although it has been more than twenty years since the first medical cannabis law passed, data on medical cannabis patients is limited (Belville 2011; Caplan 2012). Even estimating the population of state-qualified medical cannabis patients in the U.S. is challenging. This is largely because the patient registry is voluntary in a state with one of the largest patient populations, California. Most who participate in California's program are not on state rolls. Estimates for California depend on which state is used as the appropriate comparison. If California's number of state certifications is similar to those issued in Maine, where the registry is anonymous, the number of medical cannabis patients in California may be more than 1.5 million. If instead, California is estimated to resemble Oregon's more conservative enrollment rate, the estimate is half that number. Using this as a possible range for California's patient population, the estimated U.S. population of medical cannabis patients who have gone through a formal qualification process is between 1.5 million and 2.3 million. This number is projected to grow substantially as new state programs are opened to patient enrollment and existing programs recognize new qualifying conditions, as Colorado did in 2017 with PTSD. As of July 2018, Arkansas, Florida, Ohio, North Dakota, Oklahoma, Pennsylvania, and West Virginia are each implementing programs but are not yet enrolling or fully serving patients, and Maryland dispensaries have just begun distributing medicine. With a combined population of more than 60 million, those new states may add another million or more registered patients to the U.S. total. One countervailing factor that may push down the number of patients registering is the growing number of states with full legalization for adult cannabis use. Each of the states that now permit adult use, as Colorado now does, had a medical program in place prior to legalization and preserved some privileges for patients under full legalization. Those privileges are not without cost. The process of qualifying and registering as a patient remains laborious, entails a fee, and creates a record of the person as a federal lawbreaker—all factors that serve to discourage participation in the programs, as the patients interviewed here will describe. When cannabis is available at retail storefronts to anyone with a photo ID establishing age, many patients who would qualify for the medical program will opt to save time and money and protect their privacy.[5]

Colorado's state program offers better resources for researchers than many states; the Department of Public Health and Environment (CDPHE) publishes a monthly report that provides the numbers of patients in the Colorado system along with basic demographics. An archive dating back to January 2009 is publicly available on the CDPHE website, allowing enrollment to be tracked over time (see Figure 1.1). Still, this data is thin. It includes the number of patients who have applied, the number currently registered, and the summary statistics on qualifying conditions, gender, county of residence, and average age. No information is provided on age distribution, race, education, or other common demographic categories (CDPHE 2013).[6]

Overall, there is a lack of basic demographic information and health profiles on patients and programs (Kamin 2012; Reiman 2006; Nunberg et al. 2011; Aggarwal et al. 2012). One challenge has been that most states were not collecting data on even the most basic level, such as patient numbers, aggregates on conditions and diseases treated, or patient age distributions (Caplan 2012). Prior to this study, social science research about medical cannabis patients and programs in the U.S. has been conducted almost entirely in California (Chapkis and Webb 2008; Reiman 2006, 2007; O'Connell and Bou-Matar 2007; Nunberg et al. 2011; Reinarman et al. 2011; Mikuriya 2004; Harris et al. 2000; Janichek and Reiman 2012). The exception is recent work in economics on Colorado and medical geography studies on patients and services in Washington state (Anderson and Rees 2013; Aggarwal 2008; Aggarwal et al. 2012).

Even so, when studies are looked at across settings, a robust portrait of the medical cannabis patient emerges. Medical cannabis populations range across the entire adult range, but the most prevalent group, and the typical average age, is in the late 30s or early 40s (Aggarwal 2008; Aggarwal et al. 2012; Coomber, Oliver, and Morris 2003; Harris et al. 2000; Hathaway and Rossiter 2007; Hathaway, Comeau, and Erickson 2011; Janichek and Reiman 2012; Nunberg et al. 2011; Ogborne et al. 2000; Reiman 2006; Swift, Gates, and Dillon 2005). Every study finds that there are more men than women, typically at a ratio of roughly 2:1.

Individuals tend to seek out medical cannabis to treat similar conditions and symptoms. There are prominent cases of rare, difficult-to-treat disorders that respond positively to cannabis, but most qualifying patients are living with one or more of the following conditions: chronic pain (especially neuropathic pain and migraines), cancer, multiple sclerosis, glaucoma, nausea, depression, muscle spasms including menstrual cramps, digestive disorders, seizure disorders, HIV/AIDS, and musculoskeletal disorders such as arthritis

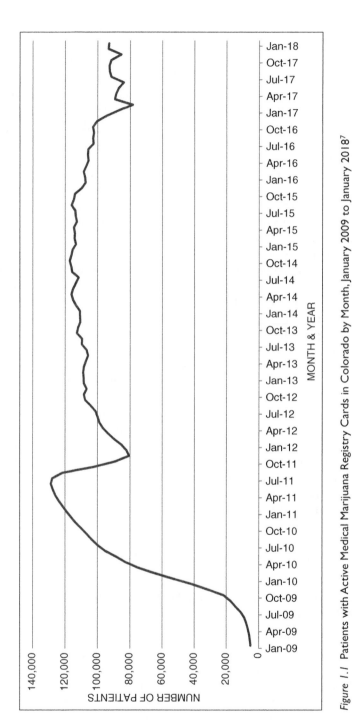

*Figure 1.1* Patients with Active Medical Marijuana Registry Cards in Colorado by Month, January 2009 to January 2018[7]

and fibromyalgia. A study in California, where physicians are not limited by a list of qualifying conditions established by lawmakers, found the most frequent reasons physicians recommended medical cannabis were back, neck, and spinal pain, followed by sleep disorders, anxiety or depression, and muscle spasm (Reinarman et al. 2011). Rates were relatively low for cancer, HIV, glaucoma, and multiple sclerosis. Chronic pain was by far the most common reason for a recommendation, and many patients note the widespread use of cannabis for pain, both historically and in other areas of the world (Caplan 2012; Swift, Gates, and Dillon 2005; Gallagher et al. 2003; Ware et al. 2003; Ogborne et al. 2000; Grinspoon 2001; Lucas 2012). Medical cannabis users are more likely to suffer from multiple conditions than the general population and use drugs at a significant rate—both prescription medications and licit and illicit recreational substances. Medical cannabis users report higher rates of tobacco use but lower levels of alcohol use than the general population (Reinarman et al. 2011).

Patients consistently report using cannabis as a substitute for prescription drugs (Corroon, Mischley, and Sexton 2017; Lucas and Walsh 2017; Lucas et al. 2016; Nunberg et al. 2011). This "substitution effect" means those who find cannabis helpful often voluntarily decrease their use of both prescribed pharmaceuticals and recreational substances (Reiman 2006; Mikuriya 2004; Swartz 2010; Lucas 2012). As will be explored in chapter 5, patients use many substances as medications, including prescribed pharmaceuticals, over-the-counter remedies, herbal and homeopathic remedies, and nonmedical recreational substances such as alcohol.

Medical cannabis patients share similar health attitudes and therapeutic aims with those who seek out other forms of complementary and alternative care. Those include dissatisfaction with the options of traditional biomedicine, a desire for "more natural" treatment options, and a desire to have more control (Coomber, Oliver, and Morris 2003; Bottorff et al. 2011; Reiman 2006; Hathaway and Rossiter 2007; Swift, Gates, and Dillon 2005; Ware et al. 2003; Feldman and Mandel 1998; Astin 1998; Barrett et al. 2003; Bishop and Lewith 2010). In fact, studies have found that medical cannabis patients are more likely to have used complementary and alternative care than the general population (Fogarty et al. 2007; Reiman 2006; Reinarman et al. 2011).

## Conditions That Qualify Under State Medical Cannabis Programs

Except for Oklahoma, each of the medical cannabis programs in the U.S. lists specific conditions for which patients can qualify to participate, with California, Massachusetts, and the District of Columbia[8] also including catch-all language that allows physicians to recommend cannabis for any other serious medical condition for which cannabis may be helpful. States vary considerably in what they define as qualifying conditions, though most recognize eight: severe pain, severe nausea, seizures, multiple sclerosis or muscle spasms, glaucoma, cachexia (better known as wasting syndrome), HIV/AIDS, and cancer (MPP 2012). Those eight are the original qualifying conditions specified in Colorado's Amendment 20.[9]

Colorado law also aligns with policies in most medical cannabis states in specifying that the managing government agency—usually but not always the state health department—can approve additional medical conditions if evidence warrants. Under Colorado's protocol, citizens can file paperwork to request such a review. At least thirteen additional conditions have been submitted for inclusion.[10] All have been rejected by the Colorado Department of Public Health and Environment, including four separate attempts to include post-traumatic stress disorder (PTSD) (CDPHE 2013). After the last rejection of PTSD in 2015, affected Colorado patients turned to the courts and then the legislature. In early 2017, the Colorado legislature passed a bill to add PTSD, which Governor John Hickenlooper signed into law in June 2017. Colorado is one of nineteen states to add PTSD as a qualifying condition between 2012 and 2017, bringing the total to twenty-two, largely due to a concerted national lobbying effort by veterans, for whom PTSD is a more prevalent condition than the general population.

Other states have approved qualifying conditions other than the core eight, either in their initial legislation or through amendment procedures. The most common of these, other than PTSD, are amyotrophic lateral sclerosis (ALS or Lou Gehrig's Disease) and Crohn's disease. ALS has been approved in sixteen states and Crohn's in fourteen. Some states specify umbrella conditions that capture multiple diagnoses. New Jersey, for instance, does not specify Crohn's disease but is one of three states that accepts patients with irritable bowel syndrome (IBS), a diagnosis with which Crohn's is often grouped as a subtype. Other approved conditions, with the number of states approving in parentheses, include: Hepatitis C (12), Alzheimer's disease (10), Parkinson's disease (7), spinal nerve injury involving spasticity (6), Tourette's (4), Huntington's disease (3), traumatic brain injury (3), and nail patella syndrome (2). Similar to the overlap between IBS and Crohn's diagnoses that may qualify in some states, some explicitly specify spinal injury/peripheral neuropathy as a qualifying condition, while most states allow these conditions to qualify under severe pain. A handful of conditions are recognized in single states, including anorexia, decompensated cirrhosis, lupus, migraine, spinal stenosis, muscular dystrophy, and others. Four states allow any patient who enters hospice or is diagnosed with a terminal illness to participate (ASA 2017).

The Colorado registry has processed a cumulative total of 342,976 new applications as of the end of 2016, the last time they reported a total. The composition of patients has remained relatively steady over time. Based on CDPHE statistics from January 2018, the average age of patients in Colorado is currently forty-four years of age (forty-three for men, forty-six for women) (CDPHE 2018). Sixty-two percent of patients are men. No statistical information regarding race for Colorado's patient population is available from CDPHE. An overwhelming 93 percent of currently registered patients qualify due to chronic severe pain, often in combination with other qualifying conditions. The next largest categories are muscle spasms (29 percent) and severe nausea (13 percent), then cancer (4 percent), PTSD (4 percent), and seizures (3 percent), with cachexia and glaucoma at roughly 1 percent of qualifying individuals (CDPHE 2017a).

For the duration of this study, Colorado's medical cannabis program stood alone in many respects. Because of the timing of Colorado's medical cannabis boom in late 2009, the state was able to learn some important lessons from its predecessors, most notably California and the other West Coast states. The regulatory structures in these states—or lack thereof—and their successes and failures have provided insights for how to create this type of regulation. As we discuss in chapter 2, since 2010, Colorado has come to be considered a leading state on the issue. As of early 2018, it is still the state with the most comprehensive statewide regulations currently in use and is one of only a few states with a functioning dispensary system for obtaining cannabis. It also stands as the first state with an operating commercial market for legalized adult use. Many states are still deciding what counts as medical cannabis, how to regulate it, and how to define patients. In states that have passed such compassionate use laws, many are still in early stages of determining the type of infrastructure and regulations they will adopt for their program. Colorado's role as a flagship state is influencing the shape of programs around the country. Forty-six states now have a medical cannabis law on the books that protects some patients, with robust access programs in thirty states and the District of Columbia, and almost all are actively working through what form their programs should take in an environment that continues to change rapidly.

### Patients in Colorado: Demographics and Health Characteristics

The forty patients in this study range in age from thirty to late sixties, with an average age of 46.6. The sample consists of twenty-eight men (70 percent of sample) and twelve women (30 percent of sample) with a diverse set of conditions ranging from moderate neuropathic pain and migraines to stage-4 cancer, HIV, and spinal injuries. Nearly all patients in the sample reported chronic severe pain; only eight patients (20 percent) reported another qualifying condition—HIV/AIDS, cancer, or muscle spasm—as the primary qualifying condition. Nearly all patients reported having secondary non-qualifying conditions from which they also derived benefit from the medicinal use of cannabis. These included conditions as diverse as Hepatitis C, bipolar disorder, insomnia, anxiety disorder, diabetes, depression, and PTSD. Racial diversity was minimal, with only five patients reporting any race or ethnicity other than white, often in combination as a multiracial identification that included white and another race. While the theoretical sampling approach used in this study does not attempt to achieve a representative demographic sample, this interview sample has the same approximate distribution of age, gender, and medical conditions reported for the entire patient population in state of Colorado (see Table 1.2).

Table 1.2 A Summary of Patients in this Study with Demographic Comparisons to the State Registry

| Geographic Location[11] | Sample (#) | Sample (%) | CO Registry (%)[12] |
|---|---|---|---|
| Denver Metro Area (Including Suburbs) | 17 | 42.5% | 47.5% |
| Colorado Springs Metro Area | 11 | 27.5% | 14% |
| Boulder/Front Range Area | 8 | 20% | 13.5% |
| Fort Collins and Surrounding Area | 2 | 5% | 5% |
| Other (Western Slope & Pueblo) | 2 | 5% | 6% |
| *Primary Qualifying Condition[13]* | | | |
| Cachexia (Wasting Syndrome) | 0 | 0% | 1% |
| Cancer | 3 | 7.5% | 3% |
| Glaucoma | 0 | 0% | 1% |
| HIV/AIDS | 4 | 10% | 1% |
| Muscle Spasm | 12 | 30% | 17% |
| Seizures | 1 | 2.5% | 2% |
| Severe Pain | 36 | 90% | 94% |
| Severe Nausea | 9 | 22.5% | 11% |
| *Gender* | | | |
| Women | 12 | 30% | 32% |
| Men | 28 | 70% | 68% |
| *Race* | | | |
| White | 36 | 90% | |
| Nonwhite | 4 | 10% | |
| *Age* | | | Average age: 41 |
| 30–39 years | 10 | 25% | |
| 40–49 years | 14 | 35% | |
| 50–59 years | 10 | 25% | |
| 60–69 years | 6 | 15% | |
| *Education (highest level)* | | | |
| High School Graduate | 9 | 22.5% | |
| Some College | 12 | 30% | |
| Associate Degree/Trade School | 5 | 12.5% | |
| Bachelor's Degree | 9 | 22.5% | |
| Professional Degree | 5 | 12.5% | |
| *Marital Status* | | | |
| Single | 11 | 27.5% | |
| Married | 20 | 50% | |
| Divorced/Separated | 9 | 22.5% | |
| *Sexual Orientation* | | | |
| Heterosexual | 36 | 90% | |
| Gay/Lesbian | 4 | 10% | |
| *Parent Status* | | | |
| Total with Kids | 27 | 67.5% | |
| Kids Under 18 Living with Patient | 8 | 20% | |

Sample n = 40, Statewide Registry (January 2013) N = 108,656

Because this study focuses on midlife patients, the sample is on average slightly older than the entire population of medical cannabis patients in Colorado. In the patient interviews, more serious conditions may also be overrepresented, which may indicate a bias in terms of which patients were more willing to volunteer for interviews. For similar reasons, the interviews may also include a higher proportion of individuals who engage in activism on medical cannabis issues than the general population of registered patients, but a handful of those interviewed reported keeping their medical marijuana patient status private and did not report participation in public advocacy.

There are more men than women in this sample, in proportion with other studies and the overall Colorado patient population. While no information on educational level of the overall medical marijuana patient population was available from the Department of Public Health and Environment, and few other studies report this information, those in the study sample who claimed some college education approximates educational levels reported by the total population census numbers on Colorado (Census 2012) but is slightly higher proportionally than samples from comparable studies in other states (Aggarwal 2008; Aggarwal et al. 2012; Janichek and Reiman 2012). Marital status of the study sample also reflects proportions found among Colorado's general population (Census 2012).

The interviews in this book were completed before the 2012 passage of Amendment 64 that legalized all adult use of cannabis in Colorado. This constitutional amendment allows anyone twenty-one or older to possess, consume, and grow cannabis in limited amounts and in non-public spaces. Although it does not formally alter the rules for medical use under Colorado's Amendment 20, it has had significant effects on the state's program. It is unclear how state legalization will fare over time, given that cannabis remains illegal at the federal level for all but approved research uses, which are exceedingly rare. But public opinion and political momentum are in the plant's favor.

Understanding patients has never been more important than now. Medical cannabis has always been subject to the accusation that it was a "ruse" with the real purpose of legalizing recreational use. On the other side, medical cannabis activists have been known to claim that "all use is medical." Wherever the truth lies on this, one thing is clear: As a consequence of criminalization, there are key differences between medical use and recreational use of cannabis that are often lost when the two are lumped together into one totalizing category. Through interviews with patients and providers, this book attempts to better understand behavior by medical users as existing laws weather unpredictable political developments and recreational use states open access to all. Ultimately, it makes a case for the need to differentiate between recreational and medical uses. Looking at the medical use of cannabis through the lens of medicalization processes can help us understand why.

## Notes

1. The term "single story" is borrowed from novelist Chimamanda Ngozi Adichie's 2009 TEDGlobal Talk. "The Danger of a Single Story." www.ted.com/talks/chimamanda_adichie_the_danger_of_a_single_story.
2. Delaware, Florida, Iowa, Missouri, North Carolina, Oklahoma, South Carolina, Tennessee, Texas, Utah, Virginia, and Wyoming were the other "CBD-only" states that enacted their laws between 2013 and 2015, though Florida's law in being expanded to allow more types of medical cannabis products in light of a voter initiative passed in 2016, and voters in Oklahoma in July 2018 enacted a far more expansive program that allows the full range of medical cannabis products for any condition a physician deems appropriate. Indiana enacted a restrictive CBD law in 2017.
3. Conrad, Peter, and Joseph Schneider 1998 [1980]. *Deviance and Medicalization: From Badness to Sickness.* Philadelphia: Temple University Press.
4. Several countries have recognized cannabis as a medicine, in most cases allowing doctors to prescribe it as they would other medications. Method of access or distribution varies considerably, from simply allowing personal cultivation to filling prescriptions in pharmacies. Most recently, Mexico and Greece announced new programs in July 2017. Other countries that allow medical use are Canada, the Czech Republic, Finland, Israel, Germany, the Netherlands, Portugal, and Spain. The United Nations in 2017 convened a special session to consider requests to modify the classification of cannabis in international agreements.
5. That effect is evident in Colorado. As of the beginning of 2016, four years after the advent of adult access, the number of patients registered has dropped steadily from a 2011 pre-legalization peak of 128,698 patients—or 30 out of every 1,000 people in the state—to 93,372 as of January 2018 (CDPHE statistics can be found online at www.colorado.gov/pacific/cdphe/2017-medical-marijuana-registry-statistics).
6. The lack of social science research may be addressed soon. Colorado is devoting a portion of the tax revenue from cannabis sales to funding research (though to date the money has gone exclusively to clinical research, much as California has funded clinical research program from 1999 to 2010), and new academic centers for the study of cannabis are springing up at American universities, including Colorado State University, Pueblo (https://www.csupueblo.edu/institute-of-cannabis-research/index.html); Humboldt State University in northern California (www2.humboldt.edu/hiimr/); UCLA (https://www.uclahealth.org/cannabis/), and the University of California, Irvine (https://californiahealthline.org/news/new-uc-irvine-center-to-study-the-highs-and-lows-of-pot/). Information about Colorado's research program: www.colorado.gov/pacific/cdphe/marijuana-research.
7. Based on the publicly provided data from the Colorado Department of Public Health and Environment statistics. www.colorado.gov/pacific/cdphe/medical-marijuana-statistics-and-data.
8. To simplify descriptions for the rest of this chapter, the District of Columbia, while not a state, is counted as one in national numerical totals of state medical marijuana programs.
9. Constitution, State of Colorado. 2000. *Medical Use of Marijuana*, Article XVIII, Section 14 Cl. 2.
10. Conditions petitioned and rejected in Colorado: asthma, atherosclerosis, bipolar disease, Crohn's disease, diabetes mellitus types 1 and 2, diabetic retinopathy, Hepatitis C, hypertension, Methicillin-Resistant Staphylococcus Aureus (MRSA), opioid dependence, severe anxiety, clinical depression, Tourette's syndrome, and PTSD.
11. Statewide percentages by region are based on combined county numbers for the area described. Percent is out of all counties. Unrepresented counties each have 2 percent or fewer of the state's registered patients.

12. Registry numbers from the September 2012 report provided on the CDPHE website: www.colorado.gov/pacific/cdphe/medicalmarijuana.
13. Patients may report more than one qualifying condition, so state registry numbers do not total to 100 percent.

## References

Adams, Glenn, and Hazel Rose Markus. 2001. "Culture as Patterns: An Alternative Approach to the Problem of Reification." *Culture & Psychology* 7(3):283.

Adler, Jonathan N., and James A. Colbert. 2013. "Medicinal Use of Marijuana: Polling Results." *New England Journal of Medicine* 368(22):e30. doi: 10.1056/NEJMclde 1305159.

Aggarwal, Sunil K. 2008. "The Medical Geography of Cannabinoid Botanicals in Washington State: Access, Delivery, and Distress." Ph.D. Dissertation, Geography, University of Washington.

Aggarwal, Sunil K. 2010. "Cannabis: A Commonwealth Medicinal Plant, Long Suppressed, Now at Risk of Monopolization." *Denver University Law Review Online*. Retrieved October 15, 2010 (www.denverlawreview.org/medical-marijuana/2010/8/23/canna bis-a-commonwealth-medicinal-plant-long-suppressed-now.html).

Aggarwal, Sunil K., Gregory T. Carter, Mark D. Sullivan, Craig ZumBrunnen, Richard Morrill, and Jonathan D. Mayer. 2009. "Medicinal Use of Cannabis in the United States: Historical Perspectives, Current Trends, and Future Directions." *The Journal of Opioid Management* 5(3):153–68.

Aggarwal, Sunil K., Gregory T. Carter, Mark D. Sullivan, Craig ZumBrunnen, Richard Morrill, and Jonathan D. Mayer. 2012. "Prospectively Surveying Health-Related Quality of Life and Symptom Relief in a Lot-Based Sample of Medical Cannabis-Using Patients in Urban Washington State Reveals Managed Chronic Illness and Debility." *American Journal of Hospice and Palliative Medicine* 00(0):1–9. doi: 10.1177/104990911 2454215.

Almanzar, Nelson A. Pichardo. 2003. "Framing the User: Social Constructions of Marijuana Users and the Medical Marijuana Movement." Hawaii International Conference on Social Sciences, Ellensburg, WA.

Anderson, D. Mark, Benjamin Hansen, and Daniel I. Rees. 2015. "Medical Marijuana Laws and Teen Marijuana Use." *American Law and Economics Review* 17(2):495–528. doi: 10.1093/aler/ahv002.

Anderson, D. Mark, and Daniel I. Rees. 2013. "Medical Marijuana Laws, Traffic Fatalities, and Alcohol Consumption." *Journal of Law and Economics* 56(2):333–69.

Arnett, Jeffrey Jensen. 2000. "Emerging Adulthood: A Theory of Development from the Late Teens through the Twenties." *American Psychologist* 55(5):469–80. doi: 10.1037/ 0003-066x.55.5.469.

ASA, Americans for Safe Access et al. 2017. *Medical Marijuana Access in the United States.* Washington, DC. (www.safeaccessnow.org/medical_marijuana_access_in_the_usa).

Astin, John A. 1998. "Why Patients Use Alternative Medicine: Results of a National Study." *Journal of the American Medical Association* 279(19):1548–53. doi: 10.1001/jama. 279.19.1548.

Ayers, Stephanie L., and Jennie J. Kronenfeld. 2010. "Using Factor Analysis to Create Complementary and Alternative Medicine Domains: An Examination of Patterns of Use." *Health* 14(3):234–52. doi: 10.1177/1363459309347491.

Barker, Kristin K. 2008. "Electronic Support Groups, Patient-Consumers, and Medicalization: The Case of Contested Illness." *Journal of Health and Social Behavior* 49(1):20–36. doi: 10.1177/002214650804900103.

Barnes, Patricia M., Eve Powell-Griner, Kim McFann, and Richard L. Nahin. 2004. "Complementary and Alternative Medicine Use among Adults: United States, 2002." *Seminars in Integrative Medicine* 2:54–71. doi: 10.1016/j.sigm.2004.07.003.

Barrett, Bruce, Lucille Marchand, Jo Scheder, Mary Beth Plane, Rob Maberry, Diane Appelbaum, David Rakel, and David Rabago. 2003. "Themes of Holism, Empowerment, Access, and Legitimacy Define Complementary, Alternative, and Integrative Medicine in Relation to Conventional Biomedicine." *Journal of Alternative & Complementary Medicine* 9(6):937–48.

Barthwell, Andrea G., Louis E. Baxter, Timmen Cermak, Robert DuPont, Mark L. Kraus, and Petros Levounis. 2010. *The Role of the Physician in "Medical Marijuana"*. Chevy Chase, MD: American Society of Addiction Medicine (https://www.asam.org/docs/default-source/public-policy-statements/1role_of_phys_in_med_mj_9-10.pdf?sfvrsn=c2a16bb3).

Belville, Russ. 2011. "America's One Million Legalized Marijuana Users." *NORML Blog*. Retrieved October 2011 (http://blog.norml.org/2011/05/31/americas-one-million-legalized-marijuana-users/).

Benoit, Ellen. 2003. "Not Just a Matter of Criminal Justice: States, Institutions, and North American Drug Policy." *Sociological Forum* 18(2):269–94.

Bishop, Felicity L., and George T. Lewith. 2010. "Who Uses CAM? A Narrative Review of Demographic Characteristics and Health Factors Associated with CAM Use." *eCAM* 7(1):11–28. doi: 10.1093/ecam/nen023.

Bonnie, Richard J., and Charles H. Whitebread, II. 1999. *The Marijuana Conviction*. New York: The Lindesmith Center.

Booth, Martin. 2003. *Cannabis: A History*. New York: Picador.

Bostwick, J. Michael. 2012. "Blurred Boundaries: The Therapeutics and Politics of Medical Marijuana." *Mayo Clinical Proceedings* 87(2):172–86.

Bottorff, Joan L., Laura J. L. Bissell, Lynda G. Balneaves, John L. Oliffe, H. Bindy K. Kang, N. Rielle Capler, Jane A. Buxton, and Robin K. O'Brien. 2011. "Health Effects of Using Cannabis for Therapeutic Purposes: A Gender Analysis of Users' Perspectives." *Substance Use & Misuse* 46(6):769–80. doi: doi:10.3109/10826084.2010.537732.

Caplan, Gerald. 2012. "Medical Marijuana: A Study of Unintended Consequences." *McGeorge Law Review* 43:127–46.

CDC, Center for Disease Control and Prevention. 2012. "Opioid Overdoses in the United States." *Journal of Pain & Palliative Care Pharmacotherapy*:44–7.

CDC, Center for Disease Control and Prevention. 2017. *Prescription Opioid Overdose Data*. U.S. Department of Health & Human Services, Last Modified August 1, 2017. Retrieved May 13, 2018 (www.cdc.gov/drugoverdose/data/overdose.html).

CDPHE, Colorado Department of Public Health and Environment. 2013. *Medical Marijuana Registry Program Update (as of January 31, 2013)*. Colorado Department of Public Health and Environment. Retrieved March 1, 2013 (www.colorado.gov/cs/Satellite/CDPHE-CHEIS/CBON/1251593017044).

CDPHE, Colorado Department of Public Health and Environment. 2015. *Healthy Kids Colorado Survey: Marijuana*. Colorado Department of Public Health & Environment, Colorado Department of Education, and Colorado Department of Human Resources. (www.colorado.gov/pacific/cdphe/hkcs).

CDPHE, Colorado Department of Public Health and Environment. 2017a. *2017 Medical Marijuana Registry Statistics*. Colorado Department of Public Health and Environment. Retrieved August 20, 2017 (www.colorado.gov/pacific/cdphe/2017-medical-marijuana-registry-statistics).

CDPHE, Colorado Department of Public Health and Environment. 2017b. *Monitoring Health Concerns Related to Marijuana in Colorado: 2016*. Retail Marijuana Public Health Advisory Committee.

CDPHE, Colorado Department of Public Health and Environment. 2018. *Medical Marijuana Registry Statistics, 2009–2018*. Colorado Department of Public Health and Environment. Retrieved February 2018 (www.colorado.gov/pacific/cdphe/2017-medical-marijuana-registry-statistics).

Census (U.S. Census Bureau). 2012. "Selected Social Characteristics in the United States: 2007–2011 American Community Survey 5-Year Estimates for Colorado." *American Community Survey*. Washington, DC: U.S. Census Bureau.

Chapkis, Wendy, and Richard J. Webb. 2008. *Dying to Get High: Marijuana as Medicine*. New York: New York University Press.

Chasin, Alexandra. 2016. *Assassin of Youth: A Kaleidoscopic History of Harry J. Anslinger's War on Drugs*. Chicago and London: University of Chicago Press.

Clarke, Adele E., Janet K. Shim, Laura Mamo, Jennifer Ruth Fosket, and Jennifer R. Fishman. 2003. "Biomedicalization: Technoscientific Transformations of Health, Illness, and U.S. Biomedicine." *American Sociological Review* 68(2):161–94.

Cohen, Peter J. 2009. "Medical Marijuana: The Conflict between Scientific Evidence and Political Ideology: Part One of Two." *Journal of Pain & Palliative Care Pharmacotherapy* 23(1):4–25. doi: 10.1080/15360280902727973.

Cohen, Stanley. 1980. *Folk Devils and Moral Panics: The Creation of the Mods and Rockers*. 3rd ed. London: Psychology Press.

Conrad, Peter. 2005. "The Shifting Engines of Medicalization." *Journal of Health and Social Behavior* 46(1):3–14.

Conrad, Peter. 2006. "Up, Down, and Sideways." *Society* 43(6):19–20.

Conrad, Peter. 2007. *The Medicalization of Society*. Baltimore, MD: The Johns Hopkins University Press.

Conrad, Peter, and Kristin K. Barker. 2010. "The Social Construction of Illness: Key Insights and Policy Implications." *Journal of Health and Social Behavior* 51(S):S67–79.

Conrad, Peter, and Valerie Leiter. 2004. "Medicalization, Markets and Consumers." *Journal of Health and Social Behavior* 45(Extra Issue: Health and Health Care in the United States: Origins and Dynamics):158–76.

Conrad, Peter, and Joseph Schneider. 1998 [1980]. *Deviance and Medicalization: From Badness to Sickness*. Philadelphia: Temple University Press.

Conrad, Peter, and Cheryl Stults. 2008. "Contestation and Medicalization." Pp. 323–35 in *Contesting Illness: Processes and Practices*, edited by Pamela Moss and Katherine Teghtsoonian. Toronto: University of Toronto Press.

Coomber, Ross, Michael Oliver, and Craig Morris. 2003. "Using Cannabis Therapeutically in the UK: A Qualitative Analysis." *Journal of Drug Issues* 33(2):325–56.

Corroon, James M., Laurie K. Mischley, and Michelle Sexton. 2017. "Cannabis as a Substitute for Prescription Drugs: A Cross-Sectional Study." *Journal of Pain Research* 10:989–98. doi: 10.2147/JPR.S134330.

Danovitch, Itai, 2012. "Sorting through the Science on Marijuana: Facts, Fallacies, and Implications for Legalization." *McGeorge Law Review* 91(43):91–108.

Doblin, Rick, and Mark Kleinman. 1991. "Marijuana as Antiemetic Medicine: A Survey of Oncologists' Experiences and Attitudes." *American Journal of Clinical Oncology* 9(7):1314–19. doi: 10.1200/JCO.1991.9.7.1314.

Earleywine, Mitch. 2010. "Pot Politics: Prohibition and Morality." Pp. 192–213 in *Cannabis: Philosopy for Everyone*, edited by Dale Jacquette. Oxford: Wiley-Blackwell.

Eddy, Mark. 2009. *Medical Marijuana: Review and Analysis of Federal and State Policies.* Washington, DC: Congressional Research Service.

Eddy, Mark. 2010. *Medical Marijuana: Review and Analysis of Federal and State Policies.* Washington, DC: Congressional Research Service.

Fair, Brian. 2010. "Morgellons: Contested Illness, Diagnostic Compromise and Medicalisation." *Sociology of Health & Illness* 32(4):597–612. doi: 10.1111/j.1467-9566.2009.01227.x.

Feldman, Harvey W., and R. Jerry Mandel. 1998. "Providing Medical Marijuana: The Importance of Cannabis Clubs." *Journal of Psychoactive Drugs* 30(2):179–86.

Ferraiolo, Kathleen Grammatico. 2007. "From Killer Weed to Popular Medicine: The Evolution of American Drug Control Policy, 1937–2000." *Journal of Policy History* 19(2):147–79.

Figert, Anne E. 2011. "The Consumer Turn in Medicalization: Future Directions with Historical Foundations." Pp. 291–307 in *Handbook of the Sociology of Health, Illness, and Healing*, edited by Bernice A. Pescosolido, Jack K. Martin, J. D. McLeod and Anne Rogers. New York: Springer.

Fine, Gary Alan, and Michaela De Soucey. 2005. "Joking Cultures: Humor Themes as Social Regulation in Group Life." *Humor: International Journal of Humor Research* 18(1):1–22.

Fogarty, A., P. Rawstorne, G. Prestage, J. Crawford, J. Grierson, and S. Kippax. 2007. "Marijuana as Therapy for People Living with HIV/AIDS: Social and Health Aspects." *AIDS Care* 19(2):295–301.

Fox, Steve, Paul Armentano, and Mason Tvert. 2009. *Marijuana Is Safer: So Why Are We Driving People to Drink?* White River Junction, VT: Chelsea Green Publishing.

Furstenberg, Frank F., Jr., Sheela Kennedy, Vonnie C. McLoyd, Ruben G. Rumbaut, and Richard A. Settersten. 2004. "Growing Up Is Harder to Do." *Contexts* Summer:33–41.

Gallagher, Romayne, J. Allan Best, Gillian Fyles, Pippa Hawley, and Wendy Yeomans. 2003. "Attitudes and Beliefs about the Use of Cannabis for Symptom Control in a Palliative Population." *Journal of Cannabis Therapeutics* 3(2):41–50.

Galliher, John F., David P. Keys, and Michael Elsner. 1998. "Lindesmith v. Anslinger: An Early Government Victory in the Failed War on Drugs." *The Journal of Criminal Law and Criminology* 88(2):661–82.

Gerber, Rudolph J. 2004. *Legalizing Marijuana: Drug Policy Reform and Prohibition Politics.* Westport, CT: Praeger.

Giordano, Peggy C., Stephen A. Cernkovich, and Donna D. Holland. 2003. "Changes in Friendship Relations over the Life Course: Implications for Desistance from Crime." *Criminology* 41(2):293–328. doi: 10.1111/j.1745-9125.2003.tb00989.x.

Goode, Erich. 2008. "Moral Panics and Disproportionality: The Case of LSD Use in the Sixties." *Deviant Behavior* 29(6):533–43. doi: 10.1080/01639620701839377.

Goode, Erich, and Nachman Ben-Yehuda. 1994. "Moral Panics: Culture, Politics, and Social Construction." *Annual Review of Sociology* 20:149–71. doi: 10.2307/2083363.

Grant, Igor. 2010. *Report to the Legislature and Governor of the State of California Presenting Findings Pursuant to SB847 which Created the CMCR and Provided State Funding.* San Diego, CA: Center for Medical Cannabis Research, University of California-San Diego.

Grinspoon, Lester. 2001. "Commentary: On the Pharmaceuticalization of Marijuana." *International Journal of Drug Policy* 12(5–6):377–83.

Grucza, Richard A., Arpana Agrawal, Melissa J. Krauss, Jahnavi Bongu, Andrew D. Plunk, Patricia A. Cavazos-Rehg, and Laura J. Bierut. 2016. "Declining Prevalence of Marijuana Use Disorders among Adolescents in the United States, 2002–2013." *Journal of the American Academy of Child and Adolescent Psychiatry* 55(6):487–94.e6. doi: 10.1016/j.jaac.2016.04.002.

Hammersly, Richard, Richard Jenkins, and Marie Reid. 2001. "Cannabis Use and Social Identity." *Addiction Research & Theory* 9(2):133–50.

Harris, Debra, Reese T. Jones, Robin Shank, Rajneesh Nath, Emilio Fernandez, Kenneth Goldstein, and John Mendelson. 2000. "Self-Reported Marijuana Effects and Characteristics of 100 San Francisco Medical Marijuana Club Members." *Journal of Addictive Diseases* 19(3):89–103.

Harrison, Lana Debra. 1988. "The Marijuana Movement: A Study of a Cohort on the Cutting Edge." Ph.D. Dissertation, Sociology, University of Michigan, 21662.

Hasin, Deborah S., Melanie Wall, Katherine M. Keyes, Magdalena Cerdá, John Schulenberg, Patrick M. O'Malley, Sandro Galea, Rosalie Pacula, and Tianshu Feng. 2015. "Medical Marijuana Laws and Adolescent Marijuana Use in the USA from 1991 to 2014: Results from Annual, Repeated Cross-Sectional Surveys." *The Lancet Psychiatry* 2(7):601–8. doi: 10.1016/S2215-0366(15)00217-5.

Hathaway, Andrew D., Natalie C. Comeau, and Patricia G. Erickson. 2011. "Cannabis Normalization and Stigma: Contemporary Practices of Moral Regulation." *Criminology and Criminal Justice* 11(5):451–69. doi: 10.1177/1748895811415345.

Hathaway, Andrew D., and Kate Rossiter. 2007. "Medical Marijuana, Community Building, and Canada's 'Compassionate Societies'." *Contemporary Justice Review* 10(3):283–96.

Hazekamp, Arno, and Franjo Grotenhermen. 2010. "Review on Clinical Studies with Cannabis and Cannabinoids 2005–2009." *Cannabinoids* 5(special issue):1–21.

Himmelstein, Jerome L. 1983. "From Killer Weed to Drop-Out Drug: The Changing Ideology of Marihuana." *Contemporary Crises* 7:13–38.

Hudak, John. 2016. *Marijuana: A Short History.* Washington, DC: Brookings Institution Press.

Hudak, John, and Grace Wallack. 2015. *Ending the U.S. Government's War on Medical Marijuana Research.* Washington, DC: Brookings Institution Press.

Iversen, Leslie L. 2008. *The Science of Marijuana.* 2nd ed. New York: Oxford University Press.

Janichek, Jennifer L., and Amanda Reiman. 2012. "Clinical Service Desires of Medical Cannabis Patients." *Harm Reduction Journal* 9:12. doi: 10.1186/1477-7517-9-12.

Jeffreys, Diarmuid. 2004. *Aspirin: The Remarkable Story of a Wonder Drug.* New York: Bloomsbury.

Johnston, Lloyd, Patrick M. O'Malley, Jerald G. Bachman, and John Schulenberg. 2012. *Monitoring the Future National Survey Results on Drug Use 1975–2011: Volume II, College Students and Adults Ages 19–50.* Ann Arbor: Institute for Social Research, The University of Michigan.

Joy, Janet E., Stanley J. Watson, Jr., and John A. Benson, Jr., eds. 1999. *Marijuana and Medicine: Assessing the Science Base.* Washington: Institute of Medicine, National Academy Press.

Kamin, Sam. 2012. "Medical Marijuana in Colorado and the Future of Marijuana Regulation in the United States." *McGeorge Law Review* 43:147–68.

Kazemian, Lila. 2007. "Desistance from Crime: Theoretical, Empirical, Methodological, and Policy Considerations." *Journal of Contemporary Criminal Justice* 23(1):5–27. doi:10.1177/1043986206298940.

Kessler, Ronald C., R. B. Davis, D. F. Foster, Maria Van Rompay, E. E. Walters, Sonja Wilkey, Ted J. Kaptchuk, and David M. Eisenberg. 2001. "Long-Term Trends in the Use of Complementary and Alternative Medical Therapies in the United States." *Annals of Internal Medicine* 135(4):262–68.

Kondrad, Elin, and Alfred Reid. 2013. "Colorado Family Physicians' Attitudes toward Medical Marijuana." *The Journal of the American Board of Family Medicine* 26(1):52–60. doi: 10.3122/jabfm.2013.01.120089.

London, Jeffrey. 2006. "The Criminalization and Medicalization of Marijuana: A Study of Changing Deviance Designations." Ph.D. Dissertation, Sociology, University of Colorado–Boulder, AAT 3212105.

Lucas, Philippe. 2012. "Cannabis as an Adjunct to or Substitute for Opiates in the Treatment of Chronic Pain." *Journal of Psychoactive Drugs* 44(2):125–33. doi: 10.1080/02791072.2012.684624.

Lucas, Philippe, and Zach Walsh. 2017. "Medical Cannabis Access, Use, and Substitution for Prescription Opioids and Other Substances: A Survey of Authorized Medical Cannabis Patients." *International Journal of Drug Policy* 42:30–5. doi: 10.1016/j.drugpo.2017.01.011.

Lucas, Philippe, Zach Walsh, Kim Crosby, Robert Callaway, Lynne Belle-Isle, Robert Kay, Rielle Capler, and Susan Holtzman. 2016. "Substituting Cannabis for Prescription Drugs, Alcohol and Other Substances among Medical Cannabis Patients: The Impact of Contextual Factors." *Drug and Alcohol Review* 35(3):326–33. doi: 10.1111/dar.12323.

Lynne-Landsman, Sarah D., Melvin D. Livingston, and Alexander C. Wagenaar. 2013. "Effects of State Medical Marijuana Laws on Adolescent Marijuana Use." *American Journal of Public Health* 103(8):1500–6. doi: 10.2105/AJPH.2012.301117.

MacDonald, James. 2009. "Medical Marijuana: Informational Resources for Family Physicians." *American Family Physician* 80(8):782–3.

Mackie, Ken 2008. "Cannabinoid Receptors: Where They Are and What They Do." *Journal of Neuroendocrinology* 20:10–14. doi: 10.1111/j.1365-2826.2008.01671.x.

Mauro, Christine M., Paul Newswanger, Julian Santaella-Tenorio, Pia M. Mauro, Hannah Carliner, and Silvia S. Martins. 2017. "Impact of Medical Marijuana Laws on State-Level Marijuana Use by Age and Gender, 2004–2013." *Prevention Science*. doi: 10.1007/s11121-017-0848-3.

Mechoulam, Raphael. 2012. "Cannabis: A Valuable Drug That Deserves Better Treatment." *Mayo Clinical Proceedings* 87(2):107–9.

Mikuriya, Tod H. 2004. "Cannabis as a Substitute for Alcohol: A Harm-Reduction Approach." *Journal of Cannabis Therapeutics* 4(1):79–93.

MPP, Marijuana Policy Project. 2012. *Key Aspects of State and D.C. Medical Marijuana Laws*. Washington, DC: Marijuana Policy Project.

Nunberg, Helen, Beau Kilmer, Rosalie Liccardo Pacula, and James R. Burgdorf. 2011. "An Analysis of Applicants Presenting to a Medical Marijuana Specialty Practice in California." *Journal of Drug Policy Analysis* 4(1):Article 1, 18 pages.

O'Brien, Patrick. 2013. "Medical Marijuana and Social Control: Escaping Criminalization and Embracing Medicalization." *Deviant Behavior* 34(6):423–43.

O'Connell, Thomas J., and Ché B. Bou-Matar. 2007. "Long-Term Marijuana Users Seeking Medical Cannabis in California (2001–2007): Demographics, Social Characteristics, Patterns of Cannabis and Other Drug Use of 4117 Applicants." *Harm Reduction Journal* 4:16. doi: 10.1186/1477-7517-4-16.

Ogborne, Alan C., Reginald G. Smart, Timothy Weber, and Carol Birchmore-Timney. 2000. "Who Is Using Cannabis as a Medicine and Why: An Exploratory Study." *Journal of Psychoactive Drugs* 32(4):435–43.

Pedersen, Willy, and Sveinung Sandberg. 2013. "The Medicalisation of Revolt: A Sociological Analysis of Medical Cannabis Users." *Sociology of Health & Illness* 35(1):17–32. doi: 10.1111/j.1467-9566.2012.01476.x.

Reed, Jack K. 2016. *Marijuana Legalization in Colorado: Early Findings.* Colorado Department of Public Safety, Division of Criminal Justice, Office of Research and Statistics (https://cdpsdocs.state.co.us/ors/docs/reports/2016-SB13-283-Rpt.pdf).

Reiman, Amanda. 2006. "Cannabis Care: Medical Marijuana Facilities as Health Service Providers." Ph.D. Dissertation, Social Welfare, University of California, Berkeley.

Reiman, Amanda. 2007. "Medical Cannabis Patients: Patient Profiles and Health Care Utilization Patterns." *Complementary Health Practice Review* 12:31–50.

Reinarman, Craig, Helen Nunberg, Fran Lanthier, and Tom Heddleston. 2011. "Who Are Medical Marijuana Patients? Population Characteristics from Nine California Assessment Clinics." *Journal of Psychoactive Drugs* 43(2):128–35. doi:10.1080/02791072.2011.587700.

Russo, Ethan. 2002. "The Role of Cannabis and Cannabinoids in Pain Management." Pp. 357–75 in *Pain Management: A Practical Guide for Clinicians*, edited by Richard S. Weiner. Boca Raton, FL: CRC Press.

SAMHSA, Substance Abuse and Mental Health Services Administration. 2017. *Results from the 2016 National Survey on Drug Use and Health: Detailed Tables*, edited by Center for Behavioral Health Statistics and Quality (CBHSQ). North Carolina: U.S. Department of Health and Human Services.

Sampson, Robert J., and John H. Laub. 1992. "Crime and Deviance in the Life Course." *Annual Review of Sociology* 18:63–84. doi: 10.2307/2083446.

Schaefer, Eric. 1999. *"Bold! Daring! Shocking! True!": A History of Exploitation Films, 1919–1959.* Durham, NC: Duke University Press.

Schmidt, Laura A., Laurie M. Jacobs, and Joanne Spetz. 2016. "Young People's More Permissive Views about Marijuana: Local Impact of State Laws or National Trend?" *American Journal of Public Health* 106(8):1498–503. doi: 10.2105/AJPH.2016.303153.

Schnittker, Jason. 2009. "Mirage of Health in the Era of Biomedicalization: Evaluating Change in the Threshold of Illness, 1972–1996." *Social Forces* 87(4):2155–82.

Schulenberg, John, Lloyd Johnston, Patrick M. O'Malley, Jerald G. Bachman, Richard Miech, and Megan E. Patrick. 2017. *Monitoring the Future: National Survey Results on Drug Use, 1975–2016: Volume II, College Students and Adults Ages 19–55.* Ann Arbor, MI: The University of Michigan.

Settersten, Richard A. 2004. "Age Structuring and the Rhythm of the Life Course." Pp. 81–98 in *Handbook of the Life Course*, edited by Jeylan T. Mortimer and Michael J. Shanahan. New York: Kluwer Academic and Plenum Publishers.

Silver, Nate. 2010. "Are Parents Just Saying No to Marijuana Legalization?" *Five Thirty Eight, New York Times.* November 10, 2010. (https://fivethirtyeight.blogs.nytimes.com/2010/11/10/are-parents-just-saying-no-to-marijuana-legalization/).

Stolick, Matt. 2009. *Otherwise Law-Abiding Citizens: A Scientific and Moral Assessment of Cannabis Use.* Lanham, MD: Lexington Books.

Swartz, Ronald. 2010. "Medical Marijuana Users in Substance Abuse Treatment." *Harm Reduction Journal* 7:3. doi: 10.1186/1477-7517-7-3.

Swift, Art. 2017. "In U.S., 45% Say They Have Tried Marijuana." In *Gallup Poll Social Series.* Washington, DC: Gallup. (http://news.gallup.com/poll/214250/say-tried-marijuana.aspx).

Swift, Wendy, Peter Gates, and Paul Dillon. 2005. "Survey of Australians Using Cannabis for Medical Purposes." *Harm Reduction Journal* 2(1):18. doi: 10.1186/1477-7517-2-18.

Taylor, Suzanne. 2008. "Medicalizing Cannabis: Science, Medicine and Policy, 1950–2004: An Overview of a Work in Progress." *Drugs: Education, Prevention, and Policy* 15(5):462–74. doi: 10.1080/09687630802114038.

Tomes, Nancy. 2016. *Remaking the American Patient: How Madison Avenue and Modern Medicine Turned Patients into Consumers.* Chapel Hill, NC: The University of North Carolina Press.

Turner, Bryan. 2004. *The New Medical Sociology.* New York: W.W. Norton.

Vettor, Roberto, Uberto Pagotto, Claudio Pagano, and Renato Pasquali. 2008. "Here, There and Everywhere: The Endocannabinoid System." *Journal of Neuroendocrinology* 20(Suppl. 1):iv–vi.

Vickovic, Samuel G., and Henry F. Fradella. 2011. "Medical Marijuana in the News." *The Southwest Journal of Criminal Justice* 8(1):67–96.

Ware, Mark A., Crystal R. Doyle, Ryan Woods, Mary E. Lynch, and Alexander J. Clark. 2003. "Cannabis Use for Chronic Non-Cancer Pain: Results of a Prospective Survey." *Pain* 102:211–16.

Warr, Mark. 1998. "Life Course and Crime." *Criminology* 36(2):183–216.

Watkins, Elizabeth Siegel. 2007. "The Medicalisation of Male Menopause in America." *Social History of Medicine* 20(2):369–88. doi: http://dx.doi.org/10.1093/shm/hkm039.

Werner, Clint. 2011. *Marijuana Gateway to Health.* San Francisco: Dachstar Press.

Williams, J. Patrick. 2011. *Subcultural Theory: Traditions and Concepts.* Cambridge, MA: Polity Press.

Williams, Simon J., and Michael Calnan. 1996. "The 'Limits' of Medicalization? Modern Medicine and the Lay Populace in 'Late' Modernity." *Social Science & Medicine* 42(12):1609–20.

Young, Francis. 1988. "In the Matter of Marijuana Rescheduling Petition." In *Docket #86–22.* Washington, DC: U.S. Department of Justice, Drug Enforcement Administration.

Zimmer, Lynn, and John P. Morgan. 1997. *Marijuana Myths, Marijuana Facts: A Review of the Scientific Evidence.* 1st ed. New York: Lindesmith Center.

Zinberg, Norman E. 1984. *Drug, Set, and Setting.* New Haven, CT: Yale University Press.

# Chapter 2

# The Landscape of Cannabis Policy

Because of the intensity of the public concern and the emotionalism surrounding the topic of drugs, all levels of government have been pressured into action with little time for planning. Perhaps the major consequence of this ad hoc [drug] policy planning has been the creation, at the federal, state, and community levels, of a vested interest in the perpetuation of the problem among those dispensing and receiving funds. Infrastructures are created, job descriptions are standardized, "experts" are created and ways of doing business are routinized and established along bureaucratic channels. During the last several years, drug programming has become a multi-billion-dollar industry, one administering to its own needs as well as to those of its drug-using clientele. In the course of well-meaning efforts to do something about drug use, this society may have inadvertently institutionalized it as a never-ending project.

(U.S. Commission on Marihuana and Drug Abuse 1973, 27)

The twists and turns taken by the social construction of cannabis over the past century—its demonization, politicization, and now (re)medicalization—have been mirrored and reinforced by changing laws and policies that are often in conflict. Just in the past two decades, all but a handful of states in the U.S. have removed criminal penalties for some form of medical use, and nine states and the District of Columbia now allow all adults to use cannabis legally.[1] These state changes have not been matched by federal reform, producing dramatic dilemmas for patients and policymakers. The U.S. system of overlapping cannabis laws creates dizzying conflicts and contradictions. When patients decide to pursue medical cannabis, the decision involves them in international treaties, federal law, state law and regulation, and local ordinance. This chapter considers how U.S. cannabis policy has changed over time in response to voter initiatives, legislative action, court decisions, and political pressures, from an increasing criminalization to an emerging medicalization. In the process, we explain how cannabis is classified by federal and state agencies, and why that matters for patient access and research. The history of attempts to modify the federal classification illustrates some of the competing social forces of medicalization and resistance at work, a pattern that is also reflected in our account of the rollout of medical cannabis programs in Colorado and other states. We conclude with a current overview of Colorado's medical cannabis program.

The single story of criminal deviance that drove policy over the last century has been supplanted over the past two decades by a deepening recognition of medical utility and, most recently, of its increasing acceptance as a recreational drug. Since the first of the current state medical cannabis laws passed in 1996, many states and municipalities have adopted laws and policies at odds with the federal government by providing some degree of legal protection for medical cannabis use. Colorado's robust medical cannabis program, which provides immunity from arrest and prosecution for registered patients and caregivers and those operating licensed businesses, is one such model. At the other end of the state spectrum, more than a dozen states offer nothing more than an affirmative defense at trial, and that only for individuals who have documented, narrowly defined conditions. And as far as the federal government is concerned, there is no such thing as medical use at all.

## Untangling the Layers of Drug Law

The remarkable, even diametrical, differences in the legal status of cannabis at the local, state, and federal levels are possible because of the successive layers of government jurisdiction, from municipalities and states to nations and international treaty agreements (Ferraiolo 2007; Gerber 2004; Sinha 2001; Suissa 2001). In some respects, these policies are nested such that each successively smaller jurisdiction is constrained by the limits set by the larger entity.

The broad architecture of modern drug policy was established between 1948 and 1961 under the guidance and recommendations of experts at the World Health Organization (WHO), with a primary goal of controlling opium- and coca-based narcotics. In 1961, regulation was formalized at the international level through the Single Convention on Narcotic Drugs, which was amended in 1972 but not since. This policy introduced the concept of drug scheduling based on three criteria that balance considerations of medical utility with potential for harm, a topic we will delve into later in this chapter. A separate Convention on Psychotropic Substances was introduced in 1971 to regulate hallucinogenic substances such as LSD and psilocybin mushrooms, but cannabis remained under the Single Convention (Sinha 2001). The last major international treaty is the Convention Against Illicit Traffic in Narcotic Drugs and Psychotropic Substances. Introduced in 1988, this treaty sought to clarify and improve coordinated approaches to reduce international drug trafficking (Sinha 2001).

Every nation that signed the three major international drug treaties of the twentieth century has agreed to restrict drug use and enforce drug laws in their country at least as harshly as these treaties' terms. If a signatory nation enacts a less restrictive policy that does not meet the mandates of the international treaties, they face review and threat of sanction (Taylor and Jelsma 2012; Sinha 2001). This became a source of contention that indirectly implicated U.S. cannabis policies when Bolivia sought legal exemption for chewing coca leaves, a traditional practice of the indigenous peoples of the Andean highlands. In March 2012, Bolivia's President Evo Morales brandished a coca leaf at a United Nations meeting on drug policy and withdrew his country from the Single Convention. Bolivia rejoined the treaty in 2013 after winning concession from the United Nations, despite U.S. opposition. Morales and others accused the U.S. of hypocrisy in resisting such reforms, given that a number of U.S. states had legalized some type of cannabis use at that point, arguably violating the very treaties the U.S. was invoking. (The U.S. can still claim compliance with international agreements because the treaties are with the federal government, and the federal government has not altered national law that classifies all non-research uses of cannabis as a crime.)

U.S. federal drug policy regulating cannabis was initiated with the Marihuana Tax Act of 1937, but its modern incarnation dates to the Controlled Substances Act (CSA) of 1970. The CSA was an omnibus drug bill that classifies various licit and illicit substances into schedules, in accordance with the United Nation's Single Convention on Narcotic Drugs. Passage of the CSA followed a brief interlude without federal penalties for cannabis after the U.S. Supreme Court in 1969 declared the Tax Act unconstitutional.[2]

Any change to marijuana's scheduling at the federal level would not only affect many dimensions of federal policy but would reverberate up and down the layers of drug policy, from local regulation to international treaties. In the years since the passage of these policies, there have been multiple attempts to introduce a medical exception for cannabis use. Government commissions from the U.S. and other countries have been tasked with conducting reviews, many of which have aligned with professional medical and patient organizations in calling for cannabis to be rescheduled, decriminalized or descheduled, legalized, or researched further, with little to no effect (Chapkis and Webb 2008; Eddy 2009; Gerber 2004; Joy, Watson, and Benson 1999; Werner 2011).

Most U.S. states have adopted controlled substances laws that are identical or similar to the federal laws. States may add more restrictive provisions than federal law regarding providing cannabis to minors and establishing drug-free zones around schools and other public areas (NCJRS 1999). However, some states have altered, adapted, or added provisions that set lower penalties for cannabis or reclassified it. For instance, Iowa, Minnesota, and Oregon have down-scheduled cannabis under state law.

The introduction of medical cannabis laws at the state level marks a more significant rupture in the system, with total prohibition on the federal side and regulated distribution systems on the state side. These conflicting legal regimes can only coexist due to the division of responsibilities between federal and state governments and their corresponding systems of laws, with each responsible for ostensibly different areas of concern. When state and federal laws come into direct conflict—if a state law requires a person to do something illegal under federal law, or vice versa—then the U.S. Constitution says federal law reigns supreme, often called the Supremacy Clause. Every presidential administration has vigorously opposed state medical cannabis laws, but none have challenged them under the Supremacy Clause. Removing criminal penalties for medical use does not constitute such a direct conflict, nor does establishing programs that entail registering patients and licensing businesses to provide cannabis or related services to them (MPP 2008). Instead of directly challenging state medical cannabis laws, successive administrations have tried to compel states to maintain an enforcement standard through a combination of civil actions and threats of withdrawing funding for other federal resources, a strategy also used with education rules and drinking age (for example, loss of highway funds over disputes about drinking age). With state medical cannabis laws, the federal intimidation has been more intense, including threatening to jail elected officials and state employees and seize state buildings.[3] How states have responded to those threats has had significant consequences for the effectiveness of their medical cannabis programs in serving patients, as will be seen later in this chapter.

The original federalist vision of James Madison sharply restricted the reach of Congress into the day-to-day life of most Americans and notably left police power to the states, meaning the work of keeping the peace and prosecuting criminals was left to local authorities. Those original rights of the states to tend to the health and welfare of their citizens were respected even through the social upheaval of the Great Depression, as federal economic stimulus efforts were routinely struck down by courts as unconstitutional overreach by Congress. The lines of demarcation between the states and the federal government were clear until World War II, when many civil liberties were set aside in deference to the war effort. The turning point, ironically for this discussion, involved a man growing plants.

The case that opened the floodgates to greater federal regulation took place in 1942. *Wickard v. Filburn* concerned an Ohio farmer who had grown wheat to feed his livestock in excess of the eleven-acre limit set by a federal crop support program. Roscoe Filburn argued that the fine he received was unconstitutional because the extra twelve acres of wheat he grew were solely for use on his farm and had nothing to do with interstate commerce, the only aspect of his activities Congress had the authority to say anything about. Until that point, the courts had repeatedly ruled to support such as interpretation. This time, however, the Supreme Court disagreed. A unanimous court accepted the government's argument that Congress' ability to regulate interstate commerce includes commodity pricing, and Filburn's conduct had an indirect effect on price. The extra wheat he grew meant he was not buying it on the open market. By removing himself from the demand side of the supply–demand curve, he was nominally reducing the pressure on price. The effect of one individual's purchasing decision in a large national market is so insignificant as to be effectively nonexistent, but, the government argued, if aggregated over the thousands of individuals who were in a position to do the same, wheat prices could be undermined.[4]

This was the argument the government returned to sixty-three years later in defending why the blanket federal prohibition on cannabis should include medical use, even when it involved neither commerce nor crossing state lines. The 2003 case involved two women, Angel Raich and Diane Monson, who were each qualified under California's Compassionate Use Act to cultivate, possess, and use cannabis. After Monson was raided by local police and federal agents in 2002 over a personal garden of six cannabis plants,[5] the women filed suit seeking a protective injunction from arrest and prosecution by the federal government. Their attorneys argued that because neither woman bought the cannabis used in their treatment, and the cannabis never crossed state lines, their conduct could not affect interstate commerce and so should be considered beyond the reach of Congress. According to this argument, federal law was not intended to address their local medical use; it was intended to stop trafficking in illicit drugs. The women's personal medical use was an entirely different class of activity. The Ninth Circuit Court of Appeals agreed, finding the Controlled Substances Act to be unconstitutional when applied to medical cannabis within a regulated state program, and issued an injunction protecting the two women in December 2003. The government appealed that decision to the U.S. Supreme Court. After a two-year period of uncertainty in which prosecutions were put on hold and some federal medical cannabis prisoners were released pending their own appeals,[6] the government prevailed. In 2005, the U.S. Supreme Court overturned the Ninth Circuit, ruling in a 6–3 decision that the government was acting within its authority in prosecuting state-qualified medical cannabis patients because cannabis grown for personal medical use is indistinguishable from illicit cannabis, and allowing patients to opt out of the illicit market could affect supply and demand, and ultimately price. This was the same reasoning the earlier court had used to conclude that Roscoe Filburn's excess wheat cultivation affected interstate commerce, even though it never left his farm.

The composition of the Supreme Court's split decision in *Raich* would seem to defy normal ideological alignments of the court, with Justice Clarence Thomas making a rare break from Justice Antonin Scalia in joining the dissent of Justice Sandra Day O'Connor and Chief Justice William Rehnquist. Yet, it reveals what may be the nexus of this issue's breadth of political appeal. While more liberal attitudes about drug use may be commonly associated with more liberal political views, attitudes about cannabis use, medical and otherwise, tend to align with libertarianism of both left and right. This has been seen in the bipartisan sponsors of legislation in both houses of Congress, with Rand Paul (R, KY) and Cory Booker (D, NJ) in the

Senate and Dana Rohrabacher (R, CA-48) and Earl Blumenauer (D, OR-3) in the House cosponsoring various federal reform bills. We will also see this libertarianism echoed by the patients themselves in chapter 9.

Conservative jurists and legal scholars of the originalist mindset championed by Justice Scalia[7] have argued for more restraint of federal powers, which is sometimes called a return to states' rights. Devolving authority to individual states allows them more freedom to determine laws governing everything from where and how someone can carry a firearm to if and when they can obtain an abortion. Historically, the most fraught confrontation over federal versus state control of policing was seen in the constitutional challenges to the Jim Crow segregation laws of the southern states, beginning with *Brown v. Board of Education* in 1954. Many of the legislative attempts at resolving the impasse between federal law and state medical cannabis programs, such as the oft-introduced States Rights to Medical Marijuana Act, have been framed as affirming the original construction of the Tenth Amendment. Even in the absence of federal legislation that provides consistent legal protections for medical cannabis patients, states have proceeded to develop a variety of programs to protect patients and provide them with cannabis. Because the federal government cannot directly go after the state laws or programs, it has adopted a strategy of prosecuting the individuals who participate in them.

### Modern Drug Policy and Medical Use: Drug Scheduling

The Single Convention of 1961 first unveiled the concept of drug scheduling that governs modern drug policy. Schedules are a categorization scheme that involves three domains: (1) accepted medical use, (2) abuse potential, and (3) potential for public health harms through risk to safety or risk of dependence. These criteria are used to determine whether a drug requires any regulatory control. Cannabis was added to the strictest scheduling criteria in the original terms of the Single Convention, largely in response to pressure from the U.S. (Sinha 2001). Although later study by World Health Organization experts found that cannabis could have medical applications, their opinions were ignored (Gerber 2004; Sinha 2001).

The U.S. adopted drug scheduling as part of the U.S. Comprehensive Drug Abuse Prevention and Control Act of 1970. Title II of this legislation is the previously mentioned Controlled Substances Act (CSA), which includes the U.S. scheduling definitions for controlled substances (Courtwright 2004). This legislation, enacted by congress under Nixon in 1970, set regulatory measures for the manufacture, importation, possession, use, and distribution of drugs as part of our obligation under the international treaty (Taylor and Jelsma 2012; Sinha 2001). Alcohol and tobacco were exempted from the CSA based on their widespread social acceptance[8].

The CSA provisionally placed marijuana in the most restrictive Schedule I category, along with heroin and PCP (Aggarwal 2010; Gerber 2004). The legislative record makes clear that Congress intended the Schedule I classification of marijuana to be a temporary one until more information could be gathered through additional studies and review. In the U.S. scheme, Schedule I and Schedule II drugs have roughly similar risk, with the difference being Schedule I is reserved for substances that have no accepted medical applications (see Table 2.1). This helps to explain why drugs that represent more serious dangers in terms of dependence and toxicity, such as cocaine and methamphetamine, reside in lower scheduling categories than cannabis—the distinction hinges on accepted medical use.

After the CSA passed, the Nixon administration assigned further study to the U.S. Presidential Commission on Marihuana and Drug Abuse under the direction of former Governor of Pennsylvania Raymond P. Shafer. What came to be known as the Shafer Commission spent over a year and a million dollars conducting over fifty studies and collecting information from stakeholders, before presenting its findings to Congress in March 1972. The commission concluded that cannabis was far less dangerous to individuals and society than popular accounts suggested and recommended that it be decriminalized (U.S. Commission on Marihuana and Drug Abuse 1972, 1973). That call for reform was rejected by Congress and President Nixon, who both claimed that the commission's report minimized the "social costs" associated with legalization (Nahas and Greenwood 1974). As will be discussed in more detail later, such would be the fate of each of the subsequent attempts to have cannabis reclassified via formal petition. All have

*Table 2.1* Drug Scheduling Criteria from the U.S. Controlled Substances Act

| Schedule Criteria | Schedule I | Schedule II | Schedule III | Schedule IV | Schedule V |
|---|---|---|---|---|---|
| *Abuse Potential* | High | High | Low to moderate | Lower than Schedule III | Lowest |
| *Medical Access* | None | Prescription with monitoring | Prescription with limits: 6 mos/5 refills | Prescription, few refill limits | Prescription, no refill limits |
| *Safety and Dependence* | Lack of safety Risk of dependence | Known safety risks Risk of dependence | Low-moderate risk of physical dependence High risk of psychological dependence | Low risk to safety Low risk of dependence | Lowest risk factors for safety and dependence |
| *Examples* | Marijuana, heroin, LSD, mushrooms | Cocaine, opium, most opiates, methadone, oxycodone, Percocet, Ritalin | Codeine, hydro-codone, anabolic steroids, dronabinol (Marinol) | Benzodi-azepines (Xanax, Valium, Klonopin), Ambien, Lomotil | Cough suppressants with codeine, anti-convulsants, anti-diarrheals |

been rejected, often after extraordinary delays. The details of those petitions serve primarily as an index of how easily attempts to utilize the formal processes of governmental drug classification can be thwarted by a recalcitrant bureaucracy.

President Nixon's resistance to expert opinion on cannabis may seem puzzlingly at odds with his otherwise science-based approach to illicit drugs, which included the first federal funding for drug treatment. But the political utility of marijuana's associations was not lost on the Nixon White House. As Chief of Staff John Ehrlichman confided to a journalist in 1994:

> The Nixon campaign in 1968, and the Nixon White House after that, had two enemies: the antiwar left and black people. You understand what I'm saying? We knew we couldn't make it illegal to be either against the war or black, but by getting the public to associate the hippies with marijuana and blacks with heroin, and then criminalizing both heavily, we could disrupt those communities. We could arrest their leaders, raid their homes, break up their meetings, and vilify them night after night on the evening news. Did we know we were lying about the drugs? Of course we did.
>
> (Baum 2016)

### Attempts to Reschedule Cannabis

Since the passage of the federal Controlled Substances Act, there have been three notable attempts to reschedule cannabis. The first appeal was filed by a citizens' petition in 1972, led by Robert Randall, a patient whose importance will be discussed later in this chapter, and the National Organization to Reform Marijuana Laws (NORML). It requested that cannabis be rescheduled and made available by prescription (Gerber 2004; Russo et al. 2002). The ruling on this petition was delayed for sixteen years. Finally, in 1988, at the conclusion of exhaustive scientific hearings, DEA Chief Administrative Law Judge Francis L. Young ruled in favor of moving cannabis to Schedule II, stating: "By any measure of rational analysis marijuana can be safely used within a supervised routine of medical care." But administrative law rulings are not binding, and the head of the DEA rejected his recommendation (Eddy 2009; Gerber 2004). Legal challenges to that rejection wound through the courts until 1994, when the Court of Appeals for the D.C. Circuit affirmed the DEA administrator's authority to reject the ruling and petition, twenty-two years after it was filed.

A second citizen's petition was submitted the next year. In response to this petition, the DEA asked the Department of Health and Human Services (HHS) to provide an evaluation based on scientific and medical data. The HHS analysis backed the Schedule I status, and in 2001, this petition was denied (Eddy 2009).

A third citizen's petition was filed in 2002, which the DEA eventually denied in 2011 (DEA 2011a). Citizen groups, led by the patient advocacy organization Americans for Safe Access (ASA), appealed the ruling, arguing that the DEA ruled without review of recent scientific findings, rendering their verdict outdated and capricious (ASA 2012). In 2011, the rescheduling petition appeal was also denied. The DEA decision was based primarily on an assessment by the HHS that cannabis is addictive and does not have an approved level of safety; the plant's chemistry remains unknown and is not reproducible; and, most critically, the clinical evidence supporting claims of medical efficacy does not meet the stringent, "gold-standard" level of human studies needed for marketing new drugs (DEA 2011a, 2011b).

Those gold-standard studies, known as Phase III clinical trials, involve double-blind, placebo-controlled studies over several years with hundreds or even thousands of participants. Phase III clinical trials have not been undertaken with cannabis for a few reasons. One is the unusual barriers to medical research involving cannabis, more than for studying any other substance (Hudak and Wallack 2015). Another is the difficulty of devising a true placebo, since the effects of cannabis are often immediately apparent to users, and the point of a double-blind study is that neither the participants nor the researchers can know who is getting treated with the active substance and who is getting the placebo. As challenging as those barriers are to overcome, looming larger is simply the cost. Phase III clinical trials are expensive, often requiring tens of millions of dollars to conduct. That cost is typically borne by the pharmaceutical company developing the drug because, if it is approved by the Food and Drug Administration (FDA), the company will enjoy a monopoly on manufacturing and marketing it for twenty years following award of a patent. Yet patents require novel inventions or significant human intervention—a problem for patenting a plant.

Narrow interpretations of scheduling criteria have not been the chief weapon in the bureaucratic arsenal. Delays have been the hallmark of the administrative review process. Each of the succession of rescheduling petitions to go before the federal government has been met with stalling tactics. The original marijuana rescheduling petition wound through administrative channels and court challenges for twenty-two years before being laid to rest. The second rescheduling petition, filed in 1995, was not acted on for six years. The next rescheduling petition, filed by a coalition of patient advocates, took nine years and prodding by courts to receive an answer. Following that, the then-governors of Rhode Island and Washington state, Lincoln Chafee (R) and Christine Gregoire (D), petitioned the DEA to reconsider if cannabis could be classified as having legitimate medical use, as recognized in their respective states. That last petition was rejected in a 2016 letter to the governors' successors, five years after it was submitted.

### Accidental Expansion of Medical Cannabis: Robert Randall and Compassionate Use

In 1976, Robert Randall became the first modern medical cannabis patient in the United States and accomplished what no other avenue had: His criminal prosecution created a legal pathway, however narrow, to receive medical cannabis with not just the permission of the federal government but its assistance. Randall had been diagnosed with severe glaucoma as a teenager and was told he'd soon be blind, but he discovered quite by accident that cannabis reduced his intraocular pressure and halted the progression of the condition. In 1975, Randall was arrested in Washington, DC, for cultivating cannabis and was charged under federal law. U.S. District Judge James Washington accepted his common law defense of medical necessity, which was backed by careful documentation showing that cannabis controlled his glaucoma when legal pharmaceuticals could not (Ferraiolo 2007). The judge dismissed charges, ruling that the therapeutic benefit for Randall was compelling, no harm had been demonstrated, and "[m]edical evidence suggests that the medical prohibition is not well-founded" (Lee 2012). That ruling allowed Randall to do more than avoid trial and conviction. It was the basis for approving his petition to the federal government for access to the nation's one source of legal cannabis—the government's research farm at the University of Mississippi (Fichtner 2010; Russo et al. 2002; Stolick 2009; Werner 2011). Randall's outspoken criticism of federal policy and advocacy for medical access continued, and in short order the government cut off his supply. Randall filed suit against a slew of federal agencies with pro bono assistance from the distinguished D.C. law firm of Steptoe & Johnson, one of whose founders had served as Secretary of Defense in the Truman administration. Within twenty-four hours of filing, the government entered settlement negotiations that in 1978 resulted in the federal Compassionate Investigational New Drug (IND) program. On the face of it, the IND program was designed to assess not benefit but damage to Randall caused by smoking cannabis, in keeping with the self-evident mandate of the agency which runs the federal cannabis farm: the National Institute on Drug Abuse (NIDA) (Werner 2011).

Randall's activism attracted other applicants to the nascent IND program, but the government's restrictive rules for entry meant the few seriously ill patients who initially applied passed away before receiving approval. It would be 1981 before another patient successfully gained access, and enrollment only reached eight by the early 1980s (Gerber 2004; Russo et al. 2002). Of the forty-three patients who would receive government approval before the program was closed to new patients in 1992, only fifteen ever received cannabis, though Randall claimed thirty-four had successfully been enrolled (Russo et al. 2002). As of January 2018, four individuals continue to receive monthly tins of 300 cannabis cigarettes (Rosenfeld 2010).

As Randall battled the federal government in the late 1970s, there was also a push at the state level to decriminalize cannabis use and acknowledge medical uses. By 1978, eleven states had passed decriminalization measures for cannabis possession, reducing charges to a civil matter equivalent with a traffic ticket (Ferraiolo 2004; MPP 2008). Colorado and California were among them (MPP 2008). By 1991, an additional twenty-three states introduced and passed programs that allowed cannabis to be used therapeutically for specific conditions, but these programs were designed to obtain medical cannabis through a central federally approved source that would allow physicians to write prescriptions as they do for other medications. State programs adopted this approach in an attempt to harmonize them with federal laws and international treaties, but the federal government refused to supply the programs. As a result, very few of these first-wave medical cannabis programs were able to become operational for any length of time, making the laws mainly symbolic (Ferraiolo 2004; MPP 2008; Werner 2001).

Symbolic policies were not sufficient for those affected by the HIV/AIDS crisis that hit California's two largest metropolitan areas, San Francisco and Los Angeles, particularly hard. When the HIV/AIDS crisis began in the mid-1980s, Randall was instrumental in helping these patients apply to the Compassionate IND program. Facing a flood of new applications to the IND program, the George H.W. Bush administration closed the program to new patients in 1992. At the same time, the FDA added HIV/AIDS to the approved indications for prescribing dronabinol (Marinol), the synthetic THC pills brought to market in 1985 for treating nausea and vomiting associated with chemotherapy.

When the federal route to legal medical cannabis was blocked, advocates sought access at the local and state levels. In San Francisco, Dennis Peron was raided by local narcotics officers for providing cannabis to a clientele of mostly HIV-positive men in the predominantly gay Castro neighborhood (Werner 2001). Undeterred by the raid, Peron opened an aboveground cannabis club, and worked to pass a local medical cannabis initiative. That municipal initiative, Proposition P, passed in 1991 with the support of 80 percent of San Francisco voters. That local success set the stage for a grassroots ballot initiative at the state level in 1996—California's Proposition 215, the Compassionate Use Act.

Prop 215 exempted patients and their caregivers from state level criminal penalties for cannabis cultivation and possession, and allowed not-for-profit community distribution systems (Eddy 2010; Geluardi 2010). The new law also ushered in the contemporary "medical marijuana patient" identity on a broader scale (Chapkis and Webb 2008; London 2006; Feldman and Mandel 1998; Grinspoon 2001). Patients and advocates in the other western states and the Northeast swiftly followed California at the end of the 1990s and start of the 2000s, launching similar voter initiatives that all passed (Eddy 2010). Colorado became the eighth state to follow California in passing a state law that allows medical cannabis use when its voters approved a state constitutional amendment, Amendment 20, in 2000 (CDPHE 2011b; Ferraiolo 2007).

### Federal Legislative Attempts to Amend Cannabis Policy

Just as attempts to reclassify cannabis at the federal level consistent with its medical efficacy and relative safety have been derailed by selective use of evidence and bureaucratic stalling, legislative attempts have been stymied by procedural barriers that have prevented bills from being brought to a vote, even in committee. Reform bills have been introduced repeatedly in both houses of Congress since the 1970s, beginning in 1973 with the Marijuana Control Act, which would have decriminalized possession of an ounce of cannabis to an infraction on par with double parking. That bill got nowhere in 1973, nor did it advance in the subsequent Congresses to which it was introduced each year until the end of the decade. The same has been true for each of the measures that, beginning in 1981, would have created exceptions to the CSA for individual medical use or, later, shielded participants in state medical cannabis programs. Every session, bills have been introduced, only to be sent to committees where they sit without hearings or debate until the congressional term ends. This is not because the proponents of reform have lacked political capital or the issue is particularly partisan. That first reform bill, the Marijuana Control Act of 1973, was introduced in the House of Representatives by Ed Koch, a prominent Democrat who would be elected to his first of three terms as mayor of New York City four years later. The Senate companion bill to Koch's was introduced by Republican Jacob Javitz, the four-term senator from New York. The first medical measure, HR 4498, a bill "to provide for the therapeutic use of marijuana in situations involving life-threatening illnesses and to provide adequate supplies of marijuana for such use," was introduced in 1981 by a Republican from Connecticut and garnered eighty-four bipartisan cosponsors, including Newt Gingrich (R-GA), who would soon become Speaker of the House, arguably the most powerful legislative position in the federal government.

Some members of Congress, such as Gingrich, demonstrated only occasional support, but others have been tireless advocates for reform. One of the cosponsors of that first medical bill, Barney Frank (D-MA), then in his first term, would go on to sponsor a succession of bipartisan cannabis bills until he retired, thirty-two years later. Frank introduced versions of the States' Rights to Medical Marijuana Act in every Congress from 1997 to the end of his career in 2013, which would have moved cannabis to Schedule II classification and allowed states to set rules for physician recommendations or prescriptions of cannabis (Eddy 2009). Another perennial proponent of reform bills was Sam Farr (D-CA). Farr's first foray into marijuana reform legislation came in response to the 2002 federal trial of Ed Rosenthal described in the introduction. The 2003 Truth in Trials Act attempted to change federal law to allow testimony in federal prosecutions about defendants' compliance with state medical cannabis laws. Farr would finally see success in 2014 through an appropriations amendment cosponsored with Dan Rohrabacher (R-CA) that bars the Department of Justice from spending funds on interfering with state medical cannabis programs.

Dana Rohrabacher, the fourteen-term Republican congressman from Orange County who was a speechwriter for President Ronald Reagan before being elected to the House in 1989, has been a staunch supporter of legal access to medical cannabis since 2001, cosponsoring various bills and amendments year after year with Democratic Reps. Frank, Farr, Hinchey, and Blumenauer and giving impassioned speeches on the floor of the House about his mother's struggles with cancer. It was one of Rohrabacher's perennially offered amendments that finally produced the first substantial change in federal marijuana law, albeit a temporary one that relies on annual renewal.

The vehicle for reform was the funding bill for the Department of Justice (DOJ). Originally introduced in 2003 in partnership with Maurice Hinchey (D-NY), the amendment was offered six times before passing the House in 2014 as a rider on the Commerce-Justice-Science Appropriations for fiscal year 2015. The 2014 version that passed the House—called the Rohrabacher-Farr Amendment after Sam Farr (D-CA) replaced Rep. Hinchey as lead Democrat cosponsor—was not voted on by the Senate but was nonetheless included by the conference committee tasked with ironing out discrepancies between House and Senate versions of the omnibus spending bill. The amendment did not directly change the Controlled Substances Act but rather suspended its enforcement on medical cannabis by forbidding the DOJ from spending any funds on interfering with the implementation of state medical marijuana laws.

The Obama administration, despite generally supportive statements on medical cannabis from the president and White House spokesmen, would argue that the amendment only meant that the DOJ could not directly interfere with state governments by challenging their state laws (which no administration had done to date, in any case). According to the administration's logic, individual patients and those that provide medicine to them could still be prosecuted at will. The DOJ position drew a formal letter of protest from Rohrabacher and Farr, who pointed out that during debate on the amendment both those in favor and those opposed had agreed that the effect would be to end prosecutions. The DOJ had, in fact, told Congress the same thing in urging it to reject the amendment. This point is made in more detail in the 2015 amici curiae brief Reps. Rohrabacher and Farr also filed in the protracted appeals case of a California man, Charles Lynch, who had operated a medical cannabis dispensary in compliance with state law but was charged and convicted under federal law in 2008 (Rohrabacher and Farr 2015).

Once the Rohrabacher-Farr Amendment had been signed into law, the DOJ reversed itself, announcing that its previous position on the amendment's effect had not been a legal opinion or analysis, and the amendment actually changed nothing about how prosecutors could or would pursue cases. Yet the favorable vote for this amendment was in part due to successful lobbying of medical cannabis patients who had been subject to federal prosecution. One of the most notable was seventy-year-old Larry Harvey, a retired long-haul trucker and commercial fisherman from Washington state who, despite being confined to a wheelchair, traveled to

Washington, D.C. to lobby on behalf of the amendment and its potential to stop prosecutions against individual patients or caregivers such as himself and four others.

Harvey was at the center of a case that came to be known as the Kettle Falls Five, after his family farm had been raided and forty-five cannabis plants seized. Harvey, three family members, and a family friend were each charged with federal drug felonies, though all were qualified under state law to cultivate cannabis for treating medical conditions. Each faced mandatory federal prison sentences of five to ten years if convicted, a situation that is almost always enough to convince patients to take a plea deal for a reduced sentence, since everything they do to comply with state law becomes evidence against them in federal court. Yet Harvey and his family were proud, law-abiding people who, like many of the patients interviewed for this book, did not view their conduct as illegal or wrong and had hidden nothing. They had even marked their outdoor growing area with a large green cross positioned to be visible to the overflights drug task forces use to spot cannabis gardens. Harvey took that spirit of openness to Washington, DC, in April 2014 to lobby Congress with the amendment's lead sponsors, Reps. Rohrabacher and Farr. Harvey's homespun lobbying was credited by the medical cannabis patient advocacy group Americans for Safe Access, which sponsored his trip, as being instrumental in convincing Congress to add the amendment for the first time (Liszewski 2015).

From 2009 to 2013, there were 262 federal raids involving medical cannabis, and sixty individual dispensary operators have been indicted (Weissmann 2012). Since the passage of the Rohrabacher-Farr Amendment in 2014, which has been renewed or continued each year since, there have been only two. Defendants with pending cases and appeals involving state-compliant medical cannabis activities have asked courts to intervene, with increasing success. Federal courts have ruled in both criminal and civil cases that the restrictions placed by Congress on federal prosecutors are substantial. To proceed with a criminal trial or a civil injunction involving medical cannabis, prosecutors must now show in a pretrial hearing that the accused were not in compliance with state law.

In rejecting the Obama administration's argument that the amendment only prevented direct interference with state law, Senior District Judge Charles Breyer noted that the DOJ's position "tortures the plain meaning of the statute."[9] The DOJ ultimately accepted Breyer's October 2015 ruling on a civil injunction that had prevented the operation of a medical cannabis dispensary in northern California since 1998. The logic of Breyer's decision was soon extended to federal prosecutions of individuals. In August 2016, the Court of Appeals for the Ninth Circuit ruled unanimously on the combined cases of ten criminal defendants, returning all to their respective district courts to determine state law compliance before proceeding with federal prosecution.[10]

The amendment was again part of the omnibus spending bill for FY2017, but in signing the bill, President Trump included a statement saying, "I will treat this provision consistently with my constitutional responsibility to take care that the laws be faithfully executed" (Trump 2017). Attorney General Jeff Sessions also sent a letter to Congress asking them to abandon the amendment because it prevents the DOJ from "us[ing] all laws available to combat the transnational drug organizations and dangerous drug traffickers who threaten American lives" (Ingraham 2017). The contention that Congress is preventing prosecutors from enforcing the law entails some twisted logic, as the Rohrabacher-Farr Amendment is as much a law as the Controlled Substances Act. Congress has the authority to limit the enforcement of laws it has passed without expressly modifying them, as it has in suspending the CSA in relation to state-legal medical cannabis. If the Department of Justice were to ignore the express direction of Congress, a constitutional crisis would result.

## Cannabis Research and the Law

In January 1997, as California's medical cannabis law went into effect, the White House Office of National Drug Control Policy (ONDCP) asked the Institute of Medicine (IOM) to conduct a new review of the scientific evidence for medical uses of cannabis and assess its potential health benefits and risks. That review began in August 1997 and culminated in a report that concluded "[s]cientific data indicate the potential therapeutic value of cannabinoid drugs, primarily THC, for pain relief, control of nausea and vomiting, and appetite stimulation" (Joy, Watson, and Benson 1999, 5). The report acknowledges there are patients with serious medical conditions for whom cannabis is effective where all other treatments fail. The IOM recommended a full program of research and clinical trials to determine proper medical uses, a necessary step to meet rescheduling criteria. This suggestion was also ignored. In fact, nothing changed. Applications for exactly the type of research called for in the IOM report continued to be routinely denied (Fichtner 2010; Russo et al. 2002; Werner 2011).

Even researchers who overcome the unique bureaucratic barriers to studying cannabis and get federal approval are then left at the mercy of getting supply from the National Institute on Drug Abuse (NIDA), whose stated mission is to support studies related to abuse and addiction. NIDA has consistently obstructed studies investigating positive effects or medical benefit. One approved study of using cannabis in the treatment of PTSD in veterans languished seven years waiting on research materials from NIDA. Their cannabis supply is also of notoriously poor quality (Ingraham and Chappel 2017). The cannabis grown by NIDA is less potent and of fewer varieties than what is commercially available in states such as Colorado. What's worse, little care has historically been shown in preparing the cannabis that goes into the pre-rolled cigarettes NIDA provides to researchers, making stems and seeds common components. Long-standing difficulties with the Kafka-esque federal rules governing cannabis clinical research continue to stymie scientists (Aggarwal et al. 2009; Chapkis and Webb 2008; Grant et al. 2012; Grinspoon and Doblin 1995; Werner 2011).[11]

These problems prompted further petitions and litigation. In June 2001, Lyle E. Craker, Ph.D., a plant biologist at the University of Massachusetts Amherst, petitioned the federal government for a DEA license to cultivate research cannabis in a secure facility at his university. The bureaucratic rabbit hole he went down would become a decade deep before he conceded defeat. First, the DEA claimed to lose Craker's 2001 application; then they rejected his photocopy of it because it lacked an original signature. A year later, DEA returned the unprocessed original application, date-stamped the previous June. The resubmitted application would be in the hands of the DEA for nearly another year before being posted for public comment. After yet another year with no word back, Craker filed suit in July 2004 to compel a response, which the D.C. Court of Appeals orders in November 2004. The DEA rejected Craker's application in December 2004, more than forty-two months after he submitted it. Craker's appeal of that decision would result, two and a half years later, in a ruling by DEA Administrative Law Judge Mary Ellen Bittner that issuing a cultivation license to Craker would be in the public interest.[12] Following that ruling, forty-five members of the U.S. House of Representatives sent a letter to the DEA urging them to grant the license. But in January 2009, the Bush administration rejected the ruling and the application (ACLU 2010). Craker and his attorneys at the ACLU filed a motion asking the DEA to reconsider, but despite the Obama administration's rhetoric about embracing science-based policy, the request languished another two years before Craker, by then age seventy, withdrew it in 2011.

## Government Responses to State Medical Cannabis Programs

Opposition to state medical cannabis programs was a consistent theme across prior presidential administrations, but the election of Barack Obama signaled the possibility for a shift in attitudes. On the campaign trail, then-Senator Obama expressed sympathy for medical cannabis patients, citing his mother's battle with cancer, and his book *Dreams from My Father* detailed his own youthful enthusiasm for cannabis. Once elected, White House spokesmen affirmed the president's position on respecting state programs and said anyone working for the administration should be mindful of it. Yet no policy initiatives were forthcoming, and the DEA continued to not just emphatically deny any legitimate medical uses of cannabis but to conduct raids of dispensaries and related individuals and businesses, including analytic laboratories devoted to testing cannabis products for contaminants. Given the high stakes of noncompliance, many states sought clarification from Attorney General Eric Holder on what they could and could not do (Dickinson 2012; Dwoskin 2012; Kondrad and Reid 2013).

In 2009, the Department of Justice released a guidance memorandum from Deputy Attorney General David Ogden. It advised federal prosecutors that it was not the best use of resources to pursue cases where individuals or businesses were in clear compliance with their state's medical marijuana laws (Ogden 2009). The memo's guidance was informal and nonbinding, but any tolerance of state programs was a distinct departure from the policies of previous administrations. The memo produced a remarkable ripple effect, increasing efforts to pass medical cannabis policies in states without such policies and motivating greater participation in states that had existing medical cannabis policies. The largest effect was probably in Colorado (Kondrad and Reid 2013). Following the release of the Ogden memo, applications to Colorado's medical cannabis registry skyrocketed. By the end of 2010, little more than a year after the memo, the program which had seen 5,000 patients sign up over its previous eight years of existence now had more than 100,000 new medical cannabis patients on its registry (Kondrad and Reid 2013; Weinstein 2010). This was matched by a surge of storefront medical cannabis centers or "dispensaries" opening across the state, with their highest concentration in Denver, a city that had already relaxed its cannabis possession policies (Fox, Armentano, and Tvert 2009; Ingold 2011a; Reuteman 2010).

In an attempt to stem what many construed as chaos resulting from the Ogden memo, a second, clarifying memorandum was released in June 2011, this time authored by the new deputy attorney general, James Cole (Cole 2011). The Cole memo was widely seen as a significant revision of the previous memo, rather than a clarification, with major consequences for those who had opened medical cannabis dispensaries based on the Ogden memo's guidance (Dwoskin 2012; Weissmann 2012). In essence, this new memorandum distinguished between individual patients and their caregivers and medical cannabis businesses. While the federal government would not pursue individuals, the memo reopened the door to prosecution of dispensary businesses or cultivation operations, even if they complied with state laws (Dickinson 2012; Weissmann 2012). As a result, there were more raids on medical cannabis centers under Obama than during any previous administration, but most took place in states with less standardized regulation than Colorado (Dickinson 2012). California has always been the prime target for federal actions, in part due to the vagueness of the state's original law, which makes it easier to claim noncompliance (Dickinson 2012; Weissmann 2012), but scores of dispensaries operating in Oregon, Washington, Michigan, Nevada, Montana, and Colorado also received letters from federal prosecutors warning them about compliance based on various criteria (Dickinson 2012; Weissmann 2012). In January 2018, the Trump administration rescinded the Cole memo, creating new uncertainty for medical cannabis stakeholders.

The differences between state medical cannabis programs have been increased by uneven federal enforcement. In addition, federal strategies have included a prohibition on gun ownership for medical cannabis users, threats to federally insured banks that do business with cannabis dispensaries, and enforcement of provisions of the tax code that greatly increase the cost of running a cannabis business (Chun 2012; Dwoskin 2012; Ingold 2011b; Matonis 2012; Wyatt 2012). Even as the stated risk to individual patients has lowered, this is mitigated by the pressure on the supply side, because caregivers and dispensaries still face big risks, and growing for one's self also heightens risk of legal intervention at some level, whether local, state, or federal.

## Cannabis and Public Opinion

As much as the fight continues over medical access at the federal level, public opinion polls have moved in a considerably more favorable direction on cannabis over the past decades. Public opinion overwhelmingly supports medical cannabis. According to a 2010 Congressional Research Service report, twenty-three national polls posed questions about medical cannabis between 1995 and 2010, and all of them showed "substantial margins," from 60 percent to 85 percent or more in support of medical cannabis policies that make it legally available (Eddy 2010). Most recently, an April 2018 Quinnipiac University poll of registered voters put support at 93 percent (Quinnipiac 2018).

A commonplace among opponents has been to suggest that medicalized cannabis is simply a "front" or a "stepping stone" to legalize recreational use. The growing acceptance of medical use may spill over onto attitudes about recreational use. Public sentiment in favor of legalized adult use has also increased dramatically since 2010, with multiple public opinion surveys finding a majority of American adults support it. Most significant of those is the findings of the preeminent public opinion research instrument, the biennial General Social Survey (GSS) from NORC at the University of Chicago, which found those who say they "think the use of marijuana should be legal" going from 52 percent in 2014 to 57 percent in 2016. (By contrast, between 1970 and 2000, the GSS put support at under 30 percent, and below 20 percent from the mid-1980s to mid-1990s.) That public support, coupled with the hundreds of millions in tax revenue being collected by states that have implemented it and the growing regulatory experience of states with medical programs, suggests that adult use laws may not hinge on whether a state allows citizen initiatives. In addition to the eight states that currently have adult use laws courtesy of voters, the Vermont legislature in early 2017 became the first to approve such legislation. That first bill was vetoed in May 2017 by Vermont Governor Phil Scott (R), but he indicated he was open to signing a modified version, and in January 2018, just days after the Trump administration rescinded the Cole memo, he got and signed just such a bill. At the same time, the New Hampshire House gave initial approval to a recreational cannabis bill, though Governor Chris Sununu (R) has said he is opposed. Twenty-one other states considered bills to regulate adult cannabis use in 2017.

## The Structure of Medical Cannabis Regulation in Colorado

Colorado leads all states in the nation in its regulatory structure for medical cannabis (Kondrad and Reid 2013, 52). Amendment 20, Colorado's constitutional amendment, specifically exempts medical marijuana patients and their designated caregivers from criminal penalty by allowing an affirmative defense in state court cases and allowing exceptions to Colorado criminal law for patients and caregivers who possess a state registry card.[13] The amendment tasked the Colorado Department of Public Health and Environment (CDPHE) with creating and managing the state registry system. In this role, the CDPHE defines rules for patients, physicians, and caregivers, based on the terms outlined by the amendment and by subsequent legislation that tightened regulation in response to the exponential increase in Colorado's program and DOJ memos that clarified federal enforcement priorities (Cole 2011; Ogden 2009). The CDPHE rules are incorporated into the Colorado Code of Regulation 5 CCR 1006–2, which is established through the Colorado Board of Health (CDPHE 2011a). These rules have evolved over the years, including changes during this study and seven more iterations since 2012.

While the CDPHE establishes the rights of patients and defines relationships between patients, providers, and physicians, the industry's regulations are defined and managed through the Medical Marijuana Enforcement Division (MMED) of the Colorado Department of Revenue. MMED rules are not covered in the state's constitutional amendment. Instead, industry rules have evolved through stakeholder negotiations that took place after the passage of Amendment 20. A few different business structures were considered for the state's medical cannabis industry; ultimately Colorado set parameters through two legislative bills: House Bill 1284, which passed in May 2010,[14] and House Bill 1043, which passed in May 2011 (Kamin 2012).[15]

The adopted medical cannabis legislation created an architecture based on a regulated for-profit dispensary model.[16] The resulting tightly regulated market compares with how the state handles oversight of prescription drugs or alcohol, with additional rules about how production, manufacture, and retail sales sectors are integrated. The industry rules are now written into the Colorado Revised Statutes as Article 43.3 of Title 12, better known as the Colorado Medical Marijuana Code (MMED 2011). These rules detail three types of medical cannabis business licenses: production licenses for gardens (OPCs), retail licenses for dispensary outlets (also called medical marijuana centers or MMCs), and a third license to manufacture cannabis-infused products such as edibles and tinctures, called a Medical Marijuana Infused Products (MMIP) license.

The MMED rules translate the legislation that defines the proper relationships between these business types into an operational system. In addition, the MMED rules codify the obligations for privacy, confidentiality, surveillance, and record-keeping in relation to patients as defined in this legislation. Finally, the MMED manages the credentialing process for employees who work at any licensed facility in this industry and administers the mandatory "badges" for workers who pass the background check and meet program criteria. Taken together, the CDPHE and MMED regulate each type of actor in the program and the progression of the plant from seed to sale.

It is also worth noting that a provision in Colorado's HB 1284 allows municipalities to prohibit or restrict the cultivation or sale of medical cannabis within their jurisdictions[17]. As an example, Denver has created Municipal Code Chapter 24, Article 11, which specifies that no one under eighteen years of age can be a visitor in a dispensary, and dispensaries cannot be located within 1,000 feet of a school or childcare facility. Article 12 of the same chapter of the Denver Municipal Code limits or prohibits highly visible forms of public advertising and signage that promote medical marijuana facilities.[18] Other towns have issued moratoria on any new medical marijuana centers, and some have banned them outright. These choices inevitably alter the local conditions in ways that influence patient's interactions with the system and can limit access, adding another layer of law and regulation for patients to navigate in treating their conditions.

Since the rules have evolved over the period of this study, and the patients in this study entered the system at different times since the medical marijuana program's inception, patient interactions with the system vary at least in part based on the timing of that experience. Among the unchanging commonalities of the patient experience in Colorado and other medical cannabis states is the need to seek a recommendation for the use of medical cannabis from an actively licensed medical professional. Chapter 3 considers how medical cannabis patient interactions with physicians in Colorado affect the patients' sense of legitimacy.

## Notes

1. In 2012, voters in Colorado and Washington passed ballot initiatives allowing cannabis use and possession for all individuals age twenty-one and over. They were followed in 2014 by voter initiatives in Alaska, Oregon, and the District of Columbia. Four more states passed ballot measures in 2016: California, Massachusetts, Maine, and Nevada. In January 2018, the Vermont legislature became the first body of elected officials to pass such a measure, which Republican Governor Phil Scott signed into law.
2. The Marihuana Tax Act was overturned when Timothy Leary, a former psychology professor at Harvard, successfully challenged it as requiring a violation of the Fifth Amendment's protections against self-incrimination to comply. His case stemmed

from being charged in December 1965 by a border officer with violating federal law (the Marihuana Tax Act) after federal agents found a small amount of marijuana in his vehicle at the Laredo, Texas, border crossing to Mexico. Leary, as we note elsewhere in this book, figures much more prominently in the story of marijuana's medicalization because he was responsible for theorizing what is now the widely accepted understanding of drug effects as being drug, set, and setting—a combination of the chemical itself, the biochemical and psychological "set" of the individual, and the setting in which it is consumed.

3. While no U.S. Attorney has taken action yet on the many threats issued, such action would not be a first. Following a 2001 DEA raid, the federal government seized a building owned by the City of West Hollywood that had been used by the Los Angeles Cannabis Resource Center (LACRC) as a distribution point for medical cannabis. A West Hollywood city councilman was the attorney for the LACRC and helped arrange the building purchase. Three of the operators of the LACRC pleaded guilty but only received a year of probation each after the judge rejected the recommended twenty-four to thirty-month prison sentence, citing the doctrine of "lesser harm," meaning violating the law created less harm than following it.

4. Wickard v. Filburn, 317 U.S. 111 (1942).

5. The raid on Monson's property in northern California generated a tense standoff that lasted several hours between the local sheriff's deputies, who were bound by the state law with which she was in compliance, and DEA agents who insisted on destroying her garden. Both local and federal law enforcement were involved because the DEA relies on cross-deputizing local officers to help carry out search warrants (Raich v. Ashcroft, 248 F. Supp. 2d 918 (N.D. Cal. 2004)).

6. One of those affected by the decision was Bryan Epis, a Chico, California, man who in 1997 became the first state-legal patient prosecuted by federal authorities. He was convicted in 2002 for maintaining a basement garden for himself and four other patients and sentenced to a mandatory ten years in federal prison. After serving two years, he was released in 2004 on order of the Court of Appeals for the Ninth Circuit pending appeal under the *Raich v. Gonzales* decision. Epis was resentenced to ten years in 2007 but stayed free on appeal until 2010, when he returned to federal prison. He was released June 17, 2013. (Gonzales v. Raich (previously Ashcroft v. Raich), 545 U.S. 1 (2005)).

7. Justice Scalia would contort his legal reasoning to an extraordinary degree in a separate concurring opinion justifying how he could say Congress has no authority to restrict guns near schools or violence against women but can prevent patients from using cannabis within a regulated state program. (Gonzales v. Raich (03–1454) 545 U.S. 1 (2005) 352 F.3d 1222).

8. This is codified in Title 21 US Code 802.

9. United States v. Marin Alliance for Medical Marijuana, 139 F. Supp. 3d 1039 (2015).

10. U.S.A. v. Mcintosh, Article 15–10117 (2016).

11. To add to the ironies of cannabis policies, Health and Human Services, the same federal agency that evaluated and rejected the evidence for the DEA rescheduling petition on the basis of incomplete evidence of medical use, also holds the patent for medical uses of the plant's constituents, known as "cannabinoids." Patent 09/674028 "Cannabinoids as antioxidants and neuroprotectants," was filed by the HHS in 2001. (Hampson, Aidan J., Julius Axelrod, and Maurizio Grimaldi. 2001. *Cannabinoids as Antioxidants and Neuroprotectants.* Washington, DC: Department of Health and Human Services.)

12. On August 12, 2016, the DEA published in the Federal Register a solicitation for applications for additional research cannabis cultivation sites, as Judge Bittner had recommended Applications to Become Registered Under the Controlled Substances Act to Manufacture Marijuana to Supply Researchers in the United States, Article 81 FR 53846, Section Docket No. DEA-447 (2016). The DEA received twenty-five

applications for new cultivation facilities to supply researchers, but DEA officials told the *Washington Post* in August 2017 that the Department of Justice, which must approve them to move forward, has refused to take action, stymying the DEA and researchers. (Zapotosky, Matt, and Devlin Barrett. 2017. "Justice Department at Odds with DEA on Marijuana Research." *Washington Post.* (https://www.washingtonpost.com/world/national-security/justice-department-at-odds-with-dea-on-marijuana-research-ms-13/2017/08/15/ffa12cd4-7eb9-11e7-a669-b400c5c7e1cc_story.html)).

13. Constitution, State of Colorado. 2000. *Medical Use of Marijuana*, Article XVIII, Section 14, Cl. 2.

14. House Bill 10–1284: Colorado House of Representatives. 2010. *Concerning Regulation of Medical Marijuana, and Making an Appropriation Therefor* (House Bill 10–1284) Article 12–43.3–101, Section 1. Title 12. Article 43.3 (2010). House Bill 11–1043: Colorado House of Representatives. 2011. *Concerning Medical Marijuana, and Making an Appropriation Therefor* (House Bill 11–1043). Sixty-eighth General Assembly, State of Colorado, First Regular Session (June 2, 2011).

15. The production and distribution system was amended in 2013 to incorporate rules for retail sales to all adults, pursuant to Amendment 64, but since this study is concerned with the patient experience in the time leading up to that, subsequent regulatory changes are not considered here in any detail.

16. Rules for adult use retail operations, instituted beginning in 2013 after the passage of Amendment 64, are separate.

17. This provision in the law passed in 2010 can be found in Title 12 Article 43.3-101 of the Colorado Revised Statutes, known as the Colorado Medical Marijuana Code. Control through local exemption is built into many state's laws and has been exercised in townships, cities, and counties in Colorado, California, New Jersey, and Maine, according to Geoff Mulvihill's 2012 Associated Press article, "Local Governments Banning Medical Marijuana Dispensaries," which was picked up by multiple publications including the *San Diego Union-Tribune* (www.sandiegouniontribune.com/sdut-many-us-communities-are-blocking-medical-marijuana-2012jan09-story.html).

18. Denver Code. 2011. *Denver Medical Marijuana Code*, Chapter 24 Article XII (Denver. gov 2011).

## References

ACLU, American Civil Liberties Union. 2010. "Time Line: In the Matter of Lyle Craker." *www.aclu.org: American Civil Liberties Union.* Retrieved August 20, 2017 (www.aclu.org/other/time-line-matter-lyle-craker).

Aggarwal, Sunil K., Gregory T. Carter, Mark D. Sullivan, Craig ZumBrunnen, Richard Morrill, and Jonathan D. Mayer. 2009. "Medicinal Use of Cannabis in the United States: Historical Perspectives, Current Trends, and Future Directions." *The Journal of Opioid Management* 5(3):153–68.

Aggarwal, Sunil K. 2010. "Cannabis: A Commonwealth Medicinal Plant, Long Suppressed, Now at Risk of Monopolization." *Denver University Law Review Online.* Retrieved October 15, 2010 (www.denverlawreview.org/medical-marijuana/2010/8/23/cannabis-a-commonwealth-medicinal-plant-long-suppressed-now.html).

ASA, Americans for Safe Access. 2012. "Petition for Review of a Final Order of the Drug Enforcement Administration." Article No. 11–1265 (U.S. Court of Appeals 2012).

Baum, Dan. 2016. "Legalize It All: How to Win the War on Drugs." *Harper's Magazine*, April.

CDPHE, Colorado Department of Public Health and Environment. 2011a. *Medical Use of Marijuana.* 5 CCR 1006–2 Congress:18.

CDPHE, Colorado Department of Public Health and Environment. 2011b. *The Colorado Medical Marijuana Registry*. Colorado Department of Public Health and Environment. Retrieved October 1, 2011 (www.cdphe.state.co.us/hs/Medicalmarijuana/statistics.html).

Chapkis, Wendy, and Richard J. Webb. 2008. *Dying to Get High: Marijuana as Medicine*. New York: New York University Press.

Chun, Janean. 2012. "Medical Marijuana Businesses Face Risks, from Raids to Audits." in *Huffington Post*. Retrieved February 18, 2013 (https://www.huffingtonpost.com/2012/09/04/medical-marijuana-business_n_1814901.html).

Cole, James M. 2011. *Guidance Regarding the Ogden Memo in Jurisdictions Seeking to Authorize Marijuana for Medical Use*. Washington, DC: Department of Justice.

Courtwright, David T. 2004. "The Controlled Substances Act: How a 'Big Tent' Reform Became a Punitive Drug Law." *Drug and Alcohol Dependence* 76(1):9–15. doi: 10.1016/j.drugalcdep.2004.04.012.

DEA, Drug Enforcement Administration. 2011a. "Denial of Petition to Initiate Proceedings to Reschedule Marijuana: Proposed Rule." *Federal Register* 76(131):40552–89.

DEA, Drug Enforcement Administration. 2011b. *Denial of Petition to Initiate Proceedings to Reschedule Marijuana*. Vol. 21 CFR Chapter II. Washington, DC: Department of Justice.

Dickinson, Tim. 2012. "Obama's War on Pot." *Rolling Stone*. November 29, 2012. (https://www.rollingstone.com/politics/news/obamas-war-on-pot-20120216).

Dwoskin, Elizabeth. 2012. "Will the Feds Crack Down on Pot or Look the Other Way?" *Bloomberg Businessweek*. November 29, 2012. (www.businessweek.com/articles/2012-11-29/will-the-feds-crack-down-on-pot-or-look-the-other-way#p2).

Eddy, Mark. 2009. *Medical Marijuana: Review and Analysis of Federal and State Policies*. Washington, DC: Congressional Research Service.

Eddy, Mark. 2010. *Medical Marijuana: Review and Analysis of Federal and State Policies*. Washington, DC: Congressional Research Service.

Feldman, Harvey W., and R. Jerry Mandel. 1998. "Providing Medical Marijuana: The Importance of Cannabis Clubs." *Journal of Psychoactive Drugs* 30(2):179–86.

Ferraiolo, Kathleen Grammatico. 2004. "Popular 'Medicine': Policymaking by Direct Democracy and the Medical Marijuana Movement of the 1990s." Ph.D. Dissertation, Political Science, University of Virginia, AAT 3131466.

Ferraiolo, Kathleen Grammatico. 2007. "From Killer Weed to Popular Medicine: The Evolution of American Drug Control Policy, 1937–2000." *Journal of Policy History* 19(2):147–79.

Fichtner, Christopher Glenn, 2010. *Cannabinomics: The Marijuana Policy Tipping Point*. Northbrook, IL: Well Mind Books.

Fox, Steve, Paul Armentano, and Mason Tvert. 2009. *Marijuana Is Safer: So Why Are We Driving People to Drink?* White River Junction, VT: Chelsea Green Publishing.

Geluardi, John. 2010. *Cannabiz: The Explosive Rise of the Medical Marijuana Industry*. Sausalito, CA: PoliPoint Press.

Gerber, Rudolph J. 2004. *Legalizing Marijuana: Drug Policy Reform and Prohibition Politics*. Westport, CT: Praeger.

Grant, Igor, J. Hampton Atkinson, Ben Gouaux, and Barth Wilsey. 2012. "Medical Marijuana: Clearing Away the Smoke." *Open Neurology Journal* 6:18–25.

Grinspoon, Lester. 2001. "Commentary: On the Pharmaceuticalization of Marijuana." *International Journal of Drug Policy* 12(5–6):377–83.

Grinspoon, Lester, and Rick Doblin. 1995. "Marijuana, the AIDS Wasting Syndrome, and the U.S. Government." Letter to the editor. *New England Journal of Medicine* 333:670-671. https://www.nejm.org/doi/full/10.1056/NEJM199509073331020

Hudak, John, and Grace Wallack. 2015. *Ending the U.S. Government's War on Medical Marijuana Research.* Washington, DC: Brookings Institution Press.

Ingold, John. 2011a. "A Map of Colorado's Medical-Marijuana Dispensaries." *Denver Post.* October 11, 2011. (http://blogs.denverpost.com/crime/2011/09/26/a-map-of-colorados-medical-marijuana-dispensaries/1553/).

Ingold, John. 2011b. "ATF Say Medical-Marijuana Patients Are Prohibited from Owning Guns." *The Denver Post.* October 2, 2011. (https://www.denverpost.com/2011/10/02/atf-say-medical-marijuana-patients-are-prohibited-from-owning-guns/#ixzz2LIWiEHwY).

Ingraham, Chris. 2017. "Jeff Sessions Personally Asked Congress to Let Him Prosecute Medical-Marijuana Providers."*Wonkblog. Washington Post.* June 13, 2017. (https://www.washingtonpost.com/news/wonk/wp/2017/06/13/jeff-sessions-personally-asked-congress-to-let-him-prosecute-medical-marijuana-providers/).

Ingraham, Chris, and Tauhid Chappel. 2017. "Government Marijuana Looks Nothing Like the Real Stuff." *WonkBlog.* Washington Post. (www.washingtonpost.com/news/wonk/wp/2017/03/13/government-marijuana-looks-nothing-like-the-real-stuff-see-for-yourself).

Joy, Janet E., Stanley J. Watson, Jr., and John A. Benson, Jr., eds. 1999. *Marijuana and Medicine: Assessing the Science Base.* Washington: Institute of Medicine, National Academy Press.

Kamin, Sam. 2012. "Medical Marijuana in Colorado and the Future of Marijuana Regulation in the United States." *McGeorge Law Review* 43:147–68.

Kondrad, Elin, and Alfred Reid. 2013. "Colorado Family Physicians' Attitudes toward Medical Marijuana." *The Journal of the American Board of Family Medicine* 26(1):52–60. doi: 10.3122/jabfm.2013.01.120089.

Lee, Martin. 2012. *Smoke Signals: A Social History of Marijuana-Medical, Recreational, and Scientific.* New York: Simon and Schuster Inc.

Liszewski, Mike. 2015. "Remembering Larry Harvey." *Americans for Save Access.* Retrieved 2017 (https://www.safeaccessnow.org/remembering_larry_harvey).

London, Jeffrey. 2006. "The Criminalization and Medicalization of Marijuana: A Study of Changing Deviance Designations." Ph.D. Dissertation, Sociology, University of Colorado-Boulder, Boulder, AAT 3212105.

Matonis, Jon. 2012. "Credit Card Processors Discriminate against Medical Marijuana." *Forbes.* Retrieved February 18, 2013 (https://www.forbes.com/sites/jonmatonis/2012/09/29/credit-card-processors-discriminate-against-medical-marijuana/#129b29566bcc).

MMED, Medical Marijuana Enforcement Division. 2011. "Medical Marijuana Code." Article 12–43.3 (Colorado State Legislature 2011).

MPP, Marijuana Policy Project. 2008. *State-by-State Medical Marijuana Laws.* Washington, DC: Marijuana Policy Project.

Nahas, Gabriel G., and Albert Greenwood. 1974. "The First Report of the National Commission on Marihuana (1972): Signal of Misunderstanding or Exercise in Ambiguity." *Bulletin of the New York Academy of Medicine* 50(1):55–75.

NCJRS, National Criminal Justice Association. 1999. *A Guide to State Controlled Substances Acts.* Document No 184295. Washington, DC: U.S. Department of Justice (https://www.ncjrs.gov/pdffiles1/Digitization/184295NCJRS.pdf).

Ogden, David W. 2009. *Investigations and Prosecutions in States Authorizing the Medical Use of Marijuana.* Washington, DC: U.S. Government.

Quinnipiac University. 2018. "U.S. Voters Believe Comey More Than Trump, Quinnipiac University National Poll Finds; Support For Marijuana Hits New High." Retrieved May 17, 2018 (https://poll.qu.edu/images/polling/us/us04262018_ufcq23.pdf).

Reuteman, Rob. 2010. "Medical Marijuana Business Is on Fire." *USA Today.* April 20, 2010. Retrieved January 16, 2013 (https://usatoday30.usatoday.com/money/industries/health/2010-04-20-medical-marijuana_N.htm).

Rohrabacher, Dana, and Sam Farr. 2015. "United States of America V. Charles C. Lynch." Article 10–50219, 10–50264 (Reed Smith LLP 2015).

Rosenfeld, Irvin. 2010. *My Medicine.* Santa Barbara, CA: Open Archive Press.

Russo, Ethan, Mary Lynn Mathre, Al Byrne, Robert Velin, Paul J. Bach, Juan Sanchez-Ramos, and Kristin A. Kirlin. 2002. "Chronic Cannabis Use in the Compassionate Investigational New Drug Program: An Examination of Benefits and Adverse Effects of Legal Clinical Cannabis." *Journal of Cannabis Therapeutics* 2(1):3–57.

Sinha, Jay. 2001. *The History and Development of the Leading International Drug Control Conventions Congress* (www.parl.gc.ca/Content/SEN/Committee/371/ille/library/history-e.htm).

Stolick, Matt. 2009. *Otherwise Law-Abiding Citizens: A Scientific and Moral Assessment of Cannabis Use.* Lanham, MD: Lexington Books.

Suissa, Amnon J. 2001. "Cannabis, Social Control and Exclusion: The Importance of Social Ties." *The International Journal of Drug Policy* 12:385–96.

Taylor, Dave Bewley and Martin Jelsma. 2012. *The UN Drug Control Conventions: The Limits of Latitude.* IDPC Series on Legislative Reform of Drug Policies. No. 18. Available at SSRN (https://ssrn.com/abstract=2184316 or http://dx.doi.org/10.2139/ssrn.2184316).

Trump, Donald J. 2017. "Signing Statement." 2017FY Appropriations.

U.S. Commission on Marihuana and Drug Abuse. 1972. *Marihuana: A Signal of Misunderstanding: First Report of the National Commission on Marihuana and Drug Abuse.* New York: New American Library.

U.S. Commission on Marihuana and Drug Abuse. 1973. "Drug Use in America: Problem in Perspective: Second Report of the Commission on Marihuana and Drug Abuse." Controlled Substances Act: Definitions, Article 21 (2006).

Weinstein, Jack. 2010. "Growing Pains Part 2: Green Rush." October 7, 2010. *Steamboat Pilot & Today* (https://www.steamboattoday.com/news/growing-pains-entrepreneurs-cash-in-on-medical-marijuana/).

Weissmann, Jordan. 2012. "Will Obama Let Washington and Colorado Keep Their Legal Pot?" *The Atlantic,* November 9.

Werner, Clint. 2001. "Medical Marijuana and the AIDS Crisis." Pp. 17–33 in *Cannabis Therapeutics in HIV/AIDS,* edited by E. Russo. Philadelphia, PA: Haworth Integrative Healing Press.

Werner, Clint. 2011. *Marijuana Gateway to Health.* San Francisco: Dachstar Press.

Wyatt, Kristen. 2012. "Banking for Pot Shops Eyed in Colorado." *The San Diego Union-Tribune.* February 14, 2012. (www.sandiegouniontribune.com/sdut-banking-for-pot-shops-eyed-in-colorado-2012feb14-story.html

Zapotosky, Matt, and Devlin Barrett. 2017. "Justice Department at Odds with DEA on Marijuana Research, MS-13." *Washington Post.* April 15, 2017. (http://wapo.st/2flpvaE?tid=ss_tw&utm_term=.18accc6c907e).

# Chapter 3

# Becoming a Patient

In order to get involved, you have to decide: Are you going to do it fully ille-gally and make one contact with the drug dealer? There. I said the bad words. A retail vendor. A free market retail vendor. You have to decide if you're going to go to a free market retail vendor, or if you're going to go through the system and then find out that it doesn't work for you. I think most people—personally, I believe most people will try it quote unquote illegally first because of how damned easy it is to try. Patients are going to find someone they know, if they can. And if they're like me, they're going to have trouble finding somebody they know [to find a supplier].

(Andy)

The incomplete medicalization of cannabis means that its access is not com-pletely controlled through medical institutions. In medical cannabis states that do not allow recreational use, patients have the option of accessing can-nabis legally through the state's medical program or illegally through the underground market. As Andy's opening quote points out, illicit access relies on networks that some patients simply do not have. In addition to decisions about cannabis supply, would-be patients often consider factors that have little to do with medical efficacy. For instance, individuals may weigh the legal protections they gain by becoming a patient against the risks or scru-tiny associated with identifying themselves as breaking federal law. Many see increased accessibility to safely produced cannabis as a benefit but may worry about risks to their reputation, professional licensure, parental rights, or employment, as chapter 8 discusses. In other words, patients often treat the decision to use cannabis medically as a separate but interrelated decision from that of registering with the state.

When asked where they first got the idea to seek a recommendation, all forty patients in this study recounted a prompting incident that led them to realize they would qualify for a doctor's recommendation. They could all name a prior diagnosis of a clearly qualifying condition, and often they could name more than one. All but three required significant ongoing medi-cal treatment related to their condition(s). Five already used cannabis and defined that use as medical prior to seeking an official recommendation. The majority of patients had used cannabis recreationally at some point in the past, most typically during their late teens or early twenties. Half claimed they had not used cannabis since their teen or college years. About a third reported more recent cannabis use. A small subgroup had never used cannabis in any context prior to medical use. Given these different profiles, patients came to the decision to seek a medical cannabis recommendation with different levels of cannabis experience and different ideas about who used it and what dangers or benefits it could offer.

## The Four Routes for Seeking a Recommendation

Patients followed one of four routes for deciding to seek an official recommendation from a doctor and apply to the registry: Their regular physician recommended it; friends or family suggested it; the patient heard about medical cannabis indirectly and initiated more research; or the patient had nonmedical motivations to seek legal protections conferred by official patient status. The most common routes leading to recommendation were the patient's own initiative and research or the suggestions of friends and family. The latter is consistent with evidence that shows people often discuss issues of health, illness, and treatment with their families and friends (Britten 2008). The strong networks of the lifeworld help individuals determine the best course of action for managing health conditions. This includes treatment decisions in the formal sector of biomedical treatment as well as choosing treatment outside of biomedicine (Bouldin et al. 2000; Britten 2008; Cameron and Leventhal 2003; Fagerlin, Wang, and Ubel 2005). The roles of individual initiative and strong networks support the understanding that cannabis medicalization is in part accomplished through lay efforts. It is much less common for doctors to suggest cannabis than for patients to seek a recommendation.

### Physician Suggestion

Although most medical cannabis recommendations in this study were driven by patients, not all were. In eight interviews, patients reported that they arrived at the idea to try medical cannabis after their physician suggested it might work for their condition. In many of these cases, patients had either been diagnosed with a serious progressive disease for which cannabis use is well established or the doctor specialized in pain management. This interview study is not designed to draw a conclusion as to representativeness; however, no pattern emerged that clearly separated cases in which a doctor initiated the recommendation from the more common cases of patients seeking one.

For instance, four patients in the study sample were living with HIV/AIDS. Two had doctors who suggested medical cannabis use, while the other two had doctors who initially discouraged the idea when the patients broached it. Cannabis was suggested to one cancer patient, while another was prescribed the synthetic THC drug Marinol and had to negotiate for a cannabis recommendation, and a third cancer patient, who was uninsured, had no regular physician to make a suggestion. In two cases, general practitioners suggested use for pain and treatment of seizures. One woman claims to have received multiple informal suggestions from different psychiatrists who thought she would benefit from medical cannabis, but she could not recall the exact circumstances of the official recommendation. From patients' reports, it seems clear that physicians do not act uniformly when it comes to medical cannabis recommendations. This finding aligns with Kondrad and Reid's (2013) research, which reported variation in physician attitudes based on the strength of their belief that cannabis is harmful, and their prior experiences with patients. Patients in this study reported that doctors who supported medical cannabis as an effective therapy often stated personal or anecdotal reasons rather than scientific evidence to bolster their position, recounting prior experiences with patients, friends, or family members who had successfully used medical cannabis.

Travis offers an example of a medical cannabis recommendation that was doctor-initiated. Now in his early forties, Travis suffered a serious head injury as a child, when he was violently accosted by a psychologically unstable stranger who wandered onto his parent's rural property. Due to the head injuries sustained in the attack, Travis has had lifelong migraines. The seizures started in early adulthood. After twenty years on serious prescription seizure medication, Travis developed negative side effects. He tried several new combinations to control seizures. These drugs had to be coordinated with his full treatment plan, which includes multiple prescriptions for anxiety and post-traumatic stress disorder (PTSD) that developed as a result of the attack. He has been on serious anti-convulsants such as phenytoin (Dilantin) and phenobarbital. These drugs have significant counter-indications, require monitoring, and come with side effects, including dizziness and stomach pain. Travis works each day to manage stomach pain and to keep his anxiety levels low.

> I've used [cannabis] all my life—just recreational use and that. I always told my doctor about it, and we kept track of it for a long time, ever since I started having seizures. He knows that I've never had one while I was smoking it. And so he wanted to try it, and that's how I got on it. They wanted to see what it would do. It actually slowed my seizures down, but I still get sick because of all the pills I take. But the seizures, they pretty much came to about two a year, compared to about twenty a year. So it's made a big difference with the seizures. But being sick, I'm still sick at least once a month for like ten days out of the month [due to all of the medications].

Travis was one of the first patients in Colorado's medical marijuana program. He says of his doctor's recommendation:

> He was my primary care doctor for twenty years. . . . He was actually working with two other patients before me who were having seizures, and he saw that [cannabis] was working for them. He just told me, "Get the paperwork, and we'll get you on, and we'll see what it does." And he told me at that time there were some doctors that weren't signing because of the laws and stuff, but he told me he would go ahead and stand up for me in court, if need be, because my seizures were so bad at that time, and I was trying to raise my [two] girls [as a single father].

The suggestion to use medical cannabis by Travis' regular physician creates a clear sense of legitimacy for his cannabis use because it is well integrated with his regular biomedical care. Additionally, due to Travis' lengthy experience with pharmaceutical regimens, he is accustomed to an experimental approach: "These doctors don't know what's wrong. They just figure: try this, try this. If it doesn't work, we'll put you on something else." While he accepts this medical approach to his issues, Travis feels that his doctors

> don't realize [the medications] are tearing up my body and my mind. . . . With all the pills they have me on, there's times when I've been on so many pills that I almost have a stroke, so they kept me in the hospital for a couple of days.

In this light, medical cannabis offers an option with less frightening side effects and controls the seizures. His physician suggested using cannabis along with his other medications, but Travis has to decide how to manage the pharmaceutical regimen's effects on his quality of life.

> Yeah, I think it scares almost anybody. I mean, I show people the pills that I take, and it breaks a lot of people down. Then I have to tell them, imagine what I have to look at every morning when I take them. I get mad about it. I start getting mad because of the system. And how it started out with two pills, three pills, and then branched out to more and more pills and stomach operations and just worse problems from all the pills I've been taking for twenty years. . . . I've got to listen to music a lot to keep my mind focused on doing things that need to be done at home instead of concentrating on what needs to be done [to change the system for patients], by advocating and showing the bad part about the police and our judicial system. When I'm at home, I've got to use music to keep my mind off that and keep my mind just positive. Music and my marijuana works real good for getting rid of migraines and helping me eat, getting my attitude back.

## Friend and Family Suggestion

About one-quarter of patients report having specific conversations with close friends or family members in which that person explicitly suggested medical cannabis use, or actually brought them cannabis and offered it to them when they were symptomatic. In most cases, the friend or family member identified as a regular cannabis consumer; some were medical cannabis patients. Those who were neither could often reference a person that both people knew in common who had experienced relief from medical cannabis use. That this route was so common says something interesting about the likelihood a patient's network has relevant firsthand or secondhand experiences on which to base such advice. Andy's comments, quoted at the outset of this chapter, suggest that many patients with little to no prior recreational experience might find it difficult to locate a source of supply outside of the medical cannabis program, but he also first pursued a recommendation in 2005, well ahead of the curve. As more people identify more publicly with medical cannabis, the probability that one's network of friends and acquaintances contains someone with experience increases considerably.

In the introduction, Karen's story and Dale's both provide examples of suggestions from friends or family. Eileen provides another. A social user in her teens, Eileen reports a lifelong preference for cannabis over alcohol, but she stopped using cannabis in her twenties, except on rare special occasions, after marrying and having children. In the time since her days of social use, Eileen was diagnosed with rheumatoid arthritis. She was still living in a southern state with no medical cannabis program when her daughter left to attend college in Colorado. After becoming an "empty nester," Eileen attended a friend's party where people were smoking a joint. When they offered it to her, she figured why not indulge, now that her kids had left home. Quite immediately, Eileen discovered that cannabis provided considerable relief for her arthritis symptoms. Later, when she moved to Colorado, she would discover that it also worked for migraines. Eileen says of her decision to pursue a recommendation:

> Well, when I moved here in 2009, a girlfriend of mine said, "you know, you could probably [qualify for medical cannabis]"—because that's when everything was going more public, with centers and doctors and places where you could actually go. Which is great from a patient's point of view because before, it had to be like you knew somebody [who could provide cannabis].

Eileen already recognized that cannabis might have medical benefits, but the decision to become a patient was in part based on a friend's recommendation, which had helped to validate it as a reasonable, effective option. Registering was appealing because it allowed easy, consistent access without having to negotiate underground friend-of-a-friend purchases.

### The Grapevine: Research Discovery

The most common route by which patients arrived at the idea that cannabis might work for them involved a combination of hearing about its use indirectly, followed by research via the internet, books, seeking people out, or, in some cases, acquiring some cannabis to try for their symptoms. This is the most patient-driven route, since no outside person made a direct suggestion; instead, it evolved out of the patient's investigation and pursuit.

One patient who reported this route was Jason, a forty-year-old professional in finance living in an urban area of Colorado, who had been diagnosed with gastroesophageal reflux disease, or GERD, over ten years ago. This condition causes severe heartburn and acid reflux. Jason says of his diagnosis,

> I never knew what it was. I just thought I had heartburn. But it started to get to the point where I couldn't swallow food. It would get stuck in my esophagus. . . . I would choke, basically. And then at night, I would wake up with stomach acid coming into my esophagus and lungs. So, it's nasty.

In addition to being uncomfortable, the stomach acid can damage the esophagus. Jason treated his condition with prescription drugs, but they are not recommended for long-term use. Jason is a clean-cut, compact, athletic guy with short hair who dresses in smart business casual clothes. He is married, a fiscally conservative but socially liberal Republican, and a father of two. He has used cannabis socially since he was sixteen, but he never considered applying for a card. He says:

> I thought it was [only] for critically ill people, like cancer or AIDS. So, there wasn't even a thought to attempt to get a card. Then one day I was reading the local alternative weekly, and in the back—this was five years ago, I've had my license for five years—on the back of it, there was this little thing, get your medical marijuana license. And then it listed all the conditions, and GERD was on there. . . . Well, I called the ad, and it was [a local organization]. Back then, there was a doctor associated with them. So, all I had to do was go in with all my medical records, and that was it.

When asked if he ever thought about going to get his card before he realized that his condition qualified, Jason said he had not, despite the fact that he had been a longtime recreational user. For Jason to decide to apply as a patient, the key piece of information was that his specific condition qualified. He did not mention doing any further medical or legal research. Because of his recreational use, Jason was already comfortable with cannabis and believed it was safe. He didn't identify with any lifestyle associations commonly attributed to cannabis use. His lack of interest in getting a card as a nonmedical, recreational user was echoed by others. Ethically, it just wasn't acceptable behavior. That said, possessing a card does not mean that individuals who were recreational users prior to their medical use completely stop using cannabis recreationally, as we hear in chapter 8.

Gary's starting point was different. Now in his fifties, Gary had not used cannabis since his teens. He reports a more intensive research process and stronger skepticism, in part because he had not used cannabis for many years. Gary had relocated to Colorado from the Midwest after the death of his wife's father, whom they had looked after for many years. In his career, Gary had worked as a delivery truck driver until he sustained a serious back injury at work when he slipped on ice while carrying heavy cargo. After a long battle with worker's compensation and multiple applications to the Social Security Administration, he failed to receive a significant settlement but did qualify for permanent disability. Since his injury, Gary has been through several prescription drug regimens and decompressive surgeries. Most recently, he was considered for a more intrusive, electrical "pain interruption" device that, should it prove to work in a temporary "test period," would entail electrical leads being surgically inserted next to his spine to interrupt nerve pain signaling.

After moving to Colorado, Gary and his wife were out to dinner with old friends who mentioned in passing that the state had legalized medical cannabis. Although they did not specifically recommend it to him, Gary says:

> I started looking into it. I read the works of Dr. Mitch Earleywine [a psychology professor who writes about cannabis use], and I went to different sites on the internet and started doing research on it because I wanted to find out whether or not this was just a Trojan Horse for pure legalization or whether or not there were actual, like there was something to this cannabis helping people for different ailments. And I found that it helped people with neurological issues. And since my problem is neurologically based, I thought I would go ahead and apply.

Like many other patients, Jason and Gary both suffer from chronic conditions that can be disruptive to everyday life. In both cases, no one directly suggested cannabis use. Jason simply saw his condition listed in a newspaper ad. Gary heard it mentioned in a casual conversation. The "grapevine" effect functioned to raise the salience of medical cannabis use and triggered enough curiosity to prompt further investigation.

Jason and Gary had each tried various other medicines and treatments for their conditions but had failed to find a safe and effective long-term treatment option. In terms of recent use, these two men represented opposite ends of the spectrum. Jason had long been known among his close friends as a recreational user. Gary had not used cannabis since his teens and had no ongoing relationship with, or connections to, recreational use.

Jason may have been more inclined to try cannabis medically since he was already accustomed to it. For Gary, the entry barrier was more significant, but the severity of his condition and the intrusiveness of his current treatment options may have tipped the scales in favor of considering any treatment that had potential to work.

Both men shared with other patients a lack of interest in medical cannabis prior to connecting it with their own disorder. Once the connection to cannabis as a medical treatment was made, Jason was almost completely uncritical of its medical potential, an attitude that was probably driven by cannabis' normal presence in his life along with more exposure to positive information about cannabis overall. Gary, on the other hand, had not really revised his impression of cannabis. In his youth it had been fun, but, as with most "fun" things, it was probably bad for you—a message reiterated by mainstream media. Gary's lack of recent experience led him to question whether cannabis could in fact be useful to treat pain. Individual research included looking into cannabis as a medicine generally, as well as its efficacy for his *specific* condition.

### Nonmedical Motivations

Three patients cited their primary motivation to seek a recommendation as something other than medical use. Brett, a man in his fifties, and Avery, a woman in her early thirties, both sought out recommendations because they decided to pursue employment opportunities in the medical cannabis industry. Brett's story was unusual because his interest in cannabis began through an intellectual pursuit for knowledge about industrial hemp.

> I'm a very pragmatic individual. I was a commercial real estate broker for over twenty years before becoming a co-owner of a medical marijuana center. I was never a grower, never a dealer, and I was never an avid user in high school or college. I was your typical beer-drinking guy. I had a back accident in college, where I messed up my back pretty bad, and there have been times in my life where getting out of bed was a major achievement. That's the main reason I medicate. That and sleep.
>
> I was reading a spiritual text about fourteen years ago, and in the text cannabis was mentioned, how beneficial it was, and that initially opened my eyes to it. I started studying [cannabis] after that. I bought a book by Ed Rosenthal and Jack Herer, the great book of hemp, *The Emperor Wears No Clothes*. It was literally like falling down the rabbit hole. The more I read, the more fascinated and amazed and intrigued I became. I started using cannabis after being exposed to that, so thirteen, fourteen years ago? Mildly. I was still, you know, more of a beer drinker, but I was using it more from a spiritual perspective, to relax, calm down, get introspective when I went out in nature. So that's how it started. I was a

family man, married at that time. I'm not married now. I was married for fifteen years, a regular, solid, family guy, and all of a sudden, dad's coming home talking about hemp—a lot! It was a strain on our marriage. It really concerned my wife, my friends, my family members. I joined [an agricultural hemp association]. [But after medical cannabis passed in Colorado], I did not seek out a doctor's recommendation. . . . I was really not up on the process. And I did not get a card until I decided that I was going to become an owner. At that point in the ballgame, I started looking into it more and realized that I could benefit from pain management from cannabis, you know, and it would be wise for me to become familiar with that process as an owner. So that's when I applied.

Avery, a tall, soft-spoken brunette had been attacked six years before by an ex-boyfriend in a domestic violence incident, which caused recurring headaches from a cervical spine injury.

I've got issues that I've been experiencing for years, headaches that radiate down through my shoulders and back. I've been to a naturopathic doctor and a chiropractor and had been using ibuprofen and things like that for years, so I decided to try [cannabis] out and see if it could really work for pain.

She only decided to take this step, however, when she was offered a job as a trained nutritionist and yoga instructor in a medical marijuana center.

I interviewed for a job as a yoga instructor and nutrition counselor from an ad on Craigslist, and [the job was in a dispensary.] I wasn't really planning on getting [a medical marijuana card], but since I found a job. . . . I had no idea when I sat down for the interview that they offered medical cannabis. That was the first thing that they said: "Well, it's a little bit more than just nutrition and yoga. We're actually going to be a medical marijuana center, and if you want to get up and leave right now you are more than welcome to." Instead of getting up and leaving, I just decided to get my card. I didn't need to, but I decided to go ahead and get my card.

A third patient, Neil, pursued a card based on advice from his attorney after an unfortunate event in which he was arrested because the passenger in his car, an acquaintance, was carrying a significant quantity of psychedelic drugs.

I was directed by an attorney to get a card. He advised me that I should have one because I got in trouble with the law in Nevada—conspiracy for a big felony. I was coming back from Burning Man, and I gave someone who runs a dispensary a ride home. He had some mushrooms and

cannabis on him. . . . I mean, I don't know the guy personally. I gave him a ride home, and we got busted in Nevada. So, going through all that bullshit, my attorney's like, Colorado, medical marijuana, you better get a card now. So that's why. But, come to find out, it's good for pain. I've been using cannabis and not getting it from a dispensary, you know, on and off, all my adult life.

Neil is a bit less comfortable with claiming legitimacy as a medical user, though he does have a condition that qualifies, because of his perceptions of who constitutes a legitimate patient.

I use it for pain management. I have . . . just a lot of chronic pain. Sore in the back, sciatica, my knee aches—you know, that kind of stuff. It's a sensible choice, so instead of saying one thing, it was more general [pain management]. . . . I grew up in Seattle, and Seattle Hempfest started there right in the middle of my adolescence. So, that's where I got my education about it—what hemp can do for the planet and all that, that it's a medicine, and people use it who are in wheelchairs and have MS. That there are real people that need it as medicine and use it.

Neil also sees his use as having continuity with his prior recreational use and feels that he cannot distinguish the two. When asked if or how he would distinguish between recreation and medical use, he says:

No, I just wouldn't. It's like a cup of coffee. You are using it to relax, or just to have? You know? I don't use it daily—sometimes I do, but not consistently. Just to relax. But yeah, I'm sore, and it takes it away. Like when I got my wisdom teeth taken out a few days ago. I've been eating cannabis to manage the pain. So, I use it to medicate. Because as I'm older, things creak and are sore. . . . when I think about it, I'm still using it as medicine [laughs].

Brett, Avery, and Neil judged their participation in the medical marijuana program as less legitimate than others. This was largely a function of their nonmedical motivation for seeking out a card, compounded by their recent history of use and their assessment of what conditions the system is meant for. These individuals had qualifying conditions, but the diagnoses had happened years before, and nothing new had introduced a need for re-examining care decisions. These three patients had established ways to manage their conditions. They were not in the midst of a health crisis. Because they could function when symptomatic, the decision to treat the condition with cannabis seemed more discretionary than it is for people with more acute or debilitating conditions.

*It's a Family Affair*

No matter the initial motivation, once the idea of registering with a medical cannabis program is on the table, the decision is made as most health decisions are made: by deciding with family and significant others. An example is Gary's case, mentioned earlier, of a workplace back injury that led to many medications and a surgically implanted device in his spine. He exemplifies both the pragmatic and collective nature of decision-making aimed at quality of life and the willingness—even desperation—to try solutions with any probability of success.

GARY:  Every decision I've made from the time I got hurt, as far as medical treatment goes, I have always discussed with my wife. She is my partner. She is the one that puts up with me when I'm feeling like crap, when I'm moody or I'm tired the next day because I have had no sleep because I hurt. So, I discussed [the medical cannabis option] with her and shared the information with her so that she would know what I was talking about when we had these conversations about it, so we could talk about it intellectually and try to remove. . . . I didn't want there to be. . . . After reading up on [medical cannabis], I realized that there is a stigma attached to its use. Reefer madness, that type of thing. So, all the information I shared with my wife, and I'd like to think that it was a joint decision with her.

INT:  What was her initial response?

GARY:  I don't remember exactly her words, but I think the general attitude was that she was very open to it. I think that if I had told her that going out and burning a Kewpie doll on a cross in the backyard was going to help me with my pain—and there was evidence to suggest that that was going to help—that she would go for it.

Patients often want those closest to them to consult on the complex decisions involved in medical care. As is clear in Gary's case as well as Karen's in the introduction and others in this and following chapters, their spouses or others living with them are affected by decisions they make about their illness and its treatment. Their functioning, capabilities, mood, and ability to work, parent, or maintain relationships are affected by these choices.

## Giving Medical Cannabis a "Test Run"

Cannabis presents an interesting set of circumstances because of its wide availability on the underground market. Some people who contemplate medical cannabis use seek it out through friends or family networks or by directly accessing the underground market prior to receiving a recommendation. Because cannabis remains controversial and physician attitudes are not easy to predict, patients often elect to experiment with medical use to test its effectiveness *prior* to seeking a recommendation.

Prospective medical cannabis patients are not the only ones who regularly engage in "lay testing" (Britten 2008). Research shows that patients regularly test prescriptions by adjusting dosages and altering their use to assess the efficacy of the treatment as well as its side effects. What is different with cannabis is that testing often precedes rather than follows the doctor-patient consultation. This allows patients to determine whether cannabis is useful before they open themselves to reputational risks in the doctor–patient interaction or legal risks associated with identifying themselves on a government registry. It is a way of assuring that the legal risk and the potential for stigma will be worth the expense and effort.

Experimentation was more common among patients who had limited or no prior use or who had only used cannabis many years or decades before, usually during their teens. Approximately one-third of patients in this study reported engaging in some form of pre-card medical trial use. Half of experimenters acted as a direct result of a suggestion of a friend who often provided assistance with obtaining a supply. The other half made an independent decision to experiment prior to seeking a card.

Anita provides an example. A compact, fit forty-year-old woman, Anita has a professional look with an artsy-punk edge. She has been diagnosed with a rare form of multiple sclerosis (MS), caused by a lesion on the left side of her brain. This lesion grew quite suddenly, triggering a shocking onset of symptoms. One night at the end of a dinner party with friends, Anita teetered and took a dive into the host's couch as they were saying goodnight. Everyone had a justification for the gaffe. She was in heels, it was late, and she was probably just tired, or maybe she'd had more wine than she realized. Little did they know it was the first symptom of complete right-side paralysis setting in.

By morning, Anita looked like she had suffered a stroke. In some ways, the presentation was similar. With the right side of her face paralyzed, her words were mumbled. She was bedridden and then required a wheelchair for six months. Prior to this, Anita had been a teacher, but she was forced to quit her job because the seriousness of her symptoms impaired her ability to function. She was treated with high doses of prednisone, anti-inflammatory drugs, and an antidepressant to help her cope with the sudden change in her circumstances. Unable to work or maintain her parenting role in the home, she stubbornly struggled over the next six months to retrain herself to walk with a cane. Between the brain lesion, the traumatic circumstances, and the intense medication, she was no longer "herself." She moved to the basement of her home and withdrew completely from family life because, as she puts it, "I couldn't stand to be around anybody."

Recovery required years of work. For three self-described "miserable" years, she followed the protocol her doctors recommended, but the side

effects of the medications were terrible. A friend who was a medical cannabis patient became determined to convince Anita to try it. Anita was reluctant, but her friend persisted. When asked why she was resistant, Anita says:

> My job. My kids. The stigma. It's not easy to hide the smell of marijuana
> when it's being smoked. And I was skeptical that it would help because,
> at that point in time, I had pretty much decided that nothing was going
> to help.

Before trying it, she researched its use for MS and found articles that
reported "huge success rates in people who could get their THC levels up
in their blood. They just maintained a certain level. . . . So, I thought it was
worth the risk for sure." Anita had used cannabis occasionally in college,
but it wasn't something she really pursued, and when it faded out of her
social circles, she barely noticed its absence. When she decided to experiment before seeking out a recommendation, she says:

> Number one, I didn't want to expose myself to a state agency if I was
> unsure, because of my job. I didn't know the level of anonymity between
> the agencies. So, I wanted to make sure this was a path that I wanted to
> commit to before actually making the paper commitment. I knew as
> soon as I put my name on a paper, I was going to be put on the list and
> that list was going to be shared with other people.

Like other patients, Anita only requested a doctor's recommendation after
determining that it helped her condition through direct experience. Her
"trial" prior to seeking a recommendation was a method that many other
patients with limited or no prior use also employed. Another group of patients
experimented with medical use prior to receiving a recommendation because
they were living in a nonmedical state. Five patients in the study sample tried
using cannabis medically outside Colorado; many based their choice to move
to Colorado in part to apply for legal medical cannabis status.

About a fourth of the patients in this study were not consuming cannabis
regularly and did not "test" cannabis first; instead, they opted to wait until
they had official sanction to use it medically. This group included several
patients who simply relied on experiences from many years ago as an indicator that using cannabis was a safe and non-addictive. Generally, prior experience, even when it had been many years before, led to reduced fear around
initiating use for medical reasons. Instead, these users focused on the risk of
arrest or scandal. Using cannabis without a legitimate card seemed foolhardy
in their estimations. A few in this category expressed moral outlooks from
their religious beliefs or military backgrounds that led them to only try
cannabis when it was considered legal for them, even if they had little to no
prior experience.

Whether they engage in experimentation prior to registering or not, patients who decide to pursue entry to the state registry need a doctor's recommendation. Obtaining one entails interactions with physicians and the state that engage questions of identity work and legitimacy, as we see in chapter 4.

## References

Bouldin, Alicia S., Mickey C. Smith, Benjamin F. Banahan, David J. McCaffrey, and Edward M. Croom. 2000. "Herbal Supplement Information and the Consumer." *Drug Information Journal* 34(4):1339–53.

Britten, Nicky. 2008. *Medicines and Society: Patients, Professionals and the Dominance of Pharmaceuticals.* New York: Palgrave Macmillan.

Cameron, Linda D., and Howard Leventhal, eds. 2003. *The Self-Regulation of Health and Illness Behavior.* London: Routledge.

Fagerlin, Angela, Catharine Wang, and Peter A. Ubel. 2005. "Reducing the Influence of Anecdotal Reasoning on People's Health Care Decisions: Is a Picture Worth a Thousand Statistics." *Medical Decision Making* 25:398–405.

Kondrad, Elin, and Alfred Reid. 2013. "Colorado Family Physicians' Attitudes toward Medical Marijuana." *The Journal of the American Board of Family Medicine* 26(1):52–60. doi: 10.3122/jabfm.2013.01.120089.

# Chapter 4

# Cannabis and the Doctor–Patient Interaction

I had kidney cancer. With the kidney cancer, I have one kidney left. I have one chance, so it really turned me around to start doing healthy things. Get off the pain pills, which I still use in very extreme situations. For the last three years, with a doctor out of town, I've been on what they call "quality of life" medication. I can't get medication from anyone else but this doctor, but I can get anything I want from him, because there is basically nothing they can do for me. My back, neck, shoulders—I need several surgeries. So, with that said, I had to go to medical marijuana. The doctor suggested that I use medical marijuana, but the group that the doctor worked for would not allow him to write any prescription [sic] for it. Thus, the big roadblock. Doctors know that it will work, but they can't write it because they work under certain health care providers or groups that dictate, "no, you can't write that."

(Carl)

Once a patient decides to pursue a medical recommendation, a visit to a physician follows. As of now, cannabis is only connected to formal medicine through the physician evaluation. Cannabis can only be "recommended," rather than prescribed, because the federal government prohibits the prescription of drugs with a Schedule I status, as chapter 2 explained. Doctor evaluations for medical cannabis are based on several factors, including the suitability of the treatment, but also beliefs about the validity of the treatment and its potential risks, including dependence. The difference between accepted medicines and cannabis often lies in the physician's knowledge about the treatment, its appropriateness to the case, and its likelihood of being effective. Physicians and patients rely on different types of evidence to make this assessment about cannabis. The formal biomedical model demands evidence produced through clinical trial and scientific methods, while patients are willing to accept less formal and more diverse forms of evidence, such as anecdotal reports from friends and family. Kondrad and Reid's (2013) research on physician attitudes toward cannabis found that those doctors who relied primarily on results of clinical trials and professional journals for medical information found little basis for support in the mainstream literature. Patients are often aware that research on cannabis has been blocked by political forces, but the available studies support medical applications. Medical professionals may be blind to those research barriers and biases and assess relative safety and efficacy by simply weighing the quantity of studies describing negative and positive effects (Gupta 2013). This creates a gap between patients' and physicians' assessments about cannabis as a medicine (Aggarwal et al. 2009; Chan et al. 2017; Kondrad and Reid 2013). Patients come to feel they know more about the issue than their doctors, while doctors feel that patients accept unscientific evidence and harbor unrealistic expectations. These epistemological differences are a source of tensions in the doctor–patient interaction (Broom and Woodward 1996).

In relation to medical cannabis, the terms "lifeworld" and "system" usefully distinguish between the logic and actions of individuals in the context of everyday life and those of institutions (Habermas 1987). Applied to health care and medicine generally, the concepts of system and lifeworld emphasize how the perspectives of the patient or layperson differ from the expert within medical systems. Lay beliefs about health care are not just "watered down" versions of expert beliefs but incorporate different logics and considerations than those systems use to simply be efficient and effective. While medical systems often focus on symptom control, adherence, and treatment success, lifeworld considerations often seek to balance symptom management with drug side effects. Concerns of the lifeworld include being able to carry out roles and responsibilities and reach milestones at normative times according to generational expectations, such as graduating from high school, getting a job, starting a relationship, buying a home, getting married, and starting a family (Britten 2008).

Cannabis recommendations put physicians in an awkward position. Modern doctors rely on standardized products that are used in precise, relatively predictable doses, but cannabis does not conform to this structure. Because cannabis leaves the jurisdiction of formal biomedicine after the recommendation and comes in a variety of whole-plant-derived herbal forms rather than controlled dosages, most doctors can offer few instructions on how much or how often to use it, options for delivery method, or even choice of product. Ongoing management subsequent to the evaluation appointment is rare. Some physicians have identified this lack of control as a source of concern in recommending it (Kondrad and Reid 2013; Chan et al. 2017). Physicians are also acutely aware that, because it is a Schedule I drug, recommending cannabis invites professional scrutiny and potential stigma. From informal discussions with physicians, it is clear that some feel they should not recommend cannabis because they lack sufficient knowledge to recommend it for specific conditions with any level of confidence. They worry about being in compliance with the standards of practice for recommending cannabis because rules set by state medical boards can be vague, changeable, and subject to interpretation. Many doctors may simply not know what they are. Some state laws or medical board rules now explicitly state physician requirements. After years of providing little or no guidance, Colorado now has a requirement that the physician have a *"bona fide* relationship" with the patient, which means the doctor is required to conduct a physical examination of the patient and provide ongoing care. The intent of this and similar requirements in other states is to curtail "doctor mill" activities and pay-to-play schemes for entry into the state program (CO-DORA 2017a, 2017b; CDPHE 2014), efforts that appear to be largely aimed at ensuring the legitimacy of the doctor–patient interaction.

Doctors also grapple with concerns that patients may be asking for cannabis for nonmedical reasons (Barthwell et al. 2010; Merrill et al. 2002). These concerns reflect the historical framing of harm associated with cannabis and are similar to how physicians weigh the decision to prescribe opioids. Doctors vary in their awareness that cannabis' potential for physical dependence is relatively low (on a par with caffeine), but studies have been accumulating that show cannabis helps patients reduce or "exit" other more addictive and potentially harmful substances such as opioids (Armentano 2017; Lucas 2012; Markoff 2003; Piper et al. 2017; Reiman 2006).

Physicians and patients both evaluate the reputational risks and practical consequences of participating in medical cannabis programs, but they make these evaluations in different ways, in part because physicians are employing the logic of the system of medicine, and patients are using the logic of the lifeworld. Whereas the patient's decision offers direct, tangible benefit in exchange for risk, the physician may see only risk, with few or no personal or professional rewards. Medical cannabis program rules have tried to reduce or eliminate financial rewards as an incentive for doctors to engage in recommendations, placing limits on their ability to own associated businesses or operate in or near dispensaries. Doctors who recommend cannabis are subject to special surveillance, as regulatory agencies track (and often report) how many recommendations they write each year. Professionally, physicians face a multitude of practical, professional, and reputational risks, yet the only reward—the satisfaction of treating patients effectively—is intangible and only manifests if the physician believes there are medical benefits. This means that physician's personal opinions about or prior experience with cannabis treatment largely dictate their attitudes and willingness to recommend.

A 2013 survey of 520 Colorado family physicians by Kondrad and Reid (2013) found that doctors' pre-existing views on medical cannabis play a role in their willingness to recommend it. According to this survey, 46 percent of family physicians in Colorado believed that cannabis should not be recommended as a medical therapy at all, while only 19 percent agreed that doctors should recommend it (Kondrad and Reid 2013, 55). Most doctors in this study believed that cannabis use posed significant physical (61 percent) and mental health (64 percent) risks and many were unaware of or unconvinced by data that show these risks are low as compared with common pharmaceuticals. Opposition in the abstract may dissipate in the face of the needs of individual patients. In contrast to Kondrad and Reid's findings, a survey of 1,446 doctors conducted that same year by *The New England Journal of Medicine* found 76 percent would recommend using cannabis as a treatment in a hypothetical case of metastasized breast cancer (Adler and Colbert 2013). Views may also change over time. In a 2017 survey of 237 University of Colorado medical students, 49 percent expressed a belief that cannabis possesses significant benefits to physical health, and the majority agreed that medical cannabis was acceptable as a treatment for the conditions approved through the Colorado state program (Chan et al. 2017). Supporting something hypothetically as a medical student is not the same as facing down the risks in actual practice, but the shift in opinions suggests growing acceptance in the formal sector. Nonetheless, views on the risk of physical (68 percent) and mental (77 percent) harm were not lower among students, and neither was the assessment of addiction potential (88 percent report believing cannabis can be addictive). The significant moderator of opinion among medical students was not length of Colorado residency, age, gender, or other demographic categorizations; it was prior experience with cannabis—those reporting past use rated cannabis as less harmful and more helpful across measures (Chan et al. 2017).

Because patients often do not know the opinion of their primary care physician on the topic of medical cannabis, broaching the subject can create anxiety or distress. In some cases, this anxiety is grounded in prior experiences with doctors who have exerted authority in ways that were perceived as rude or dismissive (Broom and Woodward 1996). Patient concerns are consistent with the dynamics proposed by identity theory, where people seek to create and maintain a relationship in which their identities are "verified" (Burke and Stets 1999, 351). Patients may fear that introducing a polarizing topic that carries reputational risk—cannabis—may destabilize the doctor-patient relationship. They may worry the physician will engage in a reappraisal of them that marginalizes their patient identity in relation to the medical conditions for which they've sought treatment. Likewise, the response of the physician may change the patient's feelings about her or him, and that potential can be a disincentive for patients who otherwise respect their doctor and value the relationship (Stets and Burke 2014, 413).

Patients who experience rejection from their primary care physicians or specialists tend to discount the physician's knowledge base for judgment as being incomplete or biased. Such interactions can result in less trust in their physician's good will and benign intent or less confidence in the physician's competence in this and other areas (Burke and Stets 1999; Burke and Stets 2009). As this chapter discusses, the legitimacy of the cannabis patient identity relies on the verification process that takes place in the doctor–patient interaction, which is dependent on both doctor and patient upholding their respective roles and the doctor validating the identity through the recommendation process.

## Medical Cannabis as a Contested Treatment

Medical cannabis recommendations resemble doctor–patient interactions for contested illnesses. The approval or rejection by the physician is not solely a medical decision; it has political and rhetorical implications for framing the legitimacy of the issue. Doctors perceive risks related to the legal status of cannabis under federal law and often fear reprisals by employers or loss of their license to prescribe, which is granted through the federal government. As is true with the patients they serve, most problems physicians have encountered have come from the state level, but federal risk is not hypothetical.

Doctors were among the first targets. The Clinton administration's response to the passage of the first medical cannabis law was to threaten the loss of the DEA-issued prescribing license for any doctor who so much as mentioned it as a possible treatment. That threat was neutralized by court rulings in favor of physicians' First Amendment rights, but the specter of federal retaliation has remained. In reality, only doctors who have directly assisted patients with obtaining cannabis have run afoul of federal law, though the consequences have been severe. California physician Mollie Fry, M.D., for instance, was sentenced in 2007 to five years in federal prison for working with her husband, an attorney who was also imprisoned, to help patients cultivate their own medicine, something she was inspired to do by her own experience living with cancer.

While drug-prescribing licenses are federal, the right to practice medicine is managed by state medical boards that set and oversee standards of care. Since cannabis therapeutics is a contested area, the standard of care related to it has not been self-evident and has evolved quickly since the advent of state programs, which all require doctor recommendations.

Physicians who specialize in cannabinoid medicines have necessarily operated at least initially without guidance from state professional organizations. Once state medical boards established standards, however vague, investigations followed for doctors who had issued a disproportionate number of recommendations, or, in the case of Colorado, certified patients as eligible to cultivate relatively large numbers of plants.

The Colorado Department of Public Health and Environment (CDPHE), which oversees physician compliance, referred five of the state's most prolific recommendation-writing physicians for audit in 2011. Between 2009 and 2013, the state medical board suspended licenses or instigated the arrest of six physicians related to medical cannabis recommendations (Gorski 2013). In 2013, following the approval of adult use, the board turned its attention to physicians who certified patients as eligible to cultivate relatively large numbers of plants. The Colorado crackdown on plant counts is an out-growth of a provision in the law that says a patient may grow more than the six plants the law allows when the recommending doctor indicates it is medically necessary. In July 2016, the board suspended the licenses of four physicians for writing what the board considered to be excessive numbers of recommendations allowing non-cancer patients to cultivate seventy-five or more plants each. Physicians in other states have been suspended or otherwise sanctioned for recommending cannabis to what overseers deemed excessive numbers of patients or for conducting only cursory patient examinations before issuing recommendations.

These compliance issues for physicians highlight an unusual aspect of the medicalization of cannabis. Medical cannabis recommendations differ from contested illnesses because the uncertainties in doctor–patient interactions are centered on the appropriate treatment instead of the diagnosis. Medical cannabis determinations are almost always separate from initial diagnosis. Prior to seeking a recommendation through a doctor, patients usually know they qualify based on the terms set by the state, which defines and restricts medical cannabis based on qualifying conditions. This combination of assertive patients and state rules also constrains physician autonomy. The constraints on cannabis care are often treated as uniquely problematic, but in truth there are comparable situations. In an era of the "lay expert," where medical information abounds and prescription drugs are advertised directly to patients, doctors must balance patient requests for prescriptions or treatments with medical judgment under constraints imposed by the directives of HMOs, insurance reimbursement rules, and the standards of evidence-based medicine enforced by employers (Britten 2008; Dumit 2006). Perhaps the closest comparison is with determinations for disability eligibility, another scenario in which (1) physicians may be influenced by nonmedical motivations involving the state; (2) physician decisions are typically not concurrent with diagnosis; and (3) their judgment confers benefits that are located outside of the medical domain (Joffe-Walt 2013; Rainville et al. 2005). These types of evaluations determine access to benefits, whether disability insurance or medical cannabis. Such incentives for patients to gain entry raise concerns with how to set boundaries so that those for whom the programs were designed can gain access, but those who want in for illegitimate reasons are kept out. Few such gatekeeping rules existed in Colorado's medical cannabis program prior to 2010, largely because relatively few people had tried to register with the state. When patient applications flooded the system in 2009, it created pressure to better define the rules for access.

New legislation in 2010 both defined the relationship between physicians and medical marijuana centers and restructured doctor–patient interactions toward greater conformity with other types of medical interactions. These rules created organizational barriers to separate the physician recommendation from the rest of the system, including separation from direct financial involvement in the industry, or writing recommendations onsite or near dispensary locations. Many patients in this study received their first recommendation prior to the 2010 legislation and experienced the industry both before and after these divisions were in place.

## Modeling Doctor–Patient Interactions

In their study on chronic fatigue syndrome, Broom and Woodward (1996) created a model for doctor–patient interactions. They found that three types of interactions with physicians are most common under conditions of incomplete medicalization (Broom and Woodward 1996). Patterns in patients' recommendation experiences map well onto this model.

In the first type of interaction, doctors take a paternalistic attitude of "doctor knows best." They discount their patients' accounts and opinions in favor of formal medical expertise that maintains their professional monopoly on assessment and care management. This often leads physicians to reject medical cannabis as a legitimate medical treatment.

In the second type, doctors do not dismiss patient reports but express reluctance to label the patient with a certain diagnosis because it lends authority to the diagnosis when the doctor is uncertain that the label is constructive. Even though doctors in this second category do not dismiss patients' experiential accounts, they still refuse to officially label the patient. Patients' concerns are outweighed by considerations of risk from the perspective of medical expertise. Doctors who exert this type of "unintentional dominance" (Broom and Woodward 1996) might not reject cannabis as potentially useful but do not feel comfortable officially recommending its use due to its uncertain legal status and perceived potential for abuse or harm. These doctors might not encourage or discourage patients from trying medical cannabis, but when it comes to signing the official paperwork, they are unwilling or unable to do so. Ultimately, they refuse to accept responsibility for sanctioning the use of medical cannabis for the patient.

In the third instance, the doctor works with patients in what Broom and Woodward (1996) termed "constructive medicalization." These physicians are cognizant of the limitations of medical knowledge and are more willing to allow the patient's definition of the situation to contribute to their recommendations. Among this group, some physicians exhibit a greater willingness to experiment or try patient-initiated forms of treatment, while others are less willing to experiment but will serve as case managers, passing along useful information and encouraging patients to be active in independently managing their conditions. In this interaction, doctors engage in constructive medicalization by exhibiting a willingness to experiment with patient-initiated forms of treatment. These doctors are often more willing to sign a recommendation form and talk openly with patients about the medical use of cannabis. However, some doctors in this category may only offer informal support, expressing a lack of knowledge or expertise about medical cannabis that leads to a refusal to sign the recommendation.

### Which Doctor to Ask?

Medical cannabis recommendations were most commonly initiated by patients. About half of the patients interviewed in this study began the process of qualifying as a medical cannabis patient by approaching their regular physician. Some patients reported that their doctors had favorable pre-existing views, while others reported doctors who held strong views against medical cannabis use. Such differences are not surprising in light of how many Colorado physicians still held negative or skeptical opinions on the issue (Kondrad and Reid 2013). This dimension adds complexity to the doctor–patient interaction because doctors may be more or less open to cannabis as a medical option, regardless of their inclusion or dismissal of patient viewpoints, and patients often do not know the doctor's viewpoint until they broach the topic. Uncertainty about their regular doctor's opinion and the reputational risks associated with asking about medical cannabis were often nerve wracking for patients. Among those who approached their regular physicians, most were rebuffed based either on the doctor's rejection of cannabis as medicine or on claims that institutional limitations restricted the physician from making the recommendation. The other half did not approach their regular physician, instead opting to go directly to a doctor who specializes in medical cannabis recommendations. These specialty cannabis doctors were often referred to as belonging to the "doctor mill."

### "Doctor Knows Best" Interactions

Among the individuals who approached their regular physician, several encountered resistance such that the doctor's expert opinion was not swayed by the patient's claim to experiential knowledge that cannabis was effective. Andy, who has degenerative disc disease, provides a good example. The symptoms for Andy's disorder were gradual, and it took several years for him to get a diagnosis. This was a frustrating process during which he was in and out of the doctor's office looking for answers. His condition had led him to try many different treatments and medications, but he developed a sensitivity to opiates as an adult, so these drugs were off the table. When Andy decided to try medical cannabis to treat his back pain, he first asked his primary doctor for a recommendation. Andy had only smoked cannabis once as a teen, found he disliked it, and never revisited recreational use.

ANDY: I must have read some news story that reminded me that [cannabis] was an alternative. I asked my doctor would he be inclined to write a note, and he seemed very afraid of the concept. This was a D.O. [doctor of osteopathy]—very naturopathic, a very discussing kind of person, and it was almost like he clammed up immediately. . . .

INT:  So [this] was your regular doctor?

ANDY:  It was, and I wouldn't even call it a discussion. . . . I asked him if he could send me to a pain specialist, and the pain specialist he recommended wouldn't talk about it. I sensed fear, bluntly speaking, because this was in 2005. I get the feeling that things blossomed between 2005 and 2008 in the industry. Then, I think most doctors just didn't want to deal with it. So, I got on the internet and looked up the topic, and I found [a medical cannabis organization] that had doctors . . . who kind of do the rounds. . . . They were the ones that believed in it and were willing to do a physical and decide whether you're a good candidate or not, even though they weren't the ones that normally saw you for pain or anything else.

Andy's experience of trying to access cannabis through his regular health care providers, then resorting to the specialty market for an evaluation, was quite common among patients. Even though half of the patients in this study began by approaching their regular physicians, over 80 percent ended up getting recommendations through a doctor who specialized in evaluations.

## Unintentional Dominance

The second type of doctor–patient interaction Broom and Woodward (1996) describe, in which physicians remain relatively neutral to the patient but will not officially sanction them, is reflected in what happened between Wes and his primary care physician. Like Andy, Wes has never been a recreational user and had zero interest in it. He had tried cannabis a few times in his youth, but he just never noticed any intoxicating effects from cannabis use. Now in his fifties, Wes suffers from advanced diabetes. Wes says that his wife was a regular recreational cannabis user, a behavior that he had strongly disliked. He says:

I forbade her doing it [smoking pot], and she was doing it behind my back. . . . So, I told her, well, you can smoke it only on the weekends. So, she was smoking during the week behind my back, and then on weekends she would smoke it in front of me.

Around the time that Amendment 20 passed, Wes' wife was diagnosed with a musculoskeletal disorder. He noticed that on the nights and weekends when he did not complain if she used cannabis openly, she seemed less symptomatic and slept better. "That's when I started researching medical marijuana and [her condition] and I realized that it helps." At that point, he changed his mind about his wife's use, and suggested that she become a registered patient.

Once she was using it more regularly, he saw how much it helped her manage her disorder. Wes says, "that's when it was good enough for me."

Wes' story of discovering cannabis' medical applications by witnessing a spouse's treatment is similar to Karen's description from the introduction. While researching his wife's condition, Wes discovered that cannabis might also help him, based on clinical studies that show it to be effective for neuropathic pain and other symptoms associated with diabetes. So, he prepared to apply for a medical cannabis card. After downloading the paperwork from the state, he talked to a woman who worked with Colorado's medical marijuana program about approaching his physician, Dr. D., for a recommendation.

> She said, here are a couple of pieces, a couple of letters, or whatever. She sent them to me, and it was basically saying that no doctor has been reprimanded by the federal government and so on. She said, "Hand these to your physician also." And I said, "Okay." So, I went in to my primary care doctor, and I was talking to him. and he said, "Is there anything else I can do for you?" And I said, "I would like to talk to you about medical marijuana." And he goes, "What about it?" And I go, "Well, the state has a program, and if I can get a doctor to sign a piece of paper that says that I may benefit from it, I can get a card, and then I'm legal to use it."

Wes tried to pave a path for his physician by providing the legal rules, but this also may have limited the doctor's ability to object on institutional grounds within the interaction. According to Wes, Dr. D. directly expressed his skepticism about cannabis' medical benefits.

> [Dr. D.] looks at me and didn't say anything. I said, "I brought the paperwork. Would you be willing to sign it for me?" And he said, "No." And I go, "Why not?" And he said, "I don't think it works." And he says, "I don't believe in it." And I said, "I'm telling you it does work because I'm already using it." I said, "The reason you had to reduce my blood pressure medication is because of it." And he said, "Well, no, I won't sign it." And I said, "Okay, then I need a recommendation to [Dr. M] here in town, a neurologist." And he said, "What do you need to see him for?" And I said, "So I can talk to him about cannabis, because he will sign it if you won't." So, he said, "Fine," and he gave me a recommendation to go see a neurologist. I went to see the neurologist and talk to him, and he said, "Yeah, I think it's the greatest thing in the world for you, with all your conditions and all that." He gave me the once over and what have you. And he said, "Here you go, give it a try. Let me hear back from you. Good or bad, let me know how it works for you and all that." And I've had a relationship with him now since 2001.

Wes' primary care physician, Dr. D., privileged clinical evidence over Wes' experiential claims. While he would not provide a recommendation, he did provide a referral. Wes formed a relationship with another doctor, a neurologist, who supported his medical use of cannabis and believed that it could be beneficial for his conditions. Even though Dr. D., Wes' primary care physician, was unmoved by Wes' report of ongoing success when first asked about it, Wes reports Dr. D. did seem to become persuaded, but his change of attitude was slow and incremental. Despite Wes' openness about his medical cannabis use, his only additional conversations with Dr. D. on the topic were indirect.

WES: About three years after [the attempt to get a recommendation], my primary care doctor, his office girl, called me, and she said, "Wes, this is Meg at Dr. D's office. . . . Dr. D is wondering who signs your cannabis recommendation for you." And I go, "Why?" And she goes, "Well, he has a patient in the office here that he thinks may benefit from it, but he is not willing to put his name on the paperwork." And I said, "Well, it's Dr. M." And she said, "Okay, thank you." And I said, "If there's anything else he wants to know, have him give me a call."

INT: So, you think he's shifted his views?

WES: I think he has shifted his view. I don't know if he's signed any recommendations yet, but I do believe [his view changed]. I haven't talked to him personally about it. I have, of course, seen him a couple of times a year every year. He is still my primary care doctor. And he just tells me, "Keep doing what you're doing because it's working." [. . . .] When I first went to him in 2000, he called me "walking death." In fact, he had my wife and I up in arms that I wasn't going to make it six months, and here I am eleven years later, still going strong. We haven't specifically mentioned the word "marijuana" or "cannabis" in our office visits other than I give them a list of my prescriptions and medications, and it's on there, how much I use and everything. He looks at it, and he says, "Good for you," and that's about it.

Andy's and Wes' doctors both expressed discomfort or completely dismissed the suggestion that cannabis could be an appropriate treatment. In both cases, physician considerations were unrelated to the patients' recreational use history, which was negligible, nor was it related to whether their conditions "qualified" with the state. Rather, the refusals appear to be directly related to the physicians' existing opinions about the legitimacy of cannabis as a medicine, including concerns about potential professional sanction. However, when Wes' health benefited from medical cannabis use, his doctor offered vague words of support and even inquired about it on behalf of another patient, all while still avoiding any direct mention of the subject or attempting to manage his care. As we will see later in the chapter, this was a common response from physicians who did not recommend medical cannabis use but maintained an ongoing relationship with the patient.

The types of interactions physicians and patients have are not always static, stuck in one type or another. Anita was one of very few patients who persisted with her primary care doctor, despite his initial, "doctor knows best" refusal to recommend. Anita, the MS patient mentioned in chapter 3, knew that she required a plan for ongoing care, and she was stubborn about getting her primary physician on board with her treatment plan, rather than going through a referral or a specialty evaluation doctor. Anita recounts the process of obtaining a recommendation from her reluctant neurologist:

ANITA: Neurologists, usually . . . don't have any bedside manner at all. They are fairly stoic. They really don't have a sense of humor. My neurologist . . . when I brought it up . . . essentially told me that I might as well drill a hole in my head and let the pressure relieve like they used to in the dark ages. I'm guessing that was his attempt at humor? But it really felt kind of like he was making me feel stupid that I would try something so outrageous.

INT: So, clearly, he didn't believe that it was going to work at all?

ANITA: Yeah, he really didn't. And I bugged him. I brought it up in conversation at one appointment to kind of feel him out, how he was going to approach the subject. And I left it at that. . . . The next time I went, I brought it up again and got a little more information out of him. The third time I went, I said, "I have tried this and it really does seem to help with the extended issues that we are unable to control at this moment with the medication regimen you have me on."

INT: So, you wore him down?

ANITA: Yeah, I pretty much wore him down.

Because Anita persisted, an experience that began as a "doctor knows best" type of interaction changed to a more constructive one. The prolonged negotiation with her neurologist required Anita to press the issue, even after he ridiculed her suggestion. After introducing cannabis medically, Anita was able to first reduce and then phase out all other medications, including medications for pain, spasms, and depression. During this time, her brain lesion shrank by 50 percent, and she is now considered in remission. Anita does not appear ill, but she continues to use cannabis to maintain remission. When asked if her experience affected her neurologist's opinion of medical cannabis, she said, "He actually has said that he is quite impressed." Yet, she also says:

Most of my doctors now, even the ones who were in state-run agencies, aren't allowed to really do anything about medicinal marijuana because they are federally funded. Even they are like, "Well, just continue it. Just do what you are doing. I can't sign any papers for you, but just continue what you are doing."

Patient interactions with primary care physicians, which are typically of the "doctor knows best" or "unintentional dominance" types, illustrate that doctors do not necessarily accept cannabis as a medicine, even when diagnoses match those that qualify according to the state. These recommendations show that when patients want to involve their physicians, it often requires a level of determination that some patients are willing to engage in, but many are not. Patients often characterized their regular physicians as uncomfortable, dismissive, and lacking in expertise on medical cannabis. Based on patient reports, doctors often seemed to view medical cannabis as they do other complementary and alternative medicines (CAM)—with skepticism based on its lack of scientific evidence and generally as outside the purview of biomedical expertise (Ruggie 2004). Before turning to a detailed look at the type of doctors who make a practice of the "constructive medicalization" type of interaction with medical cannabis patients, it is worth considering how complex and uncertain these doctor–patient interactions can be.

## Uncertainty in the Doctor–Patient Interaction

Travis' story in chapter 3 illustrates a case in which the physician suggested medical cannabis to a patient and also signed the official recommendation paperwork. Most other cases were less straightforward, some far less so. Ultimately, primary care doctors signed very few official recommendations. In the eight cases where doctors initiated the idea that the patient try medical cannabis, half of the doctors did not sign the paperwork, mostly citing bureaucratic reasons. The bureaucracy of U.S. health care can create substantial barriers to almost all aspects of patient treatment, but especially with medical cannabis.

Take Mike's case. In his interview, Mike's husky voice is punctuated with a frequent, breathy snicker that sounds like Muttley, straight out of the cartoons. With dark blond hair to his shoulders, a day or two of scruff on his face, a plaid flannel shirt, and worn construction boots, Mike's weathered look fits with stereotypes of a modern-day mountain man. Now in his late forties, Mike was diagnosed with HIV in 1986, when he was in his early twenties. His physician informally recommended use of cannabis as a part of treatment for HIV.

> I tested positive in '86. They didn't have AZT or anything at that point. And they said, in two years, you're going to start getting sick, and you're going to die within two years after that. That's exactly what they told me. They were like, we don't want you to worry, and I'm like, well, what

are you telling me? And they were like, well, in four years you're going to be dead.

Obviously, this news changed Mike's life. He dropped out of college and moved up to the mountains to ski. As he puts it:

> Well, if I'm gonna die, I might as well ski. . . . That's what I really enjoyed doing. So, I got a job at a ski area. Basically, you get a season pass and not very much money, but you can ski every day in winter. Then in summer I would work the golf course or at some other [temporary job].

Mike may have taken an "enjoy life" approach after the shock of his diagnosis, but he wasn't fatalistic about it. He has been in treatment for HIV since 1991, and during that time he has volunteered for any and all clinical trials on experimental HIV therapies that would accept him. His treatment has involved many pills. His current regimen requires him to take eleven different medications, which adds up to twenty pills a day. Mike claims that he has taken as many as thirty pills a day. In 1995, his T-cells dropped to a dangerous level, but for most of this time, he has maintained a desirable level of health.

Mike readily admits that he has an experimental streak, which has extended to drug use and sexual choices. He has smoked cannabis daily since his teen years, with only a few breaks over the years. While he did not see his cannabis use as "medical" for most of this time, he never saw it as unhealthy, addictive, or terribly wrong.

> The first time I took AZT and have that complete, just nausea, stomach tied into knots, they tried to give me Compazine, and my feet just swelled up huge. There was absolutely nothing I could take [to help with the swelling]. My ex-wife [who is a nurse], she was at home, and she was like, "You can just smoke pot for that." Because [at the time] I was trying to avoid it. And she was like, "Pffth." I smoked a little pot, and I was like, "Wow, oh my god, that works so well!"

Mike's diagnosis of HIV, and then AIDS in 1995, predated the current medical cannabis program in Colorado. Having been in many drug studies, cannabis was hardly the only experimental drug not yet being prescribed that Mike was taking:

> When they first did AZT, they didn't know how often you even had to take doses, so they were just like, "You have to take it like every two hours or you would die." And so it was like, the alarm clock goes off at midnight, you take it, go back to sleep, two o'clock, you take a pill. You never had a decent night's sleep. And then it had these really harsh side effects once you're sick and stuff. And then they came up to me one

day and they asked me, "Do you want to be in a study?" Like, at that time—now they have names, but at that time, they were like D4t3TCDI. I was like, "Okay," and it was kind of like, "We've got these drugs, do you want to try [being in a study]?" And I was like, "Well what happens if I say no?" And they go, "Well you can do what you're doing, or stop taking meds altogether." And I was like, "Well that's not really much of a choice, I guess I'm doing it." So, then I was on study drugs for ten years, and finally the drugs I was taking as study drugs were finally getting through the approval process, and then they could finally just write prescriptions for them.

In the time predating the medical cannabis program, Mike got a prescription for Marinol (dronabinol). His health improved in the late 1990s, so he went back to college and earned a college degree. He took a job, but the job came with a health plan that did not include his doctor, who was at a teaching hospital that had cutting-edge medications, studies, and treatment.

When I was working, and I had to go to the doctor [on my work insurance plan], I had much worse coverage than when I was going to the university hospital as a Medicare patient! The [work insurance] doctor didn't know any of the meds. I was telling her which meds I'm on, and she was like, "I've never heard of that. I've never heard of that." So, it was like, "I'll get back to you." A month or a couple of weeks later, she was like, "Okay, yeah, we're going to put you on that." And over here [at the university hospital], they take HIV, and they take a sample, and they match it. They take the genetics from it and match that to the best drug combination to fight that particular strain. [The insurance doctor] didn't know which meds I was taking. It got where, after a couple of years, I just stopped taking meds at all, and then my T-cells dropped down to like 39. I lost a bunch of weight, got real sick, and went on disability with social security. Then I went back to my other doctor, and I was like, "Can you write me a thing for marijuana?" And she was like, "Yeah, it works really well for you." I would come into the office reeking of pot for years [laughs]. She goes, "I can write you a prescription for Marinol, but now, university physicians won't let the doctors at the university hospital write referrals anymore."

Mike's recommendation experience illustrates interactions in which doctors approve of cannabis use but do not officially recommend it. When he moved to primary treatment through the university hospital, he was happy with the care, but they could not sign his recommendation.

MIKE: The [university hospital] won't let physicians there write recommendations.
INT: Even for qualifying conditions like HIV or cancer?

MIKE:   It's because they have a DEA license to write prescriptions. They told me that my doctor can't write those recommendations. . . . [To my doctor,] I'm like, "If your license is under the state, and these threats are from the state. . . ." She said, "that's not where we're getting the pressure. [It's] the DEA license." That's what I'm getting from my doctor. When I went to the doctor [for a cannabis evaluation], I was like, "I've been getting these for years now. This is the first time that I've had to see a doctor *about* my doctor." It irritates me that somebody's come between me and my doctor, you know? . . . It's the federal government, is what she's saying. But then I don't know if that's actually coming from the DEA, or if it's coming from their medical association that, "Hey, I don't know, we've got all these issues with the DEA, it's up in the air, we can't risk it." Either way, [the cannabis-recommending doctor] irritated me right off the bat by saying, "Well, it's because your doctor's in the pocket of big pharmaceuticals and doesn't want to write it for you." I was like, "How dare you say that about my doctor?!" But he was the cheapest one [among the medical marijuana evaluating doctors]. . . . If I could get it for less, I would go and see a different doctor.

Mike clearly does not feel his primary doctor is at fault for his difficulties obtaining a qualifying recommendation, nor does he reject western medicine. In fact, when asked about using complementary and alternative medicine, he says flatly that all of his friends with HIV who relied on such treatments instead of western medicine died. Even though he is not entirely clear if the government or the medical institution creates the added level of bureaucracy for him to gain access to medical cannabis, Mike goes along with the requirements even while he believes cannabis should be decriminalized and the requirements should be lessened. Having a life-threatening illness frames Mike's perspective on institutional hurdles. He participates in the medical registry and is politically involved with cannabis, and both are actions that protect him as well as promote legitimacy through participation. Because Mike has a condition for which medical cannabis use is well established and for which current laws provide an affirmative defense, he suggests that the registry status is unlikely to be the deciding factor leading to legal problems.

Whether a recommendation was doctor- or patient-initiated, it is a common pattern for a doctor to claim to support medical use, as Mike's doctor does, but cite organizational constraints as a reason from refusing to sign an official recommendation. Patients recounted interactions in which doctors stated various reasons related to cannabis' legal status for not approving official paperwork. Three patients reported that their doctors cited policies related to federal funding based on their employment at a university hospital or at the Veterans Health Administration (VHA), which has a policy barring their physicians from providing patient certifications. In a fourth case, the doctor signed the initial recommendation paperwork but declined to sign the renewal for reasons that were not explained to the patient but were unrelated to his ongoing approval of cannabis use in the patient's therapy. These dynamics are found among interactions where the patient initiated the recommendation, as well as among those where the doctor informally suggested medical cannabis use but then would not formally recommend.

## The "Doctor Mill" as Constructive Medicalization

By large margins, patients from this study ended up in the specialty evaluation market, what has come to be called the "doctor mill." This term was widely used in Colorado to indicate doctors who advertise that they provide evaluations for medical cannabis and who may specialize in these evaluations either part-time or full-time. As the system in Colorado evolved, such doctors faced increasing scrutiny, including investigations and, in some cases, suspensions, as mentioned earlier in this chapter. Doctors are legally required to have a *bona fide* relationship with their patients, including performing a full medical exam in person and an assessment of medical history (Gorski 2013).

One way to see the "doctor mill" is as the third type of doctor–patient interaction, one of "constructive medicalization" in which physicians bridge the gap between biomedicine and the more patient-driven models of care found in the informal and popular sectors of complementary and alternative medicine (CAM). Patients increasingly turn to CAM treatments when they are not experiencing success with biomedicine (Nichter and Thompson 2006; Ruggie 2004; Testerman et al. 2004). Most CAM users treat it as an adjunct that, as its name says, complements the formal sector rather than rejects it (Eisenberg et al. 1998; Ruggie 2004). As Baarts and Pedersen (2009) describe, "the use of CAM represents a health strategy through which individuals struggle to gain control over their situation" (720). Like many forms of CAM, medical cannabis has self-care at its core, and patients use the "doctor mill" in ways that resemble their use of the informal sector. However, few physicians, patients, or CAM practitioners group medical cannabis with other CAM therapies, even though it is being increasing classified as one. The National Institute of Health's National Cancer Institute, the leading cancer researchers in the U.S., have listed cannabis and cannabinoids among the CAM treatments they discuss in their materials for patients and physicians.[1]

Regardless of whether patients or doctors initiated the idea that the patient should try medical cannabis, thirty-three of the forty patients in this study, over 80 percent, ended up going to a specialty evaluation doctor to receive a recommendation at least once.[2] Twenty-three patients, over half of the participants in this study, went straight to the "doctor mill" when they realized that they could qualify for a recommendation based on their diagnosed condition and the terms of the state's laws. Most of these patients verified prior to making an appointment that their condition qualified, either by researching qualifying conditions on the internet or by contacting a medical marijuana center or other medical cannabis organization to ask questions. Many sought information, referrals to doctors, or resources for locating specialty evaluation doctors, from these organizations.

Specialty doctors are crucial stakeholders in medicalization, working in parallel with the state and their patients. Medical professionals who become involved in claims for newly medicalized designations often become a specialized group, according to Conrad and Schneider (1998 [1980]). Such physicians are rarely typical of the medical profession and are often in an institutional location removed from the medical rank and file. Physicians often start out in newly medicalized areas with only loose professional coordination, but may come to work with other, similarly minded doctors to press for greater acceptance of their medical "turf" by the mainstream medical profession (268). Once these physicians have invested the success of their practice and their professional reputations in an emerging medical area, they may be quite motivated to work for greater professional acceptance in order to maintain their own prestige and financial success. Such activity is more directed toward professional development than what is typically thought of as political activism.

Recent decades have seen a wide trend toward integrating care from the informal sector with biomedical practice (Ruggie 2005). Research on CAM utilization finds that most patients do not communicate to their doctors about treatments they use in the informal or popular sectors. When surveyed, CAM-using patients usually did not inform their physicians of their CAM use unless directly asked about it because they believed that doctors would be uninterested or disapproving (Kennedy, Wang, and Wu 2008; Ruggie 2004). Patients are also aware that, when CAM treatments or holistic concerns are raised, physicians often possess little expertise, and they may be unwilling to consider patient claims or requests when they perceive these suggestions as unscientific or failing to conform to the logic of biomedicine.

Regardless, a doctor's evaluation and formal approval is required from the state to participate in medical cannabis programs. Since many regular, practicing physicians are uninformed, disapproving, or claim that institutional barriers prohibit them from making recommendations, the "doctor mill" allows patients to identify physicians for whom these particular obstacles will not define the interaction. The "doctor mill" raises suspicions of illegitimate recommendations and appropriate boundary maintenance (Nussbaum, Boyer, and Kondrad 2011). The health department, the medical community, and the media express anxiety that specialty evaluation doctors fail to adhere to professional expectations. In some cases, as discussed later in the chapter, patients report questionable practices that validate this concern. Patients care about the legitimacy of interactions with physicians, and, as we will see, they avoid specialty physicians who do not uphold their interactional expectations. However, some see the requirement to get a doctor's permission as a reflection of the overinflated idea of danger about cannabis that has been reinforced by its scheduling. Although no patients objected to the doctor-qualification requirement, many talked about overregulation. Since most patients saw cannabis as safer than not only prescription medications but other herbs and even everyday items—patients mentioned aspirin, coffee, and water—the doctor's recommendation was less about medical advice and more about meeting system obligations. Nonetheless, patients understood why the state set strict rules. Because cannabis use is still considered controversial, and such programs represent a full-scale change in the laws, a system that appears beyond reproach enhances its legitimacy.

Legitimacy concerns differ for actors employing system logic—doctors and regulators—and patients who are employing lifeworld logic. Systems such as biomedicine operate on strategic action, which is largely oriented to accomplishing the goals of the organization. Options in the formal sector may not address patients' lifeworld concerns with role functioning or quality of life as well as the informal sector. By contrast, the lifeworld—our everyday world of activity—is concerned with communicative action, which is not restricted to the success of any specific institutional goals but is instead oriented toward understanding (Britten 2008). Patients often access resources from across all health sectors to manage practical health concerns (Britten 2008).

Another similarity between cannabis evaluations and the informal sector is that patients are more likely to include their regular physician when all forms of care are used to address the same health problem. When different forms of care are used to address different health concerns, patients are less likely to inform their regular physician or include them in these choices (Ruggie 2004). While patients may access different types of care, many still "prefer to keep their two worlds of health care separate" (Ruggie 2004, 78).

Sometimes, patients opted to go directly to specialty evaluation doctors because they had no regular physician managing their care or because they did not want to disclose their interest in medical cannabis to their regular physician. Lance is a case in point. A highly decorated veteran in his early thirties, Lance was medically retired from the military after incurring a traumatic brain injury (TBI) in the course of his military service in Iraq. He reports that he had never used cannabis before. His brain injury and serious PTSD symptoms resulted in treatment with antipsychotics at levels he considered near lethal, and he became concerned that if his injuries had not killed him, the treatments would. Here, Lance begins to describe his ailments and how they happened:

> I get these headaches at the base of my skull, and it feels like someone is tightening a clamp, just crushing the skull, and nobody knows why. . . . I am kind of messed up. In 2009, I was in Iraq. A national had thrown an RKG-3 at my truck, and it struck the truck and wounded eleven people, including me. I went to sleep. You get hit with a grenade, and you go to

sleep, and if you wake up, you're alive. When I woke up, the truck was full of paper and whatnot, and [I] found out that it had struck the Freon lines and let all the Freon gas inside the truck loose. About 6 pounds of Freon gas dissolved, so we don't know how long we were asleep because that gas really got us. It took about seven minutes to get the back of the truck open and get everybody out, so everyone was exposed to the Freon gas. That caused damage. I had asthma for a while. I quit smoking and tried to do the right things, and I don't have asthma anymore, but that was incurred from that.

Lance is married, and after this event, he spent a few weeks in a trauma center before he was moved to a Warrior Transition Unit (WTU), where he spent a year and a half being medically exited from the military.

[The WTU] took real good care of me and made sure that my benefits were in order before I got out. Through the military side of the house, they took care of me. They were very sympathetic too.

Once he was out of transition and back in civilian life, things became more challenging.

I couldn't sleep for about three years. I was getting about four hours of sleep a day, but it was intermittent; it was all broken apart. It took them three years to find out it was sleep apnea. That was pretty cool, once they got that figured out, and it was interesting to be able to sleep again.

Lance begins listing all the medications he was cycled through and their dosages.

I was on more pharmaceuticals than anyone that you have probably met. Some of the levels were toxic doses that were not even prescribed at that level by the maker of the pharmaceutical. So, I looked for other alternatives. Of course, it hasn't just been medical marijuana. There is definitely an herbal side, too, for balance.

About the decision to try cannabis to treat his conditions, he says:

Well, they had me on lethal doses of antipsychotics, and it really just made me really crazy. . . . After talking to some people that I had known—my dad is a [medical cannabis] patient in California—I just thought, what could go wrong, you know? It was like, the state condones it; the feds aren't really going to come after me. So, I gave it a shot. I tried everything else [first]—like, everything else!

When asked how he found a recommending doctor, he says he searched the internet to "try to find the most legitimate place." When asked if he tried his regular physician first, he laughs as if the idea is absurd, and says, "because of my current status [as a veteran], I continued to receive government health care, so no." Although Lance did not go through his regular VHA doctors, he mentions:

> My [VHA] physicians know [about my medical cannabis use]. They condone what I am doing. Unofficially, I mean. . . . They wouldn't say, "Here's a script" [prescription], because it is not something they can do, but they're happy to see an active interest, and they're seeing results. And the results aren't coming from the pharmaceuticals anymore; they are coming from what I am doing [with the medical cannabis].

Lance's father is a medical cannabis patient, but when asked if this paved the way for him to make the decision, he says, "not at all," and that it was simply based on research into his options, many of which he had first exhausted.

Many patients thought the doctors in the specialty market were accepting of cannabis as a safe option with many healthful benefits, including uses for pain conditions that are moderate or intermittent, or for conditions not specified in the registry. Turner (2004) points out that all modern medical practices engage a form of interpretation based on current nosology, and the legitimacy of diagnoses and plans for treatment often rely on a sense that medicine is a neutral representation of fact. Doctors may feel they are working within the system to maintain their own medical judgment when interpreting diagnoses and treatment plans in the evaluation. They also may enact a kind of "constructive medicalization," allowing patient who felt it would help them into the system, in part because they saw little harm created by doing so. This constructive medicalization is an interactive process involving patients, medical professionals, and the state working in concert, though with at times conflicting agendas. By offering a form of "constructive medicalization" and operating from a more patient-driven model, the "doctor mill" may solve a problem of the lifeworld, even as it seemingly causes a problem from a system point of view.

### Negotiating Qualifying Conditions

On the whole, the patients who went directly to the "doctor mill" did not have objective diagnoses that were qualifying conditions in Colorado. Some patients had diagnosed conditions that were not on the state list but qualified on the basis of symptoms related to these conditions, rather than through the condition itself. Most qualified under severe pain, sometimes combined with severe nausea or muscle spasms. Mark exemplifies this type of case. He was diagnosed with a condition called Haglund's deformity, which results in severe neuropathic pain in one's feet. His actual diagnosis is not on the list, but neuropathic pain is a legitimately qualifying condition. Many other patients suffered injuries due to specific work or car accidents, leading to well-documented medical histories that they supplied to evaluating doctors.

Only a few patients with objective diagnoses listed explicitly as qualifying—HIV/AIDS, cancer, and glaucoma—went directly to the specialty evaluation market. One of these was Ron. Ron has cancer, but, without insurance, he has no regular medical care or primary physician. Ron received his recommendation shortly after his cancer diagnosis in 2008. Ron resides in a conservative area in Colorado, and he expressed a great deal of indignation toward local authorities who harass local doctors and patients, making it nearly impossible to get a recommendation in his county. He had to travel to Denver to get his first recommendation, and he has experienced significant police harassment in his town, despite his best attempts to be transparent and abide to the letter of the law.

> Doctors are so intimidated by the district attorney [here] and by the federal government because of [cannabis'] Schedule I status. . . . Everybody gets hassled. Any time a doctor tries to help a marijuana patient, he runs the risk of being hassled. . . . The pillars of our communities are doctors now, and they don't have a voice in medicine. The district attorney has a larger voice in treating my disease than a doctor.

In the less-embattled towns and cities of Colorado, patients with serious objective diagnoses such as HIV/AIDS and cancer report few concerns with their qualifications as medical cannabis patients, even when in practice their behaviors may mix medical and recreational uses. For instance, Tucker, a thirty-three-year-old HIV patient in Denver who admits that he sometimes uses cannabis recreationally and has only recently needed it medically for the severe nausea brought on by his HIV medication regimen, says of his recommendation:

> I walked in with a slew of things to qualify me and barely uttered one thing, and it was the magic word, because I had the golden condition, so they were like, there were no questions asked, they were like, "Pfsshh" [dismissive sound].

Quite the opposite of Ron's experience, Tucker's first recommendation was at the height of Colorado's "green rush" phase, when new patient applications were peaking but before legislation defining stricter doctor–patient rules was implemented. He asked his regular physician, who immediately declined, but, overall, he experienced few roadblocks in his recommendation experience.

In cases where recommendations are based on contested or subjectively defined conditions, patients often attend more to providing evidence of qualification. For instance, many pain patients come to the recommending physician with objective proof such as x-rays and extensive prior medical records. Again, Lance provides a good example:

> I went to see the doctor, and all I had was a digital copy of my medical records because my medical records are too big. There are over 700 pages now. It really isn't a gross exaggeration. It really is 700 pages.

Some patients report that, as the regulations tightened, medical records were not sufficient, but most patients still brought medical records to show their current prescriptions and history of injuries, surgeries, and diagnosis. These were combined with answering questions and a physical examination that offered evidence of injury or disease.

Brett relied on recent x-rays to make his case in the evaluation appointment:

> I've got x-rays and, you know, they're pretty darn good, I guess. They show pretty plainly that I definitely have back issues going on. So, for me, I wasn't really concerned whether or not they could, I guess, quote-unquote qualify.

Perhaps due to Brett's involvement on the industry side of medical cannabis, he was quick to offer a defense of patient qualifications based on pain. In doing so, Brett summarized the process by which patients translate lifeworld concerns to the language of the bureaucratic system of recommendation and qualification:

> There's been a common criticism in our industry that our patients are young males, young guys, and they're all coming in for pain. And that's accurate, but what's not being told by the story is that the initial amendment that legalized this only stated eight conditions. . . . What are you going to do? Well, okay, I don't have AIDS. I can't sleep, and I've got these migraines, and I've got nausea, and I've got IBS, or I've got post-traumatic stress syndrome. Geez, none of those qualify. I guess I'll go with pain. There's a whole slew of other conditions. Everything from sleeping and migraines and all kinds of other issues that we're not putting in there. So, everything falls back on pain. Everybody will put pain, because if we had migraines on there, or sleeping disorders, then we would pick those.

In pain conditions, patients rely on medical histories and documentation such as x-rays, prescription histories, or clear diagnoses. Many also rely on the visible proof of their own bodies when they bear clear signs of significant traumas. Darrell had records but relied primarily on his disability status and the damage to his back that was obvious upon physical examination.

> I had to bring documents that showed that I had surgery. He wanted to see my scars. He sat and had an interview like we are having. He really drove me pretty hard. But it doesn't matter to me. You've got to do it.

Darrell has had multiple surgeries due to a serious injury. He has pins and screws that create a cage around his lower back and extend through his spine. He is on permanent disability through Social Security. Darrell is forty years old and married to an older woman, with multiple step-children and a very domestic lifestyle. He has never been a "partier" and has never used alcohol. Even though he has been a cannabis user for many years, he sees his medical qualification as beyond dispute. He feels a doctor looking at his physical condition would know that he was managing pain, but if there was any question, his disability status, physical state, and prescription history corroborate his claim.

Patients who have avoided biomedicine may have more challenges to provide sufficient evidence of conditions such as chronic pain. For instance, Beth, a Jehovah's Witness, rejects western medicine and prescription drugs based on her religious beliefs, using natural remedies instead. After experiencing two traumatic injuries that left her in chronic pain, she sought out a medical recommendation for cannabis.

> I took all the medical records I could find, which since I can't do medication, I don't have anything from a doctor. So, I went and got from the massage therapist and from the chiropractor all of those records.

## Identity Work in the Recommendation Setting

Patients had different reactions to the "doctor mill." Some expressed a strong preference that the interaction comport with the conventions of the doctor's visit, because this conferred legitimacy. In many respects, these interactions illustrate expectations that align with identity theory. People have developed expectations of the structure for the doctor–patient interaction, and how individuals fulfill the role standard of "patient" and "doctor" in this interaction (Burke and Stets 2009). In the sense that role-related behaviors enact social structures, patients expect legitimate medical cannabis evaluations to maintain the conventions of a typical doctor–patient interaction, including the appearance of the doctor and the setting. When details did not correspond to the ideals of such an interaction, they attempted to ignore it, but in their interviews, they reported it as bothersome, and it often led to a decision not to return to a particular doctor.

For example, Avery, the nutritional counselor in her early thirties with headaches and chronic pain due to a domestic violence attack, notes that in her first medical cannabis evaluation, the interaction approximated a typical doctor's appointment.

AVERY: It was in a medical office that was shared with other doctors. . . . The doctor was very caring and asked me questions. So, I liked that part of it, but then the person taking the money at the end, I wasn't exactly comfortable with.

INT: The way he looked or dressed?

AVERY: I know I shouldn't. . . . It's a stereotypical kind of thing, but he didn't seem very professional. He didn't match with the rest of the setting—the doctor, and the building they were in, and things like that. I decided to go to a different doctor next time. It was just—t-shirt, jeans, the jewelry he had on. [The office] wasn't exactly organized. I could have gotten out of there without paying, but I'm not that type of person, so I was looking for the person I was supposed to pay. Up until the very last moment there, it did feel [like a normal appointment]. The doctor gave me a piece of paper, had suggestions for me. He genuinely cared.

Yvonne provides another example. A sixty-year-old grandmother and self-described earth mama, Yvonne has back issues and a diagnosis of fibromyalgia. She lives in a remote southern area of Colorado where few medical marijuana centers had opened. She sought a recommendation from her primary physician. This doctor claimed she didn't handle pain management and referred Yvonne to a specialist. The specialist claimed to be "all for it," but would not sign the recommendation either, instead sending her to a doctor specializing in medical cannabis evaluations:

It was in this really seedy rental space they have out here. . . . I asked [my] kids first, "What do you think if I get legal and smoke marijuana, medical marijuana?" So, they all know about it because they're going to smell it in the air. They said, "Sure." But they didn't want me to go [to the recommendation place]. They said it was like a back-alley abortion place. It's a seedy motel, like, it was something, and I had to laugh. [The doctor] came down [to our town] one day a week, and in the waiting room, there were only folding chairs. You went in, and he was in one room and was sitting at the end of a long banquet table, and he had his receptionist in another little area behind a table, and everybody just sat in his little waiting room. . . . He did not ask for one bit of proof. I had no medical papers with me whatsoever. I had gotten everything together that I could, and they didn't need anything.

As with other patients, Avery and Yvonne avoided returning to these places. Many patients clearly state their preferences for greater legitimacy in the recommendation interaction, represented by overall professionalism in the interaction and atmosphere of the evaluation. They were disturbed by inter-actions where doctors did not maintain the appropriate appearance of pro-fessionalism because it implied nonmedical motivations for their services. In some cases, patients may have felt that a doctor's lack of legitimacy threat-ened to make the qualification less legitimate. The legitimacy of the medical cannabis patient identity is only verified by a doctor whose identity is also legitimate.

Another reaction to doctor–patient interactions in the specialty market was to interpret the recommendation experience as a bureaucratic obliga-tion instead of a legitimate medical interaction. Patients who framed the recommendation in these terms were less concerned with getting an expert evaluation from the recommending doctor. Many felt they already had such validation from their own doctors, and some did indeed have explicit but informal approval from their primary health care providers. In these cases, the "doctor mill" was seen more as a service akin to getting a notary to sign documents than an actual medical evaluation. Participants who interpreted the interaction in this way were prone during interviews to summing up the appointment rather briefly and with less detail. They often shrugged off the interaction with some version of the saying, "it's all political." In other words, patients saw the recommendation signature as a hurdle designed more for political than medical validation. However, it is significant to note that this had very little to do with their estimation of their medical qualification or legitimacy as patients.

Neil was one of the few patients who was prompted to register with the state due to a nonmedical, legal concern. Nonetheless, he possessed a qualifying condition (sciatica), and his accounts of use included clear medical patterns. When asked whether he felt he was a legitimate patient, given his characterization of his motives as primarily nonmedical, he says:

> Honestly, I felt like I was getting a driver's license. You know, like it's my right to do that. So, I didn't feel that I was getting away with anything. But I was getting my right. My right to grow and use marijuana as a medicine. So, I didn't feel like it was like, "All right!" [said to mean "I got away with something"]. It was great. Now I was able to choose things.

Neil's ability to access medical-grade cannabis and choose products that worked best for him was a benefit, but even though he indicated that his use intertwined pain management with recreational use, he refuted any sug-gestion that this access was somehow a misuse of the system for recreational purposes. Instead, he insisted on medical framing, and used much of the same health language about cannabis use that was common to other interviews. Neil also shared with many other patients a broad frame of medical use that extended beyond his "qualifying condition" to legitimately include general-ized pain, such as pain caused by the removal of his wisdom teeth.

## Assessing Legitimacy

Patients had very different estimations of how easy or difficult it was to get a recommendation, independent of medical need. Some who entered the system prior to 2009 felt that it was stringent at the time they entered and often struggled more with figuring out how to access the system or find supply. Those who entered between the start of the "rush" period of 2009 but before the new regulations were in effect commented that it seemed easy for anyone to get a recommendation during that time. Many felt that the later regulations had helped to plug some of the "leaks" in the program, and system pressures and sanctions had moved physician interactions toward greater professionalism. Others felt there were still pockets where the barriers to entry were too low, and anyone motivated to get a card could do so, whether they technically qualified or not.

Even though there were concerns that medical professionals, as gatekeepers to the system, might be a main source of "leaks," it is important to acknowledge the role of interpretation. Doctors in general medicine, specialty doctors, the state, and affected patients had predictable differences in their interpretations of the value of medical cannabis use and who should have access to it. Disagreements on procedural details such as protocols for patient evaluations and other attendant issues are largely due to the differences in how each is positioned relative to other stakeholders. Patients expressed sympathy and gratitude for doctors who adopted this risky specialty in order to help patients. Indignation was reserved for those who appeared to be profiting from the system without truly caring for patients. This included doctors who were running unprofessional recommendation practices such that the doctor's appointment reflected neither the appropriate level of professionalism nor a desired level of patient care. Such determinations were largely based on the identity work in doctor–patient interactions. The scrutiny and criticism to which physicians in the specialty recommendation market are subjected does not negate the importance of their role. These doctors serve a critical function to the medicalization processes around cannabis. Without them, many qualifying patients would have never gained access to the system.

Patient concerns about professionalism also extended to distant players, such as the government and pharmaceutical companies, who many patients believed knowingly benefit from the lack of cannabis' availability as a natural substitute for other medications and, worse, did not care that their opposition to medical cannabis results in patient suffering. Authentic caring and ethical motivations for being in the industry mattered to patients.

The patients in this study are invested in the legitimacy of the system. Patients believe that there were important differences between medical and recreational use and prefer a clear system boundary between the two. Some patients expressed concern that the specialty recommendation market presented opportunities for illegitimate entry to the medical cannabis program. Because patients in this study saw themselves as meeting the program criteria, they were bothered by this. Patients expressed these worries *even though* many were supportive of recreational uses. Perceived cheaters detracted from their own patient status and its legitimacy in a controversial climate where such concerns are commonly in the media spotlight. However, they were reticent to accuse others of "cheating" the system. Even though several patients made comments about young, male, recreational users as the stereotypical "cheaters," they were often quick to qualify such comments, acknowledging that it is unfair to base an estimation of legitimacy on appearance. The patients interviewed for this study understood that seemingly healthy young people could indeed have unseen injuries or illnesses that are completely legitimate.

The decision to seek the formal legitimacy conferred by registering with the state program is different than choosing to use medical cannabis. This may seem obvious, but the two decisions are often treated as one. Patients who are legitimately qualified under state law *and* decide to use cannabis therapeutically may still choose not to register with the state. Even after making a decision to register, patients have a recurring opportunity to change their minds about participating since registry cards are renewed annually. Many patients base their registration decision on a sophisticated assessment of legal risks and vulnerabilities, or on the sense that the cost to participate in the system is reasonable and fair. All but one patient in this study said that knowing now how cannabis can be used in their medical treatment, they would not stop using it if the laws were rolled back. Many patients take measures such as cultivating cannabis to ensure they can be self-sufficient should the system fail.

Since the passage in 2012 of Amendment 64 legalizing all adult use in Colorado, the incentives for participating in the medical program have changed. With a broad array of quality cannabis products now available to anyone twenty-one or over, registering as a patient is less worth the various risks, costs, and bureaucratic hurdles, as reflected in the 50 percent drop in registered patients (CDPHE 2017). Broader access also removes much of the incentive for nonmedical users to pursue a medical designation and may make questioning of medical legitimacy less prevalent. As more physicians come to accept a medicalized definition of cannabis, perceive less risk in providing recommendations, and have less cause for questioning patient motives, interactions with medical cannabis-seeking patients are likely to become less contentious. More widespread acceptance of medical cannabis by physicians is critical to the consolidation of legitimacy in the path to complete medicalization.

## Notes

1. The professional associations for herbal medicine have collaborated with patient advocacy organizations on developing standards for cannabis consistent with other CAM botanicals. In 2013, the American Herbal Pharmacopeia (AHP), with funding

and technical support from the patient organization Americans for Safe Access, issued a monograph, *Cannabis Inflorescence: Cannabis Spp: Standards of Identity, Analysis, and Quality Control*, which details scientific methods for identifying, analyzing, and cultivating plants (Scotts Valley, CA, AHP). In 2014, the Cannabis Committee of the American Herbal Products Association, the leading trade organization for producers of botanical medicines and similar products, released *Recommendations for Regulators* (Silver Spring, MD, www.ahpa.org/AboutUs/Committees/Cannabis Committee.aspx) that covers best practices for all aspects of commercial cannabis operations, from cultivation and processing to manufacturing, distribution, labeling, and analytic testing. Those recommendations were also developed in collaboration with Americans for Safe Access and have subsequently been incorporated in part or in whole in the regulatory structure of several state programs. Examples include Maryland (Christopher Brown, 2015, "Americans for Safe Access Program to Provide Training for MD Medical Cannabis Compliance Inspectors." Americans for Safe Access [www.safeaccessnow.org]) and Nevada (Mike Liszewski, 2013, "Nevada Draft Dispensary Regulations Incorporate AHPA and AHP Best Practices." in *Americans for Safe Access Blog*. Americans for Safe Access. Retrieved 2017 [https://www.safeaccessnow. org/nevada_draft_dispensary_regulations_incorporate_ahpa_and_ahp_best_practices]). Patient advocates are also participating in the development of international standards for cannabis through ASTM International, an organization that produces consensus technical standards for many types of materials, products, and services (Maxwell, Jack. 2017. "The Need for Cannabis Standards." *ASTM Standardization News*. Retrieved August 2017 (www.astm.org/standardization-news/?q=features/need-cannabis-standards-mj17.html). These formal attempts to standardize best practices for all aspects of producing, distributing, and testing cannabis products all work to integrate it more completely into the realm of CAM treatments.
2. Patients must obtain a signature recommending cannabis use annually and file it with their renewal paperwork with the state.

# References

Adler, Jonathan N., and James A. Colbert. 2013. "Medicinal Use of Marijuana: Polling Results." *New England Journal of Medicine* 368(22):e30. doi:10.1056/NEJMclde1305159.

Aggarwal, Sunil K., Gregory T. Carter, Mark D. Sullivan, Craig ZumBrunnen, Richard Morrill, and Jonathan D. Mayer. 2009. "Medicinal Use of Cannabis in the United States: Historical Perspectives, Current Trends, and Future Directions." *The Journal of Opioid Management* 5(3):153–68.

Armentano, Paul. 2017. "The Evidence Is Overwhelming: Cannabis Is an Exit Drug for Major Addictions, Not a Gateway to New Ones." *Alternet.org* (www.alternet.org/drugs/evidence-overwhelming-cannabis-exit-drug-major-addictions-not-gateway-new-ones).

Baarts, Charlotte, and Inge Kryger Pedersen. 2009. "Derivative Benefits: Exploring the Body through Complementary and Alternative Medicine." *Sociology of Health & Illness* 31(5):719–33. doi: 10.1111/j.1467-9566.2009.01163.x.

Barthwell, Andrea G., Louis E. Baxter, Timmen Cermak, Robert DuPont, Mark L. Kraus, and Petros Levounis. 2010. *The Role of the Physician in "Medical Marijuana."* Rockville, MD: American Society of Addiction Medicine.

Britten, Nicky. 2008. *Medicines and Society: Patients, Professionals and the Dominance of Pharmaceuticals.* New York: Palgrave Macmillan.

Broom, Dorothy H., and Roslyn V. Woodward. 1996. "Medicalisation Reconsidered: Toward a Collaborative Approach to Care." *Sociology of Health & Illness* 18(3):357–78.

Burke, Peter J., and Jan E. Stets. 1999. "Trust and Commitment through Self-Verification." *Social Psychology Quarterly* 62(4):347–66. doi: 10.2307/2695833.

Burke, Peter J., and Jan E. Stets. 2009. *Identity Theory.* New York: Oxford University Press.

CDPHE, Colorado Department of Public Health and Environment. 2014. "Medical Use of Marijuana." Article 5 CCR 1006-2.

CDPHE, Colorado Department of Public Health and Environment. 2017. "2017 Medical Marijuana Registry Statistics." Colorado Department of Public Health and Environment. Retrieved August 20, 2017 (https://www.colorado.gov/pacific/cdphe/2017-medical-marijuana-registry-statistics).

Chan, Michael H., Christopher E. Knoepke, Madeline L. Cole, James McKinnon, and Daniel D. Matlock. 2017. "Colorado Medical Students' Attitudes and Beliefs About Marijuana." *Journal of General Internal Medicine* 32(4):458–63. doi: 10.1007/s11606-016-3957-y.

CO-DORA, Colorado Department of Regulatory Agencies. 2017a. "Policy Regarding Recommendations for Marijuana as a Therapeutic Option." Article 40–28, Section 40–28.

CO-DORA, Colorado Department of Regulatory Agencies. 2017b. "Policy Statement Regarding the Provider/Patient Relationship." Article 40–3.

Conrad, Peter, and Joseph Schneider. 1998 [1980]. *Deviance and Medicalization: From Badness to Sickness.* Philadelphia: Temple University Press.

Dumit, Joseph. 2006. "Illnesses You Have to Fight to Get: Facts as Forces in Uncertain, Emergent Illnesses." *Social Science & Medicine* 62:577–90.

Eisenberg, David M., Roger B. Davis, Susan L. Ettner, Scott Appel, Sonja Wilkey, Maria Van Rompay, and Robert C. Kessler. 1998. "Trends in Alternative Medicine Use in the United States, 1990–1997." *Journal of the American Medical Association* 280:1569–75.

Gorski, Eric. 2013. "Oversight of Colorado Medical Marijuana Doctors Remains Spotty." *The Denver Post.* August 24, 2013. (https://www.denverpost.com/2013/08/24/oversight-of-colorado-medical-marijuana-doctors-remains-spotty-2/).

Gupta, Sanjay. 2013. "Why I Changed My Mind on Weed." CNN.com (https://www.cnn.com/2013/08/08/health/gupta-changed-mind-marijuana/index.html)

Habermas, Jürgen. 1987. *The Theory of Communicative Action, Volume 2: Lifeworld and System.* Boston, MA: Beacon Press.

Joffe-Walt, Chana. 2013. "Unfit for Work: The Startling Rise of Disability in America." in *This American Life.* National Public Radio (http://apps.npr.org/unfit-for-work/).

Kennedy, Jae, Chi-Chuan Wang, and Chung-Hsuen Wu. 2008. "Patient Disclosure about Herb and Supplement Use among Adults in the U.S." *eCAM* 5(4):451–6.

Kondrad, Elin, and Alfred Reid. 2013. "Colorado Family Physicians' Attitudes toward Medical Marijuana." *The Journal of the American Board of Family Medicine* 26(1):52–60. doi: 10.3122/jabfm.2013.01.120089.

Lucas, Philippe. 2012. "Cannabis as an Adjunct to or Substitute for Opiates in the Treatment of Chronic Pain." *Journal of Psychoactive Drugs* 44(2):125–33. doi: 10.1080/02791072.2012.684624.

Markoff, Steven C. 2003. "Addictiveness of Marijuana." *ProCon.org.* Retrieved August 24, 2017 (www.procon.org/view.background-resource.php?resourceID=001492).

Merrill, Joseph O., Lorna A. Rhodes, Richard A. Deyo, G. Alan Marlatt, and Katharine A. Bradley. 2002. "Mutual Mistrust in the Medical Care of Drug Users." *Journal of General Internal Medicine* 17(5):327–33. doi: 10.1046/j.1525-1497.2002.10625.x.

Nichter, Mark, and Jennifer Jo Thompson. 2006. "For My Wellness, Not Just My Illness: North Americans' Use of Dietary Supplements." *Culture, Medicine, and Psychiatry* 30:175–222. doi: 10.1007/s11013-9016-0.

Nussbaum, Abraham M., Jonathan A. Boyer, and Elin C. Kondrad. 2011. "'But My Doctor Recommended Pot': Medical Marijuana and the Patient: Physician Relationship." *Journal of General Internal Medicine* 26(11):1364–7. doi: 10.1007/s11606-011-1840-4.

Piper, Brian J., Rebecca M. DeKeuster, Monica L. Beals, Catherine M. Cobb, Corey A. Burchman, Leah Perkinson, Shayne T. Lynn, Stephanie D. Nichols, and Alexander T. Abess. 2017. "Substitution of Medical Cannabis for Pharmaceutical Agents for Pain, Anxiety, and Sleep." *Journal of Psychopharmacology* 31(5):569–75. doi: 10.1177/0269881117699616.

Rainville, James, Glenn Pransky, Aage Indahl, and Eric K. Mayer. 2005. "The Physician as Disability Advisor for Patients with Musculoskeletal Complaints." *Spine* 30(22):2579–84.

Reiman, Amanda. 2006. "Cannabis Care: Medical Marijuana Facilities as Health Service Providers." Ph.D. Dissertation, Social Welfare, University of California, Berkeley.

Ruggie, Mary. 2004. *Marginal to Mainstream: Alternative Medicine in America*. Cambridge: Cambridge University Press.

Ruggie, Mary. 2005. "Mainstreaming Complementary Therapies: New Directions in Health Care." *Health Affairs* 24(4):980–90. doi: 10.1377/hlthaff.24.4.980.

Stets, Jan E., and Peter J. Burke. 2014. "Self-Esteem and Identities." *Sociological Perspectives* 57(4):409–33.

Testerman, John K., Kelly R. Morton, Rachel A. Mason, and Ann M. Ronan. 2004. "Patient Motivations for Using Complementary and Alternative Medicine." *Complementary Health Practice Review* 9(2):81–92.

Turner, Bryan. 2004. *The New Medical Sociology*. New York: W.W. Norton.

# Chapter 5

# Medical Cannabis Use
# in Everyday Life

After patients receive a physician's recommendation for medical cannabis, their interactions with the formal system of medicine are largely complete. Now those patients face decisions about how to integrate medical cannabis in everyday life. Medical cannabis patients must figure out, independent of direct medical advice, their routine for use in an environment that scrutinizes differences between medical and nonmedical use. This chapter is the first of three that examines how patients manage their use of cannabis as a medicine. Patients construct medical use, often experimenting in order to arrive at best practices. Even when individuals have used cannabis recreationally before and were accustomed to its effects, they still engage in experimentation when imposing new medical criteria for evaluating effects and efficacy. How do people learn to interpret drug effects and form routines of use? Some classic research in sociology has proposed useful theories to address this question.

## Drug, Set, and Setting

The now-classic theory that drug experiences are created from a combination of "drug, set, and setting" gained currency in the 1960s when Timothy Leary, a Harvard professor of psychology who became a countercultural icon, introduced the concept in relation to user experiences with LSD (Leary, Metzner, and Alpert 1964; Leary 1966). Leary's formulation that social and cultural context are significant factors in a drug's effects have a long history, going back as far as the use of psychotropics. Research on cannabis and other psychoactive drugs, such as LSD, led to the idea of measuring the influence of extra-drug, "set and setting" parameters, largely because the effects of these substances are the "most susceptible to changes in set and setting conditions" (Hartogsohn 2017, 10). Not all drugs are equally "flexible" when it comes to the interpretation of effects and the influence of extra-drug factors. When clinical psychedelic research was largely abandoned after the mid-twentieth century, the concepts of "set and setting" fell out of favor. "Nevertheless, the role of set and setting has not been absent from accounts on the extra-pharmacological construction of other, nonpsychedelic, drugs" such as tranquilizers, sedatives, and stimulants (Hartogsohn 2017, 11).

The concept of drug, set, and setting was largely developed by Norman Zinberg, the psychoanalyst, psychiatrist, and Guggenheim fellow (Hartogsohn 2013). Building upon the work of Becker and Leary, Zinberg spent much of his career researching the consumption of opiates, psychedelics, and cannabis. Zinberg's findings from interviews with drug-using subjects from over a decade of research substantially expanded the theory of "drug, set, and setting" and began to dismantle ideas common at the time about addiction's relationship with specific personality types. His influence on our understanding of addiction set the direction of much contemporary research and is evident in current approaches to clinical treatment of addicts.

According to Zinberg (1984), drug effects are not simply determined by adding a drug to a person's system and assessing results. For Zinberg, the specific drug is only one of multiple elements that determines the experience that will ensue. Even though we think of most drugs as having a predictable range of effects, each person interprets those effects in ways that have a significant impact on the experience. Zinberg argued that the interpretation of drug effects could be understood through the "extra-drug" effects from "set" and "setting," which play a critical role. Zinberg uses the term "set" to have a similar meaning to "mindset" but encompassing more; "state" is perhaps closer. Set, which is covered in detail in the next chapter, includes a person's current psychological and physiological state, such as the mood the person is in, or whether they have recently eaten, but it also takes into account more enduring qualities, such as personality and physiology.

The second extra-drug factor is "setting," which refers to the social context. Again, Zinberg's conceptualization of setting includes immediate, transient circumstances of use as well as more enduring aspects of one's environment, such as accepted broad cultural meanings associated with gender, age, or an individual's long-standing values. The role of setting in medical cannabis use is explored in chapter 7.

To illustrate the powerful role played by "set" and "setting" in influencing a drug's effects, Zinberg (1984) referenced the phenomenon of the "placebo effect," in which a person is given an inert substance that they believe to contain medication. The person who consumes the placebo has an interpretation that affects not only the subjective experience of taking the drug but often also generates physiological outcomes (Price, Finniss, and Benedetti 2008). The placebo effect is well established, but there are limits to what psychological mechanisms can achieve with medical conditions. After he experienced the effectiveness of cannabis for treating neuropathic pain in his feet from Haglund's deformity, Mark was one of several patients who commented on the difference:

> This is not a placebo kind of effect. And that really enrages me when people suggest that. You cannot "placebo effect" away this kind of pain.

This is not that kind of shit. You are not dealing with that kind of stuff. This is not a little headache or something.

In this chapter and the next two, we examine in turn Zinberg's (1984) categories of drug, set, and setting to show how all three aspects are radically altered when cannabis use is reframed from recreational to medical use. Medicalization has a transformative effect on drug, set, and setting for patient's experiences.

## Reinterpreting Cannabis the Drug

It's not the pot of the 70s anymore. It's come a long way. It really has, you know. There is medical stuff about it, because when I smoked a joint back 20–30 years ago: "Hey—this is some good Mexican." But now they got even strains that target certain symptoms. Like if you have muscle spasms, you're supposed [to] smoke one strain. If you've got headaches, you're supposed to smoke this kind. It's kind of neat, the way that it's come along.

(Dale)

Cannabis produces a predictable range of effects, but, as with other substances, the individual's interpretation of those effects matters for how they are experienced. Becker's (1953) now-classic article from the 1950s, "On Becoming a Marijuana User," was the first to capture this labeling and learning process. Becker interviewed fifty cannabis users to explore how individuals learned to use cannabis recreationally. He found that new users learned from more experienced users not only techniques for smoking cannabis, but also how to gauge the right amount to smoke and interpret cannabis' effects. According to Becker (1953), users learned to identify bodily sensations created by cannabis use as pleasurable and label them "getting high."

The sensory experience associated with cannabis consumption is not automatically or universally pleasurable. New recreational users typically anticipate enjoyable effects, but not all users interpret the experience as pleasant. As Becker (1953) explains, continued use of cannabis for recreation relies on the perception that the effects are enjoyable. This relates directly to the ability to gauge and control dosage so that the substance's effects are noticeably felt, yet not so intensely that the experience is unpleasant. In a later article, Becker (1973, 26) points out:

what a person knows about a drug influences the way he uses it, the way he interprets its effects and responds to them, and the way he deals with the sequelae of the experience. What he does not know affects his experience, too, making certain interpretations and actions impossible.

The dominant framing of cannabis use as an inebriant has encouraged individuals to interpret cannabis use in one way and to one purpose. In fact, without another available interpretation, it is challenging to interpret cannabis use outside of this framework, which emphasizes the immediate sensory experience but obscures connections between its use and medical or health-related outcomes. Many only realize the limitations of framing cannabis as an inebriant when other interpretations become available to them.

## The Expansion of Cannabis Formulations

As cannabis transitions out of an underground market and enters a regulated system, it undergoes changes that should not be underestimated. Medicalization has had many implications for cannabis the plant and the products made from it. These have included greater standardization in breeding and cultivation, diversification of breeding for different qualities that are more suited to medical than recreational purposes, and the proliferation of new products that offer greater diversity in how cannabis is consumed. Additionally, there is greater circulation of knowledge about the plant among medical consumers, who tend to learn basics about the plant and its products as a step toward formulating self-care routines. For instance, a recent study of 100 Norwegian medical cannabis patients found that they have knowledge about the cannabis plant, current science, and medical properties, as well as physiological effects, and that knowledge in these areas was more substantial among those patients with more serious medical conditions (Pedersen and Sandberg 2013).

## Selecting Medical Cannabis Varieties

First, let's consider breeding and cultivation. Until relatively recently, underground market cannabis was, by and large, undifferentiated as a product, with the exception of the once-rare "sinsemilla" designation for unfertilized and therefore seedless and more potent female flowers. That nomenclature has been abandoned as seeds are now the rarity in cannabis produced for the consumer market. Cannabis produced for the medical and connoisseur markets typically relies on rooting cuttings of female plants for propagation rather than germinating seeds, a technique that ensures genetic conformity of the plants and consistency of finished products because each plant is an identical clone of the others. This change in cultivation method has created greater control over selection, allowing a consistency of finished product that is impossible with plants grown from seeds that are necessarily genetically variable. Many patients report identifying specific varieties that work well for them, as Dale alludes to, and come to rely on being able to obtain the same cannabis over time. Over the past several decades, cannabis breeders in the Netherlands, Canada, and the U.S. have brought to market a proliferation of specialty varieties bred for a variety of characteristics. Potency and cannabinoid profile are a central concern, of course, but breeders also work to enhance such aesthetic features as aroma and taste and growth factors such as resistance to pests, time to flowering, and yield.

Cannabis is generally regarded by botanists as being a single species with three primary variants—sativa, indica, and ruderalis. Each has a characteristic phenotype, from the tall, lanky sativa to the squat, bushy indica and the diminutive, thin ruderalis. Modern varieties are often a cross of the indica and sativa subspecies, but ruderalis genetics have been increasingly incorporated because they are less dependent on seasonal changes in the length of daylight to go into flowering. Some types of cannabis are well known by their variety names, but testing has shown that many are mislabeled at point of distribution. The patients interviewed for this study possessed basic knowledge about the cannabis plant and were quick to display both general and specific variety information. Even though they were not asked questions meant to elicit their specific cannabis knowledge, more than two-thirds of the participating patients offered information about specific varieties and included information on their sativa and indica ratios. Another third mentioned the balance between THC and CBD, and just under one-quarter of patients mentioned Phoenix Tears, the high-potency cannabis oil extract some cancer patients use. Over 80 percent of patents mentioned at least one of these characteristics or discussed a specific cannabis variety for medical use. Patients can often distinguish between the effects expected from an indica or sativa and many discussed this distinction as well as their own reasons for preferring one over the other as it related to their symptoms and medical needs.

As a substance, cannabis is also medicalized through selectively breeding for the plant's medical rather than its recreational traits. Delta-9 tetrahydrocannabinol (THC), the main psychoactive constituent of the plant, has been the focus of breeding for the recreational market. In the medical market, other constituents of the plant are considered for their medical effects. In particular, cannabidiol, or CBD, typically the plant's second-most prevalent cannabinoid, has gained prominence for its health effects with no "high." Specifically, CBD has been shown to have considerable therapeutic application for conditions such as seizure disorders. In the recreational market, CBD was being bred out of the plants because it is not just a non-psychoactive cannabinoid, it functions as an antagonist to THC in the body, stepping on the "high" THC creates. CBD also exhibits anxiolytic or anxiety-reducing properties, so it functions to improve patients' ability to tolerate higher therapeutic doses of THC, which might otherwise be psychologically uncomfortable. Cannabis varieties and products touting high percentages of CBD and low or no THC have been developed along with selective extraction techniques to offer whole plant medicinal products that minimize or eliminate intoxication.

CBD is not the only constituent chemical of cannabis to receive recent attention for its therapeutic potential. Terpenes, the chemicals in the essential oils of plants that produce aroma in many plants, are commonly used in aromatherapy and scented products. These volatile unsaturated hydrocarbons are produced by cannabis in abundance and great variety, with over 200 identified. In the past few years, the terpenes that give cannabis varieties their characteristic skunky, pine, or citrus aromas have been identified as exerting a significant effect on how individual varieties of cannabis are experienced, both in terms of cognitive and therapeutic effect. Historically, the variable effects of cannabis varieties—energizing or sedating, cerebral or corporeal— have been commonly ascribed to whether a variety is a sativa or an indica, and many patients continue to do so, but such effects may instead be a result of the synergy between the terpenoids and cannabinoids (Lewis, Russo, and Smith 2017; Russo and Marcu 2017; Russo 2011). This may be because the psychotropic properties of THC affect the "set" of the user such that the terpene aromas exert a more powerful effect than they can in isolation.

## Approaching Consistency

Cannabis is a plant with natural variation, but the regulated market increases control over growing conditions that lead to plant material with greater consistency and safety as a result of food-grade gardening practices. This is supported by the best-practice standards disseminated by the American Herbal Products Association and the American Herbal Pharmacopeia, as discussed in chapter 4. Even as the number of cannabis variety and product options increase, they are becoming more internally standardized as best-practice standards are promulgated throughout the industry. New extraction processes capitalize on state-of-the-art labs and improved scientific knowledge about cannabis' biochemical properties to produce whole plant extractions with levels of standardization approaching or even equaling synthetic pharmaceutical medicines.

The leading examples of standardized dose-controlled plant extract medicines are a pair of drugs developed by GW Pharmaceuticals, a company launched in the U.K. in 1998 to develop cannabis-based medicines. GW achieves consistent cannabinoid dosing in its medicines by controlled cultivation of two varieties that are respectively THC-rich and CBD-rich. The cannabinoids are extracted and blended as needed to obtain the desired target ratios of cannabinoids. GW's first drug to market was Sativex™, which has a 50:50 balance of THC to CBD, the ratio that double-blind placebo-controlled clinical research determined to be optimal for controlling cancer pain and the muscle spasticity and neuropathic pain related to multiple sclerosis (Johnson et al. 2010; Notcutt et al. 2012; Novotna et al. 2011; Portenoy et al. 2012; Wade et al. 2010). The extract is packaged as an oromucosal spray to be administered under the tongue or inside the cheek with a patented metered-dose pump-delivery device. As of late 2017, Sativex™ has been approved for prescribed use in twenty-one countries, and ten others have recommended approval under a Mutual Recognition Procedure, though the U.S. is not among them. GW's new epilepsy drug, Epidiolex™, contains primarily CBD and is administered as an oral liquid. FDA-approved Phase 3 clinical trials with pediatric seizure patients have preliminary results showing Epidiolex™ reduced the frequency of several types of seizure, including those most difficult to treat (Devinsky et al. 2018, Curran and Beyer 2017). On June 25, 2018, the FDA approved Epidiolex™ for the treatment of two rare pediatric seizure disorders, Lennox-Gastaut syndrome and Dravet syndrome, making it the first FDA-approved cannabis-based medicine and the first medication of any kind for Dravet syndrome. Cancer treatment may be next. GW announced in February 2017 that it had obtained positive results in a Phase 2 clinical study using THC:CBD to treat recurrent glioblastoma multiforme (GBM), a highly aggressive form of brain cancer. Those treated with THC:CBD had a 30 percent better one-year survival rate compared to placebo (GW Pharmaceuticals 2017). The FDA and the European Medicines Agency (EMA) have both granted GW an Orphan Drug Designation for the treatment of glioma, making it easier to gain approval to bring it to market.

At the same time as this pharmaceutical approach was developing in the U.K., cannabis cultivators in the U.S. were seeking out CBD-rich varieties for breeding programs to reclaim diminished medicinal properties. Out of that effort came collaborations such as Project CBD in Northern California and the work of the Stanley Brothers in Colorado, whose CBD variety Charlotte's Web would gain international renown after being featured in the CNN Special Report "Weed" described in chapter 1.

### Diversification of Cannabis Products

The proliferation of standardized products that expand the methods by which cannabis can be consumed are a critical part of its medicalization. Some of these are familiar variations on traditional products. Cannabis concentrates, infused oils, and tincture formulations have lengthy histories that predate the modern era, going back hundreds and even thousands of years (Booth 2003). Tinctures suspend essential-oil extracts in alcohol. "Hemp tincture" was the standard form for commercial cannabis medicines in the western hemisphere from the incorporation of cannabis therapeutics in the nineteenth century until federal legal barriers halted U.S. production. In combination with the other forms of medicalization—better information, knowledge of specific varieties, improved consistency, knowledge about other plant components, greater product safety, and improvements in standardization—these products exist in updated and modernized versions of traditional products and are now available to patients in Colorado and some other states. From lozenges to lotions, beverages to candy chews, derivative products have become standardized, and the composition and dosages are increasingly defined and included on product labels, allowing patients to self-monitor their dosage with more accuracy.

One product in particular is worth mentioning: Phoenix Tears, also known as Rick Simpson Oil, or RSO. This product is a type of thick hash oil that is often packaged in a toothpaste-type tube, making it look a bit like anchovy paste. This product was developed by Canadian advocate Rick Simpson, who disseminates information on how to make it and offers a protocol for its medical use. Simpson's (2014) website features anecdotal accounts of remarkable success in treating a variety of serious conditions including MS, cancer, Parkinson's, and Crohn's disease, among others. Other publicity, including a movie about this product called *Run from the Cure*, has led to a broad awareness of Phoenix Tears among the medical cannabis community (Laurette 2008).

## Know Thy Medicine: Patient Knowledge

Because cannabis as a drug has changed, patients have opportunities to interact with it in new ways. The culture surrounding medical cannabis and dispensaries socializes medical cannabis patients to adopt medical language and consider the political implications of their choice of terms (Chapkis 2007; London 2006; O'Brien 2013). As Conrad (2007) points out, "the key to medicalization is definition" (5). Adoption of new rhetoric becomes a direct method by which patients collectively reframe behavior as medical. It allows the drug and its effects to be discussed in the context of one's illness and other medications and treatments without invoking frames associated with terms such as "marijuana," as we discuss in the Note on Terms at the beginning of this book. Many patients explained their rationales for rhetorical choices around terminology in ways such as Brett, Gary, and Mark:

BRETT: I have a hard time using the word *marijuana*, too, to be honest with you. . . . You know, cannabis was grown in this country. It was the most dominant crop at the turn of the century, in the 1900s, and the majority of farmers were growing it. And then they demonized the plant. They demonized the Mexican-Americans coming in, coming across the border.

GARY: I don't like to use the word *pot* because it's a negative, stereotypical thing.

MARK: I don't like the word *high*. I like the word my wife used when she tried an edible. The conservative person that she was, after like thirty minutes or an hour, whenever she felt it, she said, "Wow, I feel pretty floaty." That's a word that works . . . It's a personal but heartfelt thing. I won't say it's like using the N-word because it's not, but there's a certain stereotype that I grew up with—that it is a gateway drug, or the source of all evil. You're going to be a worthless loser sitting on the sofa all day if you partake of it. It's going to introduce you to heroin and opium. The list goes on. . . . I'm just now getting over the anger I felt for being lied to my whole life about something that could be so helpful. I wish I'd discovered it much, much sooner. So that's why I don't like that "high" kind of stereotype.

Reframing the interpretation of cannabis use from recreational to medical is in part a rhetorical act, but it is more than simply calling the plant by its proper botanical name and exchanging phrases such as "getting high" for references to "medicating." It is a way of carving out space to reject the single story of cannabis use and the many entrenched stereotypes associated with it.

Not all patients felt as strongly about terminology. Many moved flexibly between recollections of recreational use to specific details about finding appropriate medical products currently on the market. They could "code switch" seamlessly between the two rhetorical realms. This is evidence that even though the individual is burdened with medicalizing, the line remains fuzzy. As we will see in the next chapter, the distinction between medical and recreational use is a focus of much media attention and institutional boundary making, but the distinction is more institutional than individual.

Medicalization of cannabis changes behaviors, altering how cannabis is used, including the form and method by which it is consumed. A medical frame alters the amount that is consumed, the context in which it is consumed, and the expectations and outcomes attached to its use. Every patient in this study expressed some familiarity with the different methods by which cannabis can be ingested and had individual preferences when it came to the array of available products. Many expressed their wonder at first visiting a dispensary, comparing it to "a kid in a candy shop," reminiscent of the Willie Wonka moment when the children are first given admittance to the land of chocolate and candy delights. Jason is one such:

> When I first got my card and I walked into a dispensary, any dispensary, it was surreal. It was like, is this really going down? Am I seriously standing here, and this guy has got 10 pounds of weed back there? Is this actually happening? It was totally surreal.

Many patients shared Jason's experience—that disorienting moment when they first stand in a shop that sells cannabis products legally. Until that moment, the changes to the law were largely abstract. Standing before the counter displaying a stunning variety of buds, concentrates, tinctures, lotions, and candies creates a disjuncture, a first glimpse into a new, alternative reality. Many people become a bit dumbstruck in this moment, as they absorb this new combination of exotic, forbidden products in the mundane familiarity of a retail store. What was so long prohibited and hidden is now here, multiplied in a variety of styles, integrated into an everyday retail landscape. To patients who were longtime recreational users, the ideal of decriminalizing cannabis has existed mostly as a far-off, vague notion, and they had never envisioned how it would materialize. For those with little experience, it was a strange new world. Both groups expressed surprise, exhilaration, and mild apprehension. Most described their first experience as a milestone, whether the dispensary had the aura of an old hippie "head shop" or the slick affluence of an upscale spa.

The sense of wonder and profound novelty eventually receded, and the dispensary came to seem a more regular feature of life for patients, although the time frame in which this happened varied. Some felt they adjusted within a few visits to the dispensary, while others felt it took almost a year for the novelty to wear off. In keeping with the Willie Wonka effect, patients were often tempted to try everything at first, an impulse that also receded over time. Patients become excited to experiment but soon tired of the effort it takes to continually sample new products whose effects and effectiveness are uncertain. Most report that their interest shifts to identifying a variety or product that proves medically effective for them and then ensuring that this product or line of products is consistently available. Consider Leo's account:

> I was speechless. I was: "Oh my God," you know? I'd only seen stuff like this underground in Guido's trunk in the back alley up on the Hill and shit like that. It was amazing. . . . Not only that, but they know the difference between sativa and indica, and what it does for certain diseases. Now, I use indica because mine's a pain killer. That happy bullshit that you take and go to Woodstock with does not do anything except draw your attention to the pain. So, the less THC in it the better. The more CBDs, the more CBNs the better, because it kills the pain.

Leo's experience captures well the importance of consistent access to standardized varieties. A self-proclaimed, longtime regular cannabis smoker, Leo is now in his sixties and retired. He sought a medical card when a disintegrating disc in his back led to severe chronic back pain. When discussing his first-time dispensary experience, Leo recounted tales of his past recreational use at length, including some memorable exploits from his early twenties. Like many patients, Leo clearly possesses a considerable amount of insider knowledge and wisdom that is based in his experience with cannabis. Because of this history, experiencing a legitimate cannabis store was a moving, emotional experience. He had long hoped that the laws would change. Yet like many other patients, Leo soon shifted gears, gravitating toward specific varieties and products. The salient factor in his selections is their effectiveness as a medicine for his pain conditions. The varieties he had experienced as fun for socializing were not useful in the context of treating chronic pain. THC and its known contribution to the "high" were passed over in favor of the non-psychoactive constituents of the plant that enhanced pain control without interfering with functionality.

Development of specialized varieties and products and patient access to a wide selection of them are tied intimately to the emergence of regulated markets such as Colorado's. Transformations in cannabis plant genetics, cultivation techniques, and whole-plant formulations are beginning to create important distinctions between "cannabis the medicine" and "cannabis the recreational drug," but at this point they can still be virtually indistinguishable. With no clearly visible differences in name or formulation that are widely recognized in society, individual orientation and behavior become paramount for defining cannabis use as medical or social. Such distinctions are not always as simple as they sound, as the next chapters on set and setting point out, but they suggest an important corollary to the old adage "the dose makes the poison." With cannabis, the behavior makes the medicine.

## References

Becker, Howard S. 1953. "Becoming a Marihuana User." *American Journal of Sociology* 59(3):235–42.

Becker, Howard S. 1973. "Consciousness, Power and Drug Effects." *Society* 10(4):26–31.

Booth, Martin. 2003. *Cannabis: A History*. New York: Picador.

Chapkis, Wendy. 2007. "Cannabis, Consciousness, and Healing." *Contemporary Justice Review: Issues in Criminal, Social, and Restorative Justice* 10(4):443–60.

Conrad, Peter. 2007. *The Medicalization of Society*. Baltimore, MD: The Johns Hopkins University Press.

Curran, Christy, and Mike Beyer. 2017. "GW Pharmaceuticals and Its U.S. Subsidiary Greenwich Biosciences Highlight New Epidiolex (Cannabidiol) Data Released by the American Academy of Neurology." GW Pharmaceuticals (www.gwpharm.com/).

Devinsky, Orrin, Anup D. Patel, J Helen Cross, Vicente Villanueva, et al. 2018. "Effect of Cannabidiol on Drop Seizures in the Lennox-Gastuat Syndrome." *New England Journal of Medicine* 378:1888–1897.

GW Pharmaceuticals. 2017. "GW Pharmaceuticals Achieves Positive Results in Phase 2 Proof of Concept Study in Glioma," news release, February 7, 2017, (https://www.gwpharm.com/about-us/news/gw-pharmaceuticals-achieves-positive-results-phase-2-proof-concept-study-glioma).

Hartogsohn, Ido. 2013. "The American Trip: Set, Setting, and Psychedelics in 20th Century Psychology." *MAPS Bulletin* 23(1):6–9. Retrieved January 2017 (www.maps.org/news-letters/v23n1/v23n1_p6-9.pdf).

Hartogsohn, Ido. 2017. "Constructing Drug Effects: A History of Set and Setting." *Drug Science, Policy and Law* 3(0):1–17. doi: 10.1177/2050324516683325.

Johnson, Jeremy R., Mary Burnell-Nugent, Dominique Lossignol, Ganae-Motan, Richard Potts, and Marie T. Fallon. 2010. "Multicenter, Double-Blind, Randomized, Placebo-Controlled, Parallel-Group Study of the Efficacy, Safety, and Tolerability of THC:CBD Extract and THC Extract in Patients with Intractable Cancer Related Pain." *Journal of Pain and Symptom Management* 39:167–79.

Laurette, Christian, dir. 2008. *Run from the Cure: The Rick Simpson Story*. (www.youtube.com/watch?v=fQwwGPiyW9M).

Leary, Timothy. 1966. "Programmed Communication During Experiences with DMT." *Psychedelic Review* 8.

Leary, Timothy, Ralph Metzner, and Richard Alpert. 1964. *The Psychedelic Experience: A Manual Based on the Tibetan Book of the Dead.* New York: Citadel Press.

Lewis, Mark A., Ethan B. Russo, and Kevin M. Smith. 2017. Pharmacological Foundations of Cannabis Chemovars. *Planta Medica* 84(4):225–233. doi: 10.1055/s-0043-122240.

London, Jeffrey. 2006. "The Criminalization and Medicalization of Marijuana: A Study of Changing Deviance Designations." Ph.D. Dissertation, Sociology, University of Colorado-Boulder, Boulder, AAT 3212105.

Notcutt, W., R. Langford, P. Davies, S. Ratcliffe, and R. Potts. 2012. "A Placebo-Controlled, Parallel-Group, Randomized Withdrawal Study of Subjects with Symptoms of Spasticity Due to Multiple Sclerosis Who Are Receiving Long-Term Sativex® (Nabiximols)." *Multiple Sclerosis Journal* 18(2):219–28. doi: 10.1177/1352458511419700.

Novotna, A., J. Mares, S. Ratcliffe, I. Novakova, M. Vachova, O. Zapletalova, C. Gasperini, C. Pozzilli, L. Cefaro, G. Comi, P. Rossi, Z. Ambler, Z. Stelmasiak, A. Erdmann, X. Montalban, A. Klimek, P. Davies, and the Sativex Spasticity Study Group. 2011. "A Randomized, Double-Blind, Placebo-Controlled, Parallel-Group, Enriched-Design Study of Nabiximols (Sativex®), as Add-on Therapy, in Subjects with Refractory Spasticity Caused by Multiple Sclerosis." *European Journal of Neurology* 18(9):1122–31. doi: 10.1111/j.1468-1331.2010.03328.x.

O'Brien, Patrick. 2013. "Medical Marijuana and Social Control: Escaping Criminalization and Embracing Medicalization." *Deviant Behavior* 34(6):423–43.

Pedersen, Willy, and Sveinung Sandberg. 2013. "The Medicalisation of Revolt: A Sociological Analysis of Medical Cannabis Users." *Sociology of Health & Illness* 35(1):17–32. doi: 10.1111/j.1467-9566.2012.01476.x.

Portenoy, Russell K., Elena Doina Ganae-Motan, Silvia Allende, Ronald Yanagihara, Lauren Shaiova, Sharon Weinstein, Robert McQuade, Stephen Wright, and Marie T. Fallon. 2012. "Nabiximols for Opioid-Treated Cancer Patients with Poorly-Controlled Chronic Pain: A Randomized, Placebo-Controlled, Graded-Dose Trial." *The Journal of Pain* 13(5):438–49. doi: 10.1016/j.jpain.2012.01.003.

Price, Donald D., Damien G. Finniss, and Fabrizio Benedetti. 2008. "A Comprehensive Review of the Placebo Effect: Recent Advances and Current Thought." *Annual Review of Psychology* 59. doi: 10.1146/annurev.psych.59.113006.095941.

Russo, Ethan B. 2011. "Taming THC: Potential Cannabis Synergy and Phytocannabinoid-Terpenoid Entourage Effects." *British Journal of Pharmacology* 163(7):1344–64. doi: 10.1111/j.1476-5381.2011.01238.x.

Russo, Ethan B. and Jahan Marcu. 2017. "Cannabis Pharmacology: The Usual Suspects and a Few Promising Leads." In *Advances in Pharmacology, Volume 80,* edited by David Kendall and Stephen P.H. Alexander, 67-134. Amsterdam, The Netherlands: Academic Press. http://dx.doi.org/10.1016/bs.apha.2017.03.004.

Simpson, Rick. 2014. "Phoenix Tears.Ca." Retrieved June 5, 2017 (http://phoenixtears.ca/).

Wade, Derick T., Christine Collin, Colin Stott, and Paul Duncombe. 2010. "Meta-Analysis of the Efficacy and Safety of Sativex (Nabiximols), on Spasticity in People with Multiple Sclerosis." *Multiple Sclerosis Journal* 16(6):707–14. doi: 10.1177/1352458510367462.

Zinberg, Norman E. 1984. *Drug, Set, and Setting.* New Haven, CT: Yale University Press.

# Chapter 6

# Changing the Set
## Creating Medical Routines
## of Cannabis Use

When individuals adopt cannabis as a medicine, their intentions, expectations, and goals are different than those of social users. This shift affects the individual's holistic state, or "set," including psychological, emotional, and physiological dimensions, and this informs how patients determine use regimens. With pharmaceutical prescriptions, routines of use can be mandated by the system—doctor's orders on medication, dose, and timing—but even with prescriptions, those routines are often adapted. Because patients operate from a set informed by their medical condition, they often model medical cannabis use routines on what they know from the use of other medicines and use similar criteria to judge them. Our medically pluralistic environment offers multiple models from which patients can borrow rhetoric and behaviors to establish a cannabis use routine. Patients determine routines of medical cannabis use based largely on considerations grounded in lifeworld concerns, as we discussed in chapter 4, namely, the desire to "live a normal life and meet their social obligations" (Britten 2008).

Patient goals related to health typically must balance quality of life considerations with treatment options and medical advice. This entails managing effects of an illness or condition along with effects of any medicine taken to treat the illness in a way that prioritizes one's ability to function as "normally" as possible in daily life (Britten 2008; Hughner and Kleine 2008). Britten (2008) terms this balance a "minimax" strategy because it seeks to minimize both the symptoms of illness and the side effects of the treatment in order to maximize the ability to function normally. Goals and expectations as they relate to medicine taking constitute a complex influence on the experience of drugs that can be seen as a part of "set and setting."

As described in the previous chapter, set and setting are often grouped together to talk about "extra-drug" effects—that is, the effects of a drug that are variable dependent on external factors. Set and setting have separate definitions but are best understood as intertwined. The immediate, individual conditions of set and setting are shaped within the larger set of social and cultural influences, just as one's personality and belief systems are shaped by the conditions in which one grows up and lives. In this sense, "individual set and setting is always nestled within a greater collective set and setting, which is shaped by the society and culture in which a person lives and develops" (Hartogsohn 2017, 10). The importance of learning from others and "constructing shared knowledge" about how a substance may be used for social or medical purposes has been described by social scientists (Becker 1953; Becker 1973; Zinberg 1984; and Britten 2008). Many patients ask others, seek information in dispensaries, or go to the internet to work out routines for medical cannabis use that suit their particular illness or condition and needs.

Patients often formulate their ingestion method, dosage timing, and frequency of cannabis use to correspond with a minimax strategy and their own preferences, just as many manage prescription pharmaceutical medicines. Each patient learns how to handle the properties of cannabis to manage the "high" flexibly. The high is sometimes treated as a side effect to manage, sometimes as a beneficial effect, and sometimes as a signal indicating that the less obvious medical benefits have been activated. Some patients seek to avoid psychoactive effects entirely to remove any possibility of interference with functioning. Others decide to minimize them when the circumstances warrant but encourage the high when they wish to distract themselves, relax, improve mood, counteract anxiety, induce a creative mood, or enhance a sensory experience. Heavy medical users may claim that they have developed a tolerance such that they no longer experience a high from cannabis at all, and some chronic pain patients report never experiencing intoxicating effects.

## Methods of Ingestion

Arriving at a preferred delivery method often requires some experimentation with methods and products. As patients discussed their concerns about the benefits or harm related to the methods of intake, their medical use mindset was evident. All patients mentioned health considerations as a factor when determining their routines for use. Patients reported judging what works best in terms of effectiveness of medical action, speed of onset of effects, ease of use, ease of concealment, and environmental concerns such as impacts on family, work, or other constraints.

Experimentation with inhaling and eating cannabis, the two most popular forms of ingestion, is common. About two-thirds of the patients in this sample considered smoking or the non-combustion inhalation method called "vaporizing" as their primary method of ingestion. Vaporization is often preferred over smoking because it does not combust plant material and produce smoke laden with potentially hazardous or irritating byproducts. Instead, it heats plant material to the point of releasing the cannabinoid-laden oils in a vapor that can be inhaled without smoke. The remaining one-third of patients reported that they primarily ingest cannabis through edible cannabis products such as infused chocolates and candies, or they alternate between edibles and smoking. Nearly all say they smoke or vaporize at least occasionally.

A handful of patients reported disliking specific methods, or they cited reasons why some methods were not viable based on factors other than medical effectiveness. Andy offers an illustration when he flatly states, "I detest smoke. I detest smoking. Both my parents smoked [tobacco], and I hated it." For this reason, Andy avoids this method, relying primarily on edibles. Beth, a Jehovah's Witness in her sixties, suffers from chronic pain as a result of injuries from a succession of accidents. Her religious beliefs prohibit her from causing intentional harm to her body, and she only uses natural medicine. She accepts cannabis as a helpful herb, which enables her to use it, but she does not smoke it because she views smoking as harmful. Instead, she primarily uses vaporization. On the other end of the spectrum is Ken, who suffered a serious back injury that damaged his spine. Many types of edibles are made with food ingredients that he cannot tolerate.

> I pretty much can only smoke it. I used to be able to eat it, and then for some reason I wasn't able to. I'm thinking that's because of the fat in the brownies and other edibles, because my gall bladder was removed. I'm hoping I can get back to eating it, but for right now, the only way I can use it is to smoke it.

Andy, Beth, and Ken illustrate some of the different constraints on patients' choices around medical cannabis use. Some begin with few limitations but discover strong preferences and aversions through experimentation. Patients often base these evaluations on two criteria. The first criterion is related to the aesthetic experience. Some patients found they really disliked the taste of edibles, for instance, which often carry a distinctive cannabis flavor. The second, more salient criterion, is the perception of control. When patients report that they did not like specific methods, they often attribute it to a lack of predictable results, which mostly arises from difficulties with gauging dosage, a particular challenge with edible modes of delivery. Others liked those same methods because they had learned how to get consistent results. Jason, the GERD patient we heard from first in chapter 3 and again in the previous chapter, represents concerns with delivery modes well. Since he smoked recreationally for years, he is more comfortable with the dosage control he achieves through smoking than with other methods. Of other methods, he says, "I tried candy. It just tasted horrible. They're awful. Then I bought a vaporizer because I heard that it was much better for you. But the vaporizer just. . . . It's way too powerful." Jason's comments exemplify how both aesthetics and control affect patient choices.

For many patients, cost was also a concern. This was an especially important criterion for patients on fixed incomes due to disability or retirement and for those who need to budget due to limitations in their ability to work and earn money. For some, the issue arises because of the quantity of cannabis needed. Smoking is widely considered to be the most cost-effective form of use. Plant material is cheaper to purchase than formulated products or concentrates, and many patients claim that smoking stretches supply the farthest. Vaporization typically delivers only about 80 percent of the available cannabinoids, so it requires more material to produce comparable effects, and the equipment required to use vaporization techniques can be prohibitively expensive. Patients with more expendable income worried less about cost, but even they remarked on how expensive everything was in the early days of the program, a complaint that is common in many of the emerging state medical cannabis programs. Generally speaking, cannabis prices in Colorado have dropped since the industry emerged, and the state is markedly less expensive than even the more loosely regulated California market, but the cost can still be a barrier, as prices continue to reflect the various risks and financial demands of participating in the industry.

### Smoking

Even though smoking is commonly identified among physicians and patients as the riskiest method for cannabis use, it is still the most common in this study and others (O'Connell and Bou-Matar 2007; Ogborne et al. 2000; Swift, Gates, and Dillon 2005). Many patients with significant past recreational use expressed sentimental attachments to smoking cannabis. Patients such as Brett, Dale, Eileen, Karen, Tim, and Jason were among those who said they still liked to smoke, often calling it "traditional" or "old-school" to do so.

While evidence strongly suggests the risks associated with smoking cannabis have been overestimated (ProCon.org 2013; Tashkin 2013), concerns with smoking are a common theme across other medical cannabis patient studies. Smoking is arguably the most illicit, nonmedical "street" form used for many drugs—opium, cocaine, and methamphetamine have all been smoked in their recreational street forms. In addition, the closest analogy is with smoking tobacco, which is now clearly understood to be antithetical to health and is associated with enormous costs to society. One of the contemporary criticisms of medical cannabis offered by those who oppose it, both in and out of government, is that "medicine is not smoked." For these reasons, smoking on the whole seems incompatible with medicine, and in fact, may have significantly contributed to cannabis' stigma.

Even though many patients see smoking as a relevant concern, inhalation methods also have benefits that patients acknowledge. The main benefit of smoking or inhaling is the immediacy of effects. The initial effects of inhaling cannabis can be felt within a matter of fifteen to thirty seconds, with a peak effect coming in fifteen to thirty minutes and total duration of one to two hours (Grotenhermen et al. 2007). This rapid onset provides extremely useful feedback that helps patients actively titrate medical and psychoactive effects. By contrast, edible products can take as much as two to four hours to be fully felt, and the effects produced endure for four to eight hours (Grotenhermen et al. 2007). Additionally, patients with conditions such as migraines, nausea, and epilepsy benefit from a substance that can bypass the digestive system. Some patients also experience edibles as unpredictable or too powerful, producing unwelcome cognitive effects. This is because the digestive metabolic process produces a variant of THC that is far more powerfully psychoactive than the one produced by inhaling it.

Sublingual delivery methods that involve spraying or placing cannabis extracts under the tongue can absorb faster than digestion and avoid its intensifying effect. Among the sublingual options are tinctures. Tinctures were the form in which cannabis medicines were legally produced and marketed by pharmaceutical companies in the U.S. for nearly a century. They can be used by placing a drop under the tongue or in food. Sativex® and Epidiolex® are two cannabis extracts from GW Pharmaceuticals that are used as a tincture, but they are not currently available to patients in the U.S.

Interestingly, Devon and Aaron, who had each suffered from asthma, were the two patients with the fewest concerns about smoking cannabis. Both reported that their asthma stopped in their teen years when they started using cannabis, and never returned. They both attributed this directly to cannabis. Asthma is one of the few conditions for which inhaled medications are used, and this may help to more easily classify cannabis inhalation as legitimate medicine. Indeed, one of the counterintuitive indications for smoking cannabis can be asthma, as among its effects is bronchodilation (Aggarwal et al. 2009; Iversen 2008). These patients were aware of studies that showed cannabis smoking had not been correlated with lung cancer or other respiratory diseases.

Many patients in this study were previous or current tobacco smokers. Cigarette smokers tended to worry less about smoking cannabis. They did not see it as compounding their health risks. Instead, tobacco was seen as riskier, so that was the behavior patients prioritized for change. Some expressed no intention to quit smoking tobacco, so they saw little point in worrying about the dangers of smoking cannabis.

While patients stopped short of seeing smoking as "healthy," especially when compared with other available methods, they often viewed it accurately as less harmful than it has been characterized in popular media and less harmful than smoking tobacco. Those who still engaged in cannabis smoking as a primary method often mitigated risks by using specialized pipes or other devices that lessen the harshness on the throat and lungs as compared to smoking a joint. About a quarter of patients transition from smoking to vaporization, citing it as the healthier option.

### Edibles

About one-third of patients in this study prefer edibles. This was often related to the type of illness or symptoms being treated. Effects from edibles are not as immediate as smoking or vaporizing. Their benefit is in their slow and steady effects, which suits patients who wish to maintain a consistent level of cannabinoids in the system over time, such as chronic pain patients who have difficulty sleeping through the night. However, because the effect is delayed, dosing can present a problem. The slower onset, which also varies depending on the individual's stomach contents, can be misleading, resulting in an often-regrettable decision to take more before the effects are fully felt. By the time the patient realizes they have taken a stronger dose than needed or desired, they generally have a much longer wait for the psychoactive effects to subside than is the case when using inhalation methods. While there are no short-term or long-term health risks to taking an excessive dose, the psychoactive effects can be acutely uncomfortable and may cause naïve individuals to fear they are experiencing a health emergency.

Patients most commonly reported taking edibles in the evening or just before going to bed, so they slept through whatever intoxication or impairment the cannabis might produce. They also worked to achieve a specific milligram level of dosage that produced medical effects—pain control, tremor control, or seizure control—that persisted through the next day without additional intake. In this way, edibles resembled taking a medication once a day before bed and controlled symptoms with minimum disruption of productive daytime hours. Nocturnal edible use is the preferred method for individuals who use particularly large doses, such as cancer patients who use high-potency cannabis oil extracts such as Rick Simpson's Phoenix Tears to target tumor reduction.

Mark is one patient who primarily uses edibles. He tried other methods but found that edibles offered far superior control of his neuropathic pain. When he tried smoking, the effects weren't as enduring. Worsening symptoms caused disruption but so did additional smoking, since the more rapid onset of smoked cannabis can produce spikes in blood THC levels that create an acute "high" feeling, with its mental distractions, short-term memory impairment, and subsequent drowsiness as the effect tapers off. Mark likes edibles because the pain relief he seeks lasts longer and requires fewer interventions throughout the day. Prior to his medical use, Mark did not use cannabis, and even though he does not dislike being high, it is not his primary objective in using cannabis now. He and many other patients treat the high as a side effect to be managed in the course of everyday life. Depending on circumstance, patients flexibly decided when it is a desirable effect—one to emphasize rather than mitigate.

Like Mark, Julie uses edibles, but her doses are heavier, and she combines them with other methods to control restless leg syndrome, a neurological disorder that causes burning pain in the legs and often interferes with sleep. For Julie, taking cannabis at night helped to manage both problems. Because Julie works as a teacher, the ability to treat her disorder at night but function during the day without the need for other prescriptions or additional cannabis helps her to maintain normal routines and fulfill her roles. The drugs Julie had initially been prescribed for her disorder worked to manage her symptoms, but they caused side effects for which her doctor prescribed additional pharmaceuticals. When Julie reached three pharmaceuticals, she decided "no more." She did not want to take that many medications; it seemed like a dangerous spiral to keep adding medications in order to treat side effects from other medications.

Julie's choice to use cannabis as a medicine for her condition serves as a form of harm reduction, since she accurately perceives cannabis to be a much safer treatment for long-term use than the pharmaceutical drugs she has been prescribed. Many other patients, like Julie, also saw cannabis as a way to reduce or replace prescription drugs—something borne out by large-scale survey studies of medical cannabis use that find patients substitute cannabis use for other medications to a significant degree (Bradford and Bradford 2016; Lucas 2012; Reiman 2009). Patients see this as harm reduction based on perceived relative dangers of pharmaceutical drugs versus cannabis, and also as a way to reduce troubling side effects of prescribed medications.

Julie has consistently used recreational cannabis since her teens, but her recreational use patterns and levels of intake did not control her condition. It was only after she tried high-dose edibles, often combined with smoking a modest amount before bed, that cannabis effectively eliminated symptoms and allowed her to maintain an asymptomatic state. Even with high doses of cannabis, she does not worry about overdose or harmful effects during sleep, and she experiences no "hangover" from use in the morning. Like Julie and Mark, many patients benefited from a consistent routine and often only discovered that cannabis could offer significant medical benefits after exploring different intake methods and dosages. Mark and Julie exist on opposite ends of the range of tolerance that people exhibit, but both had to adjust routines to fit their tolerance and optimize their use for medical purposes.

Others such as Anita, the MS patient introduced in a prior chapter, found that their symptoms were not as easily managed by taking one large dose at night but instead responded to small doses spread throughout the day. Anita is currently in remission from MS, an outcome she attributes to her medical use of cannabis, as described in chapter 3. Directly after her MS diagnosis, Anita became overmedicated with prescriptions, which she reports left her living in an unpleasant state of mind with little quality of life or functioning. Anita had to adjust to the fact that her diagnosis meant lifetime management. She realized that the prescription medication was lowering her functionality, rather than improving it, and did not represent a long-term solution. She began to phase out medications one at a time, eventually eliminating every other drug except cannabis. She tried to phase cannabis out as well, but when she did, her symptoms started to return. Of her routine with cannabis use, she says:

> I don't smoke during the day at all. I just don't like feeling any level of high during the day. I like to be completely clearheaded and in control. So, in

the morning I have these little medicinal crackers. I pop three or four of them in the morning. They don't cause me to feel high. They don't cause me to feel intoxicated, but they do have a calming effect. Then at lunch, I will pop another couple of crackers. And then at night, before I go to bed, I either smoke a little or vaporize a little bit before bed because that's when my symptoms are the worst, at night when I'm trying to sleep.

Mark, Julie, and Anita all reported using edibles in various ways—alone, with smoking, at night, or at intervals. While these patients suffer from different conditions, all are managing chronic disorders that require long-term treatment. These three cases also show how patients' decisions about medical cannabis are made in relation to experiences with prescription drugs. While Mark's prescription medications were not causing problems for him, they presented unacceptable long-term risks. Julie's prescriptions worked but caused side effects that cascaded into more pharmaceuticals than she felt comfortable taking. For Anita, the experience was the most dramatic. The prescription drugs for her MS, in combination with the abrupt onset of her disease, brought her life to a complete halt, rendering her unable to fulfill work or family roles over an extended period of time. For her, cannabis turned out to be a path back to a normal life. Now in remission, Anita would be nearly impossible to identify as ill from a casual encounter. Anita transitioned her medical care slowly. She added self-care regimens, including diet and exercise routines, to help manage her disorder, which was tracked objectively by monitoring the brain lesion responsible for the onset of her symptoms. By the end, her treatment was largely based in self-care. This in part reflected a change in her understanding that the problem was not acute but chronic and required approaches that looked at the big picture over the long-term. Other studies on medical cannabis patients found similar patterns among preferred methods (Coomber, Oliver, and Morris 2003; Ogborne et al. 2000; Reinarman et al. 2011; Swift, Gates, and Dillon 2005).

## Amounts and Managing Effects

In contrast to recreational contexts where the goal is often to test the limits of intoxication, nearly all medical consumers report using small, controlled doses—an approach called "microdosing" (Davidson 2017; Robinson 2016; Backes 2014). Most patients worked to minimize the amount they used to the lowest level that resulted in medical effects. Small doses "sub-optimize" the high, often meaning that there was no such intoxicating effect. Microdosing treats the high as an unwanted side effect to minimize while still delivering medicinal benefits. In the last few years, medical cannabis microdosing has become a trending discussion that is influencing cannabis product development.

The minimalist approach to cannabis use aligns with Britten's (2008) account of how patients manage other types of medicines. Prescription drug users often try to reduce medication use to the minimal effective dosage. This approach to medications in general is often supported by physicians and seen as "responsible" because it lowers risk of dependence and minimizes side effects or potential health hazards, as well as costs. Patients also prefer to avoid complicated or demanding regimens. Minimizing interventions can help keep medical routines simple. In addition, medicine takers often have difficulty separating disease or illness symptoms from drug side effects. They tend to experiment, even with drugs that have specific protocols and stern warning labels, tapering on and off medications to see what symptoms return or to distinguish between symptoms and medication side effects (Britten 2008). This experimentation gives patients experiential information that can be useful for adjusting treatment if symptom profiles shift, and cannabis use is no different.

Many patients in this study expressed clear medical strategies that minimized cannabis doses and timed intake to accommodate other activities and maximize role functioning. As noted with edibles, patients who needed strong dosages to control or treat disorders often timed their intake at the end of the day. Many patients who smoked also waited for the evening to take a dose large enough to produce any significant psychoactivity. Across methods, a majority of patients reported this strategy for using cannabis. The reasons given for this are often based on role functioning. Patients view cannabis as best taken after work, parenting, or other activities that require focus were completed. Even though the high is considered a pleasurable effect at times by most, context matters. Patients often work toward routines that give them the most control over effects. Some also opt for cannabis products that emphasize non-psychoactive CBD as a buffer to manage dosing, since intoxication is usually the limiting factor in how much cannabis patients are willing to take.

Patients also adapt to the cognitive effects of cannabis, allowing them to function with little disruption from their cannabis use. This development of tolerance is similar to many prescription medications, where initial side effects such as sleepiness or excitability often subside. The effects become familiar, like background noise that patients learn to integrate into daily life. With cannabis, the tolerance is not limited to physical adaptation many other drugs trigger with chronic use but instead reflects compensatory strategies users develop to maximize functionality (Sewell, Poling, and Sofuoglu 2009).

Patients were more likely to experience psychoactive effects with evening smoking in an "off-duty" context that was associated with unwinding or having fun. A handful of patients compared it with having a glass of wine after dinner. A few with spouses reported private "nightcap" rituals in which their spouse would have a glass of wine while they had a puff of cannabis before bed. Interestingly, many patients did not enjoy alcohol and saw cannabis as a flexible substance that could be used for similar relaxation purposes but with fewer negative effects.

Paul, a retired lawyer who suffered lasting injuries as a college athlete, illustrates how patients' behaviors can range intentionally from the therapeutic minimum to the self-indulgent. As Paul aged, his previous athletic injuries evolved into a severe back condition. He consulted a top back surgeon, who said the spinal stenosis could be corrected, but the fix would only be temporary. He would likely experience chronic pain, gradually lose mobility, and probably be confined to a wheelchair within a decade. Paul sought pain management with his regular doctor, who prescribed Neurontin, but Paul found it to be "like somebody hitting me over the head." Other pharmaceuticals were no better; the effects were just too intense.

Paul had been a regular cannabis user in his teens and still sampled it on occasion when it was available at social gatherings. He liked cannabis, and since it was legal to use medicinally in Colorado, he decided to give it a try for pain management. At first he smoked it, but he eventually found that tinctures work best for him. Around five o'clock every afternoon, Paul takes a dropper-full of a standardized tincture that he purchases through his dispensary.

> I have titrated the dose pretty well, so that amount doesn't make me stupid. I can still function pretty well, and it lasts. It helps me sleep through the night, and the pain relief will last for about 24 hours, pretty close. So, if I take it other than at that time, it's either because the pain is worse— I've been out shoveling snow or something—so then I increase the dose, and sometimes I do get stupid. Sometimes if I'm going out to a concert, I'll have a little extra or take some along.

Paul found a routine that works, and, in many ways, he takes cannabis as he would a prescription drug. Paul chooses when to ingest cannabis at a level that will produce a more pronounced effect for enjoyment as a "treat." As with many patients, he also reports that cannabis is helpful for sleep, which was one of the most common non-qualifying medical purposes for which patients use cannabis. Paul characterizes the high disparagingly as being "stupid." Most of the time he prefers to minimize effects, saying: "I don't want to have pinwheels shooting out of my eyes every day."

Patients also reported many types of dosage management techniques, from the carefully measured capsules employed by Lance, to Gary and Arthur's small measuring spoons, designated to parcel out the day's predetermined dosage of plant material. Women such as Eileen, Karen, and Carmella commonly reported using a small-capacity pipe or vaporizer to limit the plant amount used, accompanied by taking only small "hits" until symptoms were managed. Neil also counted vaporizer puffs and says he did not hold in his breath for medical use, whereas he might increase the size of hits he took and how long he held it in his lungs when he desired a more pronounced recreational effect.

Frank, a retired professor in his late sixties, illustrates the concerns with functional ability and dependence that were present in many patients' descriptions of their use routines. Frank has a flair for the artistic and the entrepreneurial, and since entering retirement has helped to build a small but successful specialty software company. He has advanced-stage cancer and is undergoing chemotherapy treatment. He says that the chemo has aged him in ways that are still challenging to adjust to, though he looks youthful in t-shirt and jeans, energetic even, despite his weathered face. Cancer and chemotherapy are a huge imposition on functioning that has forced Frank to adapt. Because he has already been through a round of chemotherapy, he knows that there are days when he will be highly symptomatic and other days when he will not have any energy. When asked about his routines of cannabis use, he says:

FRANK: It depends on the day. Today is a do-nothing day. . . . That's why I scheduled you today.

INT: So [your use] depends on how you're feeling that day?

FRANK: And what you've got to do, how you're feeling. I mean, some days, you're just going, like, "I don't want to do anything, so I'll just go to the garage [where he smokes cannabis] early." Usually I try to stay [working and not take any cannabis] until three or four o'clock in the afternoon and sort of pick it up then, because that's kind of shut-down time on whatever I could do that day.

Frank's routine attempts to balance the effects of cancer, chemotherapy, and cannabis such that his cannabis use begins earlier on days when chemotherapy has already limited his ability to work or think, and he needs more symptomatic control from increased nausea or exhaustion. He also points out that sometimes it is impossible to separate all the effects clearly:

You don't know whether it's the marijuana or is it the chemo, but I found that chemo brain is really a real side effect. You have a hard time reading, a hard time comprehending. You have a hard time doing a lot of stuff. . . . If you don't make a list every day and get it crossed off, then you will tend to not get a lot of stuff done that needs to be done. I try to get up early in the morning when I'm fresh and make a list of what I'm going to do today, then try to get that done, and then I'll feel like I've had a good day if I can cross a few things off the list.

Difficulty distinguishing the effects of medications and medical conditions is a common issue for many types of illness management (Britten 2008). Frank's description emphasizes the priority patients give to functional ability. In a study of terminally ill medical cannabis patients in California, Chapkis and Webb (2008) found similar reports of cannabis use routines, which were framed in the context of enhancing productivity rather than diminishing it, in contrast to the "amotivational" cannabis stereotype. Many seriously ill patients in Chapkis and Webb's (2008) study of Women's Alliance for Medical Marijuana (WAMM) reported that, far from sapping motivation, cannabis often "enhances one's ability to function in the world." This is consistent with the findings of one of the first medical anthropology studies, which in 1975 reported regular Jamaican users employed cannabis to enhance work productivity (Rubin and Comitas 1975; Sirven and Shafer 2015). Rather than being absolute, cannabis' contribution to or detraction from functioning is a matter of dosing decisions and context.

Frequency of cannabis use is tied to disease or injury symptoms. Not all patients follow the same routines. Some used it occasionally; others were consistent. Just under a third of patients said they took cannabis first thing in the morning and used it in small amounts throughout the day to control symptoms. Others simply took cannabis as needed and did not use it daily. Eileen and Karen, for instance, both suffer migraines. They reported smoking cannabis when they sensed a migraine coming on. Similarly, other patients with conditions that varied in pain level or only involved intermittent symptoms did not form daily use habits but matched use to need. This included use to increase appetite, reduce nausea, or eliminate or reduce other types of pain.

Patient reports suggest that those with more serious progressive conditions, or multiple serious conditions, tend to take medical cannabis more frequently and consistently and enforce their routines with more rigor than those whose conditions produce intermittent symptoms or ones that vary in intensity on any given day, such as chronic pain. When patients treated cannabis as a palliative analgesic used to reduce pain from injuries or surgeries, their use seemed to correspond more closely to forms of self-care, such as taking aspirin, or to CAM routines, which are often driven by patients' perceived needs based on symptoms.

While CAM or self-care can be fluid and driven by the patient's perception of need, many biomedical routines require stricter adherence to be successful. Those with serious progressive conditions used cannabis in a way that more closely mimicked use of pharmaceutical medications, and they were more likely to see cannabis use as not just a palliative avenue to symptom relief but as a way to directly treat or even potentially cure a disease. In these cases, use is less linked to expectations of a pleasant experience or symptom relief. Whether they want to use cannabis or not—and sometimes they say they do not—they use it in the service of a larger health goal. In this way, their cannabis use shared with some biomedical treatments a sense of it being an unpleasant but necessary routine that required adherence.

Ron takes the high-potency cannabis extract Phoenix Tears as his sole treatment for cancer. He has no other form of health care. Ron is relying on cannabis to control the spread of his cancer and to potentially cure it. His decision to follow this protocol is based on considerable scientific research that shows cannabinoids can directly fight cancer. Anti-tumor properties have been demonstrated over two decades with animal models of cancer and cancer lines of all types, including cancers of the breast, bone, liver, stomach, skin, and even the extremely aggressive brain cancers known as gliomas. While human clinical trials are limited to a couple of pilot studies, preclinical research has identified the mechanisms for this action, finding cannabinoids operate on key cell signaling pathways that control the spread and survival of cancer cells (Guzmán et al. 2006; GW Pharmaceuticals 2017). Cannabinoids fight tumors primarily by preventing the cancer cells from metastasizing (antiproliferation) and reprogramming cancerous cells to die off (apoptosis) (Guindon and Hohmann 2011; NCI 2013), as well as selectively cutting off the blood supply to tumors (devascularization) (Velasco, Sánchez, and Guzmán 2016).[1] The therapeutic potential indicated by these research findings is also backed by anecdotal reports from cancer patients.

Ron has conducted research to formulate his routine. At first, he knew almost no one who could help him, but he met a few cannabis specialty physicians who were knowledgeable about the science on cannabis and cancer and knew about Phoenix Tears as a treatment. He occasionally consults with them informally.

> I had a 60 to 70 percent chance to live eight years. The nature of the disease is that when it goes from chronic, whatever that is, to acute, there really isn't anything they can do. They say that they will aggressively treat it. I have cancer in my whole body. How are you going to treat it? I'm treating it at the cellular level [with cannabis]. I'm telling each cancer cell in my body to kill themselves! And without collateral damage from chemotherapy and radiation.

Ron's estimation of cannabis as an effective medicine rests primarily on its ability to help him beat cancer but is enhanced by its relative safety and limited side effects, especially in comparison with chemotherapy, which he calls "poison," and says he would refuse. As he puts it:

RON: I don't have to take something else to counteract what this is doing. There's no harmful things going on in my body as a result of marijuana. Marijuana is benign. It can't hurt you. It can't hurt you! There are experiences that you can have with marijuana that will [he pauses and chuckles, implying a challenge], that you go through when you do the [high level] dosages that I'm doing. You just have to graduate to it. And the level that I have in me, you know, is . . . I can't get down off of the level that I have now, or I start going back into the symptoms, and it's not a very pretty thing to have happen.

INT: Do you have an intense psychoactive effect?

RON: No. I don't even get high anymore. The nature of cannabis, of THC, is the body has dosages that are . . . it's not exactly saturation, but it's like, when it gets to a saturation point, the body itself goes into a chemical reaction that transforms the [THC] from a tetra–delta nine to eleven, and tetra–delta eleven's properties work against the psychotropic effect. You can't get stoned anymore. You can't get stoned.

Ron's claim that he cannot get "high" relies on a relatively sophisticated, pseudo-scientific argument related to his understanding of cannabis' biochemical properties and its transition in the body to a metabolite. This explanation reflects his intensive lay education about his treatment, but much online heath information is inaccurate (Cline and Haynes 2001, 393). It is unclear whether Ron's subjective sense of sobriety would match others' observation of his behavior, and how either of these would correlate to clinical observation of physiological effects or mental functioning, but from a sociological point of view, it harkens back to Becker's (1953) early description of cannabis use and the importance of subjective interpretation to the experience of the high. Chapkis and Webb (2008) and Coomber, Oliver, and Morris (2003) also found a significant minority of patients reported the lessening or complete abatement of the intoxicating effects of cannabis, usually after a few months of consistent dosage. When patients claim to have developed tolerance to dosages that had at first been intoxicating, it is impossible to tease out exactly which parts of this are physiological, interpretive, or rhetorical. Nonetheless, widespread reports of this type, particularly from patients who use cannabis to treat chronic pain, suggest that those who adopt medical behaviors of use in which "the high" is not the top priority or a helpful attribute often learn to mitigate or ignore these effects to a significant degree.

By contrast, recreational users often want to avoid developing a tolerance so they continue to experience the high more profoundly. That may also be true of certain medical users who are treating conditions such as terminal illnesses, anxiety disorders, and others with a psychological component that benefits from euphoric effects. The intoxication effect returns when cannabis use is discontinued for a time and then resumed, while the compensatory strategies for mitigating cannabis intoxication are learned skills similar to riding a bicycle that can be accessed as needed, independent of how recent the experience.

## "Off-Label" Medical Uses

Nearly all patients in this study claimed to use cannabis to also treat conditions other than those for which they were deemed "qualifying" under state law, which in Colorado and other states specifies the documented medical conditions that allow individuals to register for participation in the medical cannabis program. This finding also conforms to other research, both in the general sense that patients in other studies have reported "off-label" uses, and more specifically that patients across studies report using cannabis medically for many of the same non-qualifying conditions (Aggarwal et al. 2012; Chapkis and Webb 2008; Reiman 2007). In Colorado, unapproved uses of medical cannabis include headaches, other types of pain, insomnia, and digestive issues.

The most significant off-label use of cannabis is for the treatment of mental health conditions, especially anger, depression, severe anxiety, attention deficit/hyperactivity disorder (ADHD), bipolar disorder, and post-traumatic stress disorder (PTSD).[2] For patients who use cannabis for mental health, the high may not be classified as a side effect. A mental change is the desired effect when the goal is to lift mood or shift focus, but maintaining function remains a concern. The cannabis use routine in these cases becomes organized around producing the most lucid and least disruptive mental effects that accomplish the desired goals. Varieties can be selected based on these specific effects, and dosage regimens play a role. Since managing PTSD often requires consistent treatment to prevent onset of symptoms, patients with PTSD adopted routines of use that were independent of current symptom status. For others with more episodic bouts of depression, anxiety, or anger, use was not routinized but as-needed. Mental health uses mirrored physical health treatment routines in this respect, albeit with an alternative interpretation of psychoactive effects.

Lance, the young veteran with a traumatic brain injury mentioned in chapter 4, also manages severe PTSD. As a medically retired soldier, Lance retains his appreciation for precision, a quality he applies to his routine. Lance's primary method of ingestion is hash oil capsules. Rather than spending a premium for prepackaged capsules, he buys the hash oil and gelatin caps and then packages the capsules himself at his set dosage. He says:

> I take it in the morning, and I take it at night. Just one pill. They're premeasured out so I know exact dosages. I keep a log of what I've done so I don't make myself sick or give myself diarrhea.

Although Lance has adopted a strict medicalized regimen, even going so far as to take cannabis in a pill form, he is one of only a small group of patients in this study who claims that cannabis has never had a psychoactive effect on him. He does not know for certain why, but he theorizes that it is either due to his traumatic brain injury or perhaps due to other antidepressant prescriptions that he takes. Because Lance never experimented with cannabis recreationally, he has no point of comparison and may have simply not learned to interpret the effects as intoxicating.

While Lance claims to have never experienced psychoactivity from cannabis, Carmella does. Carmella's story began in her early forties. She was working as a stocker in a big department store and noticed a burning pain in her extremities that intensified until she finally decided to see a doctor about it. Carmella claims that when she was prescribed very high doses of Gabapentin, a drug used for some forms of neuralgia and seizures, it induced bipolar disorder, which is now irreversible despite discontinued use of this drug. She had many difficulties after this diagnosis and was ultimately found to qualify for disability by the state. Carmella lives in northern Colorado with her adult daughter, who is also disabled due to a seizure disorder. They are on a very tight budget and have no car. Carmella only recently applied to register with the state after her neurologist recommended cannabis for her. Since her problems began, she has also developed severe anxiety, which limits her mobility. She is still working out her routines for cannabis use, but she has found that it greatly assists with the anxiety problems.

CARMELLA: I had anxiety really bad, and they don't prescribe marijuana for mental illness. But since I had the pain, they could prescribe it for the pain. And it helps with the anxiety.
INT: How much does it help? If you were at a ten, anxiety-wise, how much would it help in controlling that? Does it just lower it a little or take it away?
CARMELLA: It takes it away completely, because I can catch it in my head before I have a panic attack and stop the panic attack. And only because I'm stoned am I thinking that way. You think different when you're stoned.
INT: How do you think differently?
CARMELLA: I'm just more aware of things when I'm stoned, and I'm not so stressed out about what I'm aware of.

During episodes of anxiety, Carmella experiences the high from cannabis as therapeutic, leading to a better state of mind. Rather than attributing the relief from anxiety to cannabis, she sees cannabis as giving her the ability to control or stop the symptoms herself. At a later point in the interview, Carmella says that she used cannabis regularly as a teen before her daughter was born, and her life from that period is filled with good memories. Cannabis, she says, makes her feel like herself as she was back then. The mental state is like a memory of an earlier version of herself, before she suffered from anxiety, and that helps lower her current anxiety.

The "off-label" uses of cannabis described by these patients show one of the problems with legislating medical decision-making. Regulatory approaches that narrowly limit the conditions for which individuals may qualify for participation in state programs can be a barrier to effective treatment for some individuals. Medical practitioners routinely prescribe medications for off-label use, and their willingness to do so for cannabis may be little different, but cannabis recommendations can bring more professional scrutiny than all but opiate prescriptions. Narrow definitions of how and for what cannabis can be used also deny the range of patient experiences that shows how routines of care are necessarily individualized. This need to adapt treatment regimens is also true of many pharmaceutical interventions, but few drugs have such a broad spectrum and range of effects as cannabis. Some of that variability stems from learned interpretative schema that filter patient perceptions, but biology also plays a role. Cannabinoids are not stimulants or depressants that exclusively up-regulate or down-regulate bodily systems. Rather, cannabinoids are modulators whose effects depend on the biological state of the individual. As a result, the effects of cannabis are not just variable from person to person but may change over time for any given patient. This illustrates one of the challenges faced by medical practitioners who may recognize that cannabis offers therapeutic potential for their patients. Doctors cannot manage patient expectations of effects or provide the direction on dosing that is the standard for prescribing pharmaceutical drugs. Putting the decision-making onus on patients who must experiment with products that are of inconsistent potency and composition runs counter to modern medical training. Yet it is not wholly different from the feedback loop between practitioner and patient on efficacy and side effect that marks pharmaceutical use. With cannabis, patient experiences are based on multiple factors: the method, timing, and consistency of intake; the condition from which they suffer; and their sensitivity to the effects. Many patients were able to find an optimal dose in which the high was diminished but the medical benefits were still realized.

## Applying Medical Models Across Drug Types

Cannabis is not the only ostensibly recreational drug that can be medicalized. A small subgroup of patients reported patterns of prior use of other illicit drugs, or current use of alcohol, that revealed a flexible definition of drugs and medicines in which patients may use any substance in ways that conform to therapeutic medical behavior. This phenomenon was also noted by Reiman (2006), who reported that most research on this has interpreted such drug use as a way of treating emotional or psychological pain rather than physical pain or as a type of coping mechanism. However, while an association had been found between other illicit drug taking and unmet mental health needs, this was not true of recreational cannabis use (Reiman 2006). In general, studies have found that those who used alcohol and recreational cannabis at more consistent levels were also more likely to rely on treatments in the popular and informal sectors, including self-medicating with cannabis, than those who did not use alcohol or cannabis recreationally.

Patients described past use of illicit drugs that ranged from none at all to extensive experimentation with every recreational drug they could get their hands on. No one reported current use of illicit drugs, and a majority said that they do not drink. Some patients reported prior dependence problems, which were equally split between recreational drugs and prescribed pharmaceutical drugs. Some patients did not draw clear lines between drugs that conformed to either statutory or medical classifications. Medical *behavior* meant more than medical definitions: Just as people misuse prescription drugs for recreational purposes, occasionally patients reported using illicit drugs in ways that aligned more closely to medical behavior than drug abuse. One such was Arthur.

Arthur is a gay man in his late fifties. He has HIV/AIDS and also suffers from a series of other chronic pain conditions and, arguably, PTSD. Arthur recounts that he enlisted in the Army straight out of high school, a tradition of service that was common among his family members. While in the service, he experienced two vicious rapes by other men in his company, events that in many ways overshadowed the rest of his life. He reported the incidents to his superior, who basically implied that he deserved what he got and did nothing to help him. Arthur said he had dreams about a future career in forestry before that event, but after that, his dreams left him:

> When I went into the military I had a set vision of what I wanted to do . . . but after getting raped in the army, I came out not knowing. I had no sense of direction. I had no self-worth, no self-anything.

For decades, Arthur never told anyone about this, even though it defined many things about his life. He abstained from sex for a long time, and says, "It wasn't until I started doing drugs—especially acid—that allowed me to allow someone else to touch me. I wouldn't let anybody touch me. Even my sister and niece . . . And taking the acid made that all go away."

Arthur says that he spent the next twenty years taking LSD every day. He set a dose and never increased it. When asked if he was hallucinating every day, he says, "No, not at all. The sun was shining—everything was. I was happy." He took it every morning with his coffee "just like a vitamin," and no one in his life was the wiser. Arthur says he did not believe he was addicted to it because he was sure he could stop at any time, but he didn't because of the perceived benefit from using it.

> I didn't want to go back to where I was before, how I felt before. Th[e LSD] was keeping me from being there. I had times in my dreams, they [the men who raped him] were there. But it kept me from thinking about it all the time. It kept me from not letting myself feel it. It wasn't until [a few years ago] that I finally . . . it just all came out [about the rape]. Because I hadn't let it come out before that. I just . . . couldn't do it. So, I stopped taking LSD, and then [two years later], that's when it all came out.

Arthur ended up telling his doctor about his LSD use during an appointment. To Arthur, LSD had allowed him to live with the trauma he experienced, connect with others, and have romantic relationships, something that he felt would not have otherwise been possible. His use lacked the social context that marks much recreational drug use because he took it alone in controlled, consistent doses, and he told no one about his use.

While Arthur's situation may seem remarkable in both the trauma he was attempting to treat and the drug he chose to employ, clinical research dating to the 1960s suggests hallucinogens may have a role in treating a range of severe emotional responses, such as those associated with terminal illness or traumatic experiences (Grob, Danforth, and Chopra 2011; Mithoefer et al. 2011; Mithoefer et al. 2013; Ross et al. 2016). Nor is his therapeutic use of a substance associated with abuse unusual. Others such as Carl and Leo reported using alcohol in combination with Advil or other pain medications to manage severe chronic pain. While Arthur perceived his LSD use as presenting few issues with harm or dependence, Carl, who has major back issues and is in recovery from kidney cancer, knew that his alcohol use was not beneficial for his overall health or for his specific condition.

> I never really drank until all of this started, but then I started drinking quite a bit of whiskey. . . . Lots of stress, you know? And to be able to take your mind out of the loop, so you can actually get some rest and have a little peace of mind, which is kind of hard to say when you're drunk, but it just takes away a lot of stuff. You know you're not supposed to mix pain pills with alcohol, but when the pain is intense enough that you're screaming, you need to do something.

Carl says for a while he drank two or three "strong drinks" of whiskey daily. He knew in the long-term that it was terrible for his remaining kidney, and he acknowledges that it can even present immediate dangers when mixed with pain pills, but the grinding experience of chronic pain can convince individuals to make self-medication choices that doctors and family would not endorse. Carl concedes that he has recently cut back to drinking at most every other day, but he makes a point of saying that he was not a drinker before his health problems, and in his current state, he almost never goes out or drinks with others.

Finally, Carmella, who was introduced earlier in this chapter, reported beginning use of methamphetamine after the pharmaceutical drugs induced mental health problems. Her doctors changed her medications several times, but she was allergic to some drugs, and it took time to find a workable regimen. She was prescribed OxyContin, but she found that it kept her awake and instigated a manic state in which she had difficulty coping. While she has been on many heavy-hitting pharmaceutical drugs, she had only smoked cannabis during her teen years and had not tried it again until very recently when she became a registered patient. A question about drug dependence elicits that methamphetamine was her drug of choice. She quit using meth two years ago but says that she still craves it. Of her meth use, Carmella says:

CARMELLA: That started after the Neurontin made me feel bipolar. Because I started doing meth, and the meth made me feel normal. So, I was self-medicating with the meth.
INT: Did [the meth use] become a problem?
CARMELLA: Yeah, it got out of control. I was getting high for high's sake, and it was out of control.

Although Carmella and her daughter's husband used meth, her daughter did not. Asked how she quit using methamphetamine, Carmella ties it to what happened after one of her parents died.

> I had a total breakdown. I went to see the doctor. And when the doctor came in and asked me how I was doing, I just started crying and telling him how I was doing, because I was falling apart. And he told me to calm down, that I was bipolar. And he said it was because of the meth that I was [bipolar], but I know it was because of the Neurontin, because that made me feel [the bipolar symptoms], and it was first.

Carmella understood that meth was terrible for her health, strongly addictive, and inappropriate as a self-administered medication.[3] However, she also had firsthand experience with the fact that many perfectly legal prescribed drugs also present dangers. She attributes her poor judgment in using meth to altered judgment stemming from her mental health issues. The context of her use, though in her private residence, included others and blurred with a recreational "set and setting." It was the phenomenological experience of being restored to "normal" that led her to use meth and to call that use "self-medication." Carmella still regrets using it in this way because of the toll it has taken on her health and the craving addiction left her with that still requires discipline to resist.

When taken together, these patients show that subjective bodily experiences of both symptoms and drug effects may lead patients to employ coping mechanisms with nonmedical substances that still engage a self-care logic. Biomedicine imposes stringent boundaries between medication and nonmedical substances. Expert knowledge and professional experience is meant to allow physicians to give patients appropriate amounts of drugs and monitor their use such that the substances help to resolve or ameliorate medical conditions without creating additional problems. Patients may engage in a different calculus of risk to reward than medical professionals and give much less heed to a drug's formal status if, at the practical level, it serves a need that has gone unmet.

Regardless of the medical status of a drug, all substances can be used by patients to cope, calling on models of medical behavior to moderate use in the service of coping. The distinction is not that licit drugs are safe and non-addictive while illicit drugs are not. Carmella's claim that a prescription drug is responsible for her devastating long-term condition can be considered in the context of data from the Centers for Disease Control and Prevention (CDC), the Office of Disease Prevention and Health Promotion (ODPHP), and other systematic data collection on the risks of pharmaceutical drugs when used as directed, as well as the work of sociologists such as Donald Light whose work analyzes changes to the pharmaceutical industry in recent decades. Current data reveal that in the U.S., adverse drug reactions account for over one million emergency department visits, 3.5 million physician office visits, and 125,000 hospital admissions each year (ODPHP 2014). Another two million who are already in the hospital experience adverse effects from the use of prescribed drugs, prolonging stays and increasing overall health care costs. That adds up to roughly three million Americans who require medical care each year as the result of taking a medication *as prescribed*. On average, 2,460 people in the U.S. die each week from taking a drug as prescribed, making prescription drugs the fourth leading cause of death in the U.S. (Light, Lexchin, and Darrow 2013; Light 2014). Fatal drug overdoses have increased substantially over the past two decades, with a 23% increase in overdose deaths between 2010 and 2014 (Warner et al. 2014). Overdose deaths connected to prescription opioids have increased five-fold between 1999 and 2016, leading to widespread concerns of an opioid epidemic (CDC 2017). Interestingly, analysis of hospitalization records in twenty-seven states from 1997 to 2014 found that the hospitalization rate for opioid-related problems plummeted by an average of 23 percent in the nine states that implemented medical cannabis programs in that time frame, with overdoses dropping by 13 percent on average. This comports with other research that found the rate of fatal unintentional opioid overdose dropped by an average of 25 percent in states with medical cannabis laws between 1999 and 2010 (Bachhuber et al. 2014).

Many drugs have the potential to be used in medical or nonmedical ways, and, for some drugs, such as opioids, one of the main differences between their licit and illicit forms may be more the user's behaviors than the drug itself. Most drugs have clearer lines between their medical form and their street form than cannabis. The street and medical versions are more separated in appearance and name, to the extent that many people may not recognize them as pharmacologically identical (Hart 2013). Although it may be the rare patient who engages in medical behavior with putatively recreational substances such as alcohol, meth, or LSD, these cases serve to emphasize the importance of patient mindset in their adoption of medical behaviors. This is also an important way in which patients may participate in early stages of medicalization processes, expanding the range of practices and substances that can be formally recognized as therapeutic.

# Notes

1. The preclinical research on the cancer-fighting properties of cannabinoids is compelling and extensive, with more than 1,000 published peer-reviewed studies on the anti-tumor actions of synthetic cannabinoids and natural phytocannabinoids.
2. As discussed earlier in this book, PTSD was added to Colorado's list of qualifying conditions in 2017 by legislative action after multiple petitions to the state health department from veterans and other affected individuals were rejected. PTSD accounts for close to 4 percent of Colorado's registered patients as of January 2018. The list of qualifying conditions can be found the on the Colorado Department of Public Health & Environment (CDPHE) website: https://www.colorado.gov/pacific/cdphe/qualifying-medical-conditions-medical-marijuana-registry.
3. Methamphetamine and related stimulants are sometimes used to treat certain aspects of bipolar illness, particularly resistant depression, iatrogenic sedation, and comorbid attention deficit/hyperactivity disorder (ADHD). ADHD is routinely treated with amphetamines (Adderall) and methamphetamine analogs (Ritalin). These drugs are all classified as medically acceptable Schedule II substances, in contrast to the cannabis classification as too dangerous to use even under medical supervision, though it is a far safer substance by any rational measure. (Hart, Carl. 2016. "Neuroscientist: Meth Is Virtually Identical to Adderall: This Is How I Found Out." *The Influence*. Retrieved June 25, 2016 (http://theinfluence.org/neuroscientist-meth-is-virtually-identical-to-adderall-this-is-how-i-found-out/)).

# References

Aggarwal, Sunil K., Gregory T. Carter, Mark D. Sullivan, Craig ZumBrunnen, Richard Morrill, and Jonathan D. Mayer. 2009. "Medicinal Use of Cannabis in the United States: Historical Perspectives, Current Trends, and Future Directions." *The Journal of Opioid Management* 5(3):153–68.

Aggarwal, Sunil K., Gregory T. Carter, Mark D. Sullivan, Craig ZumBrunnen, Richard Morrill, and Jonathan D. Mayer. 2012. "Prospectively Surveying Health-Related Quality of Life and Symptom Relief in a Lot-Based Sample of Medical Cannabis-Using Patients in Urban Washington State Reveals Managed Chronic Illness and Debility." *American Journal of Hospice and Palliative Medicine* 00(0): 1–9. doi: 10.1177/1049909112454215.

Bachhuber, Marcus A., Brendan Saloner, Chinazo O. Cunningham, and Colleen L. Barry. 2014. "Medical Cannabis Laws and Opioid Analgesic Overdose Mortality in the United States, 1999–2010." *JAMA Internal Medicine* 174(10):1668–73. doi: 10.1001/jamainternmed.2014.4005.

Backes, Michael. 2014. *Cannabis Pharmacy: The Practical Guide to Medical Marijuana*. New York: Black Dog & Leventhal Publishers, Inc.

Becker, Howard S. 1953. "Becoming a Marihuana User." *American Journal of Sociology* 59(3):235–42.

Becker, Howard S. 1973. "Consciousness, Power and Drug Effects." *Society* 10(4): 26–31.

Bradford, Ashley C., and W. David Bradford. 2016. "Medical Marijuana Laws Reduce Prescription Medication Use in Medicare Part D." *Health Affairs* 35(7):1230–6. doi: 10.1377/hlthaff.2015.1661.

Britten, Nicky. 2008. *Medicines and Society: Patients, Professionals and the Dominance of Pharmaceuticals*. New York: Palgrave Macmillan.

CDC, Center for Disease Control and Prevention. 2017. *Prescription Opioid Overdose Data*. U.S. Department of Health & Human Services, last modified August 1, 2017. Retrieved May 13, 2018 (www.cdc.gov/drugoverdose/data/overdose.html).

Chapkis, Wendy, and Richard J. Webb. 2008. *Dying to Get High: Marijuana as Medicine.* New York: New York University Press.

Cline, R.J.W. and K.M. Haynes. 2001. "Consumer Health Information Seeking on the Internet: The State of the Art." *Health Education Research* 16(6):671–692.

Coomber, Ross, Michael Oliver, and Craig Morris. 2003. "Using Cannabis Therapeutically in the UK: A Qualitative Analysis." *Journal of Drug Issues* 33(2):325–56.

Davidson,Sara. 2017. "Why Microdosing Is Taking over Medical Marijuana." *Rolling Stone.* April 20, 2017. (https://www.rollingstone.com/culture/features/why-microdosing-is-taking-over-medical-marijuana-w477381).

Grob, Charles S., Alicia L. Danforth, and Gurpreet S. Chopra. 2011. "Pilot Study of Psilocybin Treatment for Anxiety in Patients with Advanced-Stage Cancer." *Archives of General Psychiatry* 68(1):71–8.

Grotenhermen, Franjo, Gero Leson, Günter Berghaus, Olaf H. Drummer, Hans-Peter Krüger, Marie Longo, Herbert Moskowitz, Bud Perrine, Jan Ramaekers, Alison Smiley, and Rob Tunbridge. 2007. "Developing Limits for Driving under Cannabis," *Addiction* 102(12):1910–7.

Guindon, Josée, and Andrea Hohmann. 2011. "The Endocannabinoid System and Cancer: Therapeutic Implication." *British Journal of Clinical Pharmacology* 163:1447–63.

Guzmán, M., M. J. Duarte, C. Blázquez, J. Ravina, M. C. Rosa, I. Galve-Roperh, C. Sánchez, G. Velasco, and L. González-Feria. 2006. "A Pilot Clinical Study of Delta-9-Tetrahydrocannabinol in Patients with Recurrent Glioblastoma Multiforme." *British Journal of Cancer* 95:197. doi: 10.1038/sj.bjc.6603236.

GW Pharmaceuticals. 2017. "GW Pharmaceuticals Achieves Positive Results in Phase 2 Proof of Concept Study in Glioma," news release, February 7, 2017, (https://www.gwpharm.com/about-us/news/gw-pharmaceuticals-achieves-positive-results-phase-2-proof-concept-study-glioma).

Hart, Carl. 2013. *High Price: A Neuroscientist's Journey of Self-Discovery That Challenges Everything You Think You Know about Drugs and Society.* New York: Harper Perennial.

Hart, Carl. 2016. "Neuroscientist: Meth Is Virtually Identical to Adderall: This Is How I Found Out." *The Influence.* Retrieved June 25, 2016 (http://theinfluence.org/neuroscientist-meth-is-virtually-identical-to-adderall-this-is-how-i-found-out/).

Hartogsohn, Ido. 2017. "Constructing Drug Effects: A History of Set and Setting." *Drug Science, Policy and Law* 3:1–17. doi: 10.1177/2050324516683325.

Hughner, Renee Shaw, and Susan Schultz Kleine. 2008. "Variations in Lay Health Theories: Implications for Consumer Health Care Decision Making." *Qualitative Health Research* 18(12):1687–703. doi: 10.1177/1049732308327354.

Iversen, Leslie L. 2008. *The Science of Marijuana.* New York: Oxford University Press.

Light, Donald W. 2014. "New Prescription Drugs: A Major Health Risk with Few Offsetting Advantages." Harvard University, Edmond J. Safra Center for Ethics, Blog June 27, 2014, (https://ethics.harvard.edu/blog/new-prescription-drugs-major-health-risk-few-offsetting-advantages).

Light, Donald, Joel Lexchin, and Jonathan J. Darrow. 2013. Institutional Corruption of Pharmaceuticals and the Myth of Safe and Effective Drugs." *Journal of Law, Medicine, and Ethics* 14(3):590–610.

Lucas, Philippe. 2012. "Cannabis as an Adjunct to or Substitute for Opiates in the Treatment of Chronic Pain." *Journal of Psychoactive Drugs* 44(2):125–33. doi: 10.1080/02791072.2012.684624.

Mithoefer, Michael C., Mark T. Wagner, Ann T. Mithoefer, Lisa Jerome, and Rick Doblin. 2011. "The Safety and Efficacy of ±3,4-Methylenedioxymethamphetamine-

Assisted Psychotherapy in Subjects with Chronic, Treatment-Resistant Posttraumatic Stress Disorder: The First Randomized Controlled Pilot Study." *Journal of Psychopharmacology* 25(4):439–52. doi: 10.1177/0269881110378371.

Mithoefer, Michael C., Mark T. Wagner, Ann T. Mithoefer, Lisa Jerome, Scott F. Martin, Berra Yazar-Klosinski, Yvonne Michel, Timothy D. Brewerton, and Rick Doblin. 2013. "Durability of Improvement in Post-Traumatic Stress Disorder Symptoms and Absence of Harmful Effects or Drug Dependency after 3,4-Methylenedioxymethamphetamine-Assisted Psychotherapy: A Prospective Long-Term Follow-up Study." *Journal of Psychopharmacology* 27(1):28–39. doi: 10.1177/0269881112456611.

National Cancer Institute. 2013. *Cannabis and Cannabinoids*. Washington, DC: National Institutes of Health. Retrieved February 10, 2013 (https://www.cancer.gov/about-cancer/treatment/cam/hp/cannabis-pdq).

O'Connell, Thomas J., and Ché B. Bou-Matar. 2007. "Long-Term Marijuana Users Seeking Medical Cannabis in California (2001–2007): Demographics, Social Characteristics, Patterns of Cannabis and Other Drug Use of 4117 Applicants." *Harm Reduction Journal* 4:16. doi: 10.1186/1477-7517-4-16.

ODPHP, Office of Disease Prevention and Health Promotion. 2014. *National Action Plan for Adverse Drug Event Prevention*. Washington, DC: U.S. Department of Health and Human Services. (https://health.gov/hcq/ade.asp).

Ogborne, Alan C., Reginald G. Smart, Timothy Weber, and Carol Birchmore-Timney. 2000. "Who Is Using Cannabis as a Medicine and Why: An Exploratory Study." *Journal of Psychoactive Drugs* 32(4):435–43.

ProCon.org. 2013. "Does the Regular Smoking of Marijuana Cause Lung Cancer or in Any Way Permanently Injure the Lungs?" (http://medicalmarijuana.procon.org/view.answers.php?questionID=000234#answer-id-001033).

Reiman, Amanda. 2006. "Cannabis Care: Medical Marijuana Facilities as Health Service Providers." Ph.D. Dissertation, Social Welfare, University of California, Berkeley.

Reiman, Amanda. 2007. "Medical Cannabis Patients: Patient Profiles and Health Care Utilization Patterns." *Complementary Health Practice Review* 12(1):31–50. doi: 10.1177/1533210107301834.

Reiman, Amanda. 2009. "Cannabis as a Substitute for Alcohol and Other Drugs." *Harm Reduction Journal* 6(35). doi: 10.1186/1477-7517-6-35f.

Reinarman, Craig, Helen Nunberg, Fran Lanthier, and Tom Heddleston. 2011. "Who Are Medical Marijuana Patients? Population Characteristics from Nine California Assessment Clinics." *Journal of Psychoactive Drugs* 43(2):128–35. doi: 10.1080/02791072.2011.587700.

Robinson, Melia. 2016. "'Microdosing' Is the Future of Marijuana." *Business Insider*, October 17.

Ross, Stephen, Anthony Bossis, Jeffrey Guss, Gabrielle Agin-Liebes, Tara Malone, Barry Cohen, Sarah E. Mennenga, Alexander Belser, Krystallia Kalliontzi, James Babb, Zhe Su, Patricia Corby, and Brian L. Schmidt. 2016. "Rapid and Sustained Symptom Reduction Following Psilocybin Treatment for Anxiety and Depression in Patients with Life-Threatening Cancer: A Randomized Controlled Trial." *Journal of Psychopharmacology* 30(12):1165–80. doi: 10.1177/0269881116675512.

Rubin, Vera, and Lambros Comitas. 1975. *Ganja in Jamaica: A Medical Anthropological Study of Chronic Marihuana Use*. Scotch Plains, NJ: Mouton De Gruyter/MacFarland.

Sewell, R. Andrew, James Poling, and Mehmet Sofuoglu. 2009. "The Effect of Cannabis Compared with Alcohol on Driving." *The American Journal on Addictions* 18(3):185–93.

Sirven, Joseph, and Patricia O. Shafer. 2015. "Medical Marijuana and Epilepsy". Retrieved January 7, 2017. (www.epilepsy.com/learn/treating-seizures-and-epilepsy/other-treatment-approaches/medical-marijuana-and-epilepsy).

Swift, Wendy, Peter Gates, and Paul Dillon. 2005. "Survey of Australians Using Cannabis for Medical Purposes." *Harm Reduction Journal* 2(1):18. doi: 10.1186/1477-7517-2-18.

Tashkin, Donald P. 2013. "Effects of Marijuana Smoking on the Lung." *Annals of the American Thoracic Society* 10(3):239–47.

Velasco, G., C. Sánchez, and M. Guzmán. 2016. "Anticancer Mechanisms of Cannabinoids." *Current Oncology* 23(Suppl. 2):S23–S32. doi: http://doi.org/10.3747/co.23.3080.

Warner, Margaret, James P. Trinidad, Brgham A. Bastian, Arialdi M. Miniño, and Holly Hedegaard. 2014. "Drugs Most Frequently Involved in Drug Overdose Deaths: United States, 2010–2014." *National Vital Statistics Reports* 65(10):1–15.

Zinberg, Norman E. 1984. *Drug, Set, and Setting.* New Haven, CT: Yale University Press.

# Chapter 7

# The Power of Place
## Changes to Setting

The third category that defines the effects of a drug is setting. Setting is intimately connected to the "set" of the individual, and how it is changed when individuals adopt routines of use to reflect medical goals. Much like set, setting can be thought of in both an immediate sense of physical location—a hospital, a nightclub, a hike in the woods—and a larger contextual sense of one's location within a patchwork of immediate and enduring social elements— things such as the drug laws, the role of police, media coverage, and the social dynamics that come to bear on the current experience. Because medical cannabis patients themselves are largely responsible for devising their own medical use routines, the immediate setting in which cannabis use takes place is an important cue that often distinguishes recreational and medical uses. Perhaps one of the biggest differences or shifts in use routines is the greater likelihood that individuals will use cannabis when they are alone, rather than in a social context or other settings that may be construed as "recreational." For most patients, this one criterion serves as a simple heuristic to explain the difference between medical and nonmedical uses, as we'll hear in this chapter. But it is not the only one.

We also propose that the life course illuminates important aspects of the medicalization of cannabis. Age serves as a type of broad, all-encompassing setting in which substance use takes place. Age and life course are related, but life course indicates more than age; this concept captures one's aging in relation to social and historical events. It includes how the experience of events is connected to the age at which they are experienced. Life course also considers how aging is tied to expectations about the roles one will inhabit— student, spouse, parent—in relation to what is normative for each generation and culture. For example, the age of marriage has gradually moved to older ages over each successive generation. In the generation before Baby Boomers, called the Silent Generation, 65 percent of those aged eighteen to thirty-two were married, compared with 48 percent of Baby Boomers. Rates for Generation X were 36 percent, and for Millennials only 26 percent in this age range were married (Pew Research Center 2014). The change in normative marital age exemplifies how our "lives are socially structured" and age matters as a "social phenomenon" (Settersten 2004; ACHI 2005). Life course helps to establish the salience of recreational or medical frames, and it defines the meaning of those frames. Age-appropriate leisure activities shift over different phases within the life course, and cannabis use is no different.

Most of the midlife medical cannabis patients in this study had seminal experiences with recreational cannabis use in their teens, or they decided not to use cannabis recreationally. At midlife, people are generally expected to occupy different social roles than they did in their teens and early adulthood, as seen in some of the patient interviews recounted in earlier chapters. This also means many other aspects of setting have likely changed, possibly including how individuals understand their own identity in the context of their roles, and the experience of their own bodies. Aging creates differences in how much focus is placed on health generally. Such changes offer the individual a new vantage point from which to interpret cannabis use. For patients currently in midlife, attitudes about cannabis are often grounded in experiences and cultural ideas that were prominent during their teens and early twenties. In what follows, we consider how the setting immediately surrounding cannabis use becomes defined as medical. Then we expand to look at the larger change of setting related to life course that affects the decision-making, attitudes, and perceptions of patients in midlife.

## Using Cannabis Alone

Medical routines of use change the setting by largely shifting normative expectations of cannabis use from a group activity to an individual one. Aaron, a cannabis user since his early teens, is now in his early thirties. Aaron says he went through a phase of heavy cannabis use when he was young, then effortlessly transitioned into a casual cycle of cannabis use over his adult life. As a recreational user, Aaron would go through periods when he would smoke cannabis a few times a week and then segue almost accidentally into six months where he didn't consume any cannabis at all. In 2005, Aaron was in a serious car accident that left him with chronic pain from back and neck injuries. After this accident, he noticed that he had started using cannabis more often, in part because he just felt better when he did—it lowered his pain, put him in a better mood, and improved his sleep. In 2008, Aaron sought a formal medical recommendation and became a patient within Colorado's system. Despite his significant history of recreational use, he says, "I never even smoked alone before I got my card."

Medical uses of cannabis are regularly attributed to the setting, which is tightly connected to the motivation or purpose for taking it. While most patients report recreational cannabis use as a social activity among friends, often becoming more and more associated with special occasions as they aged and social use was less common, patients typically engage in medical cannabis use by themselves. This one factor—the presence or absence of another person—is often used by patients to differentiate recreational cannabis use from medical use. Ingesting cannabis alone, often timed around other role requirements such as work, parenting, driving, or simply daytime productivity, helped to define use as intended for "treatment," rather than having a "treat." It was when patients departed from their established routine of medical use, especially when this involved using it with others, that setting most clearly marked whether use was medical or not.

## Setting and the Distinction Between Medical and Recreational Uses

Cannabis use, writ large, has medical and recreational manifestations. At the institutional level, these differences have important consequences for how cannabis is researched, what products are developed, and where cannabis appears in society. At the level of the individual and each specific instance of use, the boundaries between medical and recreational use—between feeling better and feeling good—can blur and break down. Once patients understand use as being not harmful, maybe even healthful, the awareness of negligible risk often carries across all uses, regardless of the purpose. Similarly, even when cannabis use is to mitigate chronic pain or other serious symptoms, there is no clear line that can distinguish between surcease of pain and simple pleasure: Few joys are as pure or profound as relief from suffering.

Some patients define recreational use as any deviation from routine or any increase in dosage meant to enhance the psychoactive effects. However, because medical cannabis use routines are self-determined, decisions about use are often made and viewed flexibly. Many patients identify whether any specific use of cannabis is recreational or medical based on the setting or other contextual cues. When asked to explain the difference between medical and recreational uses, patients would say things like "recreational is something you do with friends" or make reference to social activities such as use before attending concerts or going to the movies.

Patients were not homogenous in how they drew the boundaries for medical and recreational use. Some made few contextual distinctions. Gary, for instance, keeps it simple: "To me, the only difference between a recreational user and one that uses it for medicine would be that they have a medical condition, whatever that may be, that they would benefit from it." Gary's definition is disconnected from context, dosage, and all distinctions but patient status. If someone has a medical condition, their use is medical, with no qualifications on how, where, or when it is used. In his view, no medical condition, no medical use; but if the person has a medical condition, it confers the mantle of medical legitimacy for that person, regardless of the context in which it is taken. Gary's youthful use had been in a social context, but decades later, his current social circles do not use cannabis, providing less readily available examples that might cause him to qualify his definition.

This type of context-free definition was more common among patients who, like Gary, were contending with serious, ongoing, or progressive diseases.

In the presence of serious illness, *all* use is medical, even in social contexts. Often in such cases, the "patient" role claims a much larger part of the person's lifeworld and interferes with role functioning in many ways, often profoundly so. Individuals in these circumstances have to adapt to new limitations, which sometimes remove roles, or significantly revise expectations about what one can do or how much one can do on any given day. When illness affects all facets of life and the patient role is hard or impossible to escape, it is easy for both the patient and observers to interpret cannabis use across all circumstances as medical.

Many patients in middle age with serious disorders were unlikely to maintain a social life that included scenarios where use was purely social, without any medical overtones. For instance, Arthur, the therapeutic LSD user, suffers from multiple conditions, including HIV/AIDS. In addition to his medicalized LSD use, Arthur claims to have indulged in his fair share of substances for recreational purposes over the years. Yet when asked if any of his current cannabis use is recreational, he says no.

INT: How would you decide that it is or isn't?
ARTHUR: Because I'm not using it to get high. I'm not sitting here constantly smoking. It's like two or three hits and I'm fine for hours. So, for me, that's what it's for. I don't need to constantly smoke it. It's not recreation for me. It's more medicinal.

When Arthur is asked if he ever uses cannabis in social settings or with other people, he says he does use it with his neighbors, but he lives in a subsidized apartment building where his neighbors are also on disability due to serious health conditions.

My neighbors, we get together, and we all smoke together because smoking by yourself, you tend to smoke more than you need. When you're with a group of people, everybody's having a good time. We're all there for the same reason. We need to eat, you know? We want to eat, so we've got to give ourselves the "munchies." So, being that the three of us are poor and, you know, being hippies—what do hippies do? You *share* when one doesn't have one and the other one does. So, we all get together, and we share.

For Arthur, social smoking was simply collective medical use. It took place among others who were using for medical purposes, so, in his thinking, the use remained medical even though it included an overlay of social enjoyment because the socializing is predicated on the common routine of care for serious medical conditions. None of them would be there absent their medical condition, and the purpose of getting together and using cannabis was not socializing but treatment. In this context, the social aspect of cannabis use is more like carpooling to chemo than hosting a party.

For Arthur and many other people in this type of circumstance, state rules about qualifying conditions were irrelevant to their judgment of legitimacy. They would note that a person had a condition that could benefit from cannabis use, but they were often unconcerned with the other person's status as an "official" patient with the state, especially among people in their regular social circles. As seen from the lifeworld perspective of patients, system distinctions that offer uneven access or treat differently people who have similarly "valid" reasons to seek cannabis as a treatment often come to seem so arbitrary they would be ridiculous if applied to friends or family. If a person accepts that cannabis use can be medical, and someone has a medical condition that may benefit from use, that overrides the "rules" on qualifying conditions, which are often seen as an improper fit with medical reality. The political bureaucracy of access has not caught up to the reality of people's experiences of the plant's broad efficacy and relative safety.

In fact, once patients accept that cannabis is a medicine, some adopt the view of medical cannabis pioneer Dennis Peron that "all use is medical"— meaning not just their use but that of all cannabis consumers. A subset of patients proposed that many recreational users are inadvertent or unconscious medical users who just don't yet recognize the underlying utility of their attraction to cannabis. This view of chronic cannabis users as unwitting patients was shared by Tom O'Connell, M.D., whose late-career turn to specialty cannabis practice led him to gather intake questionnaires from more than 7,000 Californians who sought recommendations from him. Dr. O'Connell claimed to have identified a pattern of undiagnosed Attention Deficit Disorder and childhood trauma among otherwise healthy young men who approached him for recommendations. The pattern was so consistent he became convinced that their cannabis use that began as adolescents was self-treatment, but they preferred to be seen as cheating the system than accept the stigma that came with admitting to having a disorder (O'Connell and Bou-Matar 2007).

The "all use is medical" definition of cannabis use that prioritizes biological effects accepts that cannabis as a substance is a medicine, and its ingestion, regardless of circumstance, has physiological effects that are medicinal in nature. The similarity between the cannabinoids produced by the cannabis plant and those produced by the body's endogenous cannabinoid system (ECS) to regulate immune function and other critical biological systems lend credence to that view. Cannabinoid deficiency syndrome has been proposed as an explanation for certain autoimmune disorders, so a predilection for the phytocannabinoids produced by the plant may well be an indicator of imbalance in the body's ECS, whatever the underlying source of the dysfunction (Russo 2004; Russo 2016).

Other patients took less of a blanket classification approach to defining what constitutes legitimate medical use and made more distinctions in social circumstances. When patients were using cannabis as a tool for symptom control rather than an overall strategy for disease management, they were more likely to make distinctions as to when their own use was medical. In situations where pain or other symptoms threaten to be disruptive to their other plans, patients may feel conflicted about whether taking cannabis will be less or more of an interference. They often wish they could get the medical benefit without any psychoactive effect, at least some of the time. Travis, for instance, uses cannabis to prevent seizures, but he also relies on it to help with appetite and depression issues. Travis receives disability and does not work but is the main custodial parent of his two middle school–age daughters. The parent role demands that he exert careful management over his routines in order to be the type of parent he wishes to be. As much as he needs to control his cannabis use to be functional, it is at least as important to prevent seizures, which frighten and traumatize his children. For obvious reasons, Travis sometimes wishes that the medical benefit came without other effects:

> There's times when I don't even want to be high, but I have to smoke to get that appetite back, or to get that depression gone, or to get that anxiety away, to get that scared feeling of just like, I'm going to have a seizure. To let my girls know that I'm on it just so that they feel relaxed that I'm not going to have a seizure. It's treated like medicine now.

Travis strikes a careful balance and keeps copious records to help him titrate his dosages and maximize his ability to fulfill his role as a parent. He does not use cannabis around his children and is not casual about recreational cannabis use. Due to the seriousness of his condition, as well as the seriousness with which he treats his role as a parent, Travis says he no longer hangs out with friends using cannabis. He uses his selected medicinal cannabis products only and does not wish to try other kinds. He sees all of his use as medical, and the rigorous regimen he has developed reflects that.

Most patients found they enjoyed the high so long as it didn't interfere with accomplishing goals, and some learned to see that as a "treat" at times, not just a treatment. However, this "recreational" use aimed at enhancing wellbeing often does not look like risky use or anything that could be considered "partying." At times, the circumstances and mechanics of recreational use differ very little from medical use, save the patient's own sense of why they are using it. Is it being used to reduce pain or to enhance pleasure? Even when patients confront this question, they may find it difficult to split hairs, since the two are often inextricably linked. Indeed, the two experiences may stem from a similar biochemical cascade.

Patients medical use can also extend into contexts they understand as recreational. Paul, the retired lawyer, uses cannabis tincture to control back and leg pain by following a routine in which he takes a specific amount each afternoon. He mentioned that he would increase the dose if he was experiencing more pain than usual—still a medically oriented decision. However, he had times when he called his use "recreational," and this was almost entirely characterized by increasing dosage to enjoy a social event or enhance sensory pleasure, not in response to stronger symptoms. In a context where he planned to engage in a different activity, he would not appreciate "getting stupid," as he calls it, because it would make that activity harder to accomplish. For Paul, cannabis use would be a necessary part of any of these activities to control his symptoms, but context dictates dose.

Beth, a chronic pain patient in her sixties, offers another example of when medical use and recreational use blur. When Beth is asked if any of her use is recreational, she says:

> I'm kind of back-and-forth with that. While I would like to be able to tell you that I only medicate when I hurt, I can also tell you that at my age, you pretty much hurt most of the time. So, I could always in reality tell you, "Yes, I take it for pain, and that's the only reason." But I'll choose to relieve my pain like fifteen minutes before *Frasier* comes on [starts laughing], because what do they say about laughter? It's the *best* medicine!

Not everyone felt it was necessary to make firm distinctions between recreational and medical uses in their own personal behavior. Dale described the issue as less of an "either/or" situation and more a case of "both/and." When asked about recreational and medical use, Dale says:

> Well, actually I'm using it. I'm doing both now [generally speaking] because recreationally, as I said, I don't drink. So, I just smoke it to be sociable or whatever, and, I do it medically because it helps. It really does help.

In Paul and Dale's case, a recreational aspect was an added benefit that could be accessed when it was desirable to do so, but it was not necessarily at odds with their medical use. Rather, it was a way to incentivize or extend treatment to also include a "treat," but only as the occasion warranted. In everyday life, productivity ranked over indulgence with few exceptions, and many patients were clear that they didn't want to be high most of the time. To be a treat, it has to be special, not constant.

Mike's sense of ambiguity about this captures many other reactions as well:

> It's really hard to classify the difference. . . . I don't know. I really don't know. Because I use it all the time. I don't know. If you're using it to

expand your mood, and the doctor would have you on mood enhancers anyway, am I using it medicinally or recreationally?

Mike's point raises some interesting interpretive problems that may help to explain why the medical/recreational line is at times blurry. If an individual substitutes cannabis for another medication, whether prescribed or potentially prescribed, does that make it medical use? Is medical use limited to the state-defined reasons for use as directed by a physician? Since competing definitions of qualifying conditions exist, is use for PTSD only "medical" once a state that acknowledges that use, or only if the person has a formal diagnosis? This question is far from hypothetical. In just the first six months since Colorado added PTSD to its qualifying condition list, those with the disorder became more than 3.5 percent of those registered. How is their cannabis use prior to June 2017 to be classified?

In the lifeworld, official designations may create difficulties in categorizing uses appropriately, but this is in part because the categories themselves do not capture patient behavior very accurately. Nor do they capture effects. These questions sidestep the issue of tolerance. If cannabis use does not create a "high," can it be recreational? In truth, consistent use of cannabis, even at low levels, often results in gaining a sense of familiarity with its effects that mitigates impairment. Patients learn to navigate the mental effects without experiencing the high as a functional barrier, leading some to claim they cease to get high altogether. For a few patients, the distinction between recreational and medical was personally meaningless because the patient either did not experience the high or had developed such a tolerance through medical use that a recreational "high" was unlikely. It was easy for these patients to credibly claim that all their use was medical. While routines of use seem to affect how recreational use is attributed, it is likely that individual patients had different pre-existing opinions about cannabis as a medicine and whether recreational use is acceptable.

Some patients come to interpret intoxicating effects as an indicator that cannabis is "working" therapeutically. This is consistent with how the effectiveness of other medications are judged. Managing medication has been shown to differ based on a patient's sense of what their body is telling them. In the literature on medical adherence, patients tend to adapt pharmaceutical use based on experiential cues, largely based on symptoms and their cessation. This is why the "high" in the context of medical use may come to serve as a cue of effectiveness. While no patients directly interpreted their medical cannabis use in this way, many made comments about "listening to your body" to make determinations of dosage.

Yvonne's comments about using CBD may help to point to the way the discernible effects from the cannabis "high" come to be valued information. Yvonne tried using capsules that were formulated to be rich in

CBD (cannabidiol), the non-psychoactive constituent of the cannabis plant touted for having medicinal properties without the high. Of her experience, Yvonne says:

> I spent thirty dollars on those [CBD pills], and I didn't see anything from that. I didn't get any relief. But now I'm reading this magazine that says you have to take CBDs over a period of time. So, I'm going to try it again and take it over time, keep taking it, and see if that helps.

Many medications share the lack of immediate effects that Yvonne reports with CBD. By contrast, the immediate feedback Yvonne receives from whole-plant cannabis in terms of both the "high" sensation and the immediate reduction of pain or other symptoms may become conflated such that the high becomes a signal that cannabis is having an effect. The patient develops an interoceptive awareness and learns to gauge subtle variations in effects to determine the correct dosage amount. This feedback loop of effects allows patients to exert control over dosing decisions that cannot be managed by someone else. This aspect of direct management and feedback through immediate discernible effects reveals medical cannabis use to be radically phenomenological.

Megan, a manager at a patient advocacy organization who worked closely with patients and had previously worked as an associate at a dispensary, said that she had decided to stop using the term "recreational" altogether, opting for terms like "social," or "adult" use instead. When asked why, she said:

> Well, in part because I don't really think that it's the best word to describe what people are doing when they're choosing marijuana socially. . . . I don't know that I've settled necessarily on the best word for it, but "recreational" implies in the minds of many people a lack of consideration, a lack of responsible behavior. And I think that you can use marijuana as an adult responsibly, outside of the medical context and inside of the medical context, and I think that people, individuals, are able to do that. I've seen people use marijuana medically and occasionally do so non-medically, as well—the same individual—and it works for them. I think that's okay. I don't think that there's a problem with that.

Whether the modifier for "use" is "recreational," "social," or simply "adult," the implication is that the setting matters greatly for whether particular effects are being sought solely for enjoyment. When one wishes to carry out work- or family-related tasks, stronger effects from cannabis can be stressful. On the other hand, when the goal is sociability, sensory enjoyment, relaxation, or even sleep, these effects can enhance the experience and even enhance health by supporting stress reduction.

## Age as a Setting

As we've seen, individuals enter medical cannabis use from different starting points. This is determined in part because of differences in use over the life course. Of the forty patients in this study, nearly all had used cannabis recreationally and, of those, almost all had done so primarily during teen or college years. Only two patients never tried cannabis at all; however, another five were practically never-users in that they tried it only once or twice in their early adult years, decided it was not for them, and never engaged in further recreational use prior to becoming medical cannabis users. The prevalence of prior use fits with estimates of lifetime use rates for those thirty and over at between 65 percent and 80 percent. Other studies also found that many patients had tried recreational cannabis use at least once, but the majority were not using cannabis immediately prior to adopting medical use (Hammersly, Jenkins, and Reid 2001; Reinarman et al. 2011).

Aside from the seven individuals who reported little to no recreational use, the remaining patients in this study used cannabis recreationally over a period of time in their teens. Those adolescent experiences are part of those individuals' life courses, which are embedded in and shaped by the times and places in which they occurred (Pavalko and Willson 2011). Each age cohort has a unique experience and recall the same historical events differently, in part based their age at the time the events happened. When recounting cannabis use in their teens and twenties, many patients mentioned how different things were back then. First off, they characterized the 1970s and 1980s as a time when everyone was using cannabis, but the cops weren't busting everyone. As Dale put it, "You've got to realize, I lived through the 80s when doing drugs was cool [he laughs]." This environment of relaxed drug use was still relevant to many patients, who had long held the opinion that cannabis was not dangerous. Many patients in the study who were in their late forties or older claimed at least a tangential connection to "hippies," even if they admitted on further questioning that they were not themselves hippies, but more just proximal to them at a formative age. A small minority of patients, mostly among those who did not use in their teens, said they disliked hippies at that time, but their attitude had mostly softened. Whether this was a function of elapsed time or of their own current cannabis use is hard to say. These patients still did not see themselves as stereotypical cannabis users or identify with them. A few still felt that they did not want to be around people who typified these groups, but that attitude was rare.

Not only did this group hold onto stereotypes of cannabis users, they also often volunteered rebuttals to stereotypes about cannabis that were probably more advertised during their use as young adults than they are now. The clear favorite was the gateway drug theory, mentioned by just under half of all patients interviewed. Any patients who brought it up indicated they thought it lacked any merit. A few based this on their own disinterest in any recreational drugs other than cannabis. However, many had tried other drugs but insisted that this was unrelated to cannabis use, at least as far as they were concerned. Rather, they attributed a willingness to try many things in their youth, including drugs, as more an expression of a curious attitude and a sense of invulnerability that characterized youth. Andy, Karen, Aaron, and a handful of others were willing to consider that there was merit to a gateway theory, but said that the gateway drug was alcohol, not cannabis. Carl said cannabis use was a gateway "to the presidency," but otherwise the theory was wrong. This echoes a message that has circulated widely among activists, who point out the youthful cannabis use of Presidents Obama, Clinton, and George W. Bush.

Mike and Ken, both of whom had used other drugs, said any gateway effect was "all about education," or essentially it was a result of categorizing cannabis as a deviant recreational drug, which led them to see it in the same category as other, harder drugs. Ken, a chronic pain patient, felt that if teens who tried cannabis found that they'd been lied to about its dangers, then they might believe that was the case with other drugs as well. Mike related it to himself with a different message. He said, "The only reason it would be a gateway drug is because the people I went to to get it, I'd get exposed to other drugs that way." Glenn even went so far as to not just reject the notion that cannabis is a gateway drug, but to say he thinks we will end up treating other drug addiction with cannabis. In fact, this substitution effect of cannabis for harder drugs has been found in several studies (Lucas 2012; Reiman 2006). Pioneering medical cannabis physician Tod Mikuriya used it to treat alcoholic patients, and at least one addiction recovery center employs cannabis to treat severe addiction to other drugs (Forster 2017).

About half of the patients in this study had followed an "on-time," normative trajectory for cannabis use, starting in their teens and discontinuing use in their twenties or thirties, often based on life course transitions such as work, school, or becoming a parent. Hathaway found similar patterns among life course and exiting cannabis use (Hathaway, Comeau, and Erickson 2011). When cannabis disappeared from social circles, many patients report not seeking it out. It wasn't a conscious decision; changes to the setting changed use. Women in the sample were especially likely to report stopping use when they had children. Of the nine women interviewed who had children, half reported quitting use of recreational cannabis when they became mothers; two reported quitting before having children, related to college. By contrast, men more often reported discontinuation of use due to work and drug testing. Although the sample is not representative, more men than women in this study reported intermittent and continuous ongoing use over adulthood.

Reintegrating cannabis use at midlife challenged patients' views of on-time use over the life course. As Hammersly, Jenkins, and Reid (2001) note, "cannabis may be more a signifier of the type of social setting than the identity of the participants" (140). Patients expressed concerns with perceptions others might have of their use. In part, they did not want to be subject to stereo-types as "stoners," but it also seems many did not want to be perceived as acting in a way that was deviant with midlife. This was revealed as concerns with being perceived as "responsible," or "mature." These perceptions were interconnected with use patterns and frames fitting with medical use. Many made statements about being in control and being mature or responsible. As an example, Beth states, "If you're completely in control of what you're doing, which means that your desires are not controlling you, absolutely you can regulate yourself with no problem."

Some people interviewed had used cannabis socially more recently and had less concern with stigma because use was normal in their social group. Many of their closest friends and even family already knew they used cannabis occasionally, but their identity and level of use often changed after the medical designation. Patients often verified with their closest relationships that they had their support prior to becoming medical cannabis patients. Interestingly, many had spouses who did not use cannabis medically or recreationally but supported the use of their partners, often because they just wanted the person to feel good, out of pain, or otherwise "normal." There were some exceptions to this. Occasionally spouses were uncomfortable with any cannabis use, and couples adopted a "don't ask, don't tell" policy about it.

Many patients made comparisons with their youthful use in order to draw distinctions from it. At their current stage of life, health concerns had become a more pressing issue than in their youth. Especially among patients in this sample, all of whom had health issues, risk assessments had adjusted since their youthful days. As Backett (1992) points out in her article on lay health moralities among middle-class families, health becomes a part of the lifeworld intimately tied to family and the domestic context: "Over the years, their lives had altered so that supposedly health-damaging behaviors such as excessive drinking and smoking or lack of concern about diet were no longer possible, desirable, or appropriate" (429). For people at midlife, it wasn't that these behaviors were "reproachable" or "unhealthy" in and of themselves, it was that they were "inappropriate" in the current social context. Reaching midlife reconfigures the role of health in making lifestyle determinations, perhaps especially for those who have developed significant chronic illness or experienced injuries with lasting effects. As Carl says:

> You have to regulate yourself. If you have to go to work at seven o'clock in the morning, you can't just sit there and get totally ripped all night long and then expect to be crisp the next day, like we used to when we were in high school. We'd party all damn night, and we were bullet-proof. We're not bulletproof anymore.

The many comments patients in this study made relating to maturity, responsible use, and regulating one's self—in contrast to teen behavior—may act as a form of "normification," defined by Goffman as a way of performing expected behaviors that match the age group setting in order to meet expectations and appear non-deviant. Hathaway, Comeau, and Erickson's (2011) work on stigma and cannabis found that there were two common "normifying" discursive formulations among cannabis users: "narratives of self-restraint and transformation." For the midlife patients in this study who made the transition to medical cannabis use, narratives of restraint and transformation have been at the core of adapting cannabis use to medicine and to midlife. The focus shifts to responsible adult use. This is enabled in part by alterations to the drug form to make consistent dosage easier. Yet, because cannabis use is radically individual and phenomenological, and its responsible medical use is more defined by adaptations to set and setting, integrating it into care is about behaving like an adult and using in responsible amounts at responsible times.

Patients did not define cannabis use in moralistic terms in which medical uses are positive but recreational uses are negative. Many patients who presented themselves as highly principled medical users still felt that there were appropriate ways to use cannabis for fun, relaxation, and enjoyment. Some said that because these "fun" forms of use mitigated stress, they were really more on a continuum with medical use rather than oppositional to it. Patients at midlife felt they were capable of making good choices about this based on their responsibility in other aspects of life, and the experience and judgment they had acquired at midlife.

In this and the previous two chapters, we have argued that neither the pharmacological effects of a drug nor its legal status adequately define that drug's effects. The classic concept of drug, set, and setting has provided a structure by which to analyze the shift to medical cannabis use as much more than simply changing the language from one of "getting high" to "medicating." Medical use changes behaviors and experiences. Because cannabis is incompletely medicalized, patients contribute to medicalization through the adoption of self-imposed behaviors, and these behaviors follow patterns that are seen in other self-care, CAM, and pharmaceutical drug regimens. Patients express a preference for natural solutions, seek to minimize use, and form routines that exert control over functioning in the lifeworld by balancing symptom management with drug effects. Some may actually find the high to be useful feedback that indicates the medicine is working. In addition, patient use of cannabis moves to solo settings that conforms to how other medical substances are typically used. Setting plays a broad role—midlife patients often simply no longer find themselves in the recreational settings common to teens and young adults where social cannabis use is prevalent. It is more normative for those over thirty, when they do engage in social use, to do so in more moderate ways and often in private settings. In its most radical interpretation, medical cannabis use illustrates that a substance is neither medical nor recreational until we decide how to incorporate it into our routines.

## References

ACHI, Association for Community Health Improvement. 2005. *A Community Indicators Report: Selected Stories from the 2004 Community Indicators Conference.* Chicago, IL: Health Research and Educational Trust.

Backett, Kathryn. 1992. "Taboos and Excesses: Lay Health Moralities in Middle Class Families." *Sociology of Health & Illness* 14(2):255–74.

Forster, Katie. 2017. "Medical Marijuana Used to Treat Heroin and Cocaine Addiction at Los Angeles Rehab Centre." *The Independent.* May 22, 2017. (www.independent. co.uk/news/health/medical-marijuana-heroin-cocaine-addiction-treat-los-angeles-rehab-centre-high-sobriety-joe-schrank-a7748626.html).

Hammersly, Richard, Richard Jenkins, and Marie Reid. 2001. "Cannabis Use and Social Identity." *Addiction Research & Theory* 9(2):133–50.

Hathaway, Andrew D., Natalie C. Comeau, and Patricia G. Erickson. 2011. "Cannabis Normalization and Stigma: Contemporary Practices of Moral Regulation." *Criminology and Criminal Justice* 11(5):451–69. doi: 10.1177/1748895811415345.

Lucas, Philippe. 2012. "Cannabis as an Adjunct to or Substitute for Opiates in the Treatment of Chronic Pain." *Journal of Psychoactive Drugs* 44(2):125–33. doi: 10.1080/02791072.2012.684624.

O'Connell, Thomas J., and Ché B. Bou-Matar. 2007. "Long-Term Marijuana Users Seeking Medical Cannabis in California (2001–2007): Demographics, Social Characteristics, Patterns of Cannabis and Other Drug Use of 4117 Applicants." *Harm Reduction Journal* 4:16. doi: 10.1186/1477-7517-4-16.

Pavalko, Eliza K., and Andrea E. Willson. 2011. "Life Course Approaches to Health, Illness, and Healing." Pp. 449–64 in *Handbook of the Sociology of Health, Illness, and Healing*, edited by Bernice A. Pescosolido, Jack K. Martin, J. D. McLeod and Anne Rogers. New York: Springer.

Pew Research Center. 2014. *Millennials in Adulthood: Detached from Institutions, Networked with Friends.* Washington, DC: Pew Research Center.

Reiman, Amanda. 2006. "Cannabis Care: Medical Marijuana Facilities as Health Service Providers." Ph.D. Dissertation, Social Welfare, University of California, Berkeley.

Reinarman, Craig, Helen Nunberg, Fran Lanthier, and Tom Heddleston. 2011. "Who Are Medical Marijuana Patients? Population Characteristics from Nine California Assessment Clinics." *Journal of Psychoactive Drugs* 43(2):128–35. doi: 10.1080/0279 1072.2011.587700.

Russo, Ethan. 2004. "Clinical Endocannabinoid Deficiency (CECD): Can This Concept Explain Therapeutic Benefits of Cannabis in Migraine, Fibromyalgia, Irritable Bowel Syndrome and Other Treatment-Resistant Conditions?" *Neuro Endocrinology Letters* 25(1–2):31–9.

Russo, Ethan. 2016. "Clinical Endocannabinoid Deficiency Reconsidered: Current Research Supports the Theory in Migraine, Fibromyalgia, Irritable Bowel, and Other Treatment-Resistant Syndromes." *Cannabis Cannabinoid Research* 1(1): 154–65. doi: 10.1089/can.2016.0009.

Settersten, Richard A. 2004. "Age Structuring and the Rhythm of the Life Course." Pp. 81–98 in *Handbook of the Life Course*, edited by Jeylan T. Mortimer and Michael J. Shanahan. New York: Kluwer Academic and Plenum Publishers.

# Chapter 8

# Stereotypes, Stigma, and Mitigating Risk

> Name another issue responsible for such barbaric laws that is discussed as a joke by politicians and leaders. There is none. . . . If you were talking about a crime that actually warranted the repressive laws of prohibition, it wouldn't be something you'd be laughing about. Politicians don't joke about arson, rape, murder, robbery, embezzlement. These are truly serious crimes. If a crime is serious enough to have police regularly smash into homes and hold taxpayers at gunpoint, put them in jail, take their kids, take their homes, well, that would not be a laughing matter. . . . These are the most serious things a government can do to its citizens in a society.
>
> (Marc Emery, Canadian cannabis political activist and entrepreneur who was incarcerated in the U.S. between 2010 and 2014 for selling mail-order cannabis seeds to U.S. buyers. (Emery 2011))

Throughout this book, we have asserted that cannabis use has been framed as a single story, one in which all use is lumped together as deviant, problematic, and intended for intoxication. The medical cannabis identity undermines the single story of cannabis and the characterization of its users, challenging a century of propaganda that has justified the criminalization of cannabis users. The harsh criminal penalties and pervasive social stigma historically attached to cannabis use have encouraged most users to hide it. The emergence and growing acceptance of the medical cannabis patient identity has produced modifications to state marijuana laws and changes to federal policies, as described in chapter 2, that have encouraged more Americans to claim the identity. Yet self-identifying continues to entail substantial risks. No matter how compelling the medical necessity of using cannabis may be for any individual, becoming a medical cannabis patient makes that person a federal law breaker subject to a host of life-ruining possibilities. Registering with a state program requires individuals to identify themselves as users of a still largely illicit drug, and supply state agencies with all the evidence needed for everything from criminal prosecution to loss of employment, personal property, professional license, public benefits, and parental rights. These risks make many wonder if it would not be better to remain hidden from the authorities. Cannabis users operating outside a formal system of access that requires registration have that option. Cannabis use is a concealable stigma, also sometimes called an invisible stigma because it is not observable, a quality it shares with other behaviorally based stigmas. The concealable nature of cannabis use is significant because in the eight decades during which cannabis has been illegal, concealment has been crucial to protection from risk. Participating in medical cannabis programs requires patients to do the opposite and identify themselves to state officials who can be compelled to provide patient information to federal prosecutors. This type of legal jeopardy and surveillance is not distinct from stigmatization. As Scambler (2006) points out, "stigmatization is more often than not mixed in with, even secondary to, exploitation and oppression." Stigma is part of a nexus that typically combines the threat of discrediting judgments with other forms of disadvantage in the distribution of power and resources (Link and Phelan 2001; Scambler 2006). This chapter discusses risks that patients face, how they perceive and manage those risks, and decisions to disclose their patient status.

## Identifying with Cannabis: Practical Risks

The media often portrays medical cannabis as a choice made spontaneously and casually, but, as we have seen in prior chapters, there are many steps and deliberations involved. There are also many ongoing practical risks associated with becoming a medical cannabis patient beyond its legal categorization. Growing cannabis or providing it to others increases risk of police interventions. Workplaces are not required to accommodate use, and cannabis is the most likely substance to be detected in an employment-related drug test. In most states, if employers learn of a patients' medical cannabis use, they may choose to enforce rules related to drug use that allow termination. Unless the state has a specific provision protecting employment rights for patients—which few do—the courts have sided with employers who have fired patients, even if the employee was completely compliant with state law, and there was no evidence of cannabis use on the job. In Colorado, an unrelated state law bars employers from firing anyone for conduct away from the workplace that is legal, but even this was not enough for the Colorado Supreme Court, which ruled in a 2015 case that Dish Network had the right to terminate a disabled employee who used medical cannabis in off hours because all marijuana use is still illegal under federal law.[1]

Driving is another contested area for patients. Even though all fifty states and the District of Columbia have driving under the influence (DUI) laws that prohibit operating a motor vehicle while impaired by alcohol or other drugs, including cannabis, many states have proposed or enacted another layer of law specifically pertaining to cannabis and driving (Compton 2017). Fifteen states (of which Colorado is not one) have *per se* laws that consider any detectable trace of cannabis metabolites to be conclusive evidence of impairment for a DUI charge, even though the metabolites can remain in the body for two weeks or more after use, and any psychoactive effects are gone within hours. A 2017 report from the National Highway Traffic Safety Administration (NHTSA) concluded that there is currently no time-dependent, cognitive, or behavioral test that can measure intoxication from cannabis with any acceptable level of accuracy, and states that have adopted *per se* limits "appear to have been based on something other than scientific evidence" (Compton 2017, 28). Additional studies show medical cannabis states experienced immediate reductions in traffic fatalities among those between ages fifteen and forty-four, with additional reductions year by year in those aged twenty-five to forty-four (Anderson and Rees 2013; Santaella-Tenorio et al. 2017). The NHTSA's first large-scale study of crash risk involving drugs other than alcohol found that cannabis use did not correlate to increased risk of accident when controlled for other factors (Compton and Berning 2015). Those other factors, such as concomitant alcohol use, may confound the findings of other analyses, such as one claiming the liberalization of marijuana laws in Colorado and Washington state explain a recent rise in traffic fatalities[2] (Migova 2017). The Colorado State Patrol began experimenting with cannabis use testing devices in 2015 but has not yet found a device or method as efficient for detecting cannabis impairment as the breathalyzer is for alcohol (Garcia 2017; Hernandez 2016).

Family matters also loom large. Many states, including Colorado, have no formal parental rights protections for medical cannabis patients (ASA 2017). According to an attorney who handles many medical cannabis cases in Colorado, Child Protective Services is no longer basing child removal in Colorado solely on cannabis use, but it can be a determining factor. Medical cannabis use can also be raised in child custody hearings during or after divorces, often with devastating effect for the patient parent.

Civil protections for medical cannabis patients are being increasingly recognized as an important aspect of implementing state programs, and patients and activist organizations have focused on these issues in attempts to protect patients from discrimination (ASA 2017). However, as the Americans for Safe Access report on state medical cannabis laws summarizes:

> As of 2017 none of the state laws adopted thus far can be considered ideal from a patient's standpoint. Only a minority of states currently include the entire range of protections and rights that should be afforded to patients under the law, with some lagging far behind others.
>
> (ASA 2017, 15)

The presence of civil regulation on cannabis use is directly connected to and extends the reach of the single story and its portrayal of those who use it. To be under the influence of an illegal substance is to be irresponsible, out of control, and therefore dangerous in the workplace, on the roads, and to your children. It is even considered evidence of such an egregious lack of compliance and disregard for health that in many states a positive drug test for cannabis results in automatic disqualification for an organ transplant. Similarly, the federal Bureau of Alcohol, Tobacco, Firearms, and Explosives bans cannabis users from buying firearms, a prohibition extended to medical cannabis patients by a federal appeals court ruling in 2016, which found that even therapeutic use "raises the risk of irrational or unpredictable behavior with which gun use should not be associated."[3] Such rules about firearms and organ transplants are purportedly to combat problems associated with substance abuse, but by design they focus instead on whether the individual has engaged in any use, for any purpose, at any time. Medical need, even when recognized by the rules of a state program, is often no excuse.

These factors influence patients' choices to disclose use to family, friends, coworkers, or mainstream medical professionals. Patients often become more politically active, but those who feel vulnerable to risk may avoid political activity or any explicit associations with medical cannabis in order to mitigate the threat of losing employment opportunities, parental rights, education access, health care, or other social welfare benefits. Certainly, these factors influence decisions about how and when to use medical cannabis.

## Stereotype, Stigma, and Identity Work

The terms *stereotype* and *stigma* are familiar, but elaborating their meanings and differences may help define what's at stake here. For our purposes, stereotypes are generalizations that circulate at the level of the group or larger culture. This is key. Stereotypes are like memes, they circulate in the "cloud" of human knowledge, and we may know many without knowing exactly how we know them (LeBel 2008). Certainly, we are aware of them even when we don't subscribe to them. It is hard to overestimate the degree to which our cultural learning relies on association. While associations offer a huge cognitive benefit that allows us to build complex knowledge efficiently and helps us understand what is going on around us, it can also lead to unintended biases. Stereotypes are distorted forms of association because they over-specify a trait by assuming all members of a group possess it, and often flatten any other associations so that diversity is obscured (LeBel 2008; Zerubavel 1997).

By contrast, stigma is the devalued characteristic, defined through a process of labeling that takes place at the level of the interaction. Stigmatization is interpersonal, an act that takes place between people, in which associations and stereotypes are applied to a specific person or group. While stereotypes are a part of the cultural lexicon and are changeable just as culture changes, stigmatization is a matter of interpreting norms within a culture and evaluating an individual's or group's fit or lack of fit with those expectations—an interpersonal "activation" of the stereotype (LeBel 2008; Major and O'Brien

2005; Pescosolido and Martin 2015). For this reason, stigmas reflect cultural judgments such as stereotypes, and are shaped and reshaped by culture and social context (Pescosolido and Martin 2015). When stigma "activates" a negative social judgment, it is discrediting to the individual (Goffman 1986 [1963]).

Stigma can apply to various identities, of which cannabis use is only one. Some identities, such as age, gender, race, and invisibility of disability or illness can increase the potential for stigmatization if they fit with the stereotypes of recreational cannabis users. Others, including race, ethnicity, sexual preference, poverty, or low educational levels, can be marginalizing in and of themselves, and may compound the degree to which a patient is subject to negative effects of stigma (Goffman 1986; Hathaway 1997; Hathaway 2004; Looby and Earleywine 2010; Quinn 2005).

Medical cannabis patients vary in the degree to which they may possess other identities that compound stigma or buffer it, but all patients possess at least one other identity that is subject to stigmatization: They each have an illness that qualified for the "patient" designation.

Medical cannabis programs are generally structured such that a legitimate claim to medical cannabis relies on a legitimate claim to an illness. All infirmity can be discrediting, but illnesses vary in the degree to which they are stigmatized. People are increasingly expected to take responsibility for their health or illness, as well as the lifestyle choices that may contribute to health, a topic explored more in chapter 10 (Broom et al. 2014). At least one study has found that attitudes of the general public about medical cannabis use were mediated by the degree to which an illness was stigmatized, combined with the degree to which responsibility for contracting the disease could be seen as due to the individual's personal decisions. When illnesses were seen as attributable to an individual's non-normative life choices, they aroused less sympathy and less support for medical cannabis use (Lewis and Sznitman 2017). Sentiments also vary depending on the seriousness and objectivity of the disease diagnosis. When it comes to patients with serious, objectively determined diagnoses such as cancer, cultural attitudes about medical cannabis use are often strongly sympathetic, as shown in polls of the public and physicians (Adler and Colbert 2013; Doblin and Kleinman 1991; Gillespie 2001). These patients are clearly exempted from being associated with cultural "stoner" stereotypes (Eddy 2010). However, as medical conditions become more subjectively defined and appear less life-threatening or serious, the claim to the medical cannabis identity also becomes easier to question.

Most of the medical cannabis patients in this study are contending with serious chronic illnesses or injuries that are stressful and stigmatizing in and of themselves. The combination of stigmas is particularly problematic for managing health concerns. Contemporary research has found indications that stigmatization has "a direct detrimental influence on mental and physical health stemming from exposure to chronic stress, including experiences of discrimination" (Ahern, Stuber, and Galea 2007, 188). Managing the threat of stigma becomes itself a risk factor that patients must manage, and medical cannabis use compounds the risk of stigmatization.

### Negotiating Chronic Illness

One could look at almost any of the patients in this sample and have no idea they suffer from an illness or injury. Only two patients out of the forty had any visible disease or disability: Zane uses a wheelchair due to an amputation, and Wes is legally blind and uses a cane for walking assistance. Of the other thirty-eight patients, none appeared to be ill upon casual encounter. It took their willing disclosure to learn of the invisible presence of HIV, cancer, epilepsy, multiple back surgeries, and other conditions.

As in Karen's story about her husband from chapter 1, many patients describe a process of adjustment to chronic conditions in which they slowly come to terms with the meaning of their illness or injury. Most people experiencing symptoms or an adverse event start out with an expectation that everyday roles and obligations will only be temporarily disrupted. This aligns with the classic conceptualization of the "sick role," in which it is socially acceptable to suspend normal social role expectations when ill, but at the price of recognition that illness is "undesirable," and the sick person should be working to recover "as expeditiously as possible" (Conrad and Schneider 1998 [1980], 247). Most assume that injury or illness will be resolved by identifying the problem and receiving treatment, after which they can resume normal activities.

Chronic illness revises the sick role because it often spans a long period of time and may not be resolvable even with continuous treatment. This creates a dynamic in which the boundaries of the sick role are not clearly defined (Burnham 2012; Rosenberg 2009; Turner 2004; Varul 2010). Because the sick role extends exemptions and special treatment, those invoking it can be suspected of other motives, especially if claims to sickness are intermittent and ongoing, and the type of illness has no obvious manifestation that legitimates its presence or absence (Burnham 2012). This is corroborated by research on pain and its treatment, which finds that patients, practitioners, and those closely related to the patient all experience tensions, frustration, discomfort, and distress in interactions about how to manage pain and balance consideration of pain with other factors (Crowley-Matoka and True 2012).

It takes time for patients to realize that there is no "going back to normal," and many resist this change in status and the potential role loss and stigma that it may bring. When faced with finding a "new normal" that potentially includes inhabiting the stigmatizing role of illness or disability—or cycling in and out of it with much greater frequency over a long period of time, perhaps the rest of their lives—many patients resist such labeling and the role loss that it may entail. Successfully fulfilling one's roles as, for example, student, parent, spouse, and worker is tied to self-esteem and to one's perceptions of success (Stets and Burke 2014; Stryker and Burke 2000). Experiencing one's self through one's roles is deeply emotional and meaningful. It is also inter-relational in that the connections and relationships each person has with others is tightly bound to the fulfillment of roles, serving as a form of identity verification that supports positive feelings about oneself and a sense of being dependable to family, friends, and colleagues (Stets and Carter 2012).

It is not surprising that people fight to maintain the roles that give meaning to their lives (Burke and Stets 2009; Stets and Carter 2012; Stryker and Burke 2000). Those faced with role loss can range in response from acceptance and self-stigmatization to outright challenges that reject characterizations of illness as stigmatizing on the whole. Between acceptance and outright challenge is the use of deflection strategies, in which the individual may acknowledge that illnesses are stigmatizing but insist that the characterizations do not fit in their specific case (Thoits 2011). Many patient interviews reveal elements of this process, when patients work to maintain roles, resist stigma, and deflect labels in the face of illness. To the extent that cannabis allows one to maintain functional health, it becomes a tool for resisting role loss. Ironically, the more successful it is, the less "legitimately medical" the person's cannabis use may appear.

For those who became officially designated with a disability status through the state, the process of adjustment and acceptance is often gradual. Forty percent of patients in this study qualified for some form of disability. Qualifying for disability benefits is a lengthy process that is often psychologically taxing because it confronts the individual with being disabled—a label that signifies role changes and limitations that can be accompanied by a sense of loss, both of identity and of plans for the future.

Billy exemplifies this gradual acceptance of disability. On the weekend that Billy graduated from high school, he and his closest friend from school went out to celebrate, but the night would change the rest of both of their lives. Billy got behind the wheel drunk and wrecked his car horribly. His injuries were very bad. Billy's friend lived, but he was also permanently disabled by the accident. After months in a coma, Billy spent over a year in rehab, learning to do everything over again. He lives with a traumatic brain injury that limits his abilities in many ways. Nevertheless, he was brought up in a hardworking farm family that taught a spirit of Midwestern perseverance, and he put his mind to assiduously relearning many skills with a goal of living independently from the care of his loving family. Billy rejected the disability label for years. He recounts a stubborn determination to finish a culinary degree from a prestigious school. Although he was successful in earning his degree, he just could not hold a job. The amount of multitasking under time constraints required by working in restaurant kitchens was beyond his capacity. After nearly ten years and, according to him, over 100 jobs, Billy finally conceded. He had a disability as a result of his accident, and he was not capable of working like others. It was on one hand a relief and, on the other, a huge blow that he counterbalances with his pride in finishing college and maintaining an apartment independently. He says:

> I have accepted the fact that I am disabled. I went through and I fought for so long. Every time I got back up to fight, they would knock me down, and "Oh, you're not disabled." So, I had to hit that wall where I was just done. I couldn't go anymore.

For many years, Billy paid a high price for resisting the disability label, as his inability to hold a steady job left him constantly struggling economically. Even now, his funds are very meager, and he has to budget carefully to make his money last, but going on disability has stabilized his life a great deal. Having experienced homelessness and hardship, Billy focuses on the simple, positive aspects of maintaining a stable residence:

> I am happy getting what I do. I don't have to move every month or two. I *have* stuff. I have a bed. I have a couch. I have, you know, TVs. I've always had TVs. You can stick a TV in the back of your vehicle. But couches, loveseats, dishes . . . I have a home, you know?

Still, it was very hard for him to accept being disabled, because to him, this designation indicated that he could never live a normal life. Perhaps more importantly, as a young man, admitting disability had seemed like giving up on his aspirations to achieve many of the same normative life-course milestones that most hope to reach. Eventually resistance gave way to an acceptance and adjustment of his expectations, finding new criteria by which to measure his success and buoy his self-esteem.

Yvonne's illness came later than Billy's. By the time she became ill, she had already been married, had children, and worked in a career. Rather than stopping her short of her dreams for a normal adulthood, Yvonne saw disability more as a sign that her productive adult life was coming to an end. Middle age was giving way to becoming prematurely "old." Yvonne not only resisted the disability label, she initially rejected her diagnosis altogether:

> For years, I had burning in my neck and shoulders. I thought it was from sitting at the computer, and it's fibromyalgia. I got diagnosed back in . . . gee, it was probably 2008 or 2009. I apparently had it a long time, they said. I never related the pain to anything except sitting at the computer too long. . . . I didn't believe in fibromyalgia, to be honest. I didn't believe it was really anything more than an excuse to be lazy. I kept saying "No, it's not," to anything [my doctor said]. That's why she sent me upstairs to get tests . . . because I didn't believe it. I said, "No, it's not that." [My doctor] was like, "Yeah, I think it is." I said, "No."

Although resistant, Yvonne begrudgingly accepted her diagnosis over time. Fibromyalgia prevented her from returning to a normal work life, and her resistance to accepting the limitations of chronic illness led her to postpone applying for disability.

> It took me a good year before I would consider signing up for disability. It took my cousin, a nurse, to talk me into it. . . . I didn't want to use it as an excuse, you know, I wanted to—well, it was a lot to say you were disabled. That was hard for me.

She often opted not to take medications, despite being in pain, citing concerns with dependency. In addition to fibromyalgia, Yvonne was diagnosed with Crohn's disease. Like Billy, she attributes her eventual willingness to apply for disability to difficulties maintaining a job due to illness symptoms.

> I lost my job because, basically, I was up in the bathroom all the time. But half the time, they did not even know I was gone, it was so fast there and back, and the bathroom was there by my desk. So, at the same time, I was very tired. I was so tired. It hit all at once.

Yvonne had worked for most of her adult life as a self-professed driven high achiever, but her illness interfered with her job. In the end, it was the culmination of several crises among family members, including the death of a parent, that led her to accept that things had changed and normal functioning was no longer possible.

Role disruption is often an important part of the process when redefining life after serious injury or chronic illness (Charmaz 1999). Other stories, such as that of Karen and Mateo in chapter 1 and Anita in chapter 5, illustrate the pattern of interference that illness has for the lifeworld. Parenting, spousal, and work role changes highlight how illness experiences are highly personal but also affect family and friends—one's close network—who often also must make adjustments.

In interesting ways, the fear of being stigmatized as ill or as a cannabis user are similar: both include anxiety about being labeled as lazy or incompetent. Many of those interviewed described ways they fought to fulfill valued roles even when such efforts became challenging. In fact, in Billy's and Yvonne's accounts, their attachments to being perceived as hardworking, honest, and productive while avoiding being labeled helpless or victims led them to cling tenaciously to work roles and suffer economically as a result. The sick role provides an exemption from everyday functioning, including expressions of suffering, but it is meant to be short lived. When sick role behaviors are prolonged, they connect to tropes of stigma and stereotype threat. While behaviors related to illness or suffering may be genuine, the individual often learns to hide them to protect against being seen as incompetent, lazy, old, or malcontent. Managing perceptions and protecting against judgment or intervention may lead to actions that appear irrational, such as not accepting clear diagnoses or persisting in roles at work or home despite underperformance or disruption.

Role obligations are meaningful. They demarcate our place in the world in relation to others—as husbands and wives, parents, children, students, and professionals in the work world. Much of our world revolves around these roles and the sense of belonging and responsibility to others they engender. Generally, fulfilling roles creates a sense of satisfaction and meaning in our lives. Role functioning is central to the medical cannabis patient experience. Patients may buffer the negative effects of stigma on self-esteem by challenging assumptions about the cannabis user identity or by deflecting the relevance of that identity for them personally (Thoits 2011).

## Making Trade-Offs: Medical Cannabis and Employment

Several patients described how they carefully concealed cannabis use in relation to their employment. Job threats may be related to drug testing that can result in being fired or denied employment. Consider Andy's case. Andy worked in IT. He had to go on a business trip with his boss, but travel often made his degenerative disc disease flare up, causing his upper back to knot up painfully and, if left untreated, he also got an excruciating headache. He would usually use cannabis for such flare-ups, which reduced or eliminated the symptoms without significant loss of functional time, but both the travel and the presence of his boss made cannabis a difficult option, so he concealed a tiny amount of tincture in a medicine bottle and brought along Vicodin, just in case he had any difficulties. Andy tended to have pretty bad side effects from using Vicodin, so he hoped that he would not need it. The situation was compounded by the fact that Andy had worked to conceal his illness from his company because he feared it might prevent him from being promoted or convince them to phase him out. He had seen this happen to someone else.

> [This was] the first time [my boss] ever saw me with a bad day [from illness]. We were in a hotel; we have adjoining hotel rooms. [I] actually did take an Ambesol bottle, dump the Ambesol out, and put tincture in the Ambesol bottle. So, that's all that I had. Then, usually that's not enough for long-term pain problems, [so] I also had Vicodin with me because I couldn't take my [regular cannabis] medicine. So, I have the Vicodin, and you'll recall I hate the crap. So, I woke up on a bad day. They were under a lot of pressure, and I had to excuse myself about an hour into the day. I said, "I've got to take a break," and I told [my boss]. I didn't *want* to tell him, "Hey look, I'm basically handicapped. I'm going to have bad days for the rest of my life. I'm going to not be able to work some days." I don't want to tell him that because I don't want the negative backlash

that exists in the real world. Do I say, "Now I'm covered by the Americans with Disabilities Act"? Well, I'm not that kind of person. I'm not going to push that kind of crap down somebody's throat. I just expect to be treated like a human being, right?

Similar to Yvonne and Billy, Andy refused to invoke any special privilege or be seen as incapable as a result of illness, but for Andy, this meant he felt compelled to hide his illness altogether. He would prefer not to invoke "rights" but simply be extended decent treatment. He pointed out that, because pain is not visible to others, they often lack understanding and are not sympathetic:

> [Andy pretends to be an unsympathetic coworker, in a whining voice]: "Ohhhh, he's got a headache." [back to normal voice] People who have never had serious pain don't understand it. And so, I . . . well, I had a bad day, and I had to excuse myself. . . . He saw me in pain, and I went to the room, and I sat there, just having a fit [of painful back spasms]. And I took that Vicodin. It made me feel worse. That's what happens sometimes with opiates for me—they don't help. I don't like taking them anyway because they screw up the receptors in your brain and all that, and I just don't want them. Anyway. I had a bad day. And two weeks later he told me, I'm going to have to switch you over to contractor's tasks. And after that point, I practically didn't hear anything from him again. He wouldn't ever directly, um, address me or anything. It was all like standoffish, and so on and so forth. Then, after about six months, he said, "I don't have any more work for you." I think it was entirely because of that event.

The management of two concealed identities in Andy's case created an untenable situation in which his inability to take medicinal cannabis due to several limiting factors left him so he could not manage and therefore could no longer conceal his medical condition. Because he had made a strategic decision to conceal his medical problems at work, his boss had little context to understand his actions, and, ultimately, Andy felt it was directly responsible for him losing his job. Other patients recounted similar situations where legal limitations on cannabis combined with the desire to maintain the appearance of health in social situations created impossible trade-offs.

### Legal Problems

The most negative consequence from cannabis use is often getting arrested. Medical cannabis has created new pathways for safe access and use, but many patients perceive the coexistence of criminalized cannabis to be the most dangerous aspect of being a patient. Criminalization policies create conditions for harassment or arrest, and in towns or cities where local government or law enforcement are less supportive of the state's laws, it may lead to blocked access (ASA 2017).

This has been a concern for Ron. Because he is treating cancer using a highly concentrated product that is not commercially produced, he has to maintain access to substantial plant material, which means grow his own or find a friendly source. He says, "The only problems I've had with the medicine is not having access to it." That said, Ron has also experienced harassment and arrest. He had difficulty maintaining cannabis access while also managing the legal complications and expenses from his arrest, including the potential of going to jail. A small business owner whose business folded after he fell ill, Ron had no health insurance and relied solely on cannabis for treatment. His anger at his predicament is clear:

> [The District Attorney] took my medicine and told me to die. I said, "I have a doctor's recommendation to do exactly what I'm doing." He said, "I don't even care about that." That's what's going on. So, every day I fight for my *right* to fight for my *life*. It'd be nice if all I had to do was get up every morning and fight cancer. They've got my medicine! They won't give it to me! I have to beg people on the street to have enough medicine. It puts me in situations when I run out where I think I'm gonna die, and then the symptoms that I go through—it's not . . . it shouldn't happen. And these people just continue to refuse to accept the facts! The science! Because of greed, because of misinformation. And de-education.

After this interview, Ron's case was dropped, and his medicine was returned to him, but it had not been properly stored, rendering it useless. Six months after this interview, Ron contacted us to say his blood tests had improved considerably, and his blood count numbers had lowered by half from their peak, closer to normal readings.

Ron's case was particularly egregious, but he was far from alone. Of the patients in the sample, about a quarter reported either some form of police encounter or the burglary of plants. Two other patients faced charges and court battles at the same level of seriousness as Ron's case. Other patients reported less disruptive problems, but the incidents clearly heightened their fears and sense of vulnerability. Darrell had an interaction with the police that endangered his health when the cops raided his garden based on an anonymous tip, even though his garden was found to be within the guidelines and no files were charged:

> I was well within my rights. I was not charged. There are no pending charges. But my house got raided, and they knocked my door down. They threw a flash grenade into my house. They knew I had dogs.

They burnt the tail on one of my older dogs . . . and they hurt my little dog. . . . They made them poop themselves, literally. . . . After the flash grenade went off, they were running in and saying "Get down, get down!" [I said,] "Okay. I'm disabled. I'm disabled, I'm not going to fight you. . . . Nobody's going to fight you, just settle down. . . ." They had thirteen SWAT members in my house with automatic weapons pointing in my face, screaming "Get down!" I'm petrified for my animals. They [the SWAT team] ended up pushing me down to the floor, and they ripped my shirt off of me and told me to crawl. I had [injured] my leg back [over the summer]. . . . My knee is trashed, and my other knee [had a major injury a few years before] as well. They grabbed me by my fingertips and were dragging me across my kitchen floor, scarred my knees up. . . . I have pins and screws in my lower back with a cage. I've got four long bolts that are this long [indicates 6–8 inches] and look like they belong in a fence. . . . I have to get three MRIs now. I've got pain shooting down; my neck is numb; and my arms hurt because I can't stretch like they had me stretched. And I kept telling them, I am not going to fight you. . . . They said they were there for an "overgrow." They kept us detained in handcuffs for twenty-five minutes until the detective got there, and then they go down, and they had already been down in the basement. They knew I was well within my rights, the rights of my medical card. They tore half of my Mylar [a type of reflective material] down off my one room so they could look to see if anything was behind it. I was dumbfounded for what happened. And scared to death, too. . . . I didn't even get an apology. . . . Nobody's fixing my door. My house is trashed. . . . And we're still cleaning it up. We were at twenty-two plants, and I'm allowed twenty-four. I have a license for twenty-four. So, they ended up just leaving, and I haven't heard anything else.

For Darrell, the negative consequence of having registered as a medical marijuana patient was not only the stress and fear created by the raid but the police officers' actual physical handling of his dogs, his belongings, and, most importantly, his body without concern for his disability. Ultimately, the police presented much more danger to him than he thought cannabis ever would. He feared the ease with which something like this could happen, and he suspected that the raid resulted from a person he knew calling in an anonymous tip for malicious personal reasons, but he could not prove it. He worried that, were another raid to happen, police would injure him, his home, or his dogs further, perhaps irreparably. In the end, he considered pressing charges or pursuing civil damages but decided against it, in part because he is chronically ill and poor, and he lacked the energy or funds required for a protracted battle.

Not all law enforcement encounters are so traumatic. Most patients will not have a direct interaction with law enforcement, and those that do may involve nothing more than a polite check of documentation. The differences in types of legal encounter reflect the unpredictable variability in officer attitudes toward medical cannabis, coupled with the layers of law that allow completely different responses to the medical cannabis patient identity. Some law enforcement officers are sympathetic, and some departments have clear policies on handling medical cannabis. But the legitimacy of the patient identity and the conduct associated with it, including details such as the quantity of medicine you're allowed to possess, are subject to considerable interpretation. Compounding the challenge is the fact that almost all local law enforcement is cross-deputized as federal drug agents by the DEA because federal agencies don't have enough manpower to handle raids without local reinforcements. This means that the officers themselves are caught between their sworn duty to state and federal laws (though courts have ruled state law comes first for state officers). Most problematically for patients, the close relationships those local officers form with their federal counterparts mean that federal charges for patients are all too often just a phone call away.[4]

A few patients went above and beyond to show they were cooperative with law enforcement. Karen's account of her run-in with the DEA, as described in the introduction, may have been instigated when someone completing repairs on their home saw her cannabis garden and decided to report it to the authorities. The interaction she had with the authorities was very civil. Against all advice they had ever received, Karen and her husband allowed federal agents in bulletproof vests to enter their home and look around without a warrant. After a visual inspection, they told Karen that she was in compliance with state law, but before they left, they said they would inform local law enforcement. Although they never did, this prompted Karen to try to manage the situation by going directly to her local police station to address the issue head-on. Karen ultimately ended up assisting the department with local trainings on medical marijuana in Colorado.

Karen's situation turned out in her favor despite federal involvement. When comparing the two results of anonymous tips in the cases of Darrell and Karen, the outcomes were profoundly different. Based on the facts of each case, one might expect the experiences to be switched, for at least a couple of reasons. Darrell is more clearly and verifiably disabled, while Karen and her husband appear able-bodied. The law enforcement in Darrell's case were state authorities who are sworn to uphold state law, whereas those in Karen's incident were federal agents who owe no allegiance to state law and could have been expected to invoke federal laws. Yet the drastically different outcomes underline the reasons that patients experience fear around police intervention—interpretation of the law is at the discretion of each officer, unit, and agency and may be enforced based on the attitude or whim of individuals.

In both cases, the patients appealed to human connection in the law enforcement encounter. Darrell pleads with the officers, trying to give them basic information to avoid injury to himself or his dogs. Karen acts against legal advice and her own first instinct and allows the officers to enter her home, in large part because she believes they will see that she is a good person, not a criminal drug dealer, and she is acting in compliance with state and local policies. This naïve hope that law enforcement will see the situation from the patient perspective, or at least see the person as an upstanding citizen who is normal and non-deviant, assumes that law enforcement will draw the line between guilt and innocence in the same place as the patient. This sense of being in the right—morally, legally, and in terms of social standing—may lead to a false sense of confidence in how police will interpret the situation. When this goes wrong, patients report a great deal of disbelief and anger.

More than half of patients reported an interaction with officials that led them to fear that the police would take some action against them, driving home the tentative legal status of being a patient. Heightening these fears is a very real vulnerability. As noted at the start of this chapter, "cannabis user" is largely a concealable identity until registering as a legal patient. Once that threshold is crossed, the usual strategy of concealment has been compromised. The things patients need to do to participate in a medical cannabis program—the documentation, the registration, the transparency with authorities—all provide evidence that can be used against the patient, from simple harassment to loss of employment, property, children, and freedom. Even if patients judge the risk of these outcomes to be unlikely, fear still runs deep because most patients understand well the lack of protections they have, should law enforcement become involved.

For many patients, being placed in a position of fearing their government elicited an attitude of defiance and outrage. The police often only managed to further entrench divisions by treating patients as criminals, which offended patients and reinforced their sense of being in the right. Even if the police were willing to use might over right, patients were undeterred. In fact, those who had experienced run-ins with the law not only persisted but were more stubbornly determined to exercise their rights. Claiming the quasi-public identity of the medical cannabis patient requires a commitment that invests the individual in defending it. The formal steps they take to comply with the law can yield a sense of entitlement. They are the law-abiding cannabis users, so treating them like the criminal ones comes as an insult. What's more, for any seriously ill or injured patients for whom cannabis is the medicine of last resort, medical necessity easily overwhelms any claim that cannabis is deviant, dangerous, or otherwise wrong and worthy of punishment.

While secrecy has been the hallmark of cannabis use defined by criminality and undesirable stereotypes, medical use has created a legitimate pathway for claiming cannabis use without tainting one's identity, or at least not in the same way. Much like the gay rights movement, medical cannabis users have revised a tainted or spoiled identity by shifting from closeted behaviors to proclamations of pride. Research on the gay rights movement has shown collective identity to be fundamental for enabling political engagement (Britt and Heise 2000), and much the same may be said of the patient community. When patients identify as cannabis users, they participate in revising the language and meanings associated with cannabis use in ways that challenge persistent negative cultural stereotypes. The next chapter discusses the ways that patients cope with the threat of stereotype, both individually and collectively.

## Notes

1. A handful of states have begun to incorporate civil protections for employment in non-sensitive positions.
2. How can these studies come up with completely different figures and conclusions based on largely the same data? Research methods in all studies can help clarify how accidents were counted: what years, and what cases were included. As an example, the study that claimed to find an increase counts as "marijuana-involved" accidents any in which the driver had cannabis metabolites present, even though many of the identified drivers were alcohol impaired, and metabolite tests do not show if a person is currently intoxicated.
3. Wilson v. Lynch. No. 14-15700. August 31, 2016.
4. The informal referral of what were originally state cases to the federal side has occurred with some frequency in California. In several cases, state charges were dropped after patients showed compliance with state law, but then the evidence migrated to federal prosecutors who brought charges in a venue that allows no defense based on medical necessity or state compliance. One egregious case involved an assistant district attorney asking a defense attorney to discuss dismissal of state charges in the judge's chambers; once the attorneys were out of the courtroom, waiting U.S. Marshals seized the two patients. At least one other case involved a medical cannabis defendant being seized from a state courtroom by federal agents. (www.canorml.org/costs/federal_medical_marijuana_cases_resolved).

## References

Adler, Jonathan N., and James A. Colbert. 2013. "Medicinal Use of Marijuana: Polling Results." *New England Journal of Medicine* 368(22):e30. doi:10.1056/NEJMclde1305159.

Ahern, Jennifer, Jennifer Stuber, and Sandro Galea. 2007. "Stigma, Discrimination and the Health of Illicit Drug Users." *Drug and Alcohol Dependence* 88:188–96.

Anderson, D. Mark, and Daniel I. Rees. 2013. "Medical Marijuana Laws, Traffic Fatalities, and Alcohol Consumption." *Journal of Law and Economics* 56(2):333–69.

ASA, Americans for Safe Access. 2017. *Medical Marijuana Access in the United States.*

Britt, Lory, and David R. Heise. 2000. "From Shame to Pride in Identity Politics." Pp. 252–68 in *Self, Identity, and Social Movements*, edited by Sheldon Stryker, Timothy J. Owens and Robert W. White. Minneapolis: University of Minnesota Press.

Broom, Alex, Carla Meurk, Jon Adams, and David Sibbritt. 2014. "My Health, My Responsibility? Complementary Medicine and Self (Health) Care." *Journal of Sociology* 50(4):515–30. doi: 10.1177/1440783312467098.

Burke, Peter J., and Jan E. Stets. 2009. *Identity Theory*. New York: Oxford University Press.

Burnham, John C. 2012. "The Death of the Sick Role." *Social History of Medicine* 25(4): 761–76. doi: 10.1093/shm/hks018.

Charmaz, Kathy. 1999. "Stories of Suffering: Subjective Tales and Research Narratives." *Qualitative Health Research* 9(3):362–82.

Compton, Richard. 2017. *Marijuana-Impaired Driving: A Report to Congress.* DOT HS 812 440 Washington, DC: National Highway Traffic Safety Administration (https://www.nhtsa.gov/sites/nhtsa.dot.gov/files/documents/812440-marijuana-impaired-driving-report-to-congress.pdf).

Compton, Richard, and Amy Berning. 2015. *Drug and Alcohol Crash Risk: Traffic Safety Facts.* Washington, DC: National Highway Transportation Safety Administration (NHTSA).

Conrad, Peter, and Joseph Schneider. 1998 [1980]. *Deviance and Medicalization: From Badness to Sickness.* Philadelphia: Temple University Press.

Crowley-Matoka, Megan, and Gala True. 2012. "No One Wants to Be the Candy Man: Ambivalent Medicalization and Clinician Subjectivity in Pain Management." *Cultural Anthropology (Wiley-Blackwell)* 27(4):689–712. doi:10.1111/j.1548-1360.2012.01167.x.

Doblin, Rick, and Mark Kleinman. 1991. "Marijuana as Antiemetic Medicine: A Survey of Oncologists' Experiences and Attitudes." *American Journal of Clinical Oncology* 9(7):1314–19. doi: 10.1200/JCO.1991.9.7.1314.

Eddy, Mark. 2010. *Medical Marijuana: Review and Analysis of Federal and State Policies.* Washington, DC: Congressional Research Service.

Emery, Marc. 2011. "Prison Blog #28: Injustice & Cruelty as a Laughing Matter." *Cannabis Culture.* February 28, 2011. (https://www.cannabisculture.com/content/2011/02/28/prison-blog-28-injustice-cruelty-laughing-matter).

Garcia, Adrian D. 2017. "Colorado State Patrol's Still Looking for Something as Efficient as a Breathalyzer for Marijuana." *Denverite.* January 24, 2017. (www.denverite.com/colorado-state-patrols-still-looking-something-efficient-breathalyzer-catch-drivers-high-marijuana-27334/).

Gillespie, Mark. 2001. "Americans Support Legalization of Marijuana for Medicinal Use," news release, May 15, 2001, http://news.gallup.com/poll/2902/americans-support-legalization-marijuana-medicinal-use.aspx.

Goffman, Erving. 1986 [1963]. *Stigma: Notes on the Management of Spoiled Identity.* New York: Simon and Schuster, Inc.

Hathaway, Andrew. 1997. "Marijuana and Tolerance: Revisiting Becker's Sources of Control." *Deviant Behavior* 18(2):103–24.

Hathaway, Andrew. 2004. "Cannabis Users' Informal Rules for Managing Stigma and Risk." *Deviant Behavior* 25(6):559–77. doi: 10.1080/01639620490484095.

Hernandez, Elizabeth. 2016. "Pilot Program Eyes Pot-DUI Devices." January 9, 2016. *The Denver Post* (https://www.denverpost.com/2016/01/09/pilot-program-eyes-pot-dui-devices/).

LeBel, Thomas P. 2008. "Perceptions of and Responses to Stigma." *Sociology Compass* 2(2):409–32.

Lewis, Nehama, and Sharon R. Sznitman. 2017. "You Brought It on Yourself: The Joint Effects of Message Type, Stigma, and Responsibility Attribution on Attitudes toward Medical Cannabis." *Journal of Communication* 67(2):181–202. doi: 10.1111/jcom.12287.

Link, Bruce G., and Jo C. Phelan. 2001. "Conceptualizing Stigma." *Annual Review of Sociology* 27(1):363–85. doi: 10.1146/annurev.soc.27.1.363.

Looby, Alison, and Mitch Earleywine. 2010. "Gender Moderates the Impact of Stereotype Threat on Cognitive Function in Cannabis Users." *Addictive Behaviors* 35:834–9.

Major, Brenda, and Laurie T. O'Brien. 2005. "The Social Psychology of Stigma." *Annual Review of Psychology* 56(1):393–421. doi: 10.1146/annurev.psych.56.091103.070137.

Migova, David. 2017. "Exclusive: Traffic Fatalities Linked to Marijuana are Up Sharply in Colorado. Is Legalization to Blame?" *The Denver Post* (https://www.denverpost.com/2017/08/25/colorado-marijuana-traffic-fatalities/).

Pescosolido, Bernice A., and Jack K. Martin. 2015. "The Stigma Complex." *Annual Review of Sociology* 41(1):87–116. doi: 10.1146/annurev-soc-071312-145702.

Quinn, Diane M. 2005. "Concealable Versus Conspicuous Stigmatized Identities." Pp. 83–104 in *Stigma and Group Inequality: Social Psychological Perspectives*, edited by Shana Levin and Colette Van Laar. New York: Psychology Press.

Rosenberg, Charles E. 2009. "Managed Fear." *Lancet* 373:802–3.

Santaella-Tenorio, Julian, Christine M. Mauro, Melanie M. Wall, June H. Kim, Magdalena Cerdá, Katherine M. Keyes, Deborah S. Hasin, Sandro Galea, and Silvia S. Martins. 2017. "US Traffic Fatalities, 1985–2014, and Their Relationship to Medical Marijuana Laws." *American Journal of Public Health* 107(2):336–42. doi: 10.2105/ajph.2016.303577.

Scambler, Graham. 2006. "Sociology, Social Structure and Health-Related Stigma." *Psychology, Health & Medicine* 11(3):288–95. doi: 10.1080/13548500600595103.

Stets, Jan E., and Peter J. Burke. 2014. "Self-Esteem and Identities." *Sociological Perspectives* 57(4):409–33.

Stets, Jan E., and Michael J. Carter. 2012. "A Theory of the Self for the Sociology of Morality." *American Sociological Review* 77(1):120–40. doi: 10.1177/0003122411433762.

Stryker, Sheldon, and Peter J. Burke. 2000. "The Past, Present, and Future of an Identity Theory." *Social Psychology Quarterly* 63(4):284–97. doi: 10.2307/2695840.

Thoits, Peggy A. 2011. "Resisting the Stigma of Mental Illness." *Social Psychology Quarterly* 74(1):6–28. doi: 10.1177/0190272511398019.

Turner, Bryan. 2004. *The New Medical Sociology*. New York: W.W. Norton.

Varul, Matthias Zick. 2010. "Talcott Parsons, the Sick Role and Chronic Illness." *Body & Society* 16(2):72–94. doi: 10.1177/1357034x10364766.

Zerubavel, Eviatar. 1997. *Social Mindscapes*. Cambridge, MA: Harvard University Press.

# Chapter 9

# Strategies for Managing and Changing Cannabis Stigma

There is no "typical marihuana user," just as there is no typical American. The most notable statement that can be made about the vast majority of marihuana users—experimenters and intermittent users—is that they are essentially indistinguishable from their non-marihuana using peers by any fundamental criterion other than their marihuana use.

(U.S. Commission on Marihuana and Drug Abuse 1972)

Patients may or may not fit the stereotypes of cannabis use built into the single story. As with other people who are subject to stereotypes, the issue is not whether the stereotype fits or not, but that every individual must still contend with entrenched stereotypes and the potential stigma of cannabis use. How stigma is managed, resisted, and shifted by individual medical cannabis patients is a critical aspect of medicalization.

The basic stereotypes associated with recreational cannabis users are widely known. When the accoutrements are stripped from them, they echo stereotypes that have been applied to many marginalized groups, including racial and ethnic minorities and those who identify as gay or lesbian. Most formulations characterize the targets of the stereotyping as being in some sense "dirty," lazy, unintelligent, or incompetent. However, because cannabis use is also associated with the young adult phase of the life course, stereotypes of cannabis users exaggerate qualities associated with young adults, such as lack of experience and irresponsibility, while also implying that cannabis users who have aged out of this phase of the life course are immature or "burnouts" because they have maintained inappropriate behaviors relative to their age.

As discussed in chapter 8, stereotypes are operational in society, but simply knowing what they are is not the same as subscribing to them. Knowing the stereotypes that might be invoked is a part of knowing one's culture. Stereotype and stigma intersect. A stigma is a discrediting characteristic which, when applied within an interpersonal interaction to a specific person in a specific set of circumstances, invokes a stereotype. The study of these phenomena has generated an entire literature devoted to how those subject to stigma cope or manage the identities that are vulnerable to negative evaluation. Several factors are influential in how well individuals cope with stigmatized identities.

The anticipation of stigmatization is one of the dimensions that influence how well or poorly individuals cope with a stigmatizing identity, a factor closely tied to stereotype threat (Quinn et al. 2014). Stereotype threats occur when specific, culturally available stereotypes that apply to some members of the group are brought up in the immediate performance context. The effects of invoking stereotypes have been shown to reduce working memory capacity and influence academic performance (Schmader and Johns 2003; Smith and Hung 2008). Individuals may reflexively imagine that such labels will be applied to them and adjust their appearance or visible behavior to avoid this possibility, even though no actual interaction has taken place. This also means that individuals who align with a more stereotypical portrayal because they evince more stigmatizing characteristics may feel a greater sense of "stereotype threat" than those who do not "fit the stereotype." The effects of stereotype threat do not require an interaction to be experienced. The mere possibility of such an interaction can create "the threat of being viewed through the lens of a negative stereotype, or the fear of doing something that would inadvertently confirm the stereotype" (Steele 1999, 46).

Karen provides a good anecdote that captures stereotype threat:

> There's all those little names that are out there. I've even had a guy say that, "Well, I don't want my customers to know that I'm going to get my [medical cannabis] license." Oh no! But yet that man, who has had numerous back surgeries, is always in pain, has done all the other drugs, saw they didn't work, and *still* he doesn't want anybody to know. Because there's that mindset, and people are judgmental.

Stereotype threat has been identified in patient interactions with health care providers. Patients have higher distrust of physicians and may avoid care if they fear being judged about identity in terms of race, social class, weight issues, or aging (Abdou et al. 2016; Aronson et al. 2013). At least one study has looked at differential effects of stereotype threat on male and female cannabis users, suggesting that males are more likely to fit stereotypes and therefore more likely to exhibit performance impairments due to stereotype threat (Looby and Earleywine 2010).

Research on stigma has argued that the "salience" and "centrality" of the identifying characteristic are two additional aspects, after anticipation of stigma, that influence the degree to which individuals are affected (Quinn and Chaudoir 2009; Quinn et al. 2014; Thoits 2011). Individuals who consume cannabis socially and only occasionally may feel little personal connection to a cannabis user identity and, as a result, only identify with cannabis users when they choose to selectively invoke this identity (Burke and Stets

2009; Quinn 2005; Quinn et al. 2014). In other words, centrality and salience are both low. Occasional cannabis users may only identify as such in the moment of the "vulnerable present," when cannabis is being consumed. Episodic cannabis use does not generally lead individuals to include cannabis consumption as a relevant role they occupy across social situations, and use is nearly always in the frame of the past (Hammersly, Jenkins, and Reid 2001). Future use is not planned, so such users may not ever identify as a current cannabis user and may only claim group membership in specific social contexts but not as a political identity (Ellemers, Spears, and Doosje 2002).

Unproblematic past social use is also generally not stigmatizing, especially if use was "on time" in the life course during teen or college age years. It is commonplace for individuals to recount youthful, recreational use of cannabis as a signifier of covert prestige, indicating that they were open-minded, fun-loving, mildly subversive, creative, or otherwise culturally hip in their earlier years.

The salience of "cannabis user" for the medical cannabis patient identity—that is, how often the person is prompted to think of themselves as someone who uses cannabis—is more pronounced than for most recreational users. Among patients, it may become more so for those patients who take recourse to cannabis more frequently, consistently, or urgently than others, but, as noted in the last chapter, to be a participant in the Colorado Medical Marijuana Program is to quasi-publicly identify oneself as a medical cannabis patient. The centrality of the medical cannabis patient identity appears to vary more in the sense that patients place different value on its relevance as an identity and differ in their political engagement and other types of advocacy and outreach (Quinn and Chaudoir 2009).

Diverse subcultural groups are perceived to have an association with cannabis use, but the one with which most patients at midlife must contend is the "hippie." Nearly every patient in this study treated the question about stereotypes as if the answer were self-evident and, as such, unnecessary to discuss. When pressed, most offered some variation of "dirty, unproductive hippie" as the most predominant social stereotype of cannabis users.[1]

Karen was a little more detailed and colorful:

> The whole reefer madness scenario. You know, the way the government has portrayed it, and in the movies, too—Cheech and Chong and *Pineapple Express*, and all those others . . . [cannabis users] are portrayed as just a bunch of losers, that they don't do anything, and they're not productive to society or whatever. Well, I'll tell you, I know a lot of people who are cardholders, and they are amazing people—taxpaying, productive, you know, careers—doctors, lawyers, computer geeks.

Even as Karen elaborates the stereotype, she illustrates one of the more adept rhetorical strategies common within the medical cannabis community:

to first point out *who* is doing the stereotyping—the government and the media—and, second, to immediately cite countervailing evidence that shows the stereotype is inaccurate and therefore unfair. In so doing, Karen has modeled an identified form of resisting stigma (Thoits 2011).

Karen's story in the introduction made it clear that, even though (or perhaps because) she had used cannabis as a teenager, she had internalized an idea of cannabis use as not appropriate to her roles in midlife. The degree to which stigmas of recreational use have been internalized—either as they applied to oneself or, if one was never a social cannabis consumer, to others prior to medical use—can be factors in how well one manages the medical cannabis patient identity. These have to do with one's assessment of fit with those categories based on overlapping identity characteristics of race, age, gender, occupation, and so forth. These factors each affect the degree to which any cannabis user will be affected by stereotype and may also affect the coping mechanisms used to push back against stereotypes, using the lack of fit with stereotypes as a platform to resist stigmatization.

Like Karen, Eileen reports using cannabis socially on a regular basis before having children and then after her children were grown. Eileen had developed arthritis and found out that cannabis could help with both arthritis and migraines, and she used it for symptom control before medical cannabis was an official option. Also like Karen, Eileen used her other identities as a white, professional-class woman and mother to bust stereotypes and myths.

Previous recreational cannabis users who never adopted lifestyle indicators or beliefs that aligned with the stereotypes had already established their position of resistance, and the adoption of medical use did little to change that relationship. Jason, for instance, had regularly used cannabis over his adult life. When asked if using cannabis medically had changed how he perceived his use, he said, "Not really. The only thing it's really done is made me a little more comfortable and not feel like I'm just hiding something. I just feel more comfortable now. That it's more accepted."

A fiscal conservative in the financial industries, Jason has a very clean-cut, businesslike appearance—from his haircut and tie to his choice in shoes—and has never identified with any characteristics stereotypically associated with cannabis use. Like about a quarter of the participants in this study, Jason had consistently voted Republican, "except for Obama." He expressed disdain for hippies and for the Occupy movement that had targeted his industry, saying of the protestors, "Get a job! Go get a job, instead of sitting around in the park moaning about how you don't have anything. Go get a job. There are jobs out there. You can go flip burgers."

Nothing about Jason's attitude conformed to stereotypical expectations of cannabis users.[2] Even though he had regularly used cannabis over his entire adult life, more than sixteen years, he felt it had had no influence on his political views or outlook toward others, other than his views on the specific issue of marijuana laws. Like most people in this study, Jason had no trouble easily coming up with the most common stereotypes applied to cannabis users. The adoption of the medical cannabis identity allowed him to be more open about use because it insulated him from stereotypes.

A few patients in this study maintain identification with "hippie" ethics, strongly left-leaning politics, or clothing and hairstyle choices that could be associated culturally with this group, but most knew that cannabis users didn't neatly fit this profile and vice versa. It might seem that the "hippies" would be more likely to embrace recreational cannabis culture than those like Jason, but it was not that clear cut. Some, such as Valerie, were very hippie in fashion and also in their cultural and political affiliations, but others such as Yvonne, who claims to "wear a lot of hippie garb, even to church," had a clear disdain for much of cannabis culture. Yvonne attributes her clothing choices to comfort and retirement from work rather than as representative of her politics or personality. She describes herself as more of an overachiever, a fact that made it very hard for her to accept the limitations of fibromyalgia. She says that before she "got her wings trimmed" from the physical mobility limitations that fibromyalgia creates, she had been "really judgmental . . . after being around people in Oregon" whom she saw as "lazy potheads" who didn't want to work. Overall, she was disapproving of using cannabis as a way to make claims that you could not do other things. Using it to be more functional was the appropriate moral orientation.

By contrast, others such as Julie, a school teacher, or Aaron, who worked in a job that dealt with the criminal justice system, embraced participation in recreational cannabis settings and had an affinity to cannabis culture. Julie's appearance was professional but with an edge: frosty hair, heavy mascara, and a sleeveless shirt that showed off her upper left arm tattoo. Of cannabis culture, she said:

> I like it. I think it's just my rebel spirit. I mean, I got my tattoo on my arm. . . . I'm not a rule follower, per se. I always look for holes in the rules. So, it is exciting for me to kind of rally together with the people that have helped get this through. There's a kinship to marijuana. . . . It's neat how marijuana can bridge that gap between different parts of society.

Ultimately, patients were aware of the stereotypes about cannabis users, but their own personal style choices may or may not reflect participation in the recreational or medical cannabis communities and cultures, or a rejection of them. Frank, a patient with advanced cancer, was the oldest patient in the study. He lives in an artsy house and told stories of his advanced education, college experiences, travel, and living abroad that conformed in some respects to a "bohemian" lifestyle and outlook. When asked about his views on cannabis user stereotypes and whether he believed that any of them were accurate, he said, "No, that would almost be as stupid as making comments about ethnicity. Some of it's true, but you can't just make a broadcast and have that hold up." In Frank's view, stereotypes are not a very useful way to understand yourself or the world, which allows him to simply dismiss them.

The final dimension that contributes to the effect of stigma on an individual is "outness," or the degree to which one conceals or reveals the identity to others (Quinn et al. 2014). The norm with social cannabis use has been concealment, although how vigilantly use is concealed and from whom often depends on individuals' sense of threat from judgment in their own social groups, in the form of stigma (negative judgment) or interpersonal sanctions (actions, such as excluding the person), as well as their sense of threat from the law or other institutional sanctions (Quinn et al. 2014).

Unlike recreational users who may opt to only use cannabis intermittently and whose identities are only weakly and situationally tied to cannabis, medical cannabis patients have stronger ties to the cannabis identity, though one different from those invoked by stereotype. First, they adopt a consistent, ongoing routine of cannabis use such that use is not isolated, nor is it driven by factors of social setting. Second, when patients register with the state, they establish a formal identity as a cannabis user. They are essentially now card-carrying members of a cannabis community. These two factors create stronger associations between cannabis use and identity for medical cannabis users, making flexible transitions in and out of this identity less possible. An oft-repeated behavior is more likely to translate to an element of social identity, with implications for centrality, salience, and outness, which in turn affects positioning for patient networking and political advocacy (Quinn 2005).

At the same time, the medical designation serves to weaken the connection between cannabis use and cultural stereotype and invokes the value-neutrality of medicine, even if this invocation still occupies contested space. While recreational cannabis use is typically seen as an adjunct to a lifestyle aesthetic that is subject to negative social judgment, or at least as a marker of being "conventionally unconventional," medications are generally understood to be directed at bodily states and are not dependent on one's cultural tastes, although they may be subject to moral determinations about being responsible for one's health. The incomplete medicalization of cannabis casts doubt on this distinction, since medical use cannot rely on full institutional inclusion to create the distinction from other uses.

## "Coming Out" for Cannabis: Stigma and Disclosing Use

Disclosing medical cannabis use within interpersonal interactions becomes a way of declaring its legitimacy while also allowing the patient to show they have nothing to hide from their close family and friends. In a sense, cannabis users "come out of the closet," often in stages of disclosure, starting with those to whom they are most intimately connected—spouses, children, parents, siblings, and best friends. Some will stop there, but others continue to expand the coming out process to weaker networks until it is an undifferentiated, public identity claimed by the person. An interesting effect this creates is the possibility for much more interconnected and self-aware networks. The notion of "coming out" is not restricted to identifying as gay or lesbian. The literature has examined it as a behavioral process among those with other concealable, stigmatized, and stereotyped identities, including those with mental illness, depression, autism spectrum disorder, or as an undocumented immigrant (Corrigan et al. 2010; Davidson and Henderson 2010; McKenna and Bargh 1998; Ridge and Ziebland 2012). As McKenna and Bargh (1998) point out, stigmatized individuals may like to connect with others who share their identity, but when the identity is "concealable and potentially embarrassing" due to cultural devaluation, it may be hard to easily identify others who share it. Disclosure of stigmatizing characteristics or identity requires courage, and all the more so if others have not done so first. These factors are barriers to group formation.

Anita offers an example. When asked if she has ever felt embarrassed about her medical cannabis use, she says:

> In the beginning, for sure. In my line of work [as a caregiver to those with developmental disabilities], people seem to be so hardline against it. So, I am the one in like hundreds of my peers that don't believe that way. It's hard to feel alone. Yeah, it is a very lonely place to be in the work environment, when you can't be outspoken about what you do to alleviate your symptoms. Especially when they saw me getting better. That was really difficult. "Well, what are you doing?" "Diet and exercise." "What else are you doing?" "Getting rid of my prescription medication, doing a lot of herbs." I mean, you find ingenious ways to say it without saying it.

Often, social movements can help redefine stigmatized identities in more positive or prideful terms (Britt and Heise 2000). Even those not actively participating in the social movement take cues from movement leadership in how they frame the issue and their identification with it. This has also applied to contested health-related identities (Brown et al. 2010). For instance, patients with chronic fatigue syndrome were able to collectively create a narrative about their experience and, through the transformation from a personal narrative to a collectivized one, experience a sense of confirmation that serves to support the identity as valid (Bülow 2004; Bülow 2008). This process serves a positive purpose for the individual and builds a stronger base to challenge scientific or medical authority (Brown et al. 2010). For medical cannabis users, that means finding ways to challenge the single story of deviant marijuana use. Patients offer an alternative explanation of cannabis-related science and history in order to revise their affiliation with cannabis from one of shame and embarrassment to one of pride.

Anita's initial sense of embarrassment is shared by many patients, as is its gradual turn to first acceptance and then a more confident claim to the medical cannabis patient identity. Others, like school teacher Julie, were unexpectedly "outed" through participation in activities, which forced them to have the conversation with employers or others when they might have otherwise chosen not to disclose this information. Julie describes disclosing her cannabis use to her supervisor and father, two people whose reactions she had reason to be concerned about:

> My boss knows. When I did the marijuana driving study, I was teaching here. The night before the news was on, I went into my boss' office, and I'm like, alright, I got to tell you something. You might want to fire me. He said we're not going to fire you over this. My father is a minister, and he supports what I do. He loves the fact that it . . . I have a brother that's an alcoholic, and my father has seen firsthand the difference between who's on weed and [his] son, who's an alcoholic. My brother still works at a restaurant, and I have a master's degree.

Lots of patients expressed initial embarrassment or uncertainty, but most claimed they overcame these first feelings and developed a sense of pride in being involved with medical cannabis. With that pride came a willingness to talk about cannabis with anyone who didn't present a direct threat to practical resources. Still, in the discussion, patients will offer other compensating identities such as having a higher degree or other accomplishments, in order to validate that they should be evaluated as well-meaning, non-deviant people.

Advocacy can be a strategy that proactively preempts threats of stigmatization (LeBel 2008). For instance, Andy calls himself a "good poster child for cannabis." He testifies at government hearings and participates in politics. When he was employed in the IT industry, he was very careful with the disclosure of his medical cannabis identity in order to avoid being challenged or fired on this basis. Now, he is unemployed, and this has led him to decide to use his time to be active on the issue. Many other patients expressed a sense of pride, especially with the Colorado's medical marijuana program becoming a frontrunner in the country. For instance, when asked about his attitude, Brett says, "I'm very proud. I'm extremely proud about what I'm doing. I have zero apologies or shame or anything of that type. *And* I'm very proud of Denver."

With medical cannabis, the "coming out" framework is not just a conceptual model imposed by researchers. Medical and recreational cannabis use advocates have adopted this language, and it can be found in public venues as well as conversation. Mary Anne's speech at a medical cannabis conference provides a good example. Mary Anne had left her career in social work and had recently decided to become active in cannabis advocacy, in part based on her husband's involvement in cannabis legal matters through his work as an attorney. In her first public speaking appearance among the cannabis community, Mary Anne stood on stage and said this was her "coming out speech," the first time she had announced publicly that she was a proud supporter of cannabis use. In her talk, she went on to describe how, even after attending meetings where members discussed these issues, she had been afraid to say it was normal and okay to smoke cannabis and had been content to sit on the sidelines and "watch other brave people do the work."

This speech not only explicitly invoked the "coming out" phrase but went further, using the coming out process as a model for the steps she'd taken. She acknowledged that disclosure requires a significant amount of deliberation, in which individuals anticipate the reactions of others, and that disclosure is often frightening and requires one to "be brave." Mary Anne described her experiences before coming out:

> Medical marijuana exploded, and regulations were in the news every day. At my [previous] job, there were stoner jokes every day, and people would roll their eyes, but I said nothing. Every once in a while, I would be brave enough to share something, but my coworkers would just make more jokes.

She goes on to say that people would be surprised if they knew who uses cannabis, implying the diversity that is hidden behind stereotypes. Her job had made public speech risky, but after leaving it, she felt liberated to talk about cannabis without a threat to her livelihood. Now, her job directly relates to cannabis and serving medical marijuana patients. She says that as she started identifying more publicly with the issue:

> I started thinking about how would I come out [about my cannabis affiliation] in other areas of my life—to my son, to his school, to other parents? How would I tell people what I do? It was scary and uncomfortable, so I over-thought and over-planned it.

Then one day, Mary Anne found herself in conversation with the mother of her child's good friend. This mother was one of those seemingly "perfect" women, and Mary Anne was sure she would be judged unfavorably by this woman if she disclosed the nature of her new cannabis industry job, but "when the topic came up, she [the mother] simply said, 'Wow, that's great. What do you tell your son about it?'" Mary Anne says that in all of her imagined conversations with acquaintances, she had never thought of someone asking her this question. In response, she said "My son understands the importance of patients having medications, but he's six. That's all he needs. But when he's older, I expect to tell him the truth." To that, the other mother said, "That makes sense." This, Mary Anne recounts, was when she realized that, in this ordinary location, she had "come out" to someone as a cannabis advocate, and she had not been subject to stigma. The person had not reverted to cultural stereotypes. Mary Anne describes taking more opportunities after that to identify herself as a medical cannabis patient. She ended her talk by exhorting others to "tell the truth in every conversation you have. You know that you are on the side of right. Help spread the message that it is normal to smoke marijuana."

### Pride and Privacy

Even though many patients claimed to be "out and proud" about their medical cannabis identity, there were situations where disclosure was more challenging or seemed inappropriate even for them. A few patients reported not identifying publicly out of a fear of reprisals. For instance, as a resident in public housing, Gary feels that speaking publicly or acting politically on this issue could cause him to lose his home (something about which he is correct[3]), so he is very discreet, and his only point of disclosure is through a pseudonym online.

Disclosure is not just a yes/no or an either/or proposition. Individuals must decide not only whether to disclose the cannabis use but when and how to *hide* that same information and how to *frame* that information. These factors vary across situations. While most people disclosed use in some situations, there were instances where they felt it was important to be discreet, especially when children were involved. For instance, when asked if there is any situation in which he would hide his medical cannabis use, Frank says:

FRANK: Uh, yeah. I, I've got this decision to make here in about a week from Thursday because all of my kids are bringing in their kids. They're going to go stay at [a hotel], and the kids are going to stay here. So, I've got four of them, but I don't want to go . . . I mean, the oldest is fifteen, and the youngest is one. So, I don't see how trying to convert them into any type of knowledge that . . .
INT: Because they're kids?
FRANK: Yeah, and I don't think that they have enough information to make a logical decision. Is grandpa just crazy or what?

Others were concerned not only about whether children could understand medical cannabis use, but they worried about spillover of stigma to their spouse or children. The literature refers to this as "courtesy stigma" (Birenbaum 1970). For instance, Jason says he is comfortable that his friends and family know about his use, but he would not want his medical cannabis use to be known by the parents of his child's friends. In addition, even though his in-laws know about his medical cannabis use, he would feel uncomfortable having a direct discussion about it.

INT: In what situation would you feel uncomfortable if somebody outed you as a medical marijuana user?

JASON: At my kid's school. Or in front of my in-laws. But they all know. All of them know anyway, but it's not something that I feel comfortable talking to them about.

INT: Do you think it would change their impression of you in some way?

JASON: No, because they've known me since I was sixteen, or since I was in the fourth grade. So, they know me anyway. But my kid's friends' parents don't. And I don't want them to think, "Oh gee, I can't let my kid go over to their house because their dad is a stoner."

Jason preferred not to discuss his use with acquaintances or strangers, which aligned with his desire to minimize the medical cannabis identity as a significant part of his personal story. Even though he relied on cannabis, he says:

I have never really considered marijuana to be that influential in anything really in my life, except for making me happy. Or not stressed. It's really more of a stress reliever than anything, for me. I don't have an upset stomach when I use it; I don't have heartburn; I don't get pains in my side . . . I don't agree that it's illegal. I don't think it should be.

Even though Jason had views about the politics of cannabis, he did not desire to make the issue an important part of his political identity. Likewise, even though he found it to be incredibly useful medicine for GERD, he did not want his use of cannabis to overshadow areas that he valued more for his sense of identity. Discussing his use with acquaintances felt like it identified him with the issue in a way that made him uncomfortable.

Some patients lost relationships over their medical cannabis use, usually due to religious or political beliefs of others that could not accommodate this practice within their ideologies. When asked about examples of this, Dale says:

DALE: Well, actually, my daughter. She's way into the religious stuff and goes to church every Sunday and teaches Sunday school. . . . She was raised up with a stereotype of marijuana, you know. She found out I have my card, and I haven't talked to her since.

INT: Is that [the medical cannabis] the reason why?

DALE: I imagine that's the reason why. But that sounds to me like it's a personal problem of hers, because it helps me. You know, that's her personal problem.

Unlike Jason, Dale was very outspoken about his use. Instead of controlling the identity by not talking about it, he felt it was the responsibility of others to be tolerant of his views even if they were different than their own. He felt like honesty was important, and being a patient was an integral part of his experience that had created many positive effects in his life. If his daughter could not accept this about him, she was unable to accept him. Dale did not feel he should change his behavior based on his daughter's disapproval.

A handful of patients reported conflicts with others over their use, but it was usually in more distant relationships. A few patients compartmentalized the medical cannabis identity similarly to Jason, usually based on their lack of connection with cannabis culture and its signifying aesthetics. However, many more placed at least some importance on the medical cannabis patient identity and felt it was important to take a stand on the issue. Like many others, Brett told a story of losing his best friend from high school over his involvement with the medical cannabis issue, and his attitude was much the same as Dale's, in part because the relationship was not close anymore. Like nearly all other patients, Brett checked in with his immediate family. He says that he would not have gotten involved if his children had objected. Others reported making a "family" decision with spouses and say they would probably not have decided to use cannabis had their spouse rejected the idea. A few patients such as Karen were married to other medical cannabis patients with serious disorders, but the majority had spouses who did not use cannabis medically or recreationally, despite the opportunity to do so.

While a small group of patients in this study preferred to fly completely under the radar and did not discuss medical cannabis with anyone outside of their closest relationships, the majority had adopted a proactive, educational approach and expressed a willingness to talk to anyone. Brett captures the willingness to discuss the issue:

> I try very much to gauge where the people are at. If they're completely not ready for the information, and the wall is up, I'm not going to frustrate them or myself. I've learned how to gauge and not try to force, or, you know. It just depends if they don't want to hear it. But the one thing I won't allow anybody to do is to put any kind of judgment on me or to try to give me information that's not accurate. What happens a lot of the time is that people will make up real quick, off-the-cuff remarks, like, "Oh, well, that's bad," and I won't let that stand. I have to correct the inaccuracy. But if they don't have the information, and they don't want it, God bless you. Then so be it. But I won't allow anybody to put wrong information out there.

Brett's comment shows the adamant refusal to allow stereotypes to go unnoticed or unchallenged, while simultaneously avoiding "frustrating" situations where someone is "not ready for the information." Brett illustrates the shift to pride in coming to believe that he is right—factually and morally. But aside from not allowing the perpetuation of stigma, he does not need to preach to anyone.

### Deconstructing Stigma With Normalcy

Patients often express pride in being involved with medical cannabis, but the issue with the medical cannabis identity—and this is likely true of other stigmatized identities—is that those who have it do not wish to bring *more* attention to that aspect of themselves *as an identity*. With medical cannabis there is an identity struggle. While some cannabis users proudly participate in aspects of the ongoing culture surrounding recreational use and medical advocacy, another group prefers to not emphasize this identity. Rather, they see the path forward as one of de-emphasis or "normalization." Rather than seeking recognition of their cannabis identity, they want to be treated "just like everyone else."

Tina describes this identity issue well. When asked if there is anywhere outside of work where she would feel uncomfortable identifying herself as a medical cannabis patient, she says:

TINA: No, it's who I am, and it's part of my life.
INT: Do you feel like it's become an important part of your identity to say that you are a medical cannabis patient?
TINA: Yes, but it's not my identity. I have more identities, I would say . . . that I would rather identify myself as being attached to me. It's my medicine. When I was taking Vicodin or Percocet or methadone I didn't run around making that part of my identity. However, it was obvious it was part of my identity. It was pretty bad. But no, because I think with the younger generation, it is a big part of their identity. Just the younger generations, until people grow and mature in life and find out what their true purpose and identity in this life and on this world is that, yeah, they do grab those superficial things. And to me that would be a superficial identity.
INT: The medical marijuana identity?
TINA: Yes, but then again, it is part of who I am because look at how much it has changed my life.

While some patients simply said they were comfortable or even proud of their association with medical cannabis, others, like Jason and Mike, seemed indifferent. After an HIV diagnosis during the late 1980s when Mike was in his early twenties, he lived much of the next thirty years expecting to die. In terms of his identity with medical cannabis, Mike says: "It doesn't affect my life in any way. I've always lived my life how I want." Most patients said they would identify themselves as patients to discuss or educate others on the issue, but many did not want to push their views on others. As Brett says in the earlier quote, they do not feel the need to convert anyone who "isn't ready." As we will see next in the discussion of collective responses to stigma through the medical cannabis thought community, Brett's comments also exemplify the "to each his own" attitude that is widely shared among patients.

Tina raises points that were echoed in part by some other patients, but, in identifying how the behaviors and characteristics that can be used to define identities change over time as individuals transition through the life course, she says something many others seemed to find hard to articulate. The identity of a cannabis patient at midlife is fundamentally different from someone in their teens, in part because of life experience and position in the life course but also because individuals at midlife are no longer typically engaged in as much identity experimentation as they were in young adulthood. They are more secure in their identity, and medical cannabis is simply not as important as their other roles as partner, spouse, and/or parent, or even their career or hobby pastimes. Those seeking to incorporate medical cannabis into the umbrella of normative behaviors do not deny their identity as medical cannabis users; they just do not wish to promote it to a level of importance that overshadows other aspects of their identity.

## Patients as a Thought Community

Given the risks associated with becoming a medical cannabis user described in chapter 8, identifying as a member of the group of medical users offers an interpretive framework that provides a means of building esteem and cohesion. That group membership can take a few forms. Medical cannabis activists deserve to be acknowledged for their significant accomplishments as a social and political movement, but not all medical cannabis patients consider themselves part of a social movement or become politically involved through social movement activity. What emerges from the interviews as a shared trait among people from a wide range of backgrounds is a distinctive group style and rhetoric advancing common themes, which suggests that medical cannabis patients form a "thought community."

A thought community is unlike a social movement in that its members are a more loosely connected collection of actors who are linked by a shared social role. Thought communities can be connected through kinship, work, religion, or politics but are defined by shared norms, values, ideals, and social perspectives that reflect a particular collective world view beyond individual subjectivity (Zerubavel 1997). The shared, intersubjective interpretations are not based on in-person relationships between the various members but, nonetheless, include elements that come to reflect a group style and offer tools on which individuals can draw to support their position (Arksey 1994; Eliasoph and Lichterman 2003; Rose 2007; Zerubavel 1997). The notion of thought communities is akin to Mead's (1934) concept of the generalized other in that both capture the perspectives of social collectivities that enter into the thinking of the individual (Cockerham 2005, 59). How groups form a style of interpretation around collective representations plays a key role in how culture works in everyday settings (Eliasoph and Lichterman 2003).

### Antiestablishment as a "Group Style"

Participants in this study represented the full political spectrum. Roughly one-third were Republican or Libertarian; one-third Democrat; and one-third Independent, uncertain, or unaffiliated. Culturally, they ranged from old hippies to ex-military, completely secular to devoutly religious, and well-off to abjectly poor. One clear thread ran through attitudes: a disdain for government interference in this issue and most other ones, too.

The group style among medical cannabis patients emphasizes antiestablishment views in which individuals should be free to do what they want without government interference, so long as it does not harm or disrupt others. Emphasis is placed on the fundamental rights of individuals to sovereignty over their own bodies. Patients do not want to be told by government what they can or cannot do in the privacy of their own homes. Anita describes this amorphous political orientation:

> I'm unaffiliated [with a political party] because I believe I run with the common-sense crowd, and there is no political party that follows that yet. I am very fiscally conservative but definitely more of a Constitutionalist, I believe, and that's only because I don't like all the control that we are seeing on the federal level. I'm definitely not liberal, because I'm not big on social programs. I'd like to see them [the feds] out of our hair. . . . My mother is—has always been—a registered Republican. I grew up in a Baptist home with two parents, two-point-two kids, the dog, the white picket fence: the American dream. Even my mom is on board with this whole medicinal thing because she can't see why the federal government would say that it's not helpful when she has seen what it can do. It's not a liberal or a conservative issue. It's a human issue. That [partisanship] is what we've got to let go of.

Many agreed that the issue is or should be nonpartisan, but this broadly libertarian attitude extended beyond an opinion about the balance between government authority and people's rights; it was a belief in an ethic of autonomy that extends to the treatment of others—which often meant deferring to the judgments of others. Not all patients subscribed to a strong version of this tenet, but many patients seemed to subscribe to a "to each his own" kind of mentality about life in general. Just as patients did not care for what they perceived to be the government's illegitimate role in policing their medical care, most showed a clear desire to avoid putting themselves in roles that involve enforcing the rules of the system upon others, as Andy does here:

> I consider myself a principled Libertarian. . . . If there's no victim involved, I don't care. I want to be clear about that. And [before becoming a patient] I had no interest in pot. Frankly, I really kind of looked down my nose at potheads. So even though I didn't much like potheads, I didn't think it was my business. . . . I am a legitimate patient who also does not believe that society has a right to tell recreational users that they shouldn't be using it. So, I see them both as rights.

Concerns with government overreach were bolstered by patients' concerns with government decisions about pharmaceutical drugs. Most have had considerable direct experience with multiple prescribed medications, and, in their estimation, the government's motives could not be more clearly non-medical. Patients get very heated and angry on this topic. Many had experienced side effects from pharmaceutical drugs ranging from the unpleasant to the catastrophic, a thread we pursue in the next chapter. Those interviewed share a belief that, as medical cannabis patients, they have gotten past the propaganda to more accurate information about cannabis' safety profile, medical efficacy, and other aspects. When others espouse views that cannabis or its users present dangers, patients judge these people to be misinformed and have confidence their understanding is more accurate. This supports high in-group esteem, as they see themselves as both smarter and healthier than their detractors (Ellemers, Spears, and Doosje 2002).

After discovering that cannabis was a more useful, or at least less problematic, medicine than those pharmaceuticals, many patients came to believe it had been denied them or their loved one in the service of profit, politics, and power. Patients express the view that the government's stated public health motives are not the real reasons for maintaining policies that classify cannabis as an illicit, highly dangerous drug of abuse. They do not believe that current drug laws are effective or result in anyone being safer. Rather, they see the motivations as versions of power-brokering and greed—the height of corruption in the system. Many patients voiced opinions that governmental duties of protection and public health have been subsumed by corporate interests (Waitzkin 2011).

Interestingly, patients' antiestablishment perspective spanned all political outlooks from left to right, although those who were left progressives tended to frame it in the language of civil rights, while those on the right tended to link these attitudes with small government, money, politics, and other more libertarian-leaning sentiments in which the government had little right or reason to direct its citizen's personal lives. There was no mistaking that, regardless of their politics, the cannabis issue created strong negative emotions about a perception of the government overstepping their bounds by interfering with a person's right to their own body.

Eileen, who identifies as a centrist independent with a progressive lean, characterizes it as follows:

> It has been so many years since the Seventies, and we're even more repressed than ever in many ways. Why is the federal government still against this and refused medicinal value? . . . It just doesn't make sense, and it's disheartening when you feel like it's so hard to make change. . . . But I just follow my heart with what I felt was right, and for me it became a civil rights issue more than anything else, where how much involvement should government have in our personal lives and in what we put in our body, things like that.

Eileen couches her point of view in frames that are probably more typical of the rhetoric found among Democrats and left-leaning politics with a dash of personal sovereignty. Others, such as Carl, who identifies as a lukewarm Libertarian, feels that the laws are not designed at all to serve in the interest of the people but are instead driven by economic self-interest:

> It's political. It's all it is, is political. They're trying to justify their existence. They fought it [the drug war] for so long that they will go to any extremes to make sure it remains that way. The pharmaceutical companies want to own it [cannabis], because they're losing out big. Monsanto, different people, want to control it. So, I think that it's all politics and control. And it's about money. There's tons of money being brought over the Mexican border and marijuana and cocaine and other drugs. It's all money. And I want to say the biggest thing, the reason the government is against it, the reason they're fighting—everything they do is about the money. It's not about being right or wrong. It's about the money.

Patients did not hesitate when asked if they would stop using cannabis medically were the law to change. This would not stop them. Patients were adamant that changes to the law would only affect their discretion—the degree of concealment—but they would be undeterred. Only one patient, Beth, said she would stop using cannabis if the law were reversed, and her use was no longer legal. As a Jehovah's Witness, Beth believes she is obligated to obey the laws in order to be in accord with her faith.

### Privacy and the Body

Both cannabis use and illnesses or injuries are embodied experiences. According to Bobel and Kwan (2011) "[c]ultural theorists have long asserted that social relations of power produce bodies that are disciplined and resistant" (2). Both illness and "cannabinated" states may be considered forms of "unruly bodies" (Aggarwal 2006). Medicalization is meant to transform their deviance through the social control of medicine. The exclusion of cannabis from the formal corpus of medicine may be as much about the plant's ability to create "unruly bodies" as it is about any other factor. Even as medicalization introduces control over cannabis to the medical domain, it remains layered with the control of cannabis exerted through the legal system (Medina and McCranie 2011). The intersection of legal, social, and medical categorizations of cannabis plays out on the patient body, engaging norms that surround bodies, medicine, and health. As with other norms governing our bodies, we can attempt to conform *or at least appear to*, or we can flaunt our differences (Bobel and Kwan 2011).

Cannabis states may be considered "unruly," but this characterization may rely more on different norms related to how those states are embodied in relation to set, setting, and life course than it does to a more simplistic focus on the drug's pharmacological ability to intoxicate. In a world where the use of antidepressants, opioids, and other mood-altering prescription drugs have become commonplace, the argument against cannabis' particular intoxication and mood-altering capabilities increasingly relies on cultural tradition and context rather than physiological effects. This is most stark—absurd, even—when comparing the safety profile of cannabis with the unstigmatized prescription options. Even compared to common over-the-counter medications such as Tylenol (acetaminophen) or Advil (ibuprofen), cannabis is exponentially less toxic, both in terms of fatal overdose potential and damage from long-term use.

Whatever their sentiment about cannabis intoxication, one thing was very clear among the patients in this study: They all felt strongly that they had a right to their own bodies and what they put in them. Most agree that this is true, no matter the reason, but Andy captures why the medical designation changes things:

> Basically, it's "You don't have a right to tell me I can't enjoy pot," and "How *dare* you tell me I can't have my medicine?!" So, I guess the indignation level is higher on the medicine.

While it is difficult to understand banning a leisure activity that poses few harms and is less likely to create dependence than tobacco, alcohol, or even coffee, it borders on cruel and unusual punishment to block access to a substance that can relieve pain, slow the progress of certain diseases, prevent seizures, and treat conditions for which there are no effective conventional options. Like Andy, Frank focuses on the illegitimacy of the government telling people what they can do privately with their bodies in the name of their own health, wellness, and survival:

> If you've got a goddamn debilitating disease, who is the government to tell you what you should be taking or not taking? I mean, if I firmly

believe that chocolate syrup would make me feel better, I'd go drink chocolate syrup. But don't make a law that says I can't do that. I mean, that's bullshit. Even if you believe the science or don't believe the science—which there's very little science [supporting prohibition of cannabis].

According to Frank's view, obtaining expert guidance is the prerogative of the individual, but following that guidance is supposed to be a choice that serves the individual, rather than a method by which the individual loses options and risks punishment from the state. In many ways, Gary agrees with both Andy and Frank when he says:

Why does the state have to be somebody's nanny? I don't see the purpose in that. I'm an adult. I've been around for a while. So, if I find legitimate use for a particular substance—in my case, medical cannabis—then I don't want some bean counter or some government official telling me that's bad for my health when what I have read tells me something different.

Gary's comment also points to the relevance of life course. By using terms like "nanny" and "I'm an adult," Gary emphasizes the importance of responsible adult use. His statement invokes generations of government anti-drug messaging aimed at young people, implying that, in trying to prevent teen use of cannabis, we treat everyone like children who are not yet capable of exercising sound judgment.

The group style found among medical cannabis patients emphasizes individual autonomy, a fundamental right to sovereignty over one's own body, and specifically emphasizes the illegitimacy of government actions that encroach on individual privacy. Patients share a moral agenda that establishes an alternate narrative in which cannabis patients are virtuous and the government's actions are debased. Despite a certainty about occupying the moral high ground, the "to each his own" aspect of this "group style" tends not to support traditional social movement organization and may discourage coordinated, collective action because it supports individualism over coordination, even in social actions—possibly to the detriment of the issue overall.

### Defending Medical Cannabis Against the System

Many explained cannabis' ongoing illegal status, despite proof that it had medical value, as being due to the system feeling "threatened" in terms of profit and power. Nearly every patient mentioned some version of either industry or government or both having a vested financial interest in maintaining cannabis illegality. They saw business and government as willing to say and do nearly criminally irrational things to protect their financial interests and social control. The mantra from patients on this topic was "follow the money." In essence, they were arguing that the system's interests in maintaining profit, or customers, was largely against the interest of people and their health. Beth captures what many express when she says:

BETH: There is more regulation in this one little industry than there is on Wall Street!

INT: Why do you think they're doing that?

BETH: For the same reason that they stop every kind of a cure that comes around that they can't patent—"they" being the medical world, the drug world, so be it. I mean doctors are not doctors in the true sense of the word anymore. They only know how to prescribe meds. . . . I mean, I can't remember when doctors actually fixed you, when they didn't just give you drugs and say "go home, and if that doesn't work, we'll try another drug." So *that* industry, the medical prescription industry, is against anything that is going to take patients away.

From a system perspective, curing patients is losing customers. Ongoing treatments ensure continued business, even if it is to the consumer's detriment. By contrast, cannabis aligns with lifeworld goals for health. It is natural, cheap to produce, and nontoxic. Beth speaks for this view, saying:

Cannabis in my opinion, based on my knowledge, experience, and extensive—and I mean extensive—research, other people's research, reading other people's research, it is absolutely the most human-friendly plant on the planet.

Patients consistently described the "establishment" or system's goals as antithetical to goals of wellness in the lifeworld, with cannabis portrayed as an almost heroic antidote to many of these problems. Many, like Ron, express great outrage at the moral violation of placing money ahead of life:

I think that the conspiracy is insidious. It is wrapped up into the god of this earth, money. Our society has sold its soul for money. We don't care about life anymore. We only care about money! And after we get money, we want to have power to protect the money. So, that's what's going on in our country now. We don't have medicine to help people. We've got medicines to addict people on multiple medicines that continually get one more to take care of the last symptom that the last med gave you, and then you need one more and one more. My mother, ninety years old, must have 150 different prescriptions that she has to take, for chrissakes. And how do you ever stop doing any of them, because nobody knows. The doctors don't know, and pharmaceutical companies don't care because it's just ka-ching, ka-ching, ka-ching, ka-ching. It's all about money.

Patients also take the government to task for serving as the handmaid to the pharmaceutical industry rather than protecting the interests of the people. Tina makes this connection in her critique:

> The government knows what is in these pills. They also know the good that medical marijuana, that marijuana does. They know it's medicine. They've known for years. Our founding fathers [used cannabis and hemp]. This is research that I have looked into since I've gotten sick, and it infuriates me. Not just the marijuana but hemp. Hemp provides enzymes that keep diseases out of our body, like the one I have. What's going on, really? To me, the whole reason I see behind it, I can't think of any other humane reason—and you can't put money on a human life—but that's what it is. It's about money. When they realized the money they can make off these pills? You're going to get longevity with marijuana. You're going to kill these people with the pills. When they are dead in the ground, are you still going to get money from them? No, you're going to go after the next generation. Last night Walgreens was hit again [robbed] for their pharmaceuticals. It's not just these people that are taking them that it's prescribed to, [pharmaceuticals are] on the streets. And they're worried about the marijuana being on the streets?!

Carl captures another aspect of this argument when he claims, as many patients do, that cannabis has remained illegal because the pharmaceutical industry has not yet figured out how to turn it into a commodity. He says:

> If they can't replicate it, they can't control the market. They can't have a patent on it. And that comes right down to money and money only. For pharmaceutical companies. I think pharmaceutical companies put more money into campaigns[4] and more money in to fight it [cannabis legalization] just for the reason of money. Follow the money. If we can grow a plant for ourselves, they can't tax it, other than charging us a fee to have a license to be able to do it. They can't sell it. They can't. . . . Just follow the money. My idea is just follow the money. Because it's the big pharmacies. It's getting all the politicians to fight it. That should be banned. All these contributions should be banned, totally, from unions, from pharmacies, because it's— What do they call it when you can't try a case because you're involved with it or whatever? Conflict of interest. It's a total conflict of interest, everything they're doing, every law they're making, because they're either drawing their paycheck by doing this, or they want to draw their paycheck. Ten million dollars a year is going into enforcement from our licenses.

Many believe that once cannabis is seen as capable of meeting the system's demand for making money, either through product development that the pharmaceutical industry can profit from or through government fees and taxes on use, the laws will change. Hugh, who lives with HIV, starts by discussing the pharmaceutical industry's direct-to-consumer advertising but claims that, as the system begins to draw profits from medical cannabis, the changes to the law will cascade in favor of cannabis. Hugh says of direct-to-consumer advertising of pharmaceuticals:

HUGH: It cheapens it badly. It's like when lawyers and doctors started being able to advertise . . .
INT: Like the ambulance chasers' ads?
HUGH: Yeah. I first saw that in California, but they're still not allowed in New York. You still can't do it [have those types of ads]. But what *really* got to me was to see how some of the politicians behave. Actually, in general, not just about marijuana. They all want to be on the bandwagon, and they smell the cash. The taxation money. They smell it. I know we've hit the point of no return [on medical cannabis becoming accepted] because they've got all this extra [tax] money [from fees on the cannabis industry] earmarked. They've already raided the patient medical marijuana annual fee [fund] several times. They've diverted it to the general fund.
INT: Do you think that's true of all politicians, or are there some who [will still oppose it]?
HUGH: Very few exceptions who oppose it. But those, once they smell the cash, they turn, too.

These recriminations about the system and the actions of people within it, who they see as kowtowing to money and power against the interest of human values, left patients feeling righteously defiant and stubbornly proud. Cannabis use takes on the valence of an act of civil disobedience against unjust and morally bankrupt laws. This political stance enables the cultural shift from shame to pride.

The pride self-identifying medical cannabis patients feel may be tied to a sense of special knowledge and insight on cannabis they acquired from their research, but the lack of authoritative sources in the age of the internet creates a lay expertise that mixes the scientific with the fantastical and conspiratorial. In most patient accounts, information recounted about the plant, the laws, and the policy included some parts that were objectively wrong. Even while medical cannabis patients push back against the system using the most legitimate information they can identify, the lack of available recourse to an authority, whether government or medicine, creates insularity. The thought community becomes an echo chamber of ideas, facts, and anecdotes that form a strong narrative—in this case, one that serves to counter the single story. The lifeworld's emphasis on the power of narrative allows for a lower threshold of proof than systems typically demand. The mixture of verifiable facts with less reliable information can create barriers to others believing it, often making it difficult to "sell" the idea to even potential allies, much less critics.

## Flipping the Coin from Stigma to Prejudice

It may be that the true shift in movements such as medical cannabis, gay rights, and others comes when the stigmatized identity is no longer accepted as normative, and the stereotypes are redefined as unjust. How does a stereotype lose acceptance within a culture? One step is in public identification of group members and the diversity of individuals it reveals. Stigma, as classically defined by Goffman (1986 [1963]), allows one characteristic of a person to overshadow all others in a discrediting way. Perceiving diversity within the stigmatized group breaks down the single story because that diversity erodes singular definitions on which stereotypes are founded to reveal complexities hidden within. This is especially relevant when, as with medical cannabis patients, a group was able to hide an identity but then begins to claim it. The choice of many people to claim the medical cannabis patient identity allows them to use speech, behavior, and other identifiers to serve as countervailing cases to the stereotypes, as Karen described in the introduction. This reveals what was hidden by criminalization: Cannabis users are threaded invisibly through everyone's family, workplace, and social networks. Central to this shift have been two emerging groups of medical cannabis patients: the elderly and children. Both groups defy stoner stereotypes, not least because they are well outside the normative life course for cannabis use. Medical cannabis patients in both groups also tend to occupy the least problematic subset of patients for public perception: the very seriously ill for whom other courses of treatment have been unsuccessful. The pediatric seizure cases of the sort captured by the CNN special reports are particularly difficult to fit into any drug user stereotypes: young children are innocent of ulterior motive; they cannot advocate for themselves; and the medical conditions are horrifyingly difficult to treat. As these types of patients come to dominate the public debate about access, stereotypes lose their purchase on the public imagination.

Another step in combatting stigma is to establish that the stereotype is not a freestanding or universal fact about the world but is a claim with an author and promulgators. Identifying a source demotes the stereotype from its status as a norm and links it to its messengers and their motives. Whether it is the government, corporations, or specific stakeholders who are identified as the author(s) or proponent(s), this move helps to pull back the curtain on the normative stance by showing that there are motivated "moral entrepreneurs" behind what has been presented as "universal truth" and may even highlight their historical successes in creating the status quo. Pointing out the architects of the contested "norm" helps cast it as a social construction.

This fits Foucault's idea of power that is "embodied and enacted," rather than possessed, in which "regimes of truth" are reinforced through institutions and discourse (Foucault 1991). The battle for the "truth" is a battle for who gets to set the rules, a battle of the economic and political role of the truth (Rabinow 1991).

Stereotypes begin to lose their normative status through diversification within an identity, through the communication efforts that cross networks, and through assigning authorship to stereotypes. As with stereotypes about women, people of color, and gays and lesbians that have evaporated from polite conversation, the stereotypes about cannabis users may be discarded on the sidelines of history. Those who continue to apply the stereotype by attempting to stigmatize may instead become themselves the subject of evaluation and disrepute when labeled as "prejudiced." This transformation flips the game of marked and unmarked categories. Social scrutiny shifts from the person being stigmatized to those who impose the judgment. The once-stigmatized person is now defined as a person being unfairly discriminated against. The process of labeling in order to discriminate or exclude becomes socially unacceptable—even stigmatizing in and of itself as an attitude attributed to a prejudiced person, a bigot. As with the medicalization of cannabis, this process of flipping stigmatizing representations of users to markers of intolerance and prejudice is incomplete but well on its way.

## Notes

1. This Colorado-based interview study did not capture a full spectrum of racial diversity in the recruited sample. The sample was primarily white, with a few respondents reporting multiple races or Hispanic ethnicity as reflected in the demographics reported in Table 1.2. It would take further investigation to learn if this cultural stereotype resonates with nonwhite groups, or if other common stereotypes would emerge as more prominent.
2. At least not with the most commonly stereotyped and marginalized stereotypes. Seen through the lens of the "frat boy" recreational cannabis user often buffooned in movies, he fits quite well. Much like Jason, members of this group often expect to be exempted from stigmatization—and largely have been—due to belonging to other hegemonic identities: white, male, and economically middle-class or above. As we discuss in the conclusion, these groups are often subject to less enforcement of marijuana laws than other groups. Jason's claim that his views are not affected by this choice is another indicator of his fit with this "unmarked" group.
3. Federal rules control access to public housing as well as many educational benefits such as Pell Grants for attending college. Since the federal government does not make exceptions for state medical marijuana programs, patients risk losing housing, educational funding, and other federal benefits.
4. One of the chief, nongovernmental groups pushing an anti-drug message focused primarily on cannabis use is the Partnership for a Drug-Free America, which was initially funded in the mid to late 1980s by a consortium of leading pharmaceutical makers, along with alcohol and tobacco companies. After a 1992 article in *The Nation* (www.marijuanalibrary.org/Nation030992.html) revealed this, the group dropped its alcohol and tobacco funders but still receives contributions from the pharmaceutical

industry. The same author, Cynthia Cotts, discusses the continued funding from pharmaceuticals in this 2002 drug ad exposé in the *Village Voice* (www.villagevoice.com/2002/05/21/dont-do-drug-ads/), citing a 2000 *Salon* story (www.mapinc.org/drugnews/v00/n1057/a07.html?1164) by Daniel Forbes that argues the pharmaceutical companies were motivated by medical marijuana initiatives in California and Arizona in 1996.

# References

Abdou, Cleopatra M., Adam W. Fingerhut, James S. Jackson, and Felicia Wheaton. 2016. "Healthcare Stereotype Threat in Older Adults in the Health and Retirement Study." *American Journal of Preventive Medicine* 50(2):191–8. doi: 10.1016/j.amepre.2015.07.034.

Aggarwal, Sunil K. 2006. "Embodying Forbidden Cannabinated States." (www.cannabinologist.org/library.html).

Arksey, Hilary. 1994. "Expert and Lay Participation in the Construction of Medical Knowledge." *Sociology of Health & Illness* 16(4):449–68.

Aronson, Joshua, Diana Burgess, Sean M. Phelan, and Lindsay Juarez. 2013. "Unhealthy Interactions: The Role of Stereotype Threat in Health Disparities." *American Journal of Public Health* 103(1):50–6. doi: 10.2105/AJPH.2012.300828.

Birenbaum, Arnold. 1970. "On Managing a Courtesy Stigma." *Journal of Health and Social Behavior* 11(3):196–206.

Bobel, Chris, and Samantha Kwan, eds. 2011. *Embodied Resistance: Challenging the Norms, Breaking the Rules.* Nashville, TN: Vanderbilt University Press.

Britt, Lory, and David R. Heise. 2000. "From Shame to Pride in Identity Politics." Pp. 252–68 in *Self, Identity, and Social Movements*, edited by Sheldon Stryker, Timothy J. Owens and Robert W. White. Minneapolis: University of Minnesota Press.

Brown, Phil, Rachel Morello-Frosch, Stephen Zavestoski, Laura Senier, Altman Rebecca Gasior, Elizabeth Hoover, Sabrina McCormick, Brian Mayer, and Crystal Adams. 2010. "Field Analysis and Policy Ethnography in the Study of Health Social Movements." Pp. 101–16 in *Social Movements and the Transformation of American Health Care*, edited by Jane C. Banaszak-Holl, Sandra R. Levitsky and Mayer N. Zald. New York: Oxford University Press.

Bülow, Pia H. 2004. "Sharing Experiences of Contested Illness by Storytelling." *Discourse & Society* 15(1):33–53. doi: 10.1177/0957926504038943.

Bülow, Pia H. 2008. "Tracing Contours of Contestation in Narratives about Chronic Fatigue Syndrome." Pp. 123–41 in *Contesting Illness: Processes and Practices*, edited by Pamela Moss and Katherine Teghtsoonian. Toronto: University of Toronto Press.

Burke, Peter J., and Jan E. Stets. 2009. *Identity Theory.* New York: Oxford University Press.

Cockerham, William C. 2005. "Health Lifestyle Theory and the Convergence of Agency and Structure." *Journal of Health and Social Behavior* 46:51–67.

Corrigan, Patrick W., Scott Morris, Jon Larson, Jennifer Rafacz, Abigail Wassel, Patrick Michaels, Sandra Wilkniss, Karen Batia, and Nicolas Rüsch. 2010. "Self-Stigma and Coming Out about One's Mental Illness." *Journal of Community Psychology* 38(3):259–75. doi: 10.1002/jcop.20363.

Davidson, Joyce, and Victoria L. Henderson. 2010. "'Coming Out' on the Spectrum: Autism, Identity and Disclosure." *Social & Cultural Geography* 11(2):155–70. doi:10.1080/14649360903525240.

Eliasoph, Nina, and Paul Lichterman. 2003. "Culture in Interaction." *American Journal of Sociology* 108(4):735–94.

Ellemers, Naomi, Russell Spears, and Bertjan Doosje. 2002. "Self and Social Identity." *Annual Review of Psychology* 53(1):161.

Foucault, Michel. 1991. *Discipline and Punish: The Birth of a Prison*. London: Penguin.

Goffman, Erving. 1986 [1963]. *Stigma: Notes on the Management of Spoiled Identity*. New York: Simon and Schuster, Inc.

Hammersly, Richard, Richard Jenkins, and Marie Reid. 2001. "Cannabis Use and Social Identity." *Addiction Research & Theory* 9(2):133–50.

LeBel, Thomas P. 2008. "Perceptions of and Responses to Stigma." *Sociology Compass* 2(2):409–32.

Looby, Alison, and Mitch Earleywine. 2010. "Gender Moderates the Impact of Stereotype Threat on Cognitive Function in Cannabis Users." *Addictive Behaviors* 35:834–9.

McKenna, Katelyn Y. A., and John A. Bargh. 1998. "Coming Out in the Age of the Internet: Identity 'Demarginalization' through Virtual Group Participation." *Journal of Personality & Social Psychology* 75(3):681–94.

Mead, George Herbert. 1934. *Mind, Self, and Society: From the Standpoint of a Social Behaviorist*. Chicago, IL: University of Chicago Press.

Medina, Tait R., and Ann McCranie. 2011. "Layering Control: Medicalization, Psychopathy, and the Increasing Multi-Institutional Management of Social Problems." Pp. 139–58 in *Handbook of the Sociology of Health, Illness, and Healing: A Blueprint for the 21st Century*. Handbooks of Sociology and Social Research, edited by Bernice A. Pescosolido, Jack K. Martin, Jane D. McLeod and Anne Rogers. New York: Springer.

Quinn, Diane M. 2005. "Concealable Versus Conspicuous Stigmatized Identities." Pp. 83–104 in *Stigma and Group Inequality: Social Psychological Perspectives*, edited by Shana Levin and Collette Van Laar. New York: Psychology Press.

Quinn, Diane M., and Stephenie R. Chaudoir. 2009. "Living with a Concealable Stigmatized Identity: The Impact of Anticipated Stigma, Centrality, Salience, and Cultural Stigma on Psychological Distress and Health." *Journal of Personality and Social Psychology* 97(4):634–51. doi: 10.1037/a0015815.

Quinn, Diane M., Michelle K. Williams, Francisco Quintana, Jennifer L. Gaskins, Nicole M. Overstreet, Alefiyah Pishori, Valerie A. Earnshaw, Giselle Perez, and Stephenie R. Chaudoir. 2014. "Examining Effects of Anticipated Stigma, Centrality, Salience, Internalization, and Outness on Psychological Distress for People with Concealable Stigmatized Identities." *PLoS One* 9(5):e96977. doi: 10.1371/journal.pone.0096977.

Rabinow, Paul, ed. 1991. *The Foucault Reader: An Introduction to Foucault's Thought*. London: Penguin.

Ridge, Damien, and Sue Ziebland. 2012. "Understanding Depression through a 'Coming Out' Framework." *Sociology of Health & Illness* 34(5):730–45. doi: 10.1111/j.1467-9566.2011.01409.x.

Rose, Nikolas. 2007. *The Politics of Life Itself*. Princeton, NJ: Princeton University Press.

Schmader, Toni, and Michael Johns. 2003. "Converging Evidence That Stereotype Threat Reduces Working Memory Capacity." *Journal of Personality and Social Psychology* 85(3):440–52.

Smith, Cary Stacy, and Li-Ching Hung. 2008. "Stereotype Threat: Effects on Education." *Social Psychology of Education* 11(3):243–57. doi: 10.1007/s11218-008-9053-3.

Steele, Claude M. 1999. "Thin Ice: 'Stereotype Threat' and Black College Students." *Atlantic Monthly*:44–54.

Thoits, Peggy A. 2011. "Resisting the Stigma of Mental Illness." *Social Psychology Quarterly* 74(1):6–28. doi: 10.1177/0190272511398019.

U.S. Commission on Marihuana and Drug Abuse. 1972. *Marihuana: A Signal of Misunderstanding: The Official Report of the National Commission on Marihuana and Drug Abuse.* New York: New American Library.

Waitzkin, Howard. 2011. *Medicine and Public Health and the End of Empire.* Boulder, CO: Paradigm Publishers.

Zerubavel, Eviatar. 1997. *Social Mindscapes.* Cambridge, MA: Harvard University Press.

# Chapter 10

# Beyond Medicalization
## Healthism and Pharmaceuticalization

The (re)medicalization of cannabis has been the work of a century. Medicalization as a process has been theorized with defined phases, but a strict linear progression is not apparent, nor is it clear that once medicalization is started, it is sure to finish. Medicalization also does not stand alone. It is a part of a nexus of cultural, economic, political, and environmental forces. In this final chapter, we consider medical cannabis in the context of medicalization's companion concepts, healthism[1] and pharmaceuticalization. Just as medicalization captures the process by which behaviors or substances that were previously not considered to be medical are incorporated into the realm of medicine, healthism and pharmaceuticalization refer to trends in which behaviors or conditions are grouped within the realm of health or pharmacy. A quick look at how these concepts have been developed and used will help explain how they apply to the medical use of cannabis.

Healthism indicates the trend in society by which more elements of everyday life and lifestyle are incorporated under the mandate of health. Many researchers on health and medicine have noted the significance of increased attention to health in society, paralleled by a rise of health-oriented self-help books, fitness centers, and a focus on natural health (Schuster et al. 2004). In an age when the disease burden has shifted from acute to chronic illnesses, health becomes inextricably linked to lifestyle choices, and healthful behavior takes on a moral character of individual responsibility (Cheek 2008; Conrad 2007; Greenhalgh and Wessely 2004; Turner 2004). Health maintenance and, to some degree, medical care moves toward the management of health risks (Cheek 2008; Lewis 2006). Since the 1980s, researchers have proffered healthism as a way to describe increased associations of behaviors with health, as opposed to becoming directly connected with formal medicine (Crawford 1980).

Pharmaceuticalization, on the other hand, has been identified as a process by which social, behavioral, or bodily conditions are seen as treatable with pharmaceutical drugs (Abraham 2010). The early medicalization literature gave only limited consideration to the pharmaceutical industry, paying greater attention to doctor–patient interactions, medical categories, and health care institutions. However, work in recent decades by medicalization's seminal author, Peter Conrad, along with others has made connections between many trends and medicalization, including diminished authority of doctors, increased corporatization of health care, greater consumer involvement, lower tolerance for mild health issues, increased demand for medical solutions, more technological involvement in health care, increases in direct-to-consumer advertising, greater access to health information of varying quality through the internet, and exponential increases in pharmaceutical use, especially among Americans (Ayers and Kronenfeld 2007; Clarke et al. 2003; Conrad 2005; Conrad and Barker 2010; Kivits 2009; Lewis 2006; Renahy and Chauvin 2006; Tomes 2016). Pharmaceuticalization research proposes that the greater use of prescription drugs may be a central driver of medicalization, especially since the introduction of Prozac in the late 1980s (Abraham 2010; Conrad 2007). Medicalization and pharmaceuticalization are related processes but are separable and can occur independently, as exemplified by cases when drugs become available or become more widely used in the treatment of an established medical condition (Abraham 2010). In this case, prescription drugs do not expand the domain of medicine, but they do expand the use of pharmaceutical drugs within medicine.

In previous chapters, we have argued that some patients manage routines of medical cannabis use similarly to pharmaceuticals. In evaluating medical cannabis use in relation to pharmaceuticalization and healthism, the question is: How do patients come to see their medical cannabis use? Is it primarily in terms of a medication similar to pharmaceuticals or a health behavior? Each category implies an approach that informs behaviors and attitudes toward cannabis as medicine, but are the categories mutually exclusive in this case? Looking at how patients include cannabis in each of these categories helps to elaborate cannabis' relationship with the trends of healthism and pharmaceuticalization.

## Healthism and Harms

Over the past three decades, health promotion and wellness has expanded greatly in western culture (Conrad 1994; Parusnikova 2000). The "new health morality" transforms health into a more conscious presence outside of the medical encounter. Wellness means making improvements to health through self-control, discipline, lay expertise, and self-knowledge, all suffused with an aura of morality (Kihlstrom and Kihlstrom 1999, 29). Wellness seekers engage in a discourse that blends moral aims and scientific claims around health promotion to construct a world of goods, bads, and shoulds for healthful living.

The single story of recreational cannabis use has framed it as the polar opposite of the health paradigm in popular culture, although among subcultural networks its safety has long been known (Becker 1953; Ferraiolo 2007; Harrison 1988; Himmelstein 1983; Zinberg 1984). As a recreational substance, cannabis' associations are linked to those of illicit drug use—instead of self-regulation, use is seen as impulsive and seeking a state that lessens self-control (Hathaway, Comeau, and Erickson 2011). Cannabis use is also characterized as enjoyable. This runs counter to the lay health supposition that, to be healthy, one must employ discipline and self-sacrifice, a notion that Chapkis and Webb call "pharmacological Calvinism" (Chapkis and Webb 2008; Rosenberg 2007). Health becomes a practical accomplishment due to the success of ascetic efforts, discipline, and moderation (Scheper-Hughes and Lock 1987). The corollary is that fun or enjoyable things are usually bad for you, lead to unhealthy states of illness or disease, and must be carefully moderated or abstained from altogether (Backett 1992; Chapkis and Webb 2008; Conrad 1994).

To achieve wellness, individuals must learn about health in order to determine the best choices and then exercise self-control and discipline in making those choices (Lock 1999). This may suggest that Americans face a "double-binding injunction to be self-controlled, fit, and productive workers, and to be at the same time self-indulgent pleasure-seeking consumers" (Backett 1992; Scheper-Hughes and Lock 1987, 26). Yet this dual mandate is not always a double-bind. While self-controlled and self-indulgent are distinct, oppositional constructs, there are places where health and pleasure can overlap constructively, such as when consistent sexual activity or consuming wine in moderation are defined as beneficial. CAM therapies such as yoga and massage can also be experienced as both health maintenance and indulgence (Bishop, Yardley, and Lewith 2008; Prevention 2012; Scheper-Hughes and Lock 1987, 26; Mayo Clinic Staff 2016).

Lay health theories exist in a pluralistic space with diverse information sources, and beliefs about what is healthful or how treatments function can be casual about evidence and certainty (Wang et al. 2010). Health behaviors, with their strong ties to the lifeworld, are also connected to one's social status, domestic context, and family relationships. Lay health theories frame how consumers define the meaning of "healthy" or "unhealthy." For example, consumers who define health as an absence of symptoms may make different decisions than those who view health as an optimal state (Hughner and Kleine 2008). These determinations are also relative to others in one's social networks and to the available resources in one's milieu (Christakis and Fowler 2009). Emotional states such as stress, grief, and affection are intertwined with one's close ties and social contexts but may come to be seen as directly related to one's health. Because healthism often brings medical concerns into everyday activities and relationships, it has also been referred to as the "medicalization of lifestyle" (Hughner and Kleine 2008; Lowenberg and Davis 1994, 592).

### Cannabis and Healthism

Many patients in this study see cannabis as minimally harmful or altogether lacking in physical harm to the body. Preference for cannabis among patients is often based on firsthand experience that it lacks the trade-offs of harm for benefit that many other medications involve. As discussed at length in chapter 5, the only health harm from cannabis on which the majority of physicians and patients seem to agree are those that may be associated with consuming it via smoking because of the attendant tars and other byproducts of smoke, such as an increased risk of bronchitis. The perceived risks of harm are not based on the physiological interactions with the body of any active ingredients in cannabis. Even when the "high" is seen as an undesirable consequence, patients see this as a trade-off in productivity rather than an actual physical harm. Most patients were also not concerned with dependence, in part because they had used it as teens and had no difficulty stopping. However, a few did express concerns with a dependence on its use to control pain, a problem they mostly addressed by minimizing the dose, as detailed in chapter 5. While there was broad agreement on the safety profile of cannabis, only some patients went beyond that and claimed that it was making a contribution to health.

### Healthism as a Pluralistic Space

The people in this study tried many different types of treatments to manage health from the space outside of formal health care. The most commonly reported informal treatments included hypnosis for tobacco-smoking cessation, the use of various herbs and vitamins, and chiropractic care. Lance, the young veteran with a traumatic brain injury (TBI), is one patient who, after being on medications that really scared him, has moved as much of his care regimen into the natural and self-controlled realm as possible. He describes his approach:

> Fish oil and coconut oil have been curing my depression. I'm not a clinician and neither are they. They're herbalists and naturopaths, so I'm not going to do anything foolish. . . . The first thing I did through the homeopathic thing was I started with valerian root and passion flower, and that got me to sleep for the first time in a long time, in about three years. I slept for about sixteen hours. When I woke up, I felt like a train hit me. I was like, Jesus, what happened?! I do other things, too—whole food and a whole bunch of other things. Also tried both meditation and yoga to manage symptoms, but I can't focus anymore after the TBI, so they don't help.

Lance has developed a clear preference for a health-based approach over more medical intervention. Even though his injury presents a lifelong problem, and he has to maintain formal medical care, he seems happy to trade in the pharmaceuticalized "patient" identity for the "healthy lifestyle" one.

Devon is one of many who use cannabis to manage pain and share his expressed aversion to unnatural substances and pills. Devon, a slender man in his late thirties, suffered from several bulging discs in his back in his mid-twenties. A failed operation worsened pain, mobility, and numbness, resulting in a disability designation and a heavy load of pharmaceuticals. After six months of intensive medication, he found he could not manage at a functional level because all he did was sleep. He scaled back and rediscovered cannabis as a helpful tool. After going through several different regimes of medication, Devon walked away from all pills. His skepticism and dislike for pills extends beyond pharmaceuticals to over-the-counter medications and even vitamins. Devon's idea of a healthy lifestyle included a clear preference for the raw and the natural. As he says:

> Most of the multivitamins out are just loading you full of stuff you don't need or way too much of stuff that your body is just going to kick out anyway. With me, it's more my diet. I try to eat organic. Was a veggie [vegetarian] for a long time, not anymore. But I still try to lean toward a raw-ish organic diet if I can. Statistics show that people that use cannabis recreationally instead of alcohol are much more intelligent. And I think that just coincides with the way you live your life. We are usually healthier and more conscious.

A few patients reported significant dietary changes or food restrictions, yoga and meditation, and a few idiosyncratic and obscure practices. For instance, Beth, the Jehovah's Witness, had also experienced great relief from using a form of electrotherapy. What ties these practices together is their use to promote a healthy lifestyle. Cannabis patients in this study tried many other lifestyle changes and treatments from the popular or informal sectors, but these were not based on political views—the many Republicans and Libertarians as well as the Democrats and Independents sought out health care solutions wherever they could find them.

INT: Have you ever tried any other types of treatments outside of western medicine, like acupuncture or chiropractic?

MINDY: Yeah, chiropractic, acupuncture, Chinese medicine, biofeedback, physical therapy, things like that.

INT: What was your experience?

MINDY: Just that I didn't get any long-term relief, and it was really expensive. I had to keep going back and back and back, and it wasn't really changing any of my injuries, so I just gave up on it.

Most people had tried at least one CAM modality. The ones with constant chronic pain or multiple conditions that basically took over their lives did not get much out of CAM options. The costs meant that, even if they thought it was modestly helpful, they couldn't afford to do it enough for it to seem worth it. A few of those interviewed had never tried any such treatments. These patients just shrugged and said they didn't object to it; they just never did it. While some people tried cannabis as a larger form of experimentation, others, like Devon, felt that cannabis served as a catalyst to other changes that were healthy. Brett also makes this connection when he says:

BRETT:  Cannabis encourages a healthy lifestyle.
INT:  Why is that?
BRETT:  I don't know, but I've noticed it. I think it's because I'm actually more conscious of what I'm putting in my body. Not just food wise. I've noticed that I'm more into meditation. More conscious of what I'm thinking. . . . I think that because when you're under the influence of cannabis, it heightens your senses. It heightens your level of awareness.

In these accounts, cannabis use becomes an avenue for enlightened health. It enhances healthful activities by inducing mindfulness and awareness, which can be directed toward health choices. Rather than impairing mental function, Brett and Devon clearly believe that cannabis provides them with a tool that helps them make smarter choices.

Some patients interpreted the goal of health as striving toward a normatively healthy body but maintained choices to use tobacco or alcohol and did not pursue other health behaviors such as an exercise program. If a person was going to engage in only minimal attempts at healthy behavior, they usually claimed to be eating a healthy diet. Nearly all patients pointed out that they drank very little alcohol and took great delight in pointing out how very unhealthy drinking was compared with cannabis use. This was another way that patients defined what might otherwise be stigmatizing as a measure of superiority when it came to a healthy lifestyle.

Others felt their illness or disease had rendered a normative version of "healthy" impossible, perhaps due to the nature or severity of their medical condition. One smaller group was very focused on cannabis as part of a larger, holistic view of health to include such choices as eating organically. Most, however, viewed cannabis use as more about maintaining quality of life than engaging in a healthy lifestyle.

While many patients clearly related to health as a moral issue, a few expressed strong reactions to any suggestion that cannabis fit a spiritual frame. About a fifth of patients in the sample, most who considered themselves religiously involved Christians, vehemently insisted on separation between cannabis use practices and their religious practices. Three people who were not religious but considered themselves spiritual in other ways described cannabis as a well-defined part of their spiritual practices. Most simply saw the idea as irrelevant and didn't relate to it at all, but they were fine if others did.

## Pharmaceuticalization

It is such an amazingly beneficial plant, and that's why it's illegal. It's too good. The competition's too intense. You know, the pharmaceutical industry is set

up so that there's a different pill for every ailment. That's profitable. One pill
for nausea, another pill for inflammation, another pill for pain, another pill to
handle the side effects of the other pills. Cannabis handles all of them . . . not
all, but a wide variety of them—nausea, inflammation, pain, migraines. . . .
They don't want a multipurpose medicine.

(Brett)

Brett is the dispensary owner with back issues who took up industrial hemp
as a political issue before ever trying cannabis medically. He insists that cannabis has remained illegal because it is a superior treatment that had not
been successfully monetized. As a healthy, inexpensive medication with no
downsides, and with seeds that qualify as among the most nutritionally dense
foods to be found in nature, Brett sees the illegality of cannabis as trade pro-
tectionism, plain and simple. In his view, since cannabis the plant cannot be
patented, pharmaceutical companies cannot find a way to benefit from it,
and if it were more widely available, the industry would be hard pressed to
compete with its combination of beneficial qualities.

Claims about cannabis as a medicine often placed emphasis on mind-body
connections—the importance of one's mental state or thoughts for health.
Patients were careful to distinguish that the medical effect is not a placebo,
nor is it based simply in cannabis' capability to mentally distract. While a
few conceded that the distraction from pain was helpful, many echoed what
Mark said in chapter 5 about his pain being something you can't "placebo
away." Gary is one who agrees:

Do I think it's a placebo? No. I think there's actual pharmacological
effects that it has on the body. There are studies that prove that. Not
necessarily studies in the U.S., but there are studies overseas where it
reduces pain or helps you relax or reduces muscle spasms. So, I don't
think it's a placebo. I don't think it's all in the mind.

Patients rejected the notion that the medical effects of cannabis were "just in
your head," a sentiment reminiscent of medical narratives surrounding contested illnesses (Bülow 2008). Many patients acknowledged that their illness
or chronic pain was a complex interaction of mind and body, often linked
by stress. When patients were asked what factor most affects health, many
echoed Jason's sentiment:

I think stress will kill you. Stress is the number one bad thing that people
have, mentally. If you are stressed out all the time, you are going to have
a lot of health issues. Depression. People who are depressed tend to not
be very healthy either. So, mental health is very important.

Many patients noted how physical symptoms responded to one's state of
mind. Mike even pointed out that objective measures of his T-cell count,

an important indicator for HIV patient health, directly showed mind-body effects:

> When I'm in a good mood, I'm healthier. I'm happier, and I'm healthier. When I'm down, my T-cells will reflect that, just like in the summertime. I get depressed early in the summer, and my T-cells will drop 50, 60 points. And then in the wintertime with ski season and all the snow—I just love outside, and I love the snow—my T-cells will go up.

Just as patients saw that mental states could have negative effects on the state of the body's health, many patients, especially those with serious chronic pain, also noted that it worked the other way around. Just as depression or stress could increase physical pain, pain or increased illness symptoms could cause mental stress, anxiety, and depression.

Many patients in this study reported experiencing a period of depression. Among the interviews, Ken was one of a substantial subgroup who had experienced multiple, severe bouts with depression. Ken and others associated anxiety or depression with finding out about and living with chronic conditions, due to constant physical pain or discomfort. Compounding this were newly imposed limitations, the effect these factors had on their goals or quality-of-life expectations going forward, and the implications for aging and mortality. A few patients in the sample said that the first prescriptions they were given and advised to take after receiving a serious diagnosis were antidepressants. Frank has a cancer diagnosis, and he says:

FRANK: The first thing they're going to do to you when you go through any type of deal or sickness [mimicking a doctor]: "I'll tell you what we got to do is get you on antidepressants. So, let's get you started on some antidepressants."

INT: When you have cancer, that's an automatic thing?

FRANK: Uh-huh. That's the first thing they tell you right at the start. You've gone through an operation or you've gone through a situation where you know it's terminal, the first that's prescribed to you is antidepressants. They will throw that at you. Now they don't tell you, but you better not have sex on your mind, because it won't be on your mind with antidepressants. So, they don't tell you, and talk you into taking them, and you're going like, "Shit, when was the last time I made love? I mean, there's something wrong here. This is not, not normal." So, antidepressants you want to get off of quick. You have to get off of those.

Most patients with diagnoses of serious life-threatening illnesses at the level of Frank's were prescribed antidepressants for some time. Those patients who also had mental health symptoms of depression, anxiety, or post-traumatic stress disorder (PTSD) in many cases were cycled through many different types of antidepressants. Frank did not find that the mood effects of antidepressants to be worth the trade-off for sexual function. Many found that cannabis offered relief from depression, anxiety, or anger without the forms of disorientation, sleep disorder, sexual dysfunction, or drug interaction potential of antidepressants. In evaluating the relative side effects of cannabis, Ken says, "I don't think I have any side effects. I mean, I feel a little spacey now and then. But compared to the opioids, my side effects are nada. Seriously." Ken also captures the relationship of mind-body effects well:

> I think cannabis is one hell of a better alternative [than prescription drugs]. I mean, I wake up feeling good every morning instead of sick . . . because it takes away the pain. Between the migraines and the pain . . . I have hated pain my whole life. It just disrupts your brain, it disrupts everything in your life. If you could take the pain away, why not? You could be happy again.

Mike, Jason, Frank, and Ken all express the relationship between a health condition and mental states as reflexive. The ability of cannabis to intervene in this process extends up and down the chain, improving mood and reducing pain with few costs after the fact. The one potential downside they identified was psychoactive effects that could interfere with function, but all four of these patients had prior experience with cannabis use, even if it was relatively remote, as with Ken, who had only used cannabis recreationally during his teen years. Frank had been an intermittent user over his adult life, and Mike and Jason had been consistent recreational users who enjoyed the "high," making this effect seem less of a negative in the trade-off. At times, the intoxication was seen as an unmitigated positive contribution. Those who did not enjoy the high and preferred to reduce this effect often still felt it could be managed, and getting higher than intended on occasion was seen as a small price to pay compared to the costs associated with other options. In fact, many patients were clear that, despite the rhetoric that separates medications from marijuana, many medications have mentally disorienting effects that are far more pronounced and less pleasant, so managing this characteristic is not unique to cannabis.

While many reported no adverse side effects, a few noted that they sometimes experienced anxiety, which was the most serious among the side effects reported. Patients such as Andy and Mark had experienced anxiety with cannabis on occasion, and they were more cautious in their approach to experimentation. They found that the variety of cannabis mattered considerably for this effect, which aligns with common user reports.[2] A second side effect noted by pain patients was that some varieties could actually increase the awareness of pain rather than relieve it. Patients such as Eileen and Leo found that this was often caused by using sativa-dominant varieties, because they had a stronger effect on attention. Increased attention could at times be useful, but when the focus was directed at pain, it was incompatible as a

medicine. One clinical study with induced pain found that cannabis analgesia is dose specific, so while a modest amount of cannabis relieved pain,
a higher dose produced heightened sensory experience that translated to
increased pain rather than relief (Wallace et al. 2007).

The quality of life concerns patients express help place their cannabis use
within the realm of healthism. Medicalization processes often entail a negotiation between the individual and the system of biomedicine, but healthism
processes are more firmly planted in the lifeworld, which allows quality
of life and enhancement to predominate. Some patients felt cannabis had
helped them dramatically. For some, it led to better quality of life in the face
of imminent death; for others, cannabis seemed to have kept them alive in a
time when role loss and pain might have caused them to mentally surrender.
Carl, seriously ill with kidney cancer, waxes philosophical about it:

> Well, you look at it, and everyone's going to die sooner or later. And
> you start looking at quality of life, how you want to live, and, yeah, you
> get down sometimes. When I had a little skin cancer, a little skin deal,
> it was malignant, and, you know, they got it all. And that was before all
> of this started. I freaked out. "Should I just kill myself now?" "Should I
> do this, should I do that?" And, "Oh my God, my dog's going to outlive
> me." You really start going through this "Oh me, oh my. I feel sorry for
> myself" crap. And that's very normal, now. It's very natural. So, you need
> to kind of live your life how you want to live, you know? Treat people
> how you want to be treated. And smoking pot doesn't hurt anybody.
> There should not be a damn thing wrong with it.

Carl found that cannabis helped him cope in a holistic way. It eased physical
pain, but that was not the extent of it. It also helped him experience psychological relief and reflect on his experience in a way that managed not only his
illness but his fears about whether cancer would cause his quality of life to
deteriorate. Cannabis use helped him to stop "freaking out" and shift from
feeling sorry for himself to a perspective of savoring his experience that let
him come to grips with his mortality. Others with life-threatening illnesses
in this study expressed similar sentiments, characterizing cannabis as a type
of holistic medicine. Cannabis effects are not "all in your head," but the role
of mental effects in treatment show that neither can it be reduced to a simple
one-to-one correspondence with bodily effects.

Patients with less serious conditions also saw cannabis as compatible with
a self-care approach in which subjective experience becomes a relevant indi-
cation of health needs. Several offered some version of Mark's explanation:

> I listen to my body. That's number one. I don't take anything routinely
> or say, "It's 10 o'clock in the morning, so I've got to take a dose." It's
> not like that. You really have to be in tune with your body. After a time,

anybody who has chronic pain, they learn to tune it out for a little bit. But I would say, to manage your pain really well, you have to be open to it. You have to accept it. You have to say, "Okay, I know this is going to hurt like hell, but I've got to feel it to kind of know how to manage it."

Mark's condition is serious and chronic, although not as likely to become life-threatening as Carl's. Still, Mark's emphasis on attention to symptoms and acceptance of them is a holistic approach that may mitigate the overall stress that accompanies illness.

### Cannabis, Pain, and Big Pharma

> You know what my respect for [the role of cannabis] is as an engineer? My respect for that is the human body is genetically designed by the ascent of man to respond to its environment, and cannabis is a part of that environment. Pharmaceuticals are not a part of that environment. They're wildcards. You don't know what they're going to do. The body has already figured out that that stuff exists. . . . I see naturopathy, if that is the right word, and pharmacology as being not separate. They're only separate in scientific terms. Your business, either way, that's the way I look at it for myself—like, I may get an Aleve, and I may eat a [cannabis] cookie. It's whichever works for me, whenever it works for me, and it's not what pops into my head—oh geez, this is the pharmaceutical; oh geez, this is natural.
>
> (Andy)

Between 1960 and the early 1980s, prescription drug sales were nearly flat in western countries as a proportion of gross domestic product. Then, in the period from 1980 to 2002, prescription drugs tripled worldwide to almost $400 billion. Nowhere was this increase more pronounced than in the U.S., where sales approached $200 billion. By 2007, global prescription drug sales surpassed $600 billion (Abraham 2010). Direct-to-consumer (DTC) advertising of prescriptions in the U.S. has driven sales and increased patient demand. Even for drugs without ads to drive demand, U.S. consumers have startling appetites. America is currently composed of 4.6 percent of the world's population but consumes 80 percent of the world's opioid supply and 99 percent of the global hydrocodone supply (Manchikanti et al. 2010).

The number of prescriptions has increased exponentially, and prescribed dosages per patient increased over 400 percent on average between 1997 and 2007 (Manchikanti et al. 2010). Overdose deaths from prescription analgesics has skyrocketed and is now considered at epidemic levels (CDC 2012). As noted earlier, fatal overdoses involving prescription opioids increased 400 percent between 1999 and 2015, with 33,000 deaths and half a million emergency room visits. In the U.S., middle-aged adults, the cohort for this study, have the highest prescription painkiller overdose rates (CDC 2011). Problems with opioid drugs are estimated to cost health insurers $72.5 billion annually in direct health care costs (CDC 2012; Manchikanti et al. 2010).

These trends have occurred even as the under-treatment of chronic pain has become a priority for clinicians and policymakers (Alexander, Kruszewski, and Webster 2012). The Institute of Medicine reports that chronic pain affects about 100 million American adults and costs $635 billion each year in medical treatment and lost productivity—a daunting national challenge that requires "cultural transformation" (IOM 2011). A survey by Johannes and colleagues (2010) found chronic lower back pain and osteoarthritis pain were prevalent among those reporting long-lasting pain—conditions for which cannabis often provides relief. Indeed, chronic pain is the most common qualifying condition for which patients register to use medical cannabis.

Despite huge gaps in care, widespread chronic conditions, a pain and opioid epidemic, and concerns with prescription drugs, biomedicine still treats medical cannabis as a controversial medicine of last resort, as do many patients. Cannabis is to be explored only after other options have been tried or when no treatment is available. Yet, patients often come to see cannabis as safer and more natural than pharmaceuticals or even over-the-counter drugs. Many patients feel that cannabis is overregulated and monitored more than necessary, but they also recognize that overregulation is an imperative of the political system. The transition of cannabis to a new category and a new moral standing has required strict definitions and boundaries that are unambiguously medical.

Patients in this study were greatly concerned with pharmaceutical safety and concerned with dangerous drug side effects, problems with addiction and dependence, and risks from technological interventions (Britten 2008; Williams and Calnan 1996, 1614). They often remain skeptical about "expert" medical advice on health and lifestyle and expressed that doctors do not show enough discernment and are influenced by pharmaceutical companies. The concern over doctor bias may increase their worry about prescription drugs, which were the source of much skepticism among patients—the more so the more experience they had. In most cases, these patients had already been disabused of the notion that any pharmaceutical could be a magic bullet for their illnesses. The medications had proven to be useful but sometimes only moderately so, and they often came with a cost of intense side effects or scary potential ones such as increased risk of stroke or damage to organs. Multiple prescriptions also present dangers of interaction effects, but cannabis can supplement most drugs without this concern.

Patients generally worried about taking pills in the first place. They worried even more about multiple drugs and the cumulative effect of being overmedicated or being treated as guinea pigs, as Lance describes:

> Do I have concerns with pharmaceutical drugs? Yes. All of them. All of them have terrible side effects. All of them have side effects that include

stroke, death. I mean all of the ones they have given me. Every last one of them. Seizures, I mean, and a lot of that, like that Abilify. I almost had a seizure in Home Depot. I fell on the ground, and they were like, "What happened?" I was like, "Nah, man, don't worry about it." I was like, "I'll be all right. I'm going to the hospital."

While not all patients had horror stories, the number who did have stories of overmedication were striking. Carmella had induced bipolar disorder from a prescription of Gabapentin. Arthur had adult-onset asthma that was misdiagnosed as a seizure disorder, sending him to the emergency room multiple times. He says the medication they put him on to treat the misdiagnosed condition made him crazy. By the end of Tina's experience with fibromyalgia and chronic pain, they had her on a toxic cocktail of pills that ended with methadone. She was sleeping constantly, and despite being unable to eat anything substantial, she ballooned up from her petite size to almost double her normal weight and required a cane for assistance. She claims that despite the serious nature of the drugs her physician placed her on, no one was monitoring her case.

For Tina, the turning point was when Michael Jackson died. She cried out of fear for her own life and felt desperate when she saw his grief-stricken children and thought of her own kids. Certain if she stayed on the path she was on she would meet the same end as he had, she began to taper off the drugs. The list goes on: Ken, Anita, Travis, Karen's husband, Beth's mother, Devon—all said they were overprescribed serious pain medications. These patients and others reported currently being on multiple prescriptions such as Gabapentin, Tramadol, hydrocodone-based drugs, or the muscle relaxant Flexeril. Six patients were recommended methadone, and five were briefly on it—none had good experiences. These patients all reported struggling back from a state of overmedication that was genuinely ruining their lives. Some felt that the very experience of medicines came to be associated with negative emotions, such as Travis recounts:

> I could smell the pills; I could feel them, the way they caused my stomach, just the acid in it. The more pills I put in me, the more I could feel it. It was just nasty. I could feel them. I can smell them. I can taste them. I take so many pills for my stomach just from the acid, some of them it's just nasty. So, if I can stay away from some pills, that keeps down some of the acid. And if I can smoke instead of taking that pill, then it's just a whole lot better.

With firsthand or secondhand knowledge of cases like these, many patients were wary of the pharmaceutical industry on the whole. They believe it is a corrupting influence on biomedicine that dents its image. Gary conveys some of this sentiment:

I think that there is a pharmaceutical industry [that] peddles a lot of stuff that may not be necessarily good for you, but yet there is such an incentive for the doctors to take this and pass this out to the patient or diagnose the patient has this particular problem. That way they can dose this stuff out. And I'm not against pharmaceutical medications. They have their place. They make a lot of people's lives easier to deal with. So, for me, I think that pharmaceutical medications [are like] corporate pollution. And I'm not a big ecologist, you know [what] I'm saying? But I know enough to know that there is a lot of corporate pollution going on.

Frank's description of the pharmaceutical arsenal presented to him identifies the point in serious life-threatening illness when the calculus used to balance risks and benefits to health has transformed. As a result of advanced-stage colon cancer, Frank has taken multiple courses of chemotherapy.

FRANK: [I have] colon cancer. I had it operated on. They did the transection, and it mutated, or metastasized. So, I got it on the lung and on the liver. Once you start studying cancer though, it's real funny. It's a mutant, and so what happens is it starts growing on its own, and it can sit there for a long time and decide not to do anything.

INT: The cancer?

FRANK: Yeah. There's no such thing as remission. What happens is, once you got a mutant, it'll go and just sit: "Don't feel like growing today," you know? Then, all of a sudden, when it hits, it's gonna go real quick. So, I got into it and started chemo. They will blast you with all kinds of . . . what you do in chemo is, you're always treating the side effects. . . . They don't give a shit. I mean, the guys are killing cancer. All of these fucking side effects: throwing up, loss of weight, no appetite, on and on, and on and on. They will just throw any pharmaceutical at you that you want. So, they get you on Oxycontin, and they get you on painkillers, and, geez man, you can't hold nothing down.

INT: Why would they give you Oxycontin or painkillers?

FRANK: Fuck, you're gonna die, girl! What you want? [laughter] You want *anything*, you know? Shit, dude. Shit. When I was in the hospital, they would have these nurses come in, and it would be like a drug salesman who's opened their coat [mimes opening a trench coat like a guy on the corner selling watches]. "This one's really good. . . ." and I was going like, "Damn! I've never seen a drug deal like this in my life!" But they'll throw anything at you that's on the market.

In Frank's experience, the dire situation of advanced cancer, the difficult experience of chemotherapy, and the level of pain, discomfort, nausea, and other side effects warrant physicians simply offering patients whatever they want.

The inability of biomedicine to exert control over the disease progression triggers a capitulation in which biomedicine cedes control to the patient.

Some patients started with a trusting attitude, but after firsthand experiences in which doctors introduced dangerous treatments or overmedicated them without adequate monitoring, their concession to the authority of medicine shifted to a wary, almost frightened attitude. These patients often began with hope that advancements in biomedicine might resolve their health problems, but they soon found it had greatly compounded their problems, reducing their functionality even further and resulting in endangering side effects. In previous chapters, Anita, Lance, and others reported such outcomes. Tina was perhaps one of the most severe cases of overmedication. Tina has multiple disorders, including fibromyalgia, PTSD, and severe digestive issues. After going through several increases in medication, she was placed on methadone. At her worst, she was in bed all day and unable to care for her children. While Tina has a slight frame and probably weighs just over 100 pounds at her normal weight, she says at the peak of her overmedication:

> I was 198 pounds. My hair . . . fell out. I looked sick. My kids told me, mom, you were an odd shade of gray. I had severe daily nausea. Daily. I found myself at thirty-three years old walking with a cane because of my treatment for fibromyalgia. Not because of my ailment. Fifteen pills at bedtime alone. And sometimes I would not be able to sleep after that dose. . . . It's really hard to say without crying.

Tina's experience was extreme. Tina had worked in a health care setting in the past offering patient support to cancer patients, a job she found hugely rewarding. Overall, she still aspired to work in a capacity where she could fill a healing and supportive role related to health care. While she did not blame the entire institution of biomedicine, and she knew that not all doctors would behave in the questionable ways hers had, the experience of being progressively overmedicated took years to recover from, and her attitude toward pharmaceuticals remained highly skeptical and even fearful. To her, cannabis was a great antidote, offering a natural, nontoxic treatment over which she could exert significant control and use to effectively manage much of her pain.

While several patients had experienced overmedication with biomedicine, others had not but feared such a scenario. Patients expressed a strong sense of being offended by the ability of the system to promote the use of much more dangerous drugs while prohibiting or failing to recognize the unparalleled safety record of cannabis. Leo expresses their frustration:

> You want to know what really makes me angry? I'll sit here, and I'll watch commercials about a drug made by Pfizer or whoever, and they'll sit there and go, "Well, it'll help your calluses on your feet, but it might

do this and that and that and that and that and that and that—and kill you." So, I'm going, you know, all the shit that happens on the side is worse than what the fuckin' thing cures. Two years later and you look on the TV and here's Sokolove and Sokolove, saying, "Call us, because if you ever took this drug, we're suing the hell out of those people." This makes me angry as hell. When the same drug in this bowl [pointing to the glass pipe on his end table] will work! And the federal government tells me that I can't use it because of their buddies in the drug companies? That makes me angry!

Most patients cared deeply about safety and made estimations of relative risk based on this. They felt cannabis was exponentially safer than all of these drugs. Brett brings up the therapeutic index, or TI, which is a ratio of the dose at which a drug offers medical benefits to the dose at which it is lethal 50 percent of the time (Gable 2006). Brett notes how much safer cannabis and psychedelic drugs are by this metric:

So, alcohol is four to one. Heroin is the only [recreational] drug above alcohol, it's two to one. And that's extremely toxic, way up there. The reason I'm bringing this up is, it goes right on down the line, and then at the very bottom of the lethal-to-dose ratio scale is all the psychoactive drugs, meaning Ayahuasca, peyote, psilocybin, cannabis. And so, what that tells me is that nature intentionally— You know, these are the safer drugs. The ones that are not psychoactive have way higher lethal-to-dose ratios, and the drugs that are psychoactive are way safer. So, for whatever reason, I think that what's happening there, and we're having a hard time with it, but I think we're starting to get it, especially with everything that's happening right now in our era.

As Brett notes, the ratio between a medication's therapeutic and lethal doses is of particular concern for treatment, as drugs with a narrow window are more prone to fatal mistakes. Acetaminophen (Tylenol), for example, has a very narrow range of about 4:1, while alcohol is 10:1 and morphine 70:1. Establishing an LD-50 or a therapeutic index for cannabis requires considerable conjecture, as no fatal overdose in humans has ever been recorded, and experiments with dogs and monkeys found no physiologic harm at even astronomical THC levels, those equivalent to an average human consuming more than 13,000 joints at once, or 63,000 times a standard 10 milligram therapeutic dose (Thompson et al. 1973).[3] That makes cannabis, in the words of DEA findings from rescheduling hearings in 1988, "one of the safest therapeutically active substances known to man" (Young 1988, 58).

Brett overestimates the TI for alcohol at 4:1 (the TI for Tylenol), but he is still correct that, of the most commonly used recreational drugs, only heroin is rated more dangerous than alcohol. In every estimation that patients made about cannabis' relative safety, its potential for drug interactions, or its other side effects, they adamantly expressed their belief that cannabis was a far superior choice to their pharmaceutical options. A majority were also quick to point out what a healthier choice cannabis was compared to alcohol. In fact, this perception of inherent safety was often the main justification for changing drug policies related to cannabis but not for other drugs that are potentially harmful or addictive. Lance, who says he has never experienced a high from cannabis, even goes so far as to suggest swapping the legal status of cannabis for alcohol:

> It would be fine if they got rid of alcohol. It would be a fair trade to get rid of alcohol because there is a lot of violence in alcohol. I've given up alcohol altogether because I can't drink. Because if I drink, I'll be in jail. PTSD patients should not drink.

Others, such as Devon, spoke more generally: "Yeah, I've known since I was like eighteen that tap water is more dangerous than cannabis." These estimations mitigate fear of unpleasant effects, such as anxiety, an overly stoned experience, or rapid heart rate or flutters. As a result, many patients worked to taper off other drugs when cannabis could be used effectively in its place, as Lance has:

> Currently I am on Effexor, Lamictal, some Zyrtec, and some Nexium. That's about it . . . With herbalism and medical marijuana I have gotten down, and I am pretty comfortable with [the ones I'm still on], because one's a protein pump inhibitor for your stomach, and . . . I'm allergic to dust mites and there is nothing you can really do about that. And the other two were just like an antidepressant and anti-anger thing or anxiety-type thing, and I don't think they do shit, but I am not going to stop taking them just yet.

Many patients such as Lance and Anita, who appeared earlier, reduced medicines one by one until they felt those they were taking could not be replaced by cannabis but were still necessary for symptoms. If eliminating a medication resulted in a return of symptoms, they would simply add it back in. Cannabis was used to substitute for other drugs, to wean off other drugs, and to supplement other drugs such as opioids to improve their effectiveness, allowing patients to lower dosages.

Darrell talked about his appreciation that cannabis was a more flexible therapeutic substance than many pharmaceuticals, allowing patients greater control over use routines because it is possible to skip days without resulting side effects such as withdrawal:

> [Cannabis] makes the Percocet more effective. But the problem with opiates is—If I'm not hurting, marijuana, I don't have to take. I don't

have to do it. It doesn't matter. Even if you want to for your head, it's not breaking your body down. If my Fentanyl patch is working really well when I first put it on, it kicks butt. And I really don't need Percocet, and I don't need the rest of my pills that day. But I've got to take them for maintenance. Or you get sick.

Patients largely understood proper dosages of cannabis as subjective—they know that the amount working for them might not be the same amount another person needs, or might be much less than another person requires for benefit, and that the appropriate dosage can change over time. Ultimately, they viewed cannabis as safe to experiment with in this way. As Brett puts it: "I take one puff, wait five or ten minutes, and then gauge it. I mean, you know, it requires us to be mature adults. And then if you take too much, you end up taking a nap. So? Big deal." Because of cannabis' safety, patients were free to use trial and error to arrive at a happy medium that controlled symptoms but did not impair functionality.

## Questions of Dependence

Most patients did not believe that cannabis caused physical addiction, but some worried about forming a habituated dependence. When asked about dependence, Andy said he was not addicted to cannabis; he was "addicted to not being in pain." His habits had more to do with pain management than the particular treatment, but he also says "freedom and responsibility should go hand-in-hand." Others, like Karen and Anita, noted how they monitored their use and cut back on use if they seemed to be "going overboard," as Karen describes:

There's been times where I could feel that I was maybe using too much, and I thought, "Whoa, back off." Because there's times where . . . I really just don't have the energy to do anything, and I could feel that happening within myself, and I'm like, no, I'm going to go back to being more conservative with it. Because I don't want it to not work someday. Because just like anything else, your body is going to build a tolerance. And instead of one, you're going to need two, instead of two, you're going to need three. And I don't want that at all.

While limitations on use were often self-imposed, and Karen's concern for building a physical tolerance to cannabis is largely misplaced, overall, patients prioritized personal responsibility as an important criterion in self-care regimens. Karen summed up the "set" associated with cannabis routines and risks well:

It really does boil down to you only taking what you think you're going to need. Just like anything else, it can be abused, just like anything else out there. . . . [Cannabis] is like anything else. You could drink one Pepsi a day, or you could drink a six-pack, you know? Food, anything can be abused, just about, if you're not careful.

Gary also talked about monitoring his prescription pain medication use to minimize dangers:

I don't take it twice a day, for one thing. Number two, I have dropped to—I don't want to misrepresent this—instead of taking the pink pill, which I don't remember what the milligram is, I'm taking the blue one, which is a lower milligram dosage, which has really been great because narcotics or narcotic opiate-based medications for me. It was affecting my memory. Because at that time I was going to . . . I had been on it for years, and I was finishing up my bachelor's degree, and I had a hard time concentrating. I had to read things three or four times to get it to stick. My mind was fuzzy. I used to be real sharp, real quick. Quick witted or quick with a reply or whatever. And it affects you mentally if you are on this for a long period of time.

For Gary, the concern with prescriptions was not only their physical dangers but the mental effects. In his estimation, the mental effects from medical cannabis were much more manageable for day-to-day functioning. Medical cannabis patients face a situation of incomplete medicalization, but in many ways, the medical use of cannabis is a form of harm reduction, used as an adjuvant or substitute for medicines with more serious side effects and dangers of toxicity.

### Patient Opinions of Pharmaceuticalizing Cannabis

On the whole, patients do not see cannabis as contributing to pharmaceuticalization. They also do not want to see cannabis pharmaceuticalized into standardized pills or similar formulations. Some reflected on the limitations of dronabinol (Marinol), saying it was just not very effective. Dale explains:

In its pill form, like Marinol—okay, that's synthetic THC, but it doesn't contain any of the CBNs or CBDs that marijuana contains—and so will, when you take the Marinol, just have the THC. It does not have the CBNs or CBDs. It's like making a peanut butter and jelly sandwich . . . without putting the peanut butter and jelly on it.

Other patients clearly doubt that it is possible to effectively standardize what the whole plant can do. This reflects the experiences of Carl and Mark, who feel that cannabis as a whole plant offers more holistic health assistance than any pharmaceutical compartmentalization of the plant was likely to offer.

The rejection of pharmaceuticalization also reflected the desire for more natural forms of substances. Some thought that turning cannabis into a pill form would actually make it more dangerous and much more expensive. Another point that patients raised was that pharmaceuticalization removed cannabis from the control of the patients, who can at this point grow their own medicine. Finally, the idea of pharmaceuticalization may be perceived as a loss of diversity of choice between varieties of cannabis and their unique cannabinoid and terpene profiles.

If a biomedical logic is imposed upon cannabis, the subtleties of whole-plant cannabis effects and their genetic variations are lost. So are other subtle enjoyments that are perhaps less strictly "medical" but may simply be the "treat" that incentivizes adherence to the treatment, similar to what makes CAM enjoyable but is generally lacking in medicine taking, which is seen as an unpleasant necessity. Patients compared these qualities of cannabis enjoyment and discernment to enjoying craft beers, fine wine, or other products that foster connoisseurship. This patient-centric perspective would yield to divisions based not on consumer appreciation but the one-to-one equation of biomedical medicines, in which cannabis becomes subdivided into components based on condition. Some patients simply found many of these potential changes undesirable and unneeded.

Another reason patients don't want cannabis co-opted by "Big Pharma" is their distrust of the pharmaceutical industry. Patients fear a value-added cost, not to mention greater restrictions to access, without a corresponding improvement in the value they can expect to receive. They want an ethic of care in their medical interactions, and see the profit motive of pharmaceutical companies, along with the companies' influence on physicians, as corrupting the therapeutic relationship into a capitalist transaction. The pharmaceutical companies attempt to persuade both patients and doctors to adopt a medicine. Patients are concerned that doctors resist this and only prescribe medications that are effective and not based on a capitalist model of profit.

Doctors express reluctance not only based on incomplete medicalization but because cannabis is not completely pharmaceuticalized. As an article from Nunberg and colleagues (2011) explains to a medical audience:

> For physicians who make medical cannabis recommendations, the risk of being deceived is not dissimilar to the risk of deception faced by those who prescribe oxycodone and other painkillers; however, those prescribing the latter can limit the number of pills and refills.
>
> (12)

Many patients express a preference that cannabis remain in its "natural" state as a whole plant or as a minimally processed whole plant derivative. Even when patients expressed an appreciation for biomedicine, person after person reiterated that he or she was "not a pill person" and disliked taking medications. By contrast, cannabis in its natural form allowed more individual control, and patients felt comfortable grouping it with other "health behaviors" in the lifeworld, such as eating organic food, taking ginger or other herbs, and sleeping properly.

Even as cannabis is medicalized, its current role clearly contributes to depharmaceuticalization for most patients. However, when it comes to healthism, cannabis' current primary management in the realm of self-care often leads patients to group it comfortably with other health behaviors, but not all patients make the leap from calling it minimally harmful to believing it is actually healthful. This may be more a reflection of the larger cultural narrative than any other specific cause for not adopting this view.

The well-established benefit of cannabis to those with chronic pain and other conditions for which conventional treatments are often inadequate, coupled with its ability to counterbalance trends toward pharmaceuticalization, may make an insistence on cannabis' harms seem puzzlingly irrational, especially given the serious harms associated with many approved legal prescription drugs (Cohen 2009). Its very strengths as a lifeworld medicine—its subtlety, safety, and interoceptive cues, as well as its stress-relieving qualities as a mild but enjoyable "treat"—may contribute to the difficulty of fully medicalizing cannabis. The pharmacology of cannabis has been explored in the past two decades, but the variability of the plant poses challenges to standardization. The recent trend of states requiring labeling of medical cannabis products based on analytic laboratory testing can help discerning patients make decisions, but knowing the ratio of THC to CBD or other cannabinoids and terpenes does not enable physicians to manage dosing in the way they do other medications.

Even in a scenario in which standardization of cannabis medications and their applications might be achieved and win FDA approval, patients do not want whole-plant cannabis to continue to be criminalized. Such a dichotomy is not farfetched. Synthetic THC in the form of dronabinol (Marinol) is already classified in Schedule III, while the whole plant remains in Schedule I. Just as patients see cannabis as distinct from pharmaceuticals on many important dimensions, they also seem puzzled by the idea that it might align with informal sector treatments such as chiropractic, acupuncture, or even other herbal, homeopathic, or Chinese medicine. A few patients described dreaming of a world in which cannabis simply becomes its own full-fledged branch of accepted specialty medicine rather than being subsumed into any existing system. In this vision, specialty cannabis doctors and dispensaries would remain but become more professionalized and accepted within biomedicine and society as properly medical.

The properties of the plant may make space for that possibility. Cannabis is properly considered not one medicine but rather an entire class of medicines, just as the opium plant is the basis for an entire swath of widely used pharmaceuticals. Cannabis may challenge medicine to an epistemological shift for the same reasons that it initially resisted cooptation at the turn of the twentieth century. Cannabis is simply not processed in the body in the same way as other substances, so it may be less amenable to the ways of biomedicine than most substances. Indeed, as more becomes known about the function of the endocannabinoid system (ECS) in the body and the brain, biomedicine may be asked to conform to cannabis. The wave of interest in neuromedical developments may carry cannabis to more institutional acceptance as an avenue to managing the modulatory role of the ECS in the function of brain, endocrine, and immune tissues, as well as the secretion of hormones related to reproduction and stress. Cannabis may have a leading role to play in emerging neurological treatments.

In *Our Present Complaint? American Medicine Then and Now*, medical historian Charles E. Rosenberg (2007) lists conditions that demand long-term multidimensional care or that have been resistant to available treatments such as sleep disorders, arthritis, depression, migraine, irritable bowel syndrome, and chronic back pain (128). These very conditions are among the most commonly reported conditions for which patients seek use of medical cannabis. Certainly, this context lends some perspective to the patient-driven policies allowing for medical cannabis use and suggests the potential for developing new cannabis-based treatments.

## Notes

1. Another term used in the literature is *healthicization* or *healthization,* but we have chosen to use healthism here simply because it is less awkward to spell and say.
2. THC appears to be the chemical in cannabis most responsible for producing anxiety. CBD has strong anxiolytic or anti-anxiety properties, so varieties that have higher CBD:THC ratios may be less likely to produce anxiety. Interpretation may also play a role in user reports of anxiety, as some of the physiological effects of cannabis, such as increased heart rate, can be signals of psychological stress that cause users to believe they're experiencing anxiety.
3. This estimate was obtained by calculating from the experimental dose of 9,000 milligrams THC per kilogram of body weight tested on dogs and monkeys. Assuming an average adult human weight of 70 kilograms, or 154 pounds, an equivalent dose would be 630,000 milligrams of THC. That translates to 4.2 kilograms (9.24 pounds) of cannabis with a potency of 15 percent THC. Research puts the average U.S. joint at 0.32 grams of cannabis, so the 4.2 kilograms would yield 13,129 joints. (Ridgeway, Greg, and Beau Kilmer. 2016. "Bayesian Inference for the Distribution of Grams of Marijuana in a Joint." *Drug and Alcohol Dependence* 165: 175–80. doi.org/10.1016/j.drugalcdep.2016.06.004.)

## References

Abraham, John. 2010. "Pharmaceuticalization of Society in Context: Theoretical, Empirical and Health Dimensions." *Sociology* 44(4):603–22.

Alexander, G. Caleb, Stefan P. Kruszewski, and Daniel W. Webster. 2012. "Rethinking Opioid Prescribing to Protect Patient Safety and Public Health." *Journal of the American Medical Association* 308(18):1865–66.

Ayers, Stephanie L., and Jennie Jacobs Kronenfeld. 2007. "Chronic Illness and Health-Seeking Information on the Internet." *Health* 11(3):327–47. doi: 10.1177/13634 59307077547.

Backett, Kathryn. 1992. "Taboos and Excesses: Lay Health Moralities in Middle Class Families." *Sociology of Health & Illness* 14(2):255–74.

Becker, Howard S. 1953. "Becoming a Marihuana User." *American Journal of Sociology* 59(3):235–42.

Bishop, Felicity L., Lucy Yardley, and George T. Lewith. 2008. "Treat or Treatment: A Qualitative Study Analyzing Patients' Use of Complementary and Alternative Medicine." *American Journal of Public Health* 98(9):1700–5. doi: 10.2105/ajph.2007.110072.

Britten, Nicky. 2008. *Medicines and Society: Patients, Professionals and the Dominance of Pharmaceuticals.* New York: Palgrave Macmillan.

Bülow, Pia H. 2008. "Tracing Contours of Contestation in Narratives about Chronic Fatigue Syndrome." Pp. 123–41 in *Contesting Illness: Processes and Practices*, edited by P. Moss and K. Teghtsoonian. Toronto: University of Toronto Press.

CDC, Center for Disease Control and Prevention. 2011. *Prescription Painkiller Overdoses in the U.S.* Atlanta, GA: Centers for Disease Control and Prevention.

CDC, Center for Disease Control and Prevention. 2012. "Opioid Overdoses in the United States." *Journal of Pain & Palliative Care Pharmacotherapy*:44–7.

Chapkis, Wendy, and Richard J. Webb. 2008. *Dying to Get High: Marijuana as Medicine.* New York: New York University Press.

Cheek, Julianne. 2008. "Healthism: A New Conservatism?" *Qualitative Health Research* 18(7):974–82. doi: 10.1177/1049732308320444.

Christakis, Nicholas A., and James H. Fowler. 2009. *Connected: The Surprising Power of Our Social Networks.* New York: Little, Brown and Company.

Clarke, Adele E., Janet K. Shim, Laura Mamo, Jennifer Ruth Fosket, and Jennifer R. Fishman. 2003. "Biomedicalization: Technoscientific Transformations of Health, Illness, and U.S. Biomedicine." *American Sociological Review* 68(2):161–94.

Cohen, Peter J. 2009. "Medical Marijuana: The Conflict between Scientific Evidence and Political Ideology: Part One of Two." *Journal of Pain & Palliative Care Pharmacotherapy* 23(1):4–25. doi: 10.1080/15360280902727973.

Conrad, Peter. 1994. "Wellness as Virtue: Morality and the Pursuit of Health." *Culture, Medicine, and Psychiatry* 18:385–401.

Conrad, Peter. 2005. "The Shifting Engines of Medicalization." *Journal of Health and Social Behavior* 46(1):3–14.

Conrad, Peter. 2007. *The Medicalization of Society.* Baltimore, MD: The Johns Hopkins University Press.

Conrad, Peter, and Kristin K. Barker. 2010. "The Social Construction of Illness: Key Insights and Policy Implications." *Journal of Health and Social Behavior* 51(S):S67–79.

Crawford, Robert. 1980. "Healthism and the Medicalization of Everyday Life." *International Journal of Health Services* 10(3):365–88.

Ferraiolo, Kathleen Grammatico. 2007. "From Killer Weed to Popular Medicine: The Evolution of American Drug Control Policy, 1937–2000." *Journal of Policy History* 19(2):147–79.

Gable, Robert S. 2006. "The Toxicity of Recreational Drugs." *American Scientist* 94:206–8.

Greenhalgh, Trisha, and Simon Wessely. 2004. "'Health for Me': A Sociocultural Analysis of Healthism in the Middle Classes." *British Medical Bulletin* 69(1):197–213.

Harrison, Lana Debra. 1988. "The Marijuana Movement: A Study of a Cohort on the Cutting Edge." Ph.D. Dissertation, Sociology, University of Michigan, Ann Arbor, 21662.

Hathaway, Andrew D., Natalie C. Comeau, and Patricia G. Erickson. 2011. "Cannabis Normalization and Stigma: Contemporary Practices of Moral Regulation." *Criminology and Criminal Justice* 11(5):451–69. doi: 10.1177/1748895811415345.

Himmelstein, Jerome L. 1983. "From Killer Weed to Drop-Out Drug: The Changing Ideology of Marihuana." *Contemporary Crises* 7:13–38.

Hughner, Renee Shaw, and Susan Schultz Kleine. 2008. "Variations in Lay Health Theories: Implications for Consumer Health Care Decision Making." *Qualitative Health Research* 18(12):1687–703. doi: 10.1177/1049732308327354.

IOM, Institute of Medicine. 2011. *Relieving Pain in America: A Blueprint for Transforming Prevention, Care, Education, and Research.* Washington, DC: Institute of Medicine of the National Academies.

Johannes, Catherine B., T. Kim Le, Xiaolei Zhou, Joseph A. Johnston, and Robert H. Dworkin. 2010. "The Prevalence of Chronic Pain in United States Adults: Results of an Internet-Based Survey." *The Journal of Pain: Official Journal of the American Pain Society* 11(11):1230–9.

Kihlstrom, John F., and Lucy Canter Kihlstrom. 1999. "Self, Sickness, Somatization, and Systems of Care." Pp. 23–42 in *Self, Social Identity, and Physical Health: Interdisciplinary Explorations*, Vol. 2. Rutgers Series on Self and Social Identity, edited by R. Contrada and R. Ashmore. Oxford: Oxford University Press.

Kivits, J. 2009. "Everyday Health and the Internet: A Mediated Health Perspective on Health Information Seeking." *Sociology of Health & Illness* 31(5):673–87. doi: 10.1111/j.1467-9566.2008.01153.x.

Lewis, Tania. 2006. "DIY Selves? Reflexivity and Habitus in Young People's Use of the Internet for Health Information." *European Journal of Cultural Studies* 9(4):461–79.

Lock, Margaret. 1999. "The Politics of Health, Identity, and Culture." Pp. 43–68 in *Self, Social Identity, and Physical Health: Interdisciplinary Explorations.* Rutgers Series on Self and Social Identity, edited by R. Contrada and R. Ashmore. Oxford: Oxford University Press.

Lowenberg, June S., and Fred Davis. 1994. "Beyond Medicalisation-Demedicalisation: The Case of Holistic Health." *Sociology of Health & Illness* 16(5):579–99.

Manchikanti, L., B. Fellows, H. Ailinani, and V. Pampati. 2010. "Therapeutic Use, Abuse, and Nonmedical Use of Opioids: A Ten-Year Perspective." *Pain Physician* 13(5):401–35.

Mayo Clinic Staff. 2016. "Red Wine and Resveratrol: Good for Your Heart?" Mayo Clinic Patient Care & Health Info. Retrieved May 12, 2018 (https://www.mayoclinic.org/diseases-conditions/heart-disease/in-depth/red-wine/art-20048281).

Nunberg, Helen, Beau Kilmer, Rosalie Liccardo Pacula, and James R. Burgdorf. 2011. "An Analysis of Applicants Presenting to a Medical Marijuana Specialty Practice in California." *Journal of Drug Policy Analysis* 4(1):Article 1, 18 pages.

Parusnikova, Zuzana. 2000. "Bio-Power and Healthism." *Sociologicky Casopis* 36(2):131–42.

Prevention. 2012. "7 Reasons Sex Does Your Body Good." *Prevention*, November, 2012.

Renahy, E., and P. Chauvin. 2006. "Internet Uses for Health Information Seeking: A Literature Review." *Revue D Epidemiologie Et De Sante Publique* 54(3):263–75.

Rosenberg, Charles E. 2007. *Our Present Complaint: American Medicine Then and Now.* Baltimore, MD: The Johns Hopkins University Press.

Scheper-Hughes, Nancy, and Margaret Lock. 1987. "The Mindful Body: A Prolegomenon to Future Work in Medical Anthropology." *Medical Anthropology Quarterly, New Series* 1(1):6–41.

Schuster, Tonya L., Marnie Dobson, Maritza Jauregui, and Robert H. I. Blanks. 2004. "Wellness Lifestyles I: A Theoretical Framework Linking Wellness, Health Lifestyles, and Complementary and Alternative Medicine." *Journal of Alternative & Complementary Medicine* 10(2):349–56.

Thompson, George R., Harris Rosenkrantz, Ulrich H. Schaeppi, and Monique C. Braude. 1973. "Comparison of Acute Oral Toxicity of Cannabinoids in Rats, Dogs and Monkeys." *Toxicology and Applied Pharmacology* 25(3):363–72. doi: https://doi.org/10.1016/0041-008X(73)90310-4.

Tomes, Nancy. 2016. *Remaking the American Patient: How Madison Avenue and Modern Medicine Turned Patients into Consumers*, edited by A. M. Brandt, L. R. Churchill and J. Oberlander. Chapel Hill, NC: The University of North Carolina Press.

Turner, Bryan. 2004. *The New Medical Sociology*. New York: W.W. Norton.

Wallace, Mark, Gery Schulteis, J. Hampton Atkinson, Tanya Wolfson, Deborah Lazzaretto, Heather Bentley, Ben Gouaux, and Ian Abramson. 2007. "Dose-Dependent Effects of Smoked Cannabis on Capsaicin-Induced Pain and Hyperalgesia in Healthy Volunteers." *Anesthesiology* 107:785–96. doi: 10.1097/01.anes.0000286986.

Wang, Wenbo, Hean Tat Keh, and Lisa E. Bolton. "Lay Theories of Medicine and a Healthy Lifestyle." *Journal of Consumer Research* 37(1):80–97. doi: 10.1086/649772.

Williams, Simon J., and Michael Calnan. 1996. "The 'Limits' of Medicalization? Modern Medicine and the Lay Populace in 'Late' Modernity." *Social Science & Medicine* 42(12):1609–20.

Young, Francis. 1988. "In the Matter of Marijuana Rescheduling Petition." *Docket #86–22*. Washington, DC: U.S. Department of Justice, Drug Enforcement Administration.

Zinberg, Norman E. 1984. *Drug, Set, and Setting*. New Haven, CT: Yale University Press.

# Conclusion

## Medicalization and the Future of Cannabis Medicine

If marijuana prohibition had never existed, I think that we would have marijuana on the shelves in stores, and people growing marijuana at home like they grow their tomatoes. . . . We would have countless therapies, pharmaceutical therapies based on marijuana that would be well studied and a legitimate piece of our medical lexicon. So, we are missing out on eighty years of development of an industry that would have put it into that same context that we see tomatoes and beer and wine and pharmaceuticals and the rest of it.

(Megan, patient advocacy organization manager)

We have just scratched the surface, and I greatly regret that I don't have another lifetime to devote to this field, for we may well discover that cannabinoids are involved in some way in all human diseases.

(Raphael Mechoulam, chemist who first identified THC (Sides 2015))

Cannabis is an embarrassment of riches.

(Nolan Kane, evolutionary biologist (Sides 2015))

This book has argued that cannabis and its use mark the most consequential case of social construction of the twentieth century. The dominant discourse on the plant and its users has relied on forcefully constraining the definition of cannabis to a single story, which posits that all use is criminally deviant and geared toward intoxication. Cultural dialog has limited the framework to a discussion of degrees of "harm" by creating and maintaining tight associations between cannabis and its users that rely on moral ideology over an evidence base, even as both the characterization of users and surrounding rhetoric have been transformed by cultural change and scientific claims-making. In recent years, a new story has spread from the margins to the mainstream, expanding the narrative on cannabis beyond the single story. New evidence from individual experience and scientific inquiry has propelled cannabis toward a yet-incomplete medicalization.

As we introduced at the outset of this book, medicalization has a recognizable progression that starts with redefining a morally deviant behavior into medical terms in the "definition" and "prospection" phases. Next is the moral entrepreneurship phase, in which the issue's medical territory is expanded and the importance, seriousness, and scope of the issue is emphasized. In this phase, professionals and individual patients or advocacy groups who benefit directly from its acceptance are likely to actively work on expanding these boundaries. In the fourth phase, legitimacy consolidation allows those proponents to seek formal rulings and legislation to recognize the medical definition, and the outcomes of these rulings and laws help to determine how the issue will be defined and managed, including who has access. This is where we are now in the U.S., as we see contests over cannabis' moral standing and legitimacy play out across the country.

The medicalization of cannabis is happening in the midst of a war on drugs, America's longest war, making it easy to forget that criminalization is a brief anomaly in the human history of cannabis use. Medical use has been a part of cannabis' story since before recorded history. Until the advent of the twentieth century, this use was unproblematic. Through the confluence of many circumstances outlined in chapter 2, cannabis was singled out and subsequently criminalized over the past eighty years. The moral entrepreneurship and moral panics around cannabis drew directly from the playbook of the prior century's war on opium, pushing aside nineteenth-century hemp medicines and concerns for its therapeutic potential. The contributing factors to this are well documented. They include the standardization and professionalization of medicine as a profession and, in particular, of medicines; the associations of use with undesirable categories of people, mostly on racial grounds, as it had been with opium; the aftermath of alcohol prohibition, which had created a model of federal enforcement that was easily repurposed by the enterprising Harry J. Anslinger, whose power derived from a singular mission to criminalize and demonize drug use, marijuana in particular; the mid-century culture divisions that led those in power to use marijuana as a tool in their attempt to suppress counterculture and race movements; and the contemporary apparatus of a drug war that countless politicians have relied upon to look "tough on crime" in their campaigns (Bonnie and Whitebread 1999; Chasin 2016; Ferraiolo 2007; Galliher, Keys, and Elsner 1998).

At every turn, there has been push back, but legitimacy matters. When those in authority maintain a single story that defines the rules around even what factual information can be gathered to argue against it, dissidents enter the battle at a grave disadvantage. Despite a global expansion of legitimacy through research and regulated medical cannabis programs, information that travels on lateral networks runs up against barriers in attempting to create legitimacy that the system will acknowledge. Within the lifeworld, the networks that connect information, claims, and stories about cannabis are those of family and friends, which broker legitimacy that is inherently relational. Information that spreads on strong networks—daughter to mother, brother to sister, cousin to cousin, or between close friends—begins to reveal the arbitrariness of laws that vary wildly state to state, in which one sick person is allowed access to a plant that puts another one in jail.

Despite decades of federal prohibition and more than thirty million arrests in the U.S. alone, cannabis remains the most popular illicit drug worldwide. Its use has been statistically normative among U.S. adults for the last half-century. About half of adults report trying cannabis at least once, usually in the late teen and early adult years, and even more have been exposed to the opportunity to do so or are close to people who use it. This prevalence helps explain why the core of the drug war is marijuana policy. Cannabis is the only substance used widely enough to justify annual drug war budgets in the billions (Rosenthal and Kubby 2003). Marijuana arrests account for roughly half of all drug arrests annually. The racial animus that helped launch the drug war also continues to find outlet, as highly selective enforcement strategies disproportionately affect already-marginalized groups (Drug War Facts 2012; Alexander 2010; King and Mauer 2006). The current criminal-ization policies on cannabis have stood for nearly fifty years, even as chronic pain conditions escalate, prescription drug overdoses double and then double again, and the therapeutic potential of cannabis is rediscovered and dramati-cally expanded.

The U.S. investment in the war on drugs passed the trillion-dollar mark almost a decade ago. Yet illicit drugs are now more potent, less expensive, and easier to obtain—an abject failure on all fronts of the drug war's publicly stated goals. But let's not be coy. If the drug war is instead evaluated in terms of the privately stated goals of the Nixon administration—a culture war waged for political gain—then its perpetuation makes more sense. As the analyses of Michelle Alexander (2010) and others have shown, the targeted enforcement of drug laws has had a devastatingly disproportionate impact on communities of color in the U.S., where drug use is no more likely than in white communities, but the likelihood of arrest, prosecution, and incarcera-tion is exponentially higher. Cannabis use has been defined as a marker of membership in a dangerous criminal underclass, but the victimless nature of crimes associated with it—cultivation, distribution, possession—means law enforcement is left to decide where to look for it, allowing biases conscious and unconscious to operate freely.

Although cannabis poses a low risk of harm, inappropriate handling of cannabis policy and scheduling has helped perpetuate its criminalization (Aggarwal 2010; Barnes 2000; Gwynne 2011; Riggs 2012). The successful introduction and expansion of medical cannabis across most states has chal-lenged this narrow definition, but medicalization of cannabis is far from new. Medical uses may be as old as human knowledge and use of the plant. It is mentioned in the oldest Chinese medical texts, and caches of ceremo-nial cannabis have been found in burial sites that are at least 2,400 years old (Brand and Zhao 2017; Clarke and Merlin 2013; Jiang et al. 2016). In the modern era, medical use has followed criminalization around like a ghost, haunting the single story at every turn. It was there at the congressional hearings when the Marihuana Tax Act of 1937 was introduced in the form of the American Medical Association's legislative counsel, Dr. William C. Woodard, who was the only detractor and voice of reason amid moral panic, a role for which he would pay hefty professional costs. It was there when marijuana was put in Schedule I provisionally under the Controlled Substances Act in 1970, pending further research, research which, in the form of the 1972 Shafer Commission report, found no basis for its criminalization, just as the 1944 LaGuardia Commission report and the even earlier Indian Hemp Drugs Commission report of 1894 had concluded. It was there when thirty-nine states jumped on the medical cannabis research bandwagon between 1978 and 1983, only to learn that the federal government would refuse to cooperate, leaving the programs with no legal means of supply. It was there when California defied federal prohibition to pass the first viable state medical cannabis law and the federal government commissioned the Institutes of Medicine to study the issue yet again, resulting in a 1999 report that acknowledged there were some patients and conditions for which cannabis was uniquely helpful and called for further research.

As omnipresent as the specter of medical use has been throughout the era of criminalization, institutional controls of information have meant medical successes were publicized in grassroots fashion. As those anecdotal accounts have accumulated over time, consistent profiles have emerged of cannabis as effective in treating a host of conditions, including pain, nausea, spasticity, inflammation, seizures, gastro-intestinal disorders, brain traumas, cancer, multiple sclerosis, HIV/AIDS, ALS, and Parkinson's disease. Some view skeptically the remarkable range of conditions said to be treatable with cannabis, yet pre-clinical and clinical scientific findings increasingly support patient accounts.

In the contemporary global wave that began to achieve legitimacy in 1996, medical cannabis has had its most successful run since prohibition took hold. There are many factors: the diminished authority in medicine, the rise of chronic illnesses, the expansion of alternative medicine, the shift toward a patient-consumer model, and liberalization of alternative medicine policies. Acceptance has been further aided by the rapid expansion of knowledge through basic research in many countries, beginning with identification of cannabis' main ingredient in 1964 through the discovery of the human endocannabinoid system in the 1990s. We know exponentially more about cannabis than we did a hundred years ago, when its medical use began to fall from favor along with other botanical remedies. Yet even with new discoveries, cannabis remains stubbornly defiant of the processes by which the "system" defines medicine. We've argued that medical cannabis is a case of incomplete medicalization, but it would be a mistake to think Conrad and Schneider's five-stage sequential model of medicalization is predictive. Cannabis may forever resist institutionalization because it is, in many respects, the ultimate lifeworld medicine.

The work of institutionalization nonetheless proceeds apace, driven by pharmaceutical companies and private drug-development entities, international standards organizations and botanical product trade groups, and global research consortiums and academic institutes. Institutional efforts are paralleled by "lay epidemiology" being conducted in dispensaries in Colorado and other states, where data collected from a large patient base is being used by cannabis breeders, product manufacturers, and other industry stakeholders to guide developments that become ever more sophisticated until the lines between lay and expert efforts begin to blur.

Fully pharmaceuticalized cannabis medicines could mark the entry into full medicalization. As discussed in the last chapter, this potential has some pioneering researchers excited for an entire new class of medicines to treat many conditions that currently lack effective therapeutic options. Patients share a cautious optimism about such developments but are wary that cannabis-based pharmaceuticals will not come without costs. Patients desire standardization that allows predictable effects but share the common preference for more natural medicines. The new pharmaceuticalized cannabis medicines would almost certainly entail forms of ingestion and effects so distinct from its whole plant form as to be unidentifiable. Patients worry that a bifurcation of cannabis into isolated compound medications and whole plant remedies could provide justification to continue the marginalization or even criminalization of traditional cannabis preparations and their use while Big Pharma and other forms of corporate interest swoop in and claim control over cannabis in its medicalized forms.

Patients also worry that as recreational use becomes legal, Big Tobacco or the alcohol industry will commercialize the nonmedical side. Ironically, one of the side effects of eighty years of prohibition is a distinct lack of commercialization, and this lack of corporate involvement, the homespun aspect of cannabis and its hobbyist connoisseurship, is an aspect that many patients and enthusiasts share appreciation for and do not wish to lose. Medical cannabis patients have not one battle in this arena, but two: In addition to the specter of Big Pharma claiming medical territory and alcohol and tobacco companies grabbing the recreational market, there is also the encroaching legalization of social use that many worry may produce policies that paper over the importance of medical uses and the specific needs of patients. As we have elaborated over the middle chapters of this book, medical use of cannabis involves practices that are distinct from recreational use and has led to the development of products and delivery methods that are suitable to the specific aims of therapeutic use.

As of now, cannabis has not been fully reintegrated into the medical domain, institutionally or culturally. Similarly to other conditions or treatments that are subject to contestation, this affects every aspect of the medical cannabis patient experience (Broom and Woodward 1996). Incomplete medicalization has consequences in the doctor–patient interaction, creating challenges for patient access. It affects the institutional management of cannabis, which spans the formal, informal, and popular sectors of medicine, and leaves much of the medicalization process in the hands of the individual patient. It affects the conceptualization and distinctions made between medical and recreational uses, which patients often feel pressured to monitor and define. It interacts with the cultural interpretations, stereotypes, and stigmas, where the demographic diversity of cannabis patients and the greater value-neutrality of medicine relative to recreational use has the capacity to flip the script from stigma to prejudice. Finally, incomplete medicalization contributes to an environment of uncertainty in which medical and legal forms of social control overlap but also become unpredictable, placing patients in a tenuous position where their access to cannabis as a medicine and their protection from legal repercussions become moving targets.

The ongoing contest over medical uses of cannabis is not being carried out through legislative debates in Congress (where it is denied hearings) or in academic journals (where its utility has achieved consensus). Instead, patients have become pawns in a policy debate between the states and the federal government that is being argued through militia-style raids in which homes are trashed and family members, children, and pets terrorized; through arrests, prosecutions, and incarceration; through expulsions from schools, terminations of employment, and seizures of homes, cars, and other belongings; and through loss of rights such as gun ownership, parental custody, or even access to lifesaving organ transplants. The bodies of the sick, the injured, and the dying are being used as fodder for the cannons of the drug war.

## The Effects of Cannabis Liberalization

The liberalization of cannabis laws often sets in motion a cascade of community concerns that take on the character of moral panic. Concern for children figures prominently. Some argue criminalization must be maintained because any relaxation of penalties or scheduling "sends the wrong message" to youth, who would then take up the substance without understanding its dangers. In reality, cannabis use among teens has declined to a twenty-year low nationwide, including declines in medical cannabis states (Bogdanoski 2010; Harper, Strumpf, and Kaufman 2012; Ingraham 2017a; Lynne-Landsman, Livingston, and Wagenaar 2013; Anderson, Hansen, and Rees 2015). Others warn that alcohol or other drug use will go up, or impaired driving incidents will increase. However, preliminary research on all three indicates that medical cannabis laws have the opposite effect. Traffic fatalities decrease, alcohol consumption declines, and suicide rates drop when states implement medical cannabis laws (Anderson, Hansen, and Rees 2015; Anderson, Rees, and Sabia 2012; Anderson and Rees 2013).

The hypothetical outcomes of cannabis liberalization are being sorted out as evidence accumulates. Not surprisingly, the most extreme claims opposing liberalization, with their basis in moral panic, have not come to pass. Meanwhile the costs of ongoing criminalization, which are far from hypothetical, continue to be paid. As the Trump administration revs up the drug war machine and works to roll back progress, more politicians and public figures have broken silence and stepped forward on the issue. Arrests have declined slightly and—at least for the moment—raids of those in strict compliance with state law have been largely suspended. Greater infrastructure is being built from within, in the form of advocacy groups and lobby organizations, which have professionalized and formed alliances with established advocacy groups for veterans, seniors, and various serious medical conditions, exerting more pressure on the system to support additional research and enact lasting change to the legal status of cannabis.

Further study of medical cannabis use has the potential to illuminate the importance of the extra-pharmacological effects of "set" and "setting" for all medicines. Interviews found that patients were not simply using medicalized rhetoric to reframe recreational behaviors as medical ones; rather, they employed strategies that were surprisingly consistent with behavioral patterns in the use of all types of medications, with an emphasis on the health goals of the lifeworld, including minimizing risks of toxicity and dependence while maximizing the ability to maintain role functioning and live a normal life (Britten 2008).

Diversion has been a recurring topic of concern, but "cheaters" do not invalidate the legitimacy of medical cannabis any more than the diversion of prescribed pharmaceuticals undermines the legitimacy of those medications. In fact, any regulated system that confers benefits on some while punishing others requires effective gatekeeping and is vulnerable to admitting illegitimate users. Gatekeeping often serves an important function, but views on how it operates are often overly simplistic. With medical cannabis, distinguishing those who meet the criteria of qualifying patients from those considered illegitimate "drug users" is often more complex that it seems. As chapter 4 showed, using cannabis medically cannot be conflated with registering as a patient, as these are two distinct, separable decisions, each with its own calculation of risk and benefit. Decisions to participate in Colorado's medical marijuana program were motivated by many factors. The incentives to participate have changed with the introduction of adult legal use in Colorado, and the geography of gatekeeping has changed, too. This will be a useful area for ongoing research.

This study has focused on patients at midlife and older, a group whose use has recently been increasing (Ingraham 2017b; Johnston et al. 2012). Patients at midlife focus on responsible forms of use, which include minimizing the amount used, timing use to maximize productivity, and monitoring use as a form of self-discipline. However, much of the focus for patients is on lifeworld concerns, with a recognition that one must comply with system logics to an extent, but systems often contain irrationalities that individuals must work around. Patients often saw unsanctioned "off-label" uses as legitimately medical, perhaps in part because their use still conformed to medicalized behavior to treat a condition widely understood to be helped by cannabis. System rules appeared arbitrary in the face of a loved one in pain. The idea that it was legal for them but not for a suffering elderly parent based on state of residency or other limiting factors seemed ludicrous. Most patients were adamant that they would never assist in the diversion of medical cannabis to the recreational market, or sell it to nonmedical friends or acquaintances, but they had no qualms about social use among friends without making distinctions about who was legitimate and who was not. On the whole, most patients expressed a strong sense of ethical obligation to the medical cannabis system, but no one was interested in playing cop and enforcing system rules on others.

Research on illicit psychoactive substances is experiencing a renaissance, in no small part because these substances offer novel approaches to complex chronic conditions that remain intractable. As earlier set-and-setting researchers pointed out, the effects of these substances have greater interpretive flexibility than many drugs, allowing us to better account for the significance of extra-drug factors to "optimiz[e] their patterns of use" and prevent or minimize social harms (Hartogsohn 2017, 13). The participants in this study expressed a range of responses when distinguishing between their personal cannabis use as recreational or medical, but all recognize that many substances can be used as a medicine or as a recreational intoxicant, yet cannabis differs from other substances in its relative safety. It is perhaps ironic that while the federal system enforces a definition of proven safety and efficacy that leaves cannabis in Schedule I, state programs reflect a view of the drug as safe enough that routines for use are left to patient experimentation with no medical advice or oversight. Patients are also left to create legitimacy for their medical use in the face of widespread skepticism from the media and the public, parsing differences at the individual level as a question of moral standing that they must self-police. Distinctions like this are typically made much higher up the institutional chain, rendering the medical and recreational forms of most drugs so different that they are not even recognized as the same substance.

The medicalization of cannabis has relied on patients in no small way. Patients who adopt the medical cannabis identity are already engaged in a politically meaningful act of reclaiming a spoiled identity that risks sanction. Patients find additional support from their family, friends, and others in their close networks, as well as in the medical cannabis "thought community" with its distinct group style. As with other issues that have involved spoiled identities, some medical cannabis users adopt the language of "coming out" and identity "pride" that come with reclamation, while others wish for normalization in which the use of medical cannabis blends into "normal" behaviors unworthy of special notice. Whether through pride or normalization, medical cannabis users push back against stigma by insisting that the stereotypes of cannabis users are not legitimate norms but instead are authored by biased actors with corrupt motives. To the degree that society shifts to sympathize with this viewpoint, the cultural gaze turns from the stigmatized to the stigmatizer as a perpetrator of prejudice, and the identity once spoiled is reclaimed.

## Limitations and Recommendations for Future Research

Contemporary medical cannabis use has been formally recognized through law for more than twenty years now, yet opportunities for research remain vast. This book has focused primarily on patients because understanding a lifeworld-oriented medicine such as cannabis requires examining the patients, their motives, and their behaviors. Considering medical cannabis use within the context of midlife serves an important purpose, but it does so at the expense of excluding other groups. Future research that compares and contrasts more diverse cohorts over the life course might build on the observations found here and determine if certain practices, attitudes, or styles differ by age or stage in life. This study has a broad scope but does not exhaust the possible lines of inquiry. Future studies could expand themes developed here by examining the point of view of other actors within the medical cannabis system, such as medical professionals and business operators.

While this work captures patient experiences during a pivotal moment in Colorado's history—from right after the advent of the "green rush" to just before the passage of Amendment 64—the effects on medical cannabis patients of establishing an adult use retail system in this and other states remain to be seen.

This work is not representative of the Colorado patient population, which limits its generalizability. The recruitment for this study required patients to opt in to participate, which protected the privacy rights of patients but made it more difficult to reach the full spectrum of those who have interacted with the medical cannabis system in Colorado. For instance, it was unlikely to appeal to those who had tried medical cannabis, found it did not work for them, and exited the system. Also, even though recruitment materials attempted to be inclusive, those who did not have legitimate reasons for participating in the medical cannabis program may have lacked any interest or motivation to participate. Finally, it may not have been successful in reaching those who belong to demographic groups that are the most vulnerable to stigma and are therefore reticent to disclose their use to strangers, even in the context of research.

Despite these limitations, the insights gained from this study may serve as the basis for larger-scale studies that could investigate these trends for their generalizability among patients in other states and countries. When reviewing work from Australia, the United Kingdom, the United States, and Canada, the distinct patterns among cannabis patients were striking, from attitudes and barriers to use patterns and conditions treated.

### Implications for Sociological Research

Our consideration of medical cannabis within the models and literature from sociology suggests directions for ongoing research in the sociology of health and illness. First, it offers an interesting case of incomplete medicalization that expands theories related to medicalization of contested illnesses to include a contested treatment. An especially provocative area for which this research may be relevant is the intersection of medicalization and politicized health identities. Conditions or treatments that are in the process of medicalization but are not yet completely medicalized are often not simply transitioning in relation to the medical domain. Layers of institutional social control mean the process of medicalization often involves redefinition in other domains, especially law and criminal justice. The prominence of these intersections in this study suggest it may serve as a useful direction for other studies on medicalization and theories about its processes.

Second, this work has suggested that individuals utilize medical cannabis much as they do other medications. The significance of self-care behaviors is paramount for understanding many health outcomes, yet this area has yet to be fully explored. The case of medical cannabis suggests interesting directions for exploring how people regulate health behavior and choose between more formal and flexible routines.

Finally, this work contributes to our understanding of controversial identities. The status of cannabis use is one of the largest issues that U.S. society is currently contemplating. The issue poses fundamental questions about our rights to our own bodies and what we do with them in private, much as the gay rights movement has. Stigmatized identities of this sort differ from those that form the basis of civil rights and gender equality movements because, unlike race or gender, they are based on behavioral choices that are inherently concealable and may be legally prohibited and punishable by law. This book suggests themes about concealable stigma and its relationship to identity, shame, and pride that may reveal how stereotypes, norms, and our shifting assessments of their social acceptability matter for whether groups are seen as stigmatized or as the subjects of unfair discrimination.

## Final Thoughts

Cannabis criminalization has relied on the stubborn perpetuation of illogical drug scheduling and the regular rallying of moral panic through changeable but always exaggerated claims to harm. These policies are in need of modernization to better reflect current scientific knowledge, rational policy design, and simple common sense. Considerations of cannabis laws consistently suffer idealistic errors in logic that can be found across many policies governing behaviors we wish to regulate. Policy debates often seem to assume that regulating a behavior will create or encourage it, while prohibiting it will prevent or eliminate it. In truth, regulation offers much greater control than prohibition ever can because a ban is an abdication of any meaningful control. State regulatory schemes for control of alcohol and tobacco have demonstrated that rational policy can alter behaviors and limit access. Those lessons may be applied to cannabis. As Reiman (2006) noted more than a decade ago, while the policy debate over medical cannabis drags on, "millions of patients are in need of an effective, convenient method of obtaining their medicine, and this method should be subject to the same consideration, description, and evaluation as any other health service being provided to the public" (1).

Policies should balance public concerns with scientific evidence and compassion for patient needs. Recent findings suggest that cannabis may have a role in the treatment of many difficult disorders. The potential of these applications affects much of the population. As a society, we have already begun to research and mainstream other forms of alternative medicine. Cannabis may in some ways be the most radical medicine of all, with its low toxicity, negligible risk of dependency, and its in-built "side effect" that can only be gauged in a subjective, autonomous, way. These unique qualities make it amenable to self-regulation, and interviews with patients made it clear that they took this responsibility seriously.

Conrad and Schneider (1998 [1980]) say that "in modern industrial society, only law and medicine have the legitimacy to construct and promote deviance categories with wide-ranging application" (23). The institutional control of cannabis may not be moving wholesale from one jurisdiction to another, but, like opioids, its regulation may continue to be managed through both law and medicine. The expansion of medical cannabis may help to shift public policies into a more sensible balance that acknowledges the simple truth that cannabis is just a plant. All the rest we have constructed.

# References

Aggarwal, Sunil K. 2010. "Cannabis: A Commonwealth Medicinal Plant, Long Suppressed, Now at Risk of Monopolization." *Denver University Law Review Online*. August 23, 2010. (www.denverlawreview.org/medical-marijuana/2010/8/23/cannabis-a-commonwealth-medicinal-plant-long-suppressed-now.html).

Alexander, Michelle. 2010. *The New Jim Crow: Mass Incarceration in the Age of Colorblindness*. New York: The New Press.

Anderson, D. Mark, Benjamin Hansen, and Daniel I. Rees. 2015. "Medical Marijuana Laws and Teen Marijuana Use." *American Law and Economics Review* 17(2):495–528. doi: 10.1093/aler/ahv002.

Anderson, D. Mark, and Daniel I. Rees. 2013. "Medical Marijuana Laws, Traffic Fatalities, and Alcohol Consumption." *Journal of Law and Economics* 56(2):333–69.

Anderson, D. Mark, Daniel I. Rees, and Joseph J. Sabia. 2012. "High on Life? Medical Marijuana Laws and Suicide." Vol. *Discussion Paper Series*. Bonn, Germany: IZA.

Barnes, R. Eric. 2000. "Reefer Madness: Legal & Moral Issues Surrounding the Prescription of Marijuana." *Bioethics* 14(1):16–41.

Bogdanoski, Tony. 2010. "Accommodating the Medical Use of Marijuana: Surveying the Differing Legal Approaches in Australia, the United States and Canada." *Journal of Law and Medicine* 17(4):508–31.

Bonnie, Richard J., and Charles H. Whitebread, II. 1999. *The Marijuana Conviction*. New York: The Lindesmith Center.

Brand, E. Joseph, and Zhongzhen Zhao. 2017. "Cannabis in Chinese Medicine: Are Some Traditional Indications Referenced in Ancient Literature Related to Cannabinoids?" *Frontiers in Pharmacology* 8.

Britten, Nicky. 2008. *Medicines and Society: Patients, Professionals and the Dominance of Pharmaceuticals*. New York: Palgrave Macmillan.

Broom, Dorothy H., and Roslyn V. Woodward. 1996. "Medicalisation Reconsidered: Toward a Collaborative Approach to Care." *Sociology of Health & Illness* 18(3):357–78.

Chasin, Alexandra. 2016. *Assassin of Youth: A Kaleidoscopic History of Harry J. Anslinger's War on Drugs*. Chicago and London: University of Chicago Press.

Clarke, Robert C., and Mark D. Merlin. 2013. *Cannabis: Evolution and Ethnobotany*. Berkeley and Los Angeles, CA: University of California Press.

Conrad, Peter, and Joseph Schneider. 1998 [1980]. *Deviance and Medicalization: From Badness to Sickness*. Philadelphia: Temple University Press.

Drug War Facts. 2012. *Data Table 126: Total Annual Arrests by Year and Category 1980–2011*, Lancaster, PA: Common Sense for Drug Policy. (www.drugwarfacts.org/cms/Marijuana#Total).

Ferraiolo, Kathleen Grammatico. 2007. "From Killer Weed to Popular Medicine: The Evolution of American Drug Control Policy, 1937–2000." *Journal of Policy History* 19(2):147–79.

Galliher, John F., David P. Keys, and Michael Elsner. 1998. "Lindesmith V. Anslinger: An Early Government Victory in the Failed War on Drugs." *The Journal of Criminal Law and Criminology* 88(2):661–82.

Gwynne, Kristen. 2011. "New Poll: Most Americans Consider War on Drugs a Failure and Support Legalization of Marijuana." *Alternet*. August, 10, 2011. (https://www.alternet.org/newsandviews/article/648399/new_poll%3A_most_americans_consider_war_on_drugs_a_failure_and_support_legalization_of_marijuana).

Harper, S., E. C. Strumpf, and J. S. Kaufman. 2012. "Do Medical Marijuana Laws Increase Marijuana Use? Replication Study and Extension." *Annals of Epidemiology* 22(3):207–12. doi: 10.1016/j.annepidem.2011.12.002.

Hartogsohn, Ido. 2017. "Constructing Drug Effects: A History of Set and Setting." *Drug Science, Policy and Law* 3:1–17. doi: 10.1177/2050324516683325.

Ingraham, Chris. 2017a. "Teen Marijuana Use Falls to 20-Year Low, Defying Legalization Opponents' Predictions." *WonkBlog*. Washington Post. September 7, 2017. (www.washingtonpost.com/news/wonk/wp/2017/09/07/teen-marijuana-use-falls-to-20-year-low-defying-legalization-opponents-predictions/).

Ingraham, Chris. 2017b. "More People Were Arrested Last Year over Pot Than for Murder, Rape, Aggravated Assault and Robbery-Combined." *WonkBlog*. Washington Post.

September 26, 2017. (https://www.washingtonpost.com/news/wonk/wp/2017/09/26/more-people-were-arrested-last-year-over-pot-than-for-murder-rape-aggravated-assault-and-robbery-combined/?utm_term=.7c8aae69634e).

Jiang, Hongen, Long Wang, Mark D. Merlin, Robert C. Clarke, Yan Pan, Yong Zhang, Guoqiang Xiao, and Xiaolian Ding. 2016. "Ancient Cannabis Burial Shroud in a Central Eurasian Cemetery." *Economic Botany* 70(3):213–21.

Johnston, Lloyd, Patrick M. O'Malley, Jerald G. Bachman, and John Schulenberg. 2012. *Monitoring the Future National Survey Results on Drug Use 1975–2011: Volume II, College Students and Adults Ages 19–50.* Ann Arbor, MI: Institute for Social Research, The University of Michigan.

King, Ryan S., and Marc Mauer. 2006. "The War on Marijuana: The Transformation of the War on Drugs in the 1990s." *Harm Reduction Journal* 3(1):6. Doi: 10.1186/1477-7517-3-6.

Lynne-Landsman, Sarah D., Melvin D. Livingston, and Alexander C. Wagenaar. 2013. "Effects of State Medical Marijuana Laws on Adolescent Marijuana Use." *American Journal of Public Health* 103(8):1500–6. Doi: 10.2105/AJPH.2012.301117.

Reiman, Amanda. 2006. "Cannabis Care: Medical Marijuana Facilities as Health Service Providers." Ph.D. Dissertation, Social Welfare, University of California, Berkeley.

Riggs, Mike. 2012. "Poll: 82 Percent of Americans Think the U.S. Is Losing the War on Drugs." Hit & Run Blog, Reason.com, November 13, 2012. (http://reason.com/blog/2012/11/13/poll-82-percent-of-americans-think-the-u).

Rosenthal, Ed, and Steve Kubby. 2003. *Why Marijuana Should Be Legal.* New York: Thunder's Mouth Press.

Sides, Hampton. 2015. "Science Seeks to Unlock Marijuana Secrets." *National Geographic,* June 2015.

# Research Methods

The data from this study included in-depth semi-structured interviews with forty patients between the ages of thirty and sixty-eight; unstructured interviews with eight key organizational actors; dozens to hundreds of informal conversations to learn and network; and observations at dozens of events in non-dispensary settings where medical patients or advocates met for social, political, or educational purposes related to medical cannabis.

Medical cannabis patients are a challenging population to reach (Hathaway and Rossiter 2007; O'Connell and Bou-Matar 2007). They share many of the challenges associated with recruitment for hidden populations. Due to concerns with stigma, privacy, and legality, individuals in hidden populations often have reasons to be reluctant about participation in a study. However, underrepresented populations also have motivations for participation, because they would like their group to have a voice in an issue of key importance to them (Chapkis and Webb 2008). Contradictions between state law, which allows medical use, and federal law, which maintains criminal penalties for all uses, adds significance to the protected status of patients. This perception of risk is complicated by a sense that current laws are a moving target. As the state and the federal agencies determine what constitutes legal and acceptable behavior, the rules change in ways that can alter who is safe from prosecution and who is not. At the time this data was being collected, dispensaries were being raided in record numbers, and patients were still being arrested, even in states with medical cannabis protections (Chun 2012; Dwoskin 2012). Despite widespread decriminalization and the proliferation of state medical cannabis laws in the interim, the future of enforcement remains uncertain for patients.

In addition to patients being a legally protected group, medical marijuana dispensaries are protected environments that require identification to enter and are designed to uphold patient privacy. Within dispensaries, transactions are monitored as a part of the tight regulations on patients and the industry. Based on these factors, the approach to recruitment was indirect.

It is fairly easy to reach patients who engage in activities such as political advocacy or business ventures in medical cannabis, and these individuals may also be more willing to participate in a research study, but the resulting group is also a skewed representation of all patients. Our goal became to recruit the most diverse sample of patients possible using methods that respected confidentiality. Most patients interact with the system somewhere. They get their supply from dispensaries, they follow or participate in advocacy organizations or online communities voluntarily, and they pick up the free cannabis-specific publications that are disseminated around the state. Among patients, we sought variability based on characteristics such as level of activism, public identification with cannabis issues, type and severity of illness or injury, age, and region. Our approach to recruitment may still have reached some patients more readily than others.

To reach patients for interviews we networked extensively with different outlets that served patients, including dispensaries, websites, and advocacy organizations who directly served patient populations. Observations were treated as ethnographic data, but also helped to bolster the main recruitment strategy. We cast a wide net, contacting groups and organizations located in different regions throughout Colorado. We selected organizations and dispensaries to approach in order to represent a variety of styles that are used for marketing to clientele, from ones that branded themselves in a more clinical, medical, and professionalized style, to ones that exhibited a greater overlap with recreational subculture. Covering a spectrum of organizations based on function, style, and geographic location was used as a way to maximize the variation in the patients who would hear about the study.

Organizations that decided to cooperate by advertising the study were provided a description of the study to display, publish, post, or email to their patient base. Materials instructed patients to make direct contact with the researchers by phone or email if they wished to volunteer for participation in the study. The study description said the study was about health experiences, which may have increased the likelihood of attracting patients who saw themselves as unquestionably "legitimate." To encourage more diversity in participation, recruitment materials spelled out in plain language that all patients with a doctor's recommendation were invited to participate, regardless of the seriousness of their illness or condition, or their motivations for seeking out a recommendation. This message was also emphasized when explaining the study to organizational members who posted advertisements to mitigate any potential cherry picking or other filtering effects through organizational actors' best intentions. Recruitment initiatives were renewed through personal visits, emails, and reposts of advertisements over a period of a year to ensure that locations knew details about the study and felt comfortable advertising it to their clientele based on meeting the principal researcher and having any questions about the study answered.

Several industry organizations, websites, and free specialty cannabis magazines advertised this study by posting information to their websites, announcing it in their publications, or sending recruitment text to their patient base through their own organizations' private email lists. Fliers were posted and business cards were provided. Each contained contact information but no mention of "marijuana" or "cannabis" so patients could carry them away without concerns. Word-of-mouth among organizational actors who could reach patients helped with recruitment, but this study did not employ a "snowball" approach in which participants referred other patients to the study. All patients were recruited as a result of recruitment materials they saw in one of the many places where it was advertised. This approach to patient recruitment most closely resembles a clinical study approach, where a large number of potential interviewees are informed about the study, but the rate of participation is relatively low.

While the aim of this study was not to achieve statistical representativeness, validity and bias issues are still worthy of consideration. To create a strong study, we sought to meet a few generally recognized criteria. The first was to collect enough data so that both heterogeneity and redundancy are sufficient to argue that the study has "internal generalizability," that is, that the findings adequately elaborate the concepts under study for the setting or group of interest (Maxwell 2005).

Sources on qualitative research methodology recommend that the milestone of "theoretical saturation" be used to determine the number of interviews (Charmaz 2006; Guest, Bunce, and Johnson 2006). Theoretical saturation, a term common to the grounded theory approach of qualitative analysis, is now widely adopted in research programs across several social scientific disciplines (Charmaz 2004). It is meant to indicate a point at which information collected from interview subjects is no longer expanding the theoretical categories of interest, and new interviews, rather than adding variation within these categories, prove redundant with responses from prior interviews. While one cannot be fully certain that all responses have been represented, it is important to seek a sample that encompasses diverse experiences and views and is exhaustive enough to represent the common range of responses (Charmaz 2006).

In determining sampling needs and sample size, we strived to realize two goals: completeness and the principle of similarity/dissimilarity (Blee and Taylor 2002). Completeness is described as the construction of a thorough knowledge about the topic. The goal has been to continue interviewing new participants until no new narratives or interpretations on the main topics of inquiry were emerging. At this point, the topic was considered "saturated." The principle of similarity/dissimilarity directed interviewee selection to include some similar cases in order to compare interpretations or accounts with other similarly situated participants, and to also select differently situated participants to see if accounts differ based on differences in social location or other categories (Blee and Taylor 2002).

## Recruiting Middle-Aged Patients

After an initial round of interviews, we decided to focus on patients who were middle age or older. Respondents included in this study range in age from thirty to sixty-eight years old. Since life course places importance not only on individual age but also on cohort and period—when one came of age and what one's peers were doing—the established markers for the Gen X and Baby Boomer generational groups was used to define the inclusive age range. This sampling choice was made to allow us to emphasize the importance of life course in experiences with cannabis. We wanted to focus on use by those in midlife up to and including the now aging Baby Boomer generation who were the first to experience the popularization of cannabis use in their teen and college-age years.

The choice to focus on patients at midlife fits the same criteria as many recreational use studies—study the group with highest use. The majority of medical cannabis users across states and countries are in their late thirties and early forties with the average age steadily between forty and forty-five years of age from 2009 to 2018 (CDPHE 2018; Janichek and Reiman 2012; Reiman 2007; Reinarman et al. 2011; Ware et al. 2003; Coomber, Oliver, and Morris 2003; Hathaway, Comeau, and Erickson 2011; O'Connell and Bou-Matar 2007). Two early interviews conducted in the pilot phase were with patients under thirty years of age. After electing to focus on patients over thirty years of age, these interviews were eliminated from analysis, which left a total of forty qualifying interviews with Colorado medical marijuana patients.

## Collecting Data: The Interview-Based Qualitative Approach

Interviews sought to discover what the subjects themselves experience and believe about using cannabis medicinally. In-depth, semi-structured interviews are well suited to discover emergent topics of importance for those engaged in the activity. Patient interviews resembled "life history" interviewing, which is geared toward the personal history of the individual (Creswell 2006). For the most part, patients were very forthcoming in their interviews. Most began the interview by offering a health biography, which often took the organic form of a life history that weaved in and out of the interview schedule and was driven by the patients' recounting. Other patients were more passive and let the questions drive their responses.

Areas of focus in the interview were health history, including medical history, experiences with traditional and nontraditional forms of medicine, and general beliefs about health and medicine. Patients were asked how they use medical cannabis in their day-to-day lives, how they attribute the medical significance of cannabis use, and in what ways they choose to identify themselves as medical cannabis patients. Questions also investigated the intersections between cannabis use, health care utilization, and the use of other self-initiated care using non-prescription herbal remedies. How did individuals choose particular treatments, how did they implement these treatments, and how did they assess the outcomes? Direct comparisons with complementary and alternative medicine (CAM) resonated less with patients than originally anticipated, but questions were adapted as we proceeded with data collection to allow comparisons with the literature on CAM patient populations as well as with biomedicine. In addition, questions explored the themes of medical and recreational use to find out if patients shifted their understanding of cannabis when their own status changed, and if so, how they explained this shift and saw it as significant. Patients were also asked about how they managed the identity of being a medical cannabis patient and with whom they shared information with or deliberated with about health and their medical cannabis patient status.

## Key Informant Interviews and Observation

Because changes on the ground were nearly constant, and patients mostly offer individual stories, key interviews with individuals who worked with many patients offered context and topic breadth and helped to provide accounts of broader trends seen across patients by those situated to have many interactions. Key informants and observations offered useful information regarding the business and legislative environment that surrounds patient provision, and in particular the change of rules for caregivers and dispensary operation, which affects the ways that patients can obtain a supply of medical cannabis.

Blee and Taylor (2002) describe approaches to key informant interviewing:

> The researcher questions a few well-placed informants, sometimes over an extensive period of time, to obtain descriptive information that might be too difficult or time-consuming to uncover through more structured data-gathering techniques.
>
> (105)

Within the medical marijuana community, there are many moving pieces. One reason to draw on the knowledge of key organizational actors is that they often know unpublished information or may have in-depth knowledge about how one aspect of the medical marijuana community is currently operating. A second reason to talk with key organizational actors is that many in these positions serve as the public mouthpiece for the medical marijuana community, and as such, they play a pivotal role in the cultural discourse surrounding medical cannabis, including the ability to provide grounds and factual information or rumor-level information that circulates behind assertions.

In total, eight key informant interviews were collected. Three were conducted near the outset of data collection, interspersed with the first ten patient interviews. This helped with the formulation of better patient interview questions. Specifically, because key actor interviews often had direct interaction with many patients, they had insights that we did not yet have, and that individual patients often had little cause to notice. Five of the key informant interviews were collected toward the end of data collection, interspersed with the last fifteen patient interviews. These were used to help determine that patient interviews had sufficiently captured important themes. Specifically, these final interviews were used to find out details about specific topics raised by patients and their interaction with the industry. Questions to key informants allowed themes that had emerged from patient data to be explored in more detail and probe to see if theoretical saturation had been reached based on the range of experiences and interactions that key actors could draw upon. Drawing on their own experiences, key actors often had insights that were grounded in lengthier involvements and interactions with a larger cross-section of patients than the study itself could include.

Observations included attendance at more than twenty-five medical cannabis-related functions, conferences, and events between September 2010 and November 2012, including attendance at meetings among key Colorado patient or dispensary organizations, or at public hearings regarding medical marijuana policies. Attending events throughout the time frame allowed us to "listen in" on how the medical marijuana community communicates amongst itself, discusses strategy, networks, and disseminates appropriate messages for a broader public. Events allowed us to better follow discussions in the industry about its regulation, and the concerns that both providers and patients experienced during this time. Attending multiple events of different types also made it easier to identify key organizational actors to recruit for informal interviews, and created opportunities to network with key organizational actors for assistance in patient recruitment.

Observation helped better contextualize patient interviews, allowing us to strengthen our understanding of the relationship between patient narratives and the collective, public language about the medical cannabis identities. In the words of Zussman (2004), these supplemental forms of data collection have built understanding of "people in places," acknowledging the importance of public discussion, policy debate, and the implementation of rules on individual patient's decision-making around medical cannabis.

These additional forms of data increased the reach of data collection to gain insights on patients as an aggregate population from those who regularly interacted with many patients, and to learn of developments in policy, politics, and community that were hard to access through any formal sources. Conversations at events and interviews with key actors offered another form of feedback to assess the themes emerging in the interviews, and to gauge their importance, or identify gaps. Collecting multiple forms of data and looking at patient experiences from different angles is a common recommendation for strengthening qualitative research findings (Boeije 2010; Denzin and Lincoln 2000; Hathaway and Rossiter 2007; Maxwell 2005).

## Confidentiality in Analysis

All participants in this study were assigned pseudonyms whether they wanted them or not! Some insisted that it was fine to use their real names and identities but due to the sensitive nature of the laws, the decision was made to use pseudonyms throughout. Any friends, relatives, or associated businesses named in interviews were also kept private through the use of pseudonyms. Because the site of the study is identified as Colorado, we have not invented fictitious town names but have taken care in how details between person and place are connected in ways that could possibly lead to identification.

Even as it continues to grow, medical cannabis patients remain a small community, and those in visible advocacy or business roles can be fairly easy to identify without providing names. Patients are more numerous, but some have unusual conditions or combinations of conditions that may only affect a few hundred, or even a few dozen people within the state. A condition combined with any other piece of identifying information may in some cases be enough to breach confidentiality. For these reasons, we have taken great care when recounting individual stories. We did not create composites, allowing each patient's story to retain its unique integrity, but details, especially when they entailed court cases or other public advocacy, have not been included beyond what was needed to explain the story in order to minimize identification. Specific geographic, demographic, and health information about those interviewed is provided in aggregate in Chapter 1.

## Interview Details

The forty patient interviews conducted in this study were carried out in-person and ranged in length from one to three hours. All interviews were digitally recorded and then transcribed and coded using NVivo version 10, a qualitative coding software program (NVivo 10 2012). Interview locations varied. Some interviews were conducted at the individual's home; others took place at a neutral but private location, typically a private study room at a public or university library that was local to the participant. Key interviews and observations at public locations involved a mixture of digital recording and field notes. While only a few key interviews were recorded and transcribed, extensive notes were maintained for all events, which were entered into NVivo for coding.

Patients often wanted to know the interviewer's status as a patient. Most also wanted to be sure that the research contributed to a better understanding of patients and was not intended to discredit medical cannabis or disparage its users. The interviewer's non-patient status was clearly identified and presented as friendly to medical cannabis and interested in patients. Patients were not informed about the interviewer's background before the interview out of concern that this would cause patients to make assumptions about shared knowledge and insider status, and such assumptions might encourage them to leave out information that we wanted them to include. If patients asked more about the interviewer's background and project, it was provided in more detail after the interview if it seemed appropriate to the conversation.

## Analytic Approach

This qualitative study took an inductive approach, engaging in data analysis simultaneously with data collection, and conducting interviews in stages with intermittent periods where the focus was primarily on review and initial coding using NVivo for qualitative coding analysis (NVivo 10 2012). A short post-interview survey was collected from every interviewed patient to ensure that consistent demographic and summary health information was obtained from every participant.

Qualitative codes began as "organizational codes," also referred to as "topics," which simply refer to the spheres of activity we expected to find among patients. These included things like "doctor referral experiences," or "patient diagnosis," or "family and friend reactions." They were simply categories without an assumption of what patients would say about each topic (Maxwell 2005). After interviews began, initial coding of transcripts developed analytic themes. This was followed by a period of constant coding to adjust and refine the initial themes, and was used reflexively to adjust interview questions as needed. Coding adjusted as new themes emerged or prior ones changed in response to the interview and observation data, followed by a second stage of ongoing refined coding based on the primary themes of the book, which continued to be improved after data collection ended (Charmaz 2006). Approximately twenty interviews were completed, then the data was assessed for themes, and areas that needed more development were identified (Charmaz 2004). Throughout data collection, theoretical memos were used to record insights related to relationships between interviews, observations, and relevant theories, especially as they related to complementary and alternative medicine, identity, and stigma, recreational drug use, life course, and collective identity. Theoretical memos assist with the development of themes and their relationships to the data and to one another (Charmaz 2006; Walker and Myrick 2006). Memos are often seen as a "pivotal, intermediate step between data collection and writing drafts of papers" because memos serve as the starting point for building data-driven analysis (Charmaz 2006, 72). It is considered a useful companion strategy for creating stronger validity in qualitative research (Whittemore, Chase, and Mandle 2001). Memos assisted us in recognizing important themes, noting questions or topics for further consideration to be explored in ongoing interviews, and developing theories based on interview respondents. Themes are ways of classifying discrete concepts and beginning the process of abstraction from which theory can be built (Ryan and Bernard 2003). Memos often helped capture ideas after interviews or after coding—times when we had spent time immersed in data and details, and interesting ideas arose to examine. Memos were revisited and added to periodically as interviews accumulated, and this helped to determine whether themes had applicability or could be further developed. Themes also helped point to appropriate literature for review. We also wrote memos when some aspect seemed to stick out as troublesome or problematic, in order to earmark it as something to think about further. Just as much as conceptual breakthroughs are useful for theory development, many times the parts that seemed to depart from what was expected often developed into the best ideas and insights for analysis.

## Completing the Study

In the preface, we described the thought process and circumstances that led to this research. Little could we have known when this project began as a dissertation back in 2009 that it would capture such a pivotal moment in the history of medical cannabis. The medical cannabis industry is self-conscious about its current place in history. There are a host of organizational actors who are clambering to take credit for making history, and many more who are humbly relishing the sense that they are witnessing history in the making. This research took place during the period when massive expansion of Colorado's medical cannabis program began and ended just days before the historic passage of Amendment 64, which made Colorado one of the first two states to legalize cannabis. It is our hope that, through patients' stories, we have captured both what was new and particular about this moment, as well as offered ideas that endure and help shed light on cannabis and its medical use, expanding the story to include new conversations.

## References

Blee, Kathleen M., and Verta Taylor. 2002. "Semi-Structured Interviewing in Social Movement Research." Pp. 92–117 in *Methods of Social Movement Research*, edited by B. Klandermans and S. Staggenborg. Minneapolis: University of Minnesota Press.

Boeije, Hennie. 2010. *Analysis in Qualitative Research*. Thousand Oaks, CA: SAGE Publications.

CDPHE, Colorado Department of Public Health and Environment. 2018. "Medical Marijuana Registry Statistics, 2009–2018": Colorado Department of Public Health and Environment. Retrieved February, 2018 (www.colorado.gov/pacific/cdphe/2017-medical-marijuana-registry-statistics).

Chapkis, Wendy, and Richard J. Webb. 2008. *Dying to Get High: Marijuana as Medicine*. New York: New York University Press.

Charmaz, Kathy. 2004. "Grounded Theory." Pp. 496–521 in *Approaches to Qualitative Research: A Reader on Theory and Practice*, edited by S. Nagy Hesse-Biber and P. Leavy. New York: Oxford University Press.

Charmaz, Kathy. 2006. *Constructing Grounded Theory: A Practical Guide through Qualitative Analysis*. Thousand Oaks, CA: SAGE Publications.

Chun, Janean. 2012. "Medical Marijuana Businesses Face Risks, from Raids to Audits." in *Huffington Post*. Retrieved February 18, 2013 (https://www.huffingtonpost.com/2012/09/04/medical-marijuana-business_n_1814901.html)

Coomber, Ross, Michael Oliver, and Craig Morris. 2003. "Using Cannabis Therapeutically in the UK: A Qualitative Analysis." *Journal of Drug Issues* 33(2):325–56.

Creswell, John W. 2006. "Five Qualitative Approaches to Inquiry." Pp. 53–84 in *Qualitative Inquiry and Research Design*. Thousand Oaks, CA: SAGE Publishing.

Denzin, Norman K., and Yvonna S. Lincoln. 2000. "The Discipline and Practice of Qualitative Research." Pp. 5–28 in *Handbook of Qualitative Research*, edited by N. K. Denzin and Y. S. Lincoln. Thousand Oaks, CA: SAGE Publishing.

Dwoskin, Elizabeth. 2012. "Will the Feds Crack Down on Pot or Look the Other Way?" *Bloomberg Businessweek*. Retrieved February 2013 (www.businessweek.com/articles/2012-11-29/will-the-feds-crack-down-on-pot-or-look-the-other-way#p2).

Guest, Greg, Arwen Bunce, and Laura Johnson. 2006. "How Many Interviews Are Enough? An Experiment with Data Saturation and Variability." *Field Methods* 18(1): 59–82. doi: 10.1177/1525822x05279903.

Hathaway, Andrew D., Natalie C. Comeau, and Patricia G. Erickson. 2011. "Cannabis Normalization and Stigma: Contemporary Practices of Moral Regulation." *Criminology and Criminal Justice* 11(5):451–69. doi: 10.1177/1748895811415345.

Hathaway, Andrew D., and Kate Rossiter. 2007. "Medical Marijuana, Community Building, and Canada's 'Compassionate Societies'." *Contemporary Justice Review* 10(3):283–96.

Janichek, Jennifer L., and Amanda Reiman. 2012. "Clinical Service Desires of Medical Cannabis Patients." *Harm Reduction Journal* 9:12. doi: 10.1186/1477-7517-9-12.

Johnston, Lloyd, Patrick M. O'Malley, Jerald G. Bachman, and John Schulenberg. 2012. *Monitoring the Future National Survey Results on Drug Use 1975–2011: Volume II, College Students and Adults Ages 19–50*. Ann Arbor: Institute for Social Research, The University of Michigan.

Maxwell, Joseph A. 2005. *Qualitative Research Design: An Interactive Approach*. Vol. 41, edited by L. Bickman and D. J. Rog. Thousand Oaks, CA: SAGE Publications.

NVivo 10. 2012. *NVivo Qualitative Data Analysis Software*. Qualitative coding software: QSR International.

O'Connell, Thomas J., and Ché B. Bou-Matar. 2007. "Long-Term Marijuana Users Seeking Medical Cannabis in California (2001–2007): Demographics, Social Characteristics, Patterns of Cannabis and Other Drug Use of 4117 Applicants." *Harm Reduction Journal* 4:16. doi: 10.1186/1477-7517-4-16.

Reiman, Amanda. 2007. "Medical Cannabis Patients: Patient Profiles and Health Care Utilization Patterns." *Complementary Health Practice Review* 12:31–50.

Reinarman, Craig, Helen Nunberg, Fran Lanthier, and Tom Heddleston. 2011. "Who Are Medical Marijuana Patients? Population Characteristics from Nine California Assessment Clinics." *Journal of Psychoactive Drugs* 43(2):128–35. doi:10.1080/02791072.2011.587700.

Ryan, Gery W., and H. Russell Bernard. 2003. "Techniques to Identify Themes." *Field Methods* 15(1):85–109. doi: 10.1177/1525822x02239569.

Schulenberg, John, Lloyd Johnston, Patrick M. O'Malley, Jerald G. Bachman, Richard Miech, and Megan E. Patrick. NIDA/NIH. 2017. *Monitoring the Future: National Survey Results on Drug Use, 1975–2016: Volume II, College Students and Adults Ages 19–55*. Ann Arbor, MI: The University of Michigan.

Walker, Diane, and Florence Myrick. 2006. "Grounded Theory: An Exploration of Process and Procedure." *Qualitative Health Research* 16(4):547–59. doi: 10.1177/1049732305285972.

Ware, Mark A., Crystal R. Doyle, Ryan Woods, Mary E. Lynch, and Alexander J. Clark. 2003. "Cannabis Use for Chronic Non-Cancer Pain: Results of a Prospective Survey." *Pain* 102:211–16.

Whittemore, Robin, Susan K. Chase, and Carol Lynn Mandle. 2001. "Validity in Qualitative Research." *Qualitative Health Research* 11(4):522–37. doi:10.1177/104973201129119299.

Zussman, Robert. 2004. "People in Places." *Qualitative Sociology* 27(4):351–63.

Appendix B

# Annotated Index of Patients by Pseudonym

**Aaron** Male, 33, chronic debilitating pain from back and neck injuries sustained in a car accident (193). Aaron has been a cannabis user since his early teens, when he also had asthma (136), with a phase of heavy use in young adulthood. He transitioned to casual use as an adult (158). Works a job in the criminal justice system (193). See also 167.

**Andy** Male, 47, degenerative disc disease (96). Andy had tried cannabis only once in his teens, didn't like it (96), and looked down on recreational users prior to medical use (204). In using it medically, he still does not smoke it (134) and occasionally experiences anxiety from use (224). Worked in IT with engineering background. Discusses his experiences with his recommendation (97–98) and his employer (180–1). Calls himself a "good poster child for cannabis," testifies at hearings, and participates in politics around cannabis (196). Libertarian (204). *See also* 75, 79, 99, 167, 196, 206–7, 226, 233.

**Anita** Female, 40, multiple sclerosis (MS). Anita is a fit, compact, artsy-punk educator. Sudden onset of a rare form of MS caused by lesion in left side of brain, produced right-side paralysis (86). Anita had used cannabis occasionally in college but not since. A friend persuaded her to try it to treat her MS (87), which put her in remission (100, 138). She discusses her recommendation experience (87, 100), her experience with being overmedicated with prescription drugs (138, 228, 230–2), her method for use in combination with other self-care regimens (139), and her experiences with stigma (195). Politically unaffiliated (203). See also 179.

**Arthur** Male, 58, HIV/AIDS, chronic pain issues, and PTSD. Arthur qualifies for permanent disability and lives in subsidized housing (160). His life has been overshadowed by a horrific rape that occurred when he was a young enlisted soldier in the Army (149). In his struggle to recover a sense of self-worth, Arthur reports secretly taking microdoses of LSD daily for 20 years to cope (149). Comfortable with recreational cannabis use and use of other recreational substances, Arthur says all his current use of cannabis is medical (160). He discusses his routine for use (160), his views on legitimate use (161), and his experiences with doctors and misdiagnosis (149, 228). See also 141.

**Avery**   Female, 30, cervical spine injury from being attacked by an ex-boyfriend, which caused recurring headaches and neck pain (83). Avery works as a yoga instructor and nutrition counselor in a dispensary, the choice that prompted her to get a registry card (83). She discusses her motivations for getting a medical card (82–84) and her recommendation experience (112–13).

**Beth**   Female, 62, chronic pain from injuries sustained in a series of accidents (112). A member of Jehovah's Witnesses, she is retired and a caretaker to her elderly mother. Beth discusses her choices for methods of cannabis use (134), her take on recreation and medical use (163), perceptions of cannabis users (168), the law and medicine (208), alternative therapies (220), and how medical cannabis use aligns with her religious beliefs (134, 205). See also 205.

**Billy**   Male, 31, traumatic brain injury (TBI) from a DUI automobile accident on his high school graduation night that nearly took his life and seriously injured a friend (177). Billy completed a culinary degree after the accident but after getting and losing many restaurant jobs, he realized the multitasking was too much for him and is now on permanent disability. Billy discusses his pursuit of life milestones, and his gradual acceptance of the disability designation (177–8). See also 181.

**Brett**   Male, 47, chronic pain due to a back injury (111). Brett came to cannabis through an interest in industrial hemp (84) and decided to change careers midlife and start a business in the medical cannabis industry (82). He discusses his motivations for seeking a recommendation (82), the use of terminology (127), his preferred methods for use (135) and his pride in how Colorado has implemented the cannabis programs (196). He also talks about the effect of cannabis disagreements on family and friend relationships (200). See also 202, 221–2, 231, 233.

**Carl**   Male, 54, kidney cancer and longstanding severe back and neck issues that cause chronic pain and require surgery (89). Carl discusses use of alcohol and other medications (150), the role of cannabis in coping psychologically with a terminal disease (225), the politics of medical cannabis (167), self-regulation of dosage (168), and the pharmaceutical industry (209). See also 205, 234.

**Carmella**   Female, 47, bipolar disorder and extreme anxiety (147). Carmella is on state disability and lives in subsidized housing (147). She discusses the experience of the psychoactive effects of cannabis (147), her use of other prescribed and recreational drugs including meth (150–1), long-term effects on her health from prescribed pharmaceutical drugs (152), and overmedication (152, 228). See also 141.

**Dale**   Male, 52, chronic pain from work-related injuries. Dale's story is featured in the introduction, which discusses his background and extensive prior drug use, including using and selling cannabis as a teenager (7–11). He talks about doubting the medical utility of cannabis (7, 13), activism (11, 15, 200), changes to cannabis since his youth (122, 166), his medical use now (135, 163), and the prospect of pharmaceutical forms of cannabis (234). He also describes being encouraged to try it as an alternative to opioids by a member of extended family (8, 15–16, 79), and how it affected his relationship with his daughter (198, 200).

**Darrell**    Male, 40, chronic pain from multiple major surgeries. Darrell has pins and screws in his lower back and is on permanent disability. A family man with a large family through marriage, Darrell is a lifelong abstainer from alcohol and recreational drugs but came to use cannabis to manage pain (112). He talks about his legitimacy as a patient (112), his recommendation experience (112), and a harrowing police raid of his home in which he was further injured (182–3). He also compares his experiences with cannabis and pharmaceuticals (232).

**Devon**    Male, 37, chronic pain from bulging discs in his back. After the disc problem developed in his mid-20s, a failed operation to fix it resulted in worsened pain, mobility, and numbness (219–20). Devon has a disability designation and found that he could not manage his pain with prescriptions and remain functional, so he sought out healthier alternatives (220). A recreational user in his teens, he attributes the cessation of childhood asthma to cannabis use (136). He talks about cannabis safety and health (220–2, 232) and his aversion to prescription pharmaceuticals (219, 228).

**Eileen**    Female, 52, rheumatoid arthritis and migraines (79). After becoming an empty nester, Eileen relocated to Colorado in part to have legal access to medical cannabis (79). She discusses preferred methods (135) and frequency of cannabis use (141, 143), as well as her use prior to having children and after her children reached adulthood (192). Eileen also discusses the politics of medical cannabis (205) and effects from different cannabis varieties (224).

**Eric**    Male, 47, hernia that is undertreated due to his lack of health insurance and a failed mesh implant. Although Eric is one of only three patients not directly mentioned in the text, his interview is included when discussing patients in aggregate.

**Frank**    Male, 68, advanced-stage cancer. Frank is a retired professor with an artistic and entrepreneurial streak who has helped to build a software company in his retirement years (142). An intermittent recreational user over his adult life (224), he talks about managing cancer and medications (142, 223, 229), disclosing cannabis use (198), use routines (142), stereotypes (193–4), and the government's role in cannabis regulation (206–7).

**Gary**    Male, 54, chronic pain from work-related injuries. In his work as a delivery driver, Gary slipped on the ice while carrying heavy items, causing permanent injury to his back. He discusses researching cannabis as an option (81, 85, 222), discussing it with his wife (85), his choice of terminology for the plant (127), regimens and methods for use (141), differences between teen and later life use (82, 159), definitions of medical versus recreational use (160), privacy and disclosure (198), the role of the government in cannabis regulation (207), the use of prescription medications (234), and opinions on the pharmaceutical industry (228–9).

**Glenn**   Male, 44, severe chronic neuropathic pain and muscle spasms in the neck. Glenn has had multiple surgeries and used prescription medications to manage pain. Glenn is a devout Catholic and a Republican who is briefly mentioned for his opinion on cannabis as a gateway drug (167). His interview informs what is reported in aggregate within the book.

**Hugh**   Male, 52, HIV. A longtime survivor of HIV diagnosed in the late 1980s, Hugh discusses the pharmaceutical industry (210) and the influx of newcomers with money to the medical cannabis space (210). He also talks about the politics of medical cannabis and politician behavior (210).

**Jason**   Male, 40, gastroesophageal reflux disease (GERD). Diagnosed ten years prior, Jason is a financial professional, married with small children, who considers himself a fiscally conservative, socially liberal Republican (80). Jason has used cannabis socially since his teens (80, 192). He talks about learning that he could qualify for medical cannabis due to his condition (80, 81), his recommendation experience (80), his lack of cultural or political identification with cannabis use (80, 192, 199, 200, 212n2), his first dispensary experience (128), and his choice of use method (134, 135). He also discusses choices about disclosure (192, 198–9) and cannabis's role in health (222, 224).

**Julie**   Female, 42, restless leg syndrome. Julie works as an educator at a secondary school and has been a consistent social user over her adult life. Julie discusses her method for use (137, 139), pharmaceutical medications and cannabis as a replacement for them (138, 139), cannabis safety (138), choices about disclosure (196), and opinions about cannabis culture (193).

**Karen**   Female, 53, migraines. Karen's story is the companion to Dale's in the introduction (1–7). Karen discusses how her husband, Mateo, came to use cannabis medically, followed by her adoption of medical use for migraines (1–7). Karen's story in the Introduction draws out main themes in the book (11–16) and references to her can be found throughout as those themes are developed in more depth, such as discussions about run-ins with the law (184–5), methods and amounts of use (135, 141, 143, 233), the role of family (79, 85, 98, 179, 200), adjustments after an injury or illness (176), disclosing use, stereotypes of use (167, 190–1, 211), and differences in cannabis use over the life course (192, 233).

**Ken**    Male, 47, chronic pain. Ken sustained damage to his spine that causes significant neuropathic pain. He discusses his method for use (134), the effect of inaccurate government information about cannabis (167), the effect of cannabis on depression (223–4), the comparison of cannabis with prescription medications (224), cannabis and health (224), and overmedication (228).

**Lance**    Male, 31, traumatic brain injury (TBI) and post-traumatic stress disorder (PTSD). Lance is a highly decorated military veteran who was injured in combat in Iraq, which led to his treatment at a Warrior Transition Unit for eighteen months as part of his medical retirement (107). The TBI and PTSD led to dangerous levels of overmedication, which prompted his research into alternatives (107–9, 227–8). Lance discusses his experiences with physicians, (109), his research into medical cannabis use (109), the recommendation experience (111), and his regimen for use (141, 146). He talks about the lack of intoxicating effects from his cannabis use (146, 232), his reduction in use of pharmaceutical medications (232), and the role of cannabis in his overall approach to recovering health (219). He also shares his opinions of how cannabis should be regulated (232). *See also* 230.

**Leo**    Male, 62, chronic pain. Leo has back issues with his discs, causing severe chronic pain, which he treats with cannabis. A longtime regular social cannabis user, Leo is now retired. He discusses his first experience in a dispensary (129), his knowledge of cannabis and its medicinal uses (129, 224), as well as his use of prescription medicines and other substances to control pain (150). Leo also talks about the pharmaceutical industry (230).

**Mark**    Male, 50, chronic pain. Mark has a neuropathic pain condition in his feet called Haglund's deformity. He talks about qualifying due to his condition (109), method and frequency of use (137, 225), managing effects of cannabis (121, 137), and prescription medications (139).

**Mike**    Male, 48, HIV. Like Hugh, Mike was diagnosed with HIV early, in 1986. He identifies as gay and has an ex-wife with whom he had a son. The HIV diagnosis and emerging treatments shaped Mike's life in many ways. After the diagnosis, he dropped out and became a ski bum, but after living with HIV for many years he returned to complete a college degree and pursue a career (101–2). He has participated in many university-based experimental treatments to manage his HIV. He discusses the effectiveness of cannabis for managing his symptoms (102), his medical recommendation experience (102–4), medical and recreational definitions of use (163–4), the messaging around cannabis use in society (167), how the cannabis user identity affects how he sees himself (201), and the role of cannabis use in maintaining health (222–4).

**Mindy**    Female, 45, multiple disorders including fibromyalgia, myofascial pain, bipolar disorder, and post-traumatic stress disorder (PTSD). Mindy's only appearance is when she discusses her experiences with using complementary and alternative medicines (220). Her interview information is used when reporting on patients in aggregate.

**Natalie**   Female, 33, chronic pain and spasticity. Natalie is a married stay-at-home mother of a toddler. She has chronic severe pain and muscle spasm as a result of a back injury sustained in a car accident. Although she is never identified by name in the text, her interview information is used when reporting on patients in aggregate.

**Neil**   Male, 40, chronic pain. Neil, who has sciatic pain from an injury, sought out a card based on advice from his attorney (83). He was charged with felony conspiracy when he was stopped coming home from Burning Man and a friend-of-a-friend who he was giving a ride was in possession of psychedelic mushrooms (83). He talks about his motivation to get a card (82–3), defining medical and recreational use (114), and his preferred methods for use (141).

**Paul**   Male, 64, chronic pain. A retired lawyer, Paul's injuries from college sports led, over time, to spinal stenosis, a severe back condition that threatened to put him in a wheelchair (141). Paul had used cannabis regularly in young adulthood but only very intermittently in later life. He discusses his diagnosis and prescribed medications (141), his use of cannabis tinctures and use routines (141, 163), and distinctions between medical and recreational uses (141, 163).

**Ron**   Male, 63, cancer. Ron was a small business owner who had to give up his business following his cancer diagnosis and has no medical insurance. Ron discusses the politics of cannabis in his area of Colorado (110), police harassment (110), and his difficulty securing a recommendation (110). He discusses his method and frequency of use, which includes Phoenix Tears, the Rick Simpson Oil concentrate (143). He talks about his research into cannabis for cancer (144), his inability to "get high" despite the large doses he ingests (145), and his fight with authorities to maintain access (182), as well as his outrage about cannabis laws (208).

**Tim**   Male, 33, chronic pain. Tim has a back injury from motocross and also suffers migraines. He is an unemployed mechanic who is a stay-at-home parent for his five children. Tim and his wife have a history of multiple drug use and have been in and out of trouble with the law but now only use tobacco and cannabis. Tim is only mentioned as part of a group of patients who express a preference for smoking as a delivery method for cannabis (135). His other interview information is used when speaking about patients in aggregate.

**Tina**   Female, 36, multiple diagnoses that include fibromyalgia, post-traumatic stress disorder (PTSD), and severe nausea (228). Tina discusses medical cannabis use in relation to age and identity (201, 202). She also offers opinions of the pharmaceutical industry and its relationship to cannabis law (209), and describes her experiences with overmedication (228, 230).

**Travis**   Male, 40, traumatic brain injury (TBI), seizures, migraines, anxiety, and post-traumatic stress disorder (PTSD). As a child, Travis was the victim of a violent assault from a stranger who suffered from mental illness. His head injury from the attack resulted in lifelong migraines and seizures, as well as PTSD and anxiety (77). Travis is the father of two daughters and is on permanent disability (162). He has used cannabis recreationally on and off over his adult life and discusses the pharmaceutical medications he has used to manage these conditions (77–8) as well as working with his doctor to use cannabis to control his seizures (77). He talks about health management strategies and quality of life (78, 162), including management of anxiety (162) and overmedication (228). He also describes his medical regimen and recordkeeping (162).

**Tucker**   Male, 33, HIV. Tucker, who identifies as gay, has a history of recreational use and began using cannabis to control nausea brought on by HIV medications (110). He discusses his recommendation experience at the height of the "green rush" in Colorado (110). His other interview information is used when reporting on patients in aggregate.

**Valerie**   Female, 47, post-traumatic stress disorder (PTSD) and thoracic outlet syndrome. Valerie is mentioned as an example of when a patient's cultural and political leanings align with the stereotypical expectations for a cannabis consumer (193). Her other interview information is used when reporting on patients in aggregate.

**Wes**   Male, 53, advanced diabetes. Wes was never a recreational user and detested that his wife occasionally used cannabis socially (97). Wes describes how growing awareness of the positive effects of cannabis on his wife's musculoskeletal disorder changed his attitude toward medical use for his own symptoms (97, 98). He describes his recommendation experience (97–9) and is referenced in the section on differences in the concealability of medical conditions because diabetes has left Wes legally blind (176).

**Yvonne**   Female, 60, Crohn's disease, fibromyalgia, and back issues. Yvonne, a grandmother, recounts her recommendation experience (113), her experience with CBD (164–5), and her experience of accepting her fibromyalgia diagnosis and the physical limitations that came with it in the context of losing one's social roles (178–9, 181). She is also referenced in the discussion of stereotypes related to affiliation with cannabis culture and fitting the appearance of a stereotypical cannabis user (193).

**Zane**   Male, 59, advanced diabetes. Zane has diabetes and is in a wheelchair due to multiple amputations. He is retired from an administrative job with the government and lives in state-subsidized assisted-living housing. Zane is mentioned by name (with Wes) as one of the two out of the forty patients interviewed who are immediately identifiable as disabled (176). Zane's interview data is included when patients are described in aggregate.

# Index

addiction 16, 19–20, 64, 92, 121, 167, 227
ADHD *see* attention deficit disorder
Adichie, Chimamanda Ngozi 41
adolescence 14, 23, 26, 161, 166, 202
advocacy xx, 16, 191, 194, 196, 242, 247, 254–5, 260
age: and cannabis use 14, 18, 23–4, 26, 121, 189, 192; and deviance 24; fifties 1, 7, 81–2, 97, 149; forties 9, 77, 101, 146, 166, 257; as a setting 121, 157, 166, 192; and stigma 175; teens 1, 4, 14, 24, 26, 76, 79, 81, 136, 138, 141, 147, 150, 158, 166–7, 169, 189, 191–2, 243, 246; thirties 8, 82, 107, 112, 158, 167, 220, 257; twenties 8
agents, federal drug 6, 54, 70, 184, 186
Aggarwal, Sunil 27–8, 34, 40, 55, 65, 90, 136, 146, 205, 243
aging and life course 24, 157–8, 190, 223
alcohol: abstinence from 112; dependence 9, 206, 237; as gateway drug 167; industry 245; preference for cannabis over 1, 79, 140, 220–1, 232; prohibition of xxi, 242; regulation of 18, 55, 68, 232, 251
alcohol consumption 7–8, 82, 140, 148, 150, 173, 220–1, 231–2, 241, 246, 251; and driving 172–3, 186, 246; and safety 231; as self-medicating 148, 150, 152
"all use is medical" 40, 161
amendments: federal 60–4, 68, 71, 97, 116, 262; state 37, 40, 60, 68, 111; state, Amendment 64, 40, 71, 249
Americans for Safe Access (ASA) xv, 37, 57–8, 63, 117, 173, 181–2
amotivational syndrome 27, 143
Anslinger, Harry 21, 242
anxiety: and cannabis use 36, 133, 146–7, 162, 223–4, 232, 237; in the doctor-

patient interaction 92; managing 147; as a qualifying condition 41, 146–7; *see also under* medical conditions
appetite stimulation from cannabis 13, 64
arrests for cannabis xv, 11, 57, 93, 182, 243, 246–7
attention deficit/hyperactivity disorder 30, 146, 153, 161

Baby Boomers 10, 22, 24, 157, 257
barriers: to getting a medical cannabis card 115; to legitimacy 211, 242; to medical cannabis research 58; for physicians 106; to social movement activity 195; to trying medical cannabis 16, 101, 147
Becker, Howard 121–2, 133, 145, 217
behaviors: medicalized 13–14, 110, 127, 130, 132, 145, 148–9, 152, 163, 169, 248
benefits of cannabis use 18, 26–7, 32, 59, 133, 135, 145, 159, 161, 236
Big Pharma 226, 235, 245
Big Tobacco *see* tobacco, companies
bills: legislative *see* legislation
body: cannabis effects on the 27, 124, 144–5, 161, 173, 209, 218–19, 222, 233, 237; sovereignty over one's own 203–7, 250
*bona fide* relationship 91, 105
Breyer, Charles 63
Bush, George H.W. 60; *see also under* presidential administrations

California xiv–xv, xvii, xx–xxi, 33–4, 36, 38, 41, 54, 59–60, 62–4, 66, 69–71, 108, 126, 135, 142, 161, 186, 210, 213
CAM *see* complementary and alternative medicine (CAM)
Canada 41, 123, 127, 250
cannabidiol (CBD) *see* CBD

demographics 34, 39, 92, 212, 260–1
demographics and health characteristics 38
Denver Medical Marijuana Code 69, 71
Denver Metro Area 1, 10, 39, 66, 69, 71,
    110, 196
Department of Justice see DOJ
dependence: cannabis 32, 56, 233; drug 3,
    41, 55–6, 89, 140, 142, 148, 150, 206,
    219, 227, 233, 247
depression 3, 34, 36, 100, 146, 162, 195,
    219, 222–4, 237
deviance xxi, 6, 12, 18, 20–1, 24, 29–31,
    41, 168, 171, 185, 206, 241, 251
deviant behaviors 12, 23–4, 30–1, 241
diagnosis 16, 19, 30–1, 37, 75, 80, 84,
    94–6, 102, 109–11, 113, 138, 147, 164,
    175, 178–80, 223, 229
diet 139, 168, 195, 220
direct-to-consumer advertising 210, 217,
    226
disability 3–4, 81, 94, 103, 112, 134, 147,
    160, 162, 175–9, 183, 220; invisibility
    of 175
disclosing use 176, 194, 196–8
disease control 29, 152
disorders 82, 98, 111, 137–40, 160–1, 164,
    200, 251; see also medical conditions
dispensaries xvii, 10, 62–3, 65–9, 83–4, 91,
    95, 117, 127–9, 133, 141, 165, 236, 245,
    254–5, 258–9
diversity 123, 174, 197, 211, 235, 255;
    demographic 246; racial 38, 212
"doctor mill" 14, 91, 96, 105–6, 109, 112,
    114
doctor-patient interaction 69, 86, 89–117,
    190, 216, 245
doctors 2, 4, 9, 11–13, 19, 28–30, 76–80,
    86, 89–117, 138, 141, 147–51, 178, 208,
    210, 216–17, 223, 227, 229–30, 235;
    attitudes 77, 85, 89; recommendation 9,
    75, 78, 83, 87–8, 93, 107, 182, 255
DOJ (Department of Justice) 61–4, 66,
    68, 71
dosage: 32, 108, 127, 135, 137–8, 144–5,
    159, 162, 164, 233; gauging 122, 134;
    management techniques 128, 138–9, 141,
    163, 225, 233, 247; regimens 146, 165
dronabinol see Marinol
drug abuse potential 32, 55
Drug Abuse Resistance Education
    (DARE) 24
Drug Enforcement Administration see DEA
drugs, licit and illicit 152–3

drug schedules 51–2, 55–7, 89–90,
    107, 110, 236, 243–4, 246, 248, 250;
    definitions and criteria 55–6; Schedule
    I 55, 89–90, 110; Schedule II 56–7, 61,
    153; Schedule III 56, 236; Schedule
    IV 56
"drug, set, and setting" 66; reinterpreting
    cannabis the drug 122
drug test 8, 11, 172, 174
drug war 22, 57, 205, 242–3, 246–7;
    annual budgets 243
DUI 11, 173

"to each his own" 202–3, 207
Earleywine, Mitch 81
ECS (endogenous cannabinoid system)
    27–8, 161, 237, 244
edibles 69, 84, 126–8, 133–4, 136–41
Ehrlichman, John 57
employment 13, 75, 93–4, 104, 171–2,
    180, 185–6, 196, 246
endogenous cannabinoid system see ECS
Epidiolex 136
Epis, Bryan 70
European Medicines Agency (EMA) 126
experience level with cannabis 12, 21, 122,
    129, 133, 145, 164, 208, 219, 225, 227
extracts, high-potency cannabis oil xxi,
    124–5, 137

Farr, Sam 61–3
FDA (Food and Drug Administration) 32,
    58, 60, 126; approval 26, 126, 236
Federal Bureau of Narcotics (FBN) 21
federal legislative attempts to amend
    cannabis policy 60
Figi, Charlotte 25
Filburn, Roscoe see Wickard v. Filburn
firearms 55, 174
First Amendment 93
Florida 33, 41
Food and Drug Administration see FDA
Foucault 212
Frank, Barney 61
friends and family 9, 76, 89, 198
Fry, Mollie 93

gatekeeping 29, 115, 247
gateway drug theory 27, 166–7
gay rights 185–6, 211, 250
General Social Survey (GSS) 24, 67
generations 24, 28, 157, 201, 207, 209;
    flower-child generation 24; Gen X